Hans Hartung

text by Umbro Apollonio

translated by John Shepley

Hans Hartung

Harry N. Abrams, Inc. Publishers New York

LIBRARY OF CONGRESS CATALOGING IN PUBLICATION DATA

Hartung, Hans, 1904–
Hans Hartung.

I. Apollonio, Umbro, 1911–
ND588.H34A813 759.3 72–4459
ISBN 0–8109–0163–3

Library of Congress Catalogue Card Number: 72–4459

Harry N. Abrams, Incorporated, New York
Printed and bound in Italy

"Ce que j'aime, c'est agir sur la toile."

The realm of the imagination is so vast, profound, and inexhaustible that its exploration never fails to yield new wonders and surprises. The artist, investigating its innermost recesses, and coming in contact with its supreme hoards of reality, lives the experience in a particular way, while the historical circumstances that have compelled him to set himself against the forces of convention become history themselves when, with every spiritual or formal bondage overcome, they are enshrined in works determined by a conscious choice. The perfect culmination takes place at the point where poetry and culture, instinct and thought join in an inner cohesion so absolute as to constitute both premise and message. In such a case, an iconography is established different from the one that up until that moment has been most common and accepted—or, rather, an iconography opposed to the ordinary vision and determined to confront problems in relation to the world that have so far gone unexamined, and for which it is necessary to find adequate means of expression.

It is true that the artist makes use of the lessons handed down by his predecessors, but just as he transforms his historical models, to which he cannot remain subject, he also sets in motion a dialectical energy that will have greater or lesser results in the work of others drawn to his magnetic field. On the other hand, those who can justifiably be called innovators and leaders are always rare; most stop with escapism, preferring exile, however properly expressed, to direct and responsible action on the level of absolute creation. Hans Hartung can be numbered among the few who, by virtue of their irreproachable spontaneity and sureness, tower over the conflicts that mark and trouble contemporary art.

Proof of Hartung's exceptional artistic ability can be found in his earliest works. Unlike the great majority of painters who begin by imitating either nature or models hallowed by museums, Hartung looked at both not with the purpose of learning, but in order to transfer the emotions he felt in their presence into an inner realm of his own from which their living realities could be most readily communicated.

Whether he was standing before a Goya in 1922 (he was then eighteen, having been born in 1904 in Leipzig) or a little later in front of a Rembrandt, his drawings and paintings revealed even in those years a personal formulation in which the elements of composition converged toward an image that is quite distinct from the original reference. There can be no possible doubt that already as an adolescent Hartung had his own aesthetic vision. Though later, between 1924 and 1926, he attended the academies of Leipzig and Dresden, submitting to a more rigid discipline, this was out of respect for his father's wishes, and also because of his need to refine his means of expression in order to make them more responsive to the artistic idiom that he proposed to develop. Even as a youth, Hartung had been attracted by speculative thought and scientific observation. In Leipzig he took courses in philosophy and art history. Prompted by his encounter with the Cubists, whose work he came to know in Paris in the winter of 1927, he embarked on an analysis of the problems of rhythm and proportion. He continued to interest himself in such questions until 1933, and even in those periods when he studied mathematics, he never allowed his artistic resolution to suffer. In Hartung every intellectual stimulus eventually finds its release in exemplary form—the whole being truly the aesthetic sum of the various moments that have moved the artist. His learned principles and lyrical emotion unfailingly merge, since everything is examined with an eye to a result that is the symbolic essence of vision. Few artists have achieved Hartung's stable equilibrium between intellectual reason and the imaginative ideal. His work, in its completeness of form, is extracted from that totality of relationships which is the first requirement for the unfolding of multiple meanings, meanings that are never abstract, however specific may be their absolute values. In his creative rigor and deliberate abstraction, Hartung never limits himself to a dry or artful professionalism, but reduces to one conscious and deeply felt denominator the fragments of the antitheses that constitute the dialectic within which the vital impulses of life aimlessly strive.

He was twenty-two when, having seen the works of such Expressionist painters as Marc, Kokoschka, and Nolde, he came to know those of Matisse, Picasso, and Rouault. He was deeply impressed by Marc's *Animal Destiny* of 1913, but could not help noting that its effect was primarily due to its dynamic rhythm. "The animals bothered me; I should have preferred to leave them out, for they seemed to hinder the free development of the painting." [1]

In some of his watercolors of 1922, the impetus of his vivid and lively coloring would seem to follow in the wake of Nolde; actually it is not a case of direct influence, but of a certain rapidity of execution that goes back to Slevogt and Corinth. Moreover these German Impressionists differed from the French in their heightened use of color, often neither sensitive nor refined, while their restless and agitated brushstrokes tended to have an explosive quality as though throwing off all restraint in a field of tension. If in a certain sense, structure in the French was built up by an accumulation of elements, in the Germans it resulted instead (or at least largely) from the emotional character of the brushwork. Thus, even the hurried violence of the Expressionist painters of *Die Brücke* might be traced back to those provocative rhythms with their vital inner intensity.

Hartung must surely have looked at certain works in this light—he himself makes no secret of his interest (after Rembrandt, El Greco, and Goya) in Slevogt, Corinth, Nolde, Kokoschka, and the graphic artists of *Die Brücke*—and what he retained from them was precisely this emotional pre-eminence, on a vivid level of free expression purged of every academic or conventional residue. The proofs that we have at our disposal not only affirm such a line of development, but reveal a process by which any psychological compromise and all representational tendencies have been eliminated. "With the back of the pen I drew things in which the figurative now played hardly any role. . . . It was rather the *tache* that took on its own meaning," he has said, referring to works executed between 1921 and 1923.[2]

It is a surprising but undeniable fact that all the premises on which Hartung's art was to be based were already delineated in his twenties with spontaneous and outstanding precision. Nevertheless we should not overlook a distinction that, in my opinion, serves better to define his work as it was manifested over the years. Though Hartung's priority in employing the *tache* is indisputable, ample justification for contemporary painting to recognize in him a pioneer in the technique later to be called *tachisme* or Abstract Expressionism, his work develops chiefly in the field of the sign or gesture. Hartung is a master of the emotional gesture, of that moment when the stroke becomes a conscious voice of expression within the context of the picture, not a matter of experiment, but an element in an integral space where the spheres of creative action derive from their specific form.

The order proposed by Hartung is parametric in nature, never engaging in the superfluities of private improvisation, nor, on the other hand, divorced from the dismaying events of the outside world.

One notices the way Hartung's agile strokes find their counterpart in the slashing ones of Fontana, as though paradoxically a feather touch were inflicting a gaping wound on the taut and luminously colored surface of the picture. We would even say that this element is the most important, and the one that appeared last in Hartung's work. If René de Solier was right when, referring to the drawings of 1922, he called attention to the fact that "within the drawing, the *taches* (and the white spaces that act as negatives) acquire an independent value,"[3] it is no less true that the strokes in the drawing play a role of marked importance. The artist still seeks a harmony between these two elements—sign and blot—endeavoring to coordinate them in order to polarize space by the suitable arrangement of opposites within an imagined diagram. It was something that Kandinsky, whose fascinating and proliferating tangles Hartung admired, had also tried to do. Even on this point, Hartung does not conceal his impressions. "In 1925, when I was twenty-one, I went to hear a lecture in Leipzig by Professor Kandinsky, an intelligent and important man, who spoke very capably and seriously about abstract art. My first impression at the time was simultaneously a keen disappointment and a feeling of reassurance. I mean that on the one hand I was very annoyed not to be—as I had thought—the only one to express himself by purely abstract means; on the other hand, I was happy to find a kind of confirmation of my experiments. And although I had immediately felt that Constructivism, the artistic path indicated by Kandinsky, was not the one that I myself would follow, I felt close to the great lyrical improvisations of his first abstract period—which he had shown us with lantern slides at the beginning of his lecture." [4]

Now it might be possible to question the notion that attributes responsibility to Kandinsky for the Constructivist trend, but it cannot be denied that at a certain moment his composition became a rigid scale of geometricized values—probably owing to the example of Malevich—and took the direction of a rather speculative absoluteness warmed over by the fires of lyrical emotion. This was most certainly the reason why Hartung did not go to the Bauhaus. It does not mean that he did not esteem Kandinsky or that he rejected his influence—he unquestionably made use of certain hints to spur his own work. We must remember, however, that Hartung was aiming at something more ordered, something to curb Kandinsky's reactive chaos, where constellations and entangled lines were scattered in a dynamic arrangement more improvised than structured.

Though he arrived spontaneously at a certain *tachisme* at least three decades before it made its appearance on the general artistic scene—demonstrating an expressive faculty that was later widely adopted—he always preferred an authoritative strength, a spatial situation consisting of the arrangement of perfectly focused constituent elements.

After a trip to Italy in the summer of 1926, when he traveled by bicycle as far as Sicily, he went to Paris in October, where he was to spend his winters from 1927 to 1929. His knowledge grew by direct exposure to the Impressionists, to Cézanne and Van Gogh, and the Cubist experiments of Picasso, Braque, and Léger. He examined their paintings attentively, from the technical standpoint as well as that of artistic conception, but always with a certain detachment that kept him from being subject to them. Thus there are no appreciable traces of their influence in his work.

Hartung keeps his independence at all costs, and any change that his work may undergo happens spontaneously and never with the purpose of replacing the substance of his imagination with a criterion other than that which prompts him to pursue particular stimuli. If anything, he is hostile to determined ways of formulating an image and rejects any possibility of compromising influences. It is true that between 1931 and 1933 his pictures show a unity of composition that reflects certain laws of Cubist construction, but they are not imposed as determinants. The space is a combination of formal and chromatic sectors derived from a synthesis such as the Cubists might have undertaken, but the total vision is not based on any objective motive, centering instead on entirely imaginative articulations, freed of all laws of perception. Such a painting as *T. 1932–7* seems to anticipate Poliakoff rather than to embody the themes dear to the Cubists. Similarly, in *T. 1934–2* we find that the isolated presence of formal elements and the connections between them come close to the amusing juxtapositions of Miró, whom he was not to meet until 1935.

It can and has been ascertained that even in Hartung's artistic training there were borrowings and influences from various sources, but it must be noted that these are rather a matter of vocabulary, while his syntax is extremely free, personal, and therefore exemplary in its characterization. What is striking, even in the earliest available examples of his art, is his adoption of a highly sensitive linguistic measure, intimate in its action, and never affected or caught up in a network of imitation. Moreover, when one examines the series of formal themes that Hartung has used from time to time to express the clarity of his inner vision, one is astonished at the breadth that his painting reveals over and beyond any experimental pretext. By moderating the implicit dramatic tension and muffling the echo of the accompanying crisis, he achieves a balance that appears more as a consoling hypothesis than a conceded grace. The tangles that he created in India ink in 1927 show a striking similarity to those of Pollock; some landscapes of 1925 are very close to the synthetic naturalism of De Staël; certain tumultuous developments are akin to the tortured despair of Wols; sometimes the arrangement of austere but vividly colored segments suggests the works of Baumeister; and even the luminous clarity of his backgrounds can be matched with Rothko's floating surfaces. To a still greater degree, the wriggling interlacings of Mathieu and Degotex go back to Hartung's energetic strokes, as do the massed bars of Soulages. Nor should we forget that his example has had repercussions on Vedova, Saura, Henri Goetz, Trier, and other lesser artists.

It is not my intention to indulge in a sort of paternity complex—which would perhaps be premature—or in prophecy, but it should be mentioned that the impetus provided by Hartung has stimulated modes of expression that have been exploited and merged with talent and skill by a widening circle of respectful interpreters and followers.[5] Excluding uninspired imitations, it is logical that such an outstanding example as Hartung's art should become widely diffused and be handed down in a great number of variations, and that its linguistic means be extended, for in this way it acquires importance for more than one generation and transcends the historical moment when it proudly proclaimed its break with the past. Every influential artist also triumphs by the continuity over which he presides as patron saint, and consolidates in the ranks of his followers the justifications for the cultural situation whose beginning he has supplied. Difficult as it may be to establish the precise point when it came to be acknowledged, there is no doubt that Hartung is a conscious presence in contemporary culture, one whose stature greatly exceeds the average level of other contributors to the aesthetic development taking place in our century.

In any case, it was in the thirties that, with his formative period concluded, Hartung's works reached an elevated height through a union of human emotion and stylistic quality.

During this decade his infallible powers of artistic conception were affirmed. As Gindertael has acutely observed: "the rule of forces . . . has replaced the world of forms to supply our perception with a new definition and a new representation of our universe, along with another possibility of identifying existence and the world." [6] This was the moment of his most extraordinary revelations, when the values of his vision became precise and imperative, freed now from the means of expression, but charged with energy for the sole purpose of strengthening the presence of the image. Though it is true that ever since his youth Hartung had been disencumbering himself of old conventions and cultural precepts, the sureness of his creative potentiality was so natural, spontaneous, and unassailable that nothing suggests an intention to destroy, or even any personal invective against the past. It is impossible to perceive in him any contradiction of position or reversal of situation.

The artist cannot allow himself to fall into such snares, for he participates intimately in that dialectic between sign and purpose that mobilizes a dynamic space by means of rhythm and convergence. What strikes one at first in a Hartung painting is precisely the extended space in the background, in front of which unfolds an extremely mobile ensemble of gestures. In appearance, the formulation is very similar to academic tradition, where the canvas acts as a background scene serving as the place of action and against which the actors play their parts. The spatial cavity, on the other hand, is profoundly different—in no way does it attempt a view or even the effect of a magic lantern. The forms are not superimposed but always return to the background, and the latter is related to them through a constant, dialectical interaction so as to signify the totality of space. As René de Solier has remarked:

Hartung's spatial and empirical void is without any proportional relation to the foreground (we have said that the line is not "posed"—thus there is no "departure" along a conventional horizon line), because one enters at once "into space and the void," where the attraction, an unmistakable gravitation, is manifested, though broken by the sign. The lines run upward from the bottom, then fall again, but the fall is overcome by the movement, which takes forms other than vertical attraction. Since the usual axes are destroyed, and the foreground is no longer at the mercy of a conventional and restricting horizon line (often the place of departure produces false perspectives), it is the forms and lines that hold our attention by their general organic and "unnamed" structure—in movement, however, not as on a microscope slide but in space, which is their element and the scene of the action (taking the place of attraction).

But the space offers a resistance that is partially overcome by the advance or interruption of lines—which are scattered about and replace the usual nucleus of forms. This scattered arrangement, outside the expected axis, becomes a source of attraction. In Hartung's painting, this antagonism between the two sources (of action and attraction) is characteristic.[7]

This active complexity of space, which is

never programmed but rather represented in its emotional factors, is harmonized by the dynamic and chromatic differentiation of the compositional elements. The artist himself has supplied a psychological explanation for its origin: "When I was a child, I was much influenced by lightning. At the age when most children are drawing stick figures, I filled whole notebooks, and a great many of them at that, with all the lightning flashes I had seen. Seen or not seen. From top to bottom, always lightning, lightning, lightning. Probably this is still present in my style of drawing, which very often has this zigzag aspect, of a line leaping across the page."[8] In my opinion, the transposition now does not take place so simply, nor do I see in Hartung's paintings a predominance of darting lines. Rather, I think I am right in saying that his observation of lightning brought about an inner movement that the painter still perceives (Georges Charbonnier has also pointed this out in the course of his interview with Hartung). In fact, even if he was impelled to arrest on paper the lightning flash, the most conspicuous aspect of the phenomenon, this does not mean that unconsciously, given his age, he did not notice the relation between sign and background in the sense that the flash came out of an indefinite space, and passed through and re-entered it, setting in motion lights and perspectives to the point of activating an over-all tension on the visible surface. Even bearing in mind Hartung's maxim "to see is not a total experience," there is nothing to prevent us from thinking that those visions had encouraged a figurative idea and, better still, a knowledge of the inexplicable forces of the world.

The canvas that Hartung uses to develop his ideas certainly does not resemble the common stage of nature where physical phenomena occur—it is a place whose borders are fixed from time to time as on a battlefield or in a sports arena. Between these limits, by an unerring governing principle, the events are spread over many levels, and it is precisely this distribution of individual situations and acts that provokes a sense of urgency, a high dramatic potential. But the conflict does not take place between one world and another, between an idea and a culture, between novelty and tradition—these have no meaning for Hartung's painting. Rather one is present at the normalization, in a revealing poetic key, of the action on the whole of reality, the latter being understood as man's proper dimension in which he expiates his existence at all levels.

This action is all-inclusive, not merely founded on causal relations or supported by sequences of greater or lesser importance, as though one could speak of higher and lower layers of knowledge, and neither is it stabilized in the abstraction of a preconceived idea —nothing is further from Hartung's art than any schematic program whatsoever. This is precisely because everything happens in the course of executing the picture, with inspiration, accidents, and reasoning combining in it from one moment to the next. As he says: "First . . . I feel the desire for a certain *tache*, a certain color or line. I like to act on the canvas. The first plastic signs bring others with them. The colors lead to graphic effects, which in their turn suggest *taches* whose final role may be (depending on their own expression) as well to accompany or counteract as to stabilize. . . . The work, as it goes along, forces my hand more and more and limits my choice. . . . One must let an idea ripen, push it to the maximum, concentrate on the essential . . . and still make every effort to preserve in the execution a fresh, direct, spontaneous character that is clearly the look of improvisation." [9]

From this it seems clear that if Hartung is preoccupied with formal logic, or rather with that union that compresses the individual parts into a unified whole, and which requires a certain control, he is nevertheless not averse to relying on the response generated by contact with primary elements, thus releasing a whole sequence of other stimuli. It should be noted that he stood at the beginning at the crossroads of two cultural currents—on one side, the descendants of Expressionism with all their vivid, impartial virulence, often improvised and largely composed of formulations that move from the figure to the sign; on the other, the extremely rational results of geometric Abstractionism (the *Cercle et Carré* group was founded in Paris in 1930, to be joined two years later by another, *Abstraction-Création*), which by divesting form of any possible reference to natural objects gave rise to a purism that was too often frigid and neutral.

Hartung from his early youth, and not through any suggestions from the culture around him, had understood that the problem was not to strip form of any reference to reality, to the point where it might stand for anything at all, but rather to invest it with its own meanings, self-sufficient and valid in themselves. It seemed necessary to reject the aesthetic of purist Abstractionism precisely because it erred by an excess of schematization and calculation. Even the sudden burst of lightning, which as a boy he had done his best to capture on the pages of his notebooks, was only a sign—and yet so much mystery and universality lay in its rapid appearance—a sign each time foreseeable, and each time different. This is just what Hartung wants—signs that, although corresponding to changeable circumstances, reflect a real situation of events at which, within the space of the world, man is present and by which he is emotionally penetrated, a sort of communication or correspondence between the natural cosmic event and individual human feeling. Each single element reacts immediately to the slightest contact—at the very moment when it is placed on the naked surface of the picture, it sets off vibrations to be taken up by the next element, which, in fact, it generates spontaneously. This new thrust is certainly not automatic or fortuitous, since there is no work that does not follow its own method. Thus everything in Hartung's work unfolds according to the personal and guiding pattern (though not one whose potentialities have all been unraveled) of an individual feeling that takes command of the material without preconceptions and submits it to whatever that feeling imposes.

We may therefore say that the part reserved for the intellect makes use of a rationality that is not deliberate but rather experienced at the moment, just as the improvisations of his impulsive side can sometimes be foreseen. In other words, Hartung is always in a state of vigilance, and in whatever he does there is concealed such foresight of vision as to pervade every sector and detail of the picture and subject them to tension.

Hartung's signs, never mere graphic shorthand, are charged and irradiant units, devoid of those attributes that characterize, let us say, Zen scripture. They come enclosed in a mental space that extends both widely and deeply—in a certain sense an infinite space, where the light is clear and constant, and where these graphic gestures (usually in soft black, in tangles or bundles) are placed with such categorical presence, even with their slight oscillations, that only through them does one "feel," almost physically, the limitless void with which a relationship has been established. These signs, used metaphorically or articulated in sequence, do not disturb the spatial harmony or dissolve into it; they only remove the mystery of its paradisiacal and canonical existence, making it a place where the meanings of our vital impulses reverberate and become concrete, are reintegrated, and remain suspended to form a circle in which every element has its precise place and function.

Compared with the many artists who have adopted a kind of graphic calligraphy, the Hartung sign is never the result of uncontrolled excitement; it is rather a conscious vector directed from a state of mind that has been long experienced and verified. In 1963, he confirmed what he had already explained in 1957:[10]

For me, the reality of the work is a manifestation running parallel to the life of the artist, the expression by the forces within him of everything that moves him to action, that brings into play his impulses, aims, and experiences. Often a trace of the object remains in the picture, even if unrecognizably. It manifests itself through the strength, speed, harshness or softness of his strokes. Our organic knowledge that the pulsebeat of the blood is the driving force . . . finds its parallel, its equivalent in what we create. Our psyche is nourished by memories of sensations, of experiences.[11]

From this arises the dynamic drive toward a measurable and generative relationship—sometimes with an accumulation of accents, sometimes turning on directional axes—that remains constant in his work and governs it by a rhythm that is never inert but replenishes both the tangible and inner qualities in its structure. René de Solier has rightly observed that "the whole canvas, seen in this perspective, is force, movement, space—the sum of contradictory actions or 'chain reactions,' one provoked by another. Thus the idea of motion ceases to be an idea or an empirical result."[12] In fact, wherever painting, or art in general, limits itself to a more-or-less figurative representation of tangible reality, it is only ideational and not expressive—in short, it does not emerge to become autonomous creation.

It was thus in the thirties that Hartung, with exceptional clarity, made his pictorial statement, one that has now entered the mainstream of modern culture. He thereby proposed an unparalleled stylistic method, soon to be widely shared, as we have said, by his contemporaries. His vision is based on a kinetic equilibrium of appositions, set down almost in a single burst, whose signs break up and modulate the clear surface of the canvas. These measured interruptions, in normal curves, slight trajectories, or small circles, ensure great stability. The dynamic diagram does not come alive by a series of jolts, for its harmonious layout is so deeply combined with the painter's vision as to allow only small alterations. The line is more frequently slanting than diagonal, and the rectangle is usually employed with a rib structure that expands and broadens the background. His graphic impulse is in no way a whiplash, as will be the case for others who later adopt it, though it does involve a linear leap that finds its place in a spatial context. This context is conceived in its totality by bringing together in the same creative parabola the lower layers (beneath an infinite horizon) and the higher ones (inclining direction signs), so as to connect them by indissoluble gravitation rather than linking them in succession. And it is precisely this persistent correlation, with its necessary complication and inner significance, that ensures that the work will represent a state of universal relations. Or, turning once again to René de Solier: "Space, the scene of the action, is also the surface of the group." [13]

At this point, after having produced such extraordinary work, which remained largely unappreciated until some five years later when it received its due recognition, there came a six-year interruption—the war obliged Hartung to take on other responsibilities, as serious on an ethical and human plane as they had been on the creative one. He resumed his work in 1945, displaying the same spontaneity that had appeared in the early years of his maturity. One may say besides that despite the suffering he endured, Hartung did not respond by protest or rebellion, as he might well have done, and as others were ready to do on his behalf. While freeing himself from every form of despotism, the artist had no intention of breaking an aesthetic order; he has never cared to adopt a position that might take precedence over form. Rather, through patient meditation on the torments of his mind as well as the matrices of form, expression was born to him within the image, which gloried in its indomitable *raison d'être*—the point of fusion between consciousness and subjectivity.

Around 1947, curled and tangled black lines and peremptory latticework patterns appeared without warning in the foreground, while behind them loomed an extended movement of planes in which color instilled a melting and tremulous quality—as though a landscape were to burst out beyond an iron grating. But let us not be deceived by parallels that might denote a detached place to be contemplated from this side of some boundary. Both the multiple contours of the tangles, and the chromatic phrasing they enclose, offer only a temporal sequence to be confronted on its less precarious levels, and therefore from a prearranged and absolute standpoint. It is the prominence of the gesture that acts to isolate two *tempi*, which grow and impress themselves on the viewer, interacting by their varying rhythms, but no less individualized or inspired.

There has been a complementary aspect that was always implicit in his work. This was the moment when Hartung's creative process was directed by his attraction to color, which became more explicit and accentuated than before. And it was during the last two years of the forties that he marked another stage in the growing development of an image that united existential torment with the incorruptible values of the immanence of the imagination. It appeared like a new poetic animation, with the balance of forces in the luminous texture remaining suspended and tremulous—forces that skim lightly as they project themselves in the quiet air, purified of any tangible contingency, and thus already mental.

He was to depart from this vision in his work of the sixties, where the enchantment of sign and light—the sign more isolated and definite, the light more delicate and impalpable—becomes ecstatic and indivisible, despite their clear antithesis. This dualism is converted into a concrete harmony that overwhelms all distinctions. The singular plumage that appears almost as the protagonist on the proscenium of a clear and boundless sky takes on the effect of a gradient projecting from the very atmosphere with which it competes. At the risk of being too elemental, or of reducing his expressive elements too radically, Hartung does not hold back from such comparisons—they represent a logical result of his investigation of reality, insofar as they serve to dislodge the more permanent substance of conscious life from the shell of ordinary objectivity. Emotion, immune to any contagion by outside canons, acts as the formative power. In the end these plumes re-enter the expanded space with which they collide, and much as they do not form a compact mass, as had happened and will happen again, they represent the sinuous and exposed moment when a limit is reached with no diminution of pride. An almost irreverent threat to the atmospheric expanse that they intercept, they nevertheless end by re-entering its channel.

Informal poetry has made its many suggestions and Hartung has put them to use within a measure of immediate structural syntax, but he has not merely matched the rhythm that began with a basic element. In that state it is still impatient, undisciplined, fortuitous, even instantaneous; while in Hartung the process is normative, and, though not dogmatic, has no unforeseeable solutions—the movements of the sign indicate a particular organization. In a certain sense, the intervention of the observer is not accessory; rather his existence is joined with all that is implied in the picture. Such painting is free of enigmas, because it communicates an event whose necessity is all-inclusive: it draws us into the folds of a texture where the labyrinth is ramified according to precise rules and verifiable measures. The direction of this texture is never negative, since that would presuppose a preexisting order against which to act (an *a priori* order outside human engagement), while the system is governed exclusively on its own measures. It is always the human tempo, seen and exalted as an ever-present gestation, that supplies the factors for the projecting of a positive element of knowledge. Even recent experimental trends may go back to certain beginnings initiated by Hartung. He took up the variability of phenomena within a visual objectivity that recognizes images as temporal events in whose cycle all men are involved beyond any stance of rejection or protest—an idea that always comes back to a unitary and paradigmatic measure expressed in terms of relation, progression, and generation. The optical reticle, combined and harmonized with associations of the labyrinth, offers an infinity of crossings and divergences that become sensitized by their elementary and controllable organicism. In short, it seems that Hartung has moved once again to produce a cultural situation within which the sign and the gesture, no longer emptied or expanded graphically, transform themselves into unity of movement, ready to embody the reverberations of echoes, and thus valid for their atonality and serial nature. These are anticipations with which it would be well for us not to lose contact now that the modern creative experience is being shifted into areas that seem radically to modify the presentation of the artistic phenomenon as we have so far known it. The paths of history have cracks but never irreparable breaks, and great artists do not embellish history by obstructing or resisting it—rather, they vie with it by lending it fruitful support, even though such support may still be linked to certain methods that the future may eliminate.

Hartung's latest paintings confirm this conviction. They have not only gone beyond the informal nature of their origin (whereby he was able to lay out cultural guidelines destined to be widely exploited), but reveal a method that accepts its own eventual demise, while standing ready to lend strength to other values. Instead of intricacy, we now have a sequence of primary elements, fixed within a precise channel where they arrange themselves as in a fugue, and where the light that skims over them kindles threads that extend and contract. A new dynamic mobilizes the picture, vitally participating in its development through references whose action is unmistakable because it cannot be interpreted in only its own terms. Its meanings are many, though controlled by guided possibilities. Shortly before, background areas became nebulous masses, within whose temporary softness no graphite lines appeared, though they could not help reappearing from time to time, primarily in the form of vigorously hollowed furrows. However, in recent works, those between 1965 and 1966, lines are represented as threads of light, their presence again a determinant in the sense that they resolutely command an open spatial dimension agitated by the luminous flux that invades it. There is something that recalls certain watercolors of 1922, and here once again one can only admire the extraordinary vitality of the artist, who by an accumulation of moments and references constantly deepens his inner experience.

Hartung's career, in its undaunted independence, has avoided the dangers of dogmatism that might have precluded the development of his own artistic idiom and thereby the emergence of a moment of ontological significance. His work mirrors with unquestionable authority the geographical system of the place where it emerged and was defined. Many might have preferred a detailed analysis of individual works, more precise interpretations, comparisons, and value judgments. Instead it has been my purpose to present a synthesis that would make clear, from several angles, the comprehensive meaning of Hartung's work. Others have probed, more or less deeply, the various phases of his painting, following the evidence step by step. I have preferred to attempt a comparison between the artist as individual and his relation to history in the hope that this would lead the reader to the more specialized texts—which though not quoted are listed in the bibliography—so that, instead of relying on isolated instances, he might see them in their relation to one another, to be understood not only in themselves but also against a wider cultural background. Being convinced that major creative figures are of interest not simply to art but to the whole breadth of a civilization in formation—to which art, with its pauses and advances, is one of the principal contributors—I trust that I have not evaded the task by offering this plan of interpretation of an artist whose clarity and quality of creation are among the least doubted but least discussed of this century.

UMBRO APOLLONIO

NOTES

1 Madeleine Rousseau and Ottomar Domnick, *Hans Hartung,* Domnick-Verlag, Stuttgart, 1949

2 Georges Charbonnier, *Le Monologue du peintre,* René Juillard, Paris, 1959

3 René de Solier, "Hans Hartung," *Quadrum,* No. 2, Brussels, November, 1956

4 Bernard Dorival (ed.), *Peintres célèbres contemporains,* Lucien Mazenod, Paris, 1964

5 Giuseppe Marchiori ("Hartung, l'oeuvre première," *XXe Siècle,* No. 14, Paris, June, 1960), in discussing the works between 1920 and 1924, argues that "they can be considered as the prototypes of many present experiments, or even seen as the original inspiration for a few modern painters who are very sensitive to Hartung's formal inventions (graphic and pictorial)." Gindertael, one of the most diligent interpreters of Hartung's work, remarks in his monograph (Pierre Tisné, Paris, 1960) that the artist has been widely recognized in the United States since 1936.

6 R.-V. Gindertael, "Peintres de la nouvelle génération: Hans Hartung," *XXe Siècle,* No. 7, Paris, June, 1956

7 René de Solier, "Hans Hartung," *Cahiers d'art,* XXVII/1, Paris, July, 1952

8 Georges Charbonnier, *op. cit.*

9 Roger Bordier, "Notre Enquête sur la technique ou l'improvisation travaillée. L'Art et la manière: Hans Hartung," *Art d'aujourd'hui,* Series 5, No. 2/3, Boulogne-sur-Seine, March–April, 1954

10 Pierre Volboudt, "A Chacun sa réalité: Hartung," *XXe Siècle,* No. 9, Paris, June, 1957

11 J. Claus, "Die herbe Vision: Gespräch mit H. Hartung," *Literatur Revue,* No. 12, Würzburg, 1963; reprinted in *Theorien zeitgenössischer Malerei,* Rowohlt, Reinbeck bei Hamburg, 1963

12 René de Solier, *Cahiers d'art, op. cit.*

13 René de Solier, *Quadrum, op. cit.*

Biographical Outline

1904 Hans Hartung is born on September 21 in Leipzig, where his father is a doctor; from his mother and maternal grandfather he inherits a deep musical sensibility tending primarily toward Italian, French, and German music of the seventeenth and eighteenth centuries, as well as twelve-tone and other contemporary works.

1912–14 During vacations in the Swiss Alps, he draws views of mountains. The family settles for a time in Basel, where he becomes interested in astronomy and photography, and draws views of the sun and moon. With the outbreak of war, the Hartungs return to Leipzig.

1915 Enters secondary school in Dresden where he will remain until 1924.

1917–19 Begins his career as a painter. Becomes interested in religion, and undergoes an adolescent spiritual crisis.

1921–22 Intensely interested in drawing, he passes gradually from the figurative to the abstract. Visits museums, but is also attracted by exhibitions of German Impressionists and Expressionists.

1923–24 Executes abstract watercolors, then large drawings in India ink and red chalk, to be followed at the end of 1923 and the beginning of 1924 by his first abstract canvases.

1924–26 Studies philosophy and art history at the University of Leipzig, meanwhile taking regular courses at the Leipzig and Dresden Academies of Fine Arts, and subjecting himself to strenuous technical discipline. Makes copies of El Greco, Hals, and Rembrandt. Through color reproductions, copies Matisse, and later Picasso. Beginning in 1925 he advances his technical training under Professor Kurt Wehlte (later, in 1928, he will attend Max Doerner's courses in Munich). In 1925, he attends a Kandinsky lecture in Leipzig, and is greatly impressed by a Kokoschka exhibition in Dresden; Nolde's Expressionism also has a profound effect on him.

1926 Rejects his professors' suggestions that he go to the Bauhaus. The Dresden international exhibition puts him in contact with modern painting outside Germany, in particular French Impressionist, Post-Impressionist, Fauve, and Cubist trends. Having been in the Tyrol in 1924, he now undertakes long trips, going by bicycle as far as Sicily. On his first visit to France, arrives in Paris in October.

1927–29 Spends the first part of 1927 in Paris, then some months in the south of France. He is in Paris for the next two winters, gradually discovering Cézanne and Van Gogh, Bonnard, Picasso, Braque, and Léger, and studying particularly their techniques. Attends the free Academies of Castellucho, Ranson, and Lhote with an interval, in 1928, of one semester at the Munich Academy of Fine Arts. Desultory study of engraving; continues his study of aesthetic problems. Travels to Belgium and Holland. In September, 1929, marries the young Norwegian painter Anna-Eva Bergman.

1930–31 Lives on the Côte d'Azur. Exhibits for the first time in Dresden. Cubist allusions appear in some paintings of this period.

1932 In February, exhibits three canvases at the "Young Artists" show at the Flechtheim Gallery, Berlin; later exhibits at the Blomquist Gallery in Oslo. The sudden death of his father, which seriously affects the artist's health. As a result of this and his concern over the rising power of the Nazis, he decides to leave Germany for Paris, where he entrusts some of his youthful canvases to the Galerie Jeanne Bucher.

1933–34 On Minorca in the Balearic Islands, he works assiduously to free himself of Cubist influence and return to the more instinctive painting of his youth. The canvases of 1934, by their similarity of line, derive from the ink drawings of 1922 to 1923. In financial straits because of the confiscation of his property in Germany and the impossibility of receiving help from relatives in Dresden, he leaves Minorca for Paris, then goes to Stockholm to live with his wife's family.

1935 Returns to Berlin with the hope of saving his property, but is blocked by the surveillance of the Nazis and decides to leave Germany for good. In October, with the help of Will Grohmann and Christian Zervos, he settles permanently in Paris. Becomes friendly with Hélion and meets Kandinsky, Mondrian, Domela, Magnelli, Miró, and Calder. His first Paris studio, 19 Rue Daguerre, is next to that of Goetz. Exhibits at the Salon des Surindépendants, and will do so again in 1936, 1937, 1938, and 1945.

1936 Participates in group show in May at the Galerie Pierre, with Kandinsky, Arp, Hélion, and the architect Nelson. Devotes himself to a technique similar to the "ink spot."

1937 Takes part in the international exhibition organized by Christian Zervos at the Jeu de Paume, in connection with the Paris International Exhibition of Art and Technology.

1938 Still in financial difficulties, he moves to a small studio near the Rue de la Convention. After a period of nervous exhaustion and marital difficulties divorces Anna-Eva Bergman (they will re-marry in 1957). Deprived of his German passport, his situation in Paris becomes precarious. Works for about a year in the studio of the sculptor Julio Gonzalez, whose daughter Roberta, a painter, he marries in 1939. At this time a certain Surrealist influence can be seen in his work. Exhibits at the show of twentieth-century German art at the New Burlington Galleries in London, then at other galleries in that city. In Paris, exhibits pastels and drawings with Roberta Gonzalez at the Galerie Henriette.

1939 Begins his official opposition to the Hitler regime. Though he lives somewhat in isolation, Hélion persuades him to participate in the "Réalités Nouvelles" exhibition at the Galerie Charpentier—he submits a single drawing, which is not even listed in the catalogue. With the outbreak of war in September, the artist is interned in a camp for foreign nationals. Joins the Foreign Legion in December, and goes to North Africa.

1940 After the fall of France, leaves the Legion and settles temporarily at Cahors, rejoining the Gonzalez family who have taken refuge in the south of France. (Julio Gonzalez returns to Paris in 1941, and dies there on March 27, 1942.)

1943 When the Germans occupy southern France, Hartung flees to Spain, where he is imprisoned and later interned in a concentration camp. Freed in December through American influence, he returns to North Africa and again joins the Foreign Legion.

1944 After the Allied landing in France, takes part in the Alsace offensive, is wounded at Belfort, and loses a leg.

1945 Returns to Paris and begins to paint again after a six-year interruption.

1946 Now a French citizen, Hartung is awarded the Médaille Militaire, the Croix de Guerre, and the Cross of the Legion of Honor. Exhibits at the first "Domela-Hartung-Schneider" show at the Salle du Centre des Recherches, 15 Rue Cujas, and shortly thereafter at the fifth group exhibition in the same Salle, attracting the attention of various critics, among them Charles Estienne, Wilhelm Uhde, Madeleine Rousseau, and Léon Degand. Holds a one-man show from May to June at the Gasser Gallery in Zurich. Is represented at the Salon de Mai in Paris, and at the first Salon des Réalités Nouvelles (where he will again exhibit in 1947, 1948, 1949, 1950, and 1956). The art dealer Denise René becomes interested in his work, and invites him to join a group exhibition in her gallery, "Abstract Painters," along with Deyrolle, Dewasne, Marie Raymond, and Schneider. Begins a series of engravings.

1947 Hartung has his first one-man show in Paris, on the occasion of the opening of the Galerie Lydia Conti. The director Alain Resnais makes him the subject of a film, which will be shown in 1948 during a traveling exhibition in Germany, and in 1950 at the Galerie "La Hune" in Paris to mark the publication of a Hartung monograph by O. Domnick in Stuttgart.

1948 Retrospective exhibition of drawings at the Galerie Lydia Conti, covering Hartung's work from 1922 to 1948. Takes part in a traveling exhibition of French abstract painters in Germany, and in exhibitions in Paris galleries. Is present at the Venice Biennale.

1949 With the closing of the Galerie Conti, transfers to the Galerie Louis Carré. One-man shows at the Stangl Gallery in Munich (drawings), and at the Hanover Gallery in London.

1951 Exhibition of pastels with Schneider and Lanskoy at the Galerie Carré, and later with Carré in New York, Chicago, Baltimore, and San Francisco, as part of a traveling exhibition of French avant-garde art. He is represented at the "Véhémences confrontées" show organized by Michel Tapié at the Galerie Nina Dausset, and shows three canvases at the first "Pittori d'oggi, Francia-Italia" exhibition in Turin.

1952 One-man show from February to March at the Kunsthalle, Basel. Devotes himself again to a series of engravings. Exhibits a number of canvases at the Venice Biennale.

1953 One-man shows at Reed and Lefèvre, London, and at the Marbach Gallery, Berne. Takes part in the third "Pittori d'oggi, Francia-Italia" exhibition.

1954 Exhibits fifty paintings, twenty pastels, and fifteen engravings from 1933 to 1954 at the Palais des Beaux-Arts in Brussels. He later exhibits his graphic work at the Galerie "La Hune" in Paris. Is present at the Venice Biennale, and takes part in the Ecole de Paris exhibitions at the Galerie Charpentier each year until 1958.

1955 "Documenta I" exhibition in Kassel; one-man show at the Probst Gallery, Mannheim; represented by various works in exhibitions in Lausanne, Pittsburgh, Tokyo, São Paulo, etc.

1956 Exhibition of recent work at the Galerie de France; retrospective show of drawings, 1921–38, at the Galerie Craven, Paris. Receives a Guggenheim Prize.

1957 Exhibition at the Kestner-Gesellschaft, Hannover (eighty-five paintings, 1932–56; drawings and watercolors, 1921–54), later taken to Stuttgart, Berlin, Hamburg, Cologne, and Nuremberg; one-man show at the Kleeman Gallery, New York. Present at the fifth "Pittori d'oggi, Francia-Italia" exhibition in Turin. Begins a third period of engravings, etchings, and lithographs for Berggruen in Paris and the Marbach Gallery in Berne.

1958 Exhibition of graphics at the Galleria Il Segno in Rome. Executes a new series of lithographs. Lithography exhibition at the Galerie "La Hune" in Paris. Hartung is awarded the Rubens Prize, conferred for the first time by the town of Siegen in Westphalia. One-man show at the Stangl Gallery in Munich; one-man show of pastels at the Galleria Il Segno, Rome, and another at the Galerie de France, Paris. Participates in exhibitions of modern art in Paris, Brussels, Liège, and in Denmark and Switzerland.

1959 Exhibits at the Mannheim Kunsthalle and at the Carnegie Institute of Pittsburgh. Retrospective one-man show at the museum of Antibes; exhibition of pastels in Aix-en-Provence with Anna-Eva Bergman; pastels at the Kleeman Gallery, New York; drawings at the Stangl Gallery, Munich; pastels at the Galleria La Bussola, Turin. Exhibits five canvases at the international exhibition "Documenta II" in Kassel. Takes part in the seventh "Pittori d'oggi, Francia-Italia" exhibition in Turin, and also in the opening exhibition of the Galleria d'Arte Moderna, Turin, "Modern Painting by Foreign Artists in Italian Private Collections."

1960 One-man show of twenty-one pastels at the Van de Loo Gallery, Essen. Participates in the exhibition "Antagonismes" at the Musée des Arts Décoratifs, Paris. First prize for painting at the Venice Biennale by unanimous vote of the jury.

1961 One-man show at the Galerie de France with works from 1922 to 1939.

1962 One-man show of recent works at the Galerie de France.

1963 Traveling retrospective at the Kunsthaus in Zurich, the Museum des XX. Jahrhunderts in Vienna, the Kunstverein in Düsseldorf, the Palais des Beaux-Arts in Brussels, the Stedelijk Museum in Amsterdam, with 120 canvases, 150 drawings, pastels, and gouaches, and a sculpture. One-man show at the "Im Erker" Gallery in Saint Gallen, Switzerland, with recent works; one-man show at the Franke Gallery in Munich with recent works.

1964 One-man show at the Galerie de France with fifteen paintings from 1963 to 1964.

1965 One-man show of engravings, 1921–65, at the Städtisches Museum of Brunswick, on the occasion of the publication of his catalogue of engravings and lithographs.

1966 Traveling exhibition in Spain: Sala Nebli, Madrid; Galería René Métras, Barcelona; Sala Illescas, Bilbao. One-man show of pastels and paintings on paper at the Galerie de France. Exhibition of engravings and lithographs with Anna-Eva Bergman at the "Sa Taula" Gallery, Fornells, Minorca. Exhibition at the Galleria Civica d'Arte Moderna in Turin.

1969 Retrospective at the Musée National d'Art Moderne in Paris, January 7–February 24.

Bibliography

General Works

ANDERSON, MOGENS. *Moderne Fransk Malerkunst.* Athenaeum, Copenhagen, 1948

BOURET, JEAN. *L'Art abstrait.* Club Français du Livre, Paris, 1957

BRION, MARCEL. *Art abstrait.* Albin Michel, Paris, 1956

———, et al. *Art Since 1945.* Harry N. Abrams, New York, 1958

CHARBONNIER, GEORGES. *Le Monologue du peintre.* René Juillard, Paris, 1959

CLAUS, J. *Theorien zeitgenössischer Malerei in Selbstzeugnissen.* Rowohlt, Reinbeck bei Hamburg, 1963

DIEHL, GASTON. *La Peinture moderne dans le monde.* Paris, 1961. (*The Moderns: A Treasury of Painting Throughout the World.* Crown Publishers, New York, 1961)

DORIVAL, BERNARD. *Les Peintres du XXe Siècle,* Vol. II. Pierre Tisné, Paris, 1957

GIANI, GIAMPIERO. *Arte astratta, Collezione Cavellini.* Edizioni della Conchiglia, Milan, 1958

GOTOH, SHIGEKI (ed.). *Modern Painting.* Text in Japanese, captions in Japanese and English. Tokyo, 1963

GROHMANN, WILL. *Bildende Kunst und Architektur* (*Zwischen den beiden Kriegen*). Suhrkamp, Berlin, 1953

HAFTMANN, WERNER. *Malerei im XX. Jahrhundert.* Prestel-Verlag, Munich, 1955

HUYGHE, RENÉ. *Dialogue avec le visible.* Flammarion, Paris, 1955

MARCHIORI, GIUSEPPE, and GRIBAUDO, EZIO. *La pittura straniera nelle collezioni private italiane.* Fratelli Pozzo, Turin, 1960

Metro, International Directory of Contemporary Art, 1964. Milan, 1964

NACENTA, RAYMOND. *School of Paris: The Painters and the Artistic Climate of Paris Since 1910.* New York Graphic Society, Greenwich, Conn., 1959

PONENTE, NELLO. *Modern Painting: Contemporary Trends.* Skira, Geneva, 1960

RAGON, MICHEL. *L'Aventure de l'art abstrait.* Lafont, Paris, 1956

———. *Expression et non-figuration.* Jacques Damase, Paris, 1949

SCHMIDT, GEORG. *Die Malerei in Deutschland 1918–1955.* Langewiesche-Köster, Königstein im Taunus, 1960

SEUPHOR, MICHEL. *L'Art abstrait, ses origines, ses premiers maîtres.* Maeght, Paris, 1949

———. *Dictionnaire de la peinture abstraite.* Hazan, Paris, 1957

———. *La Peinture abstraite, sa genèse, son expansion.* Paris, 1962. (*Abstract Painting: Fifty Years of Accomplishment from Kandinsky to the Present.* Harry N. Abrams, New York, 1962)

THWAITES, J. A. *Ich hasse die moderne Kunst.* Agis-Verlag, Krefeld and Baden-Baden, 1957

TRIER, EDUARD. *Zeichner des XX. Jahrhunderts.* Mann, Berlin, 1956

Monographs

AUBIER, DOMINIQUE. *Hartung.* With 30 reproductions, 12 in color. Le Musée de Poche, Georges Fall, Paris, 1961

GINDERTAEL, R.-V. *Hans Hartung.* With 117 reproductions, 40 in color. Pierre Tisné, Paris, 1960; Rembrandt-Verlag, Berlin, 1962; Universe Books, New York, 1961

GROHMANN, WILL. *Hans Hartung: Aquarelle 1922.* With 33 colorplates; text in German, English, and French. Erker-Verlag, Saint Gallen, 1966

Hans Hartung. "Plaquette" published on the occasion of the Venice Biennale. With 51 reproductions, 13 in color. Galerie de France, Paris, 1960

Hans Hartung: Dix Peintures. Published on the occasion of an exhibition of recent works, November–December, 1962. With 10 colorplates. Galerie de France, Paris, 1962

Hans Hartung: Oeuvres de 1920 à 1939. Published on the occasion of the exhibition of June–September, 1961. With 46 reproductions, 17 in color. Galerie de France, Paris, 1961

ROUSSEAU, MADELEINE, and DOMNICK, OTTOMAR. *Hans Hartung.* Preface by James Johnson Sweeney. With 56 reproductions, 12 in color; text in English, French, and German. Domnick-Verlag, Stuttgart, 1949

SCHMÜCKING, ROLF (ed.). *Hans Hartung: Werkverzeichnis der Graphik 1921–1965.* With 192 reproductions. Schmücking Gallery, Brunswick, 1965

TARDIEU, JEAN. *Sur Dix Pastels de Hartung.* With 10 colorplates. Peintres d'Aujourd'hui, Fernand Hazan, Paris, 1962

Catalogues

Brussels, Palais des Beaux-Arts. Exhibition, April 3–21, 1954. Catalogue by René de Solier

Córdoba, Galería Liceo. Exhibition of pastels. 1961. Catalogue by José de Castro Arines

Dresden, Kühl Gallery. Hartung exhibition. 1931. Preface to catalogue by Erich Lissner

Düsseldorf, Kunstverein für die Rheinlande und Westfalen, Kunsthalle. Retrospective exhibition. 1963. Preface to catalogue by Karl-Heinz Hering

Eindhoven, the Netherlands, Stedelijk van Abbemuseum. Catalogue. 1958

Hannover, Kestner-Gesellschaft. Traveling exhibition *Ausstellungsjahre 1956–1957.* January 26–March 3, 1957. Catalogue No. 4 by Werner Schmalenbach

London, Hanover Gallery. Exhibition of drawings by Hans Hartung and Peter Foldes. 1949. Preface to catalogue by Denys Sutton

Madrid, "Ateneo." Exhibition of pastels. 1961. Preface to catalogue by J. Vergara

Milan, Galleria Loenzelli. Exhibition of pastels, 1961. Catalogue by Giuseppe Marchiori

New York, Collections of the Museum of Living Art. 1942. Catalogue by A. E. Gallatin

Paris, Musée National d'Art Moderne. Exhibition. January 7–February 24, 1969

Paris, Salon des Réalités. Exhibition. 1948

Paris, Galerie Craven. Exhibition. November 17–December 15, 1956. Preface to catalogue by R.-V. Gindertael

Paris, Salon des Réalités Nouvelles. Exhibition. 1947. Catalogue by Madeleine Rousseau

Paris, Galerie Lydia Conti. Hartung exhibition. 1947. Preface by Madeleine Rousseau

Saint Gallen, "Im Erker." Exhibition of recent paintings. 1963. Preface to catalogue by Werner Schmalenbach and J. Proal

Siegen, Städtische Galerie Haus Seel. Hans Hartung exhibition (Rubens prize). 1958. Catalogue by Will Grohmann, *et al.*

Stuttgart. *Sonderausstellung französischer abstrakter Malerei in Deutschland.* 1948. Catalogue by Ottomar Domnick

Turin, Galleria Civica d'Arte Moderna. Exhibition. May–June, 1966. Organized by Luigi Malle, preface by Giuseppe Marchiori

Turin, Galleria Civica d'Arte Moderna. Exhibition. 1961. Catalogue by Giuseppe Marchiori and Ezio Gribaudo

Vienna, Museum des XX. Jahrhunderts. Retrospective exhibition. 1963. Interview with Hartung in the catalogue by Werner Hofmann

Zurich, Kunsthaus. Retrospective exhibition. 1963. Preface to catalogue by Eduard Hüttinger

Periodicals

AUBIER, DOMINIQUE. "Hans Hartung et l'urgence de peindre." *XXe Siècle,* No. 12, Paris, May–June, 1959

———. "Hartung peintre du silence," *France-Observateur,* December 31, 1958

BORDIER, ROGER. "Notre Enquête sur la technique ou l'improvisation travaillée. L'Art et la manière: Hans Hartung," *Art d'aujourd'hui,* March–April, 1954

BOZAL FERNANDEZ, V. "Hartung, Signo y significado," *Artes,* No. 76, Madrid, 1966

CLÉMENT, VIRGINIA. "Le Réel-Irréel de Hans Hartung," *Aesculape,* Paris, February, 1956

DEGAND, LÉON. "Hartung," *Aujourd'hui,* Paris, January, 1957

———. "Jean Hartung," *Juin,* Paris, 1946

DESCARGUES, PIERRE. "Les Incunables de Hans Hartung," *Les Lettres Françaises,* 17/3, Paris, 1966

DYPRÉAU, JEAN. "Hartung à Bruxelles et Amsterdam," *XXe Siècle,* No. 23, Paris, May, 1964

ESTIENNE, CHARLES. "Peintures de Hans Hartung," *Combat,* March 21, 1947

———, and DEGAND, LÉON. "Notes sur Hartung," *Art d'aujourd'hui,* No. 4, March 4, 1951
FEZZI, E. "Il limbo incantato di Hartung," *Le Arti,* No. 2, Milan, 1966
FRIGERIO, SIMONE. "Hartung," *Aujourd'hui,* No. 39, Paris, November, 1962
———. "Hartung," *Aujourd'hui,* No. 45, Paris, 1964
GHEERBANDT, B. "Lithographies de Hans Hartung," *XXe Siècle,* No. 11, Paris, 1958
GINDERTAEL, R.-V. "L'Exposition graphique et l'espace: Hans Hartung," *XXe Siècle,* Paris, March, 1958
———. "Hans Hartung," *Les Beaux-Arts,* Brussels, April 2, 1954
———. "Hans Hartung," *Cimaise,* Paris, September–October, 1956
———. "Hans Hartung e il significato dell'atto di dipingere," *i 4 Soli,* Turin, November 6, 1954
———. "Hartung aujourd'hui," *Quadrum,* No. 14, Brussels, 1963
———. "Oeuvres récentes de Hartung," *XXe Siècle,* No. 24, Paris, 1964
———. "Peintres de la nouvelle génération," *XXe Siècle,* Paris, June, 1956
———. "Peintres d'origine allemande en France. I: Les Créateurs," *Allemagne d'aujourd'hui,* Nos. 4, 5, Paris, July, October, 1957
GUÉGUEN, P. "Hans Hartung le Précurseur," *Aujourd-'hui,* No. 31, Paris, 1961
HAFTMANN, WERNER. "Mutamenti formali nell'opera di Hans Hartung," *La Biennale di Venezia,* No. 42, January–March, 1961
HODIN, J.-P. "Quand les Artistes parlent du sacré," *XXe Siècle,* No. 24, Paris, 1964
JOUFFROY, ALAIN. "Biographie des peintres: Hans Hartung," *Le Jardin des Arts,* No. 66, Paris, April, 1960
"Lines of Force" (Hans Hartung), *Time,* No. 13, April, 1957
MARCHAND, JEAN-JOSÉ. Critical notes in *Paru,* Nos. 34, 41, 43, 47, Paris, 1947
———. "Un Néo-Abstractiviste, Hans Hartung," *Le Rassemblement,* Paris, September 17, 1948
MARCHIORI, GIUSEPPE. "Hartung, l'oeuvre première," XXe Siècle, No. 14, Paris, June, 1960
RAYMOND, MARIE. Article in *Kronick van Kunst en Kultur,* Amsterdam, 1948
RESTANY, P. "Le Cas Hartung," *Prisme des arts,* Paris, November, 1956
RINGSTROM, KARL K. "Un Réaliste parmi les abstraits: Hans Hartung," *Le Jardin des Arts,* Paris, September, 1957
SÉE, J.-C. "De Gauguin à l'art d'aujourd'hui," *Combat,* January 24, 1949
SEUPHOR, MICHEL. "Hans Hartung," *Art Digest,* New York, March 1, 1955
SIBLIK, JIRI. "Dynamicky grafizmus Hans Hartunga," *Revue Svetovej Literatúry,* No. 3, Prague, 1965
SOLIER, RENÉ DE. "Hans Hartung," *Cahiers d'art,* July, 1952
———. "Hans Hartung," Quadrum, No. 2, Brussels, November, 1956
———. "Die Kunst der Geste bei Hans Hartung: der Sammler Cavellini," *Das Kunstwerk,* December 10, 1959
THWAITES, J. A. "An Exhibit in Germany" (Hans Hartung at the Kestner-Gesellschaft), *Pictures on Exhibit,* No. 6, March, 1957
VOLBOUDT, PIERRE. "A Chacun sa réalité: Hartung," *XXe Siècle,* No. 9, Paris, June, 1957
———. "Hans Hartung: une thématique de l'espace," *XXe Siècle,* No. 21, Paris, May, 1963
VOLTA, CANDIDO. "Conversazione con Hartung," *Metro,* No. 3, Milan, 1961
WESCHER, HERTA. In *Axis,* Nos. 6, 7, London, 1936

Poem

JAGUER, EDOUARD. *Les Deux Soeurs, pays de Hartung,* 1946

Films

Hans Hartung. By Alain Resnais, 1947. (The commentary by Madeleine Rousseau and the music by Antoine Duhamel could not be recorded at the time for lack of funds)
Hans Hartung. In the series "Peintres d'aujourd'hui," 1964. Produced by Jacques Simonet, directed by Suzuki, text by Camille Bourniquel

List of Illustrations

KEY TO THE CAPTIONS

A.	= watercolor	G.	= gouache
C.	= pencil	P.	= pastel
C.N.	= black chalk	S.	= sanguine
E.	= ink	Sc.	= sculpture
E.C.	= Chinese ink	T.	= oil on canvas
F.	= charcoal		

96 T. 1947–9. 28¾ × 18⅞″
97 T. 1945–27. 10¾ × 7½″
98 T. 1945–28. 10¾ × 7½″
99 T. 1947–30. 23⅝ × 28¾″
100 T. 1947–12. 57½ × 38⅛″
101 T. 1947–39. 23¼ × 39⅜″
102 T. 1947–25. 19 × 28¾″
103 T. 1948–23. 18⅛ × 21⅝″
104 T. 1948–34. 19⅝ × 24″
105 T. 1947–14. 38⅛ × 51⅛″
106 T. 1949–26. 38⅛ × 57½″
107 T. 1948–19. 38⅛ × 51⅛″
108 T. 1949–9. 35 × 63¾″
109 T. 1949–24. 38⅛ × 57½″
110 T. 1949–25. 47¼ × 47¼″
111 T. 1949–23. 38⅛ × 51⅛″
112 T. 1948–8. 19⅝ × 28¾″
113 T. 1950–46. 34⅝ × 51⅛″
114 T. 1952–50. 38⅛ × 63¾″
115 T. 1952–53. 19¼ × 31⅞″
116 T. 1951–8. 38⅛ × 57½″
117 T. 1951–5. 38⅛ × 57½″
118 T. 1952–40. 38⅛ × 51⅛″
119 T. 1952–3. 38⅛ × 51⅛″
120 T. 1955–12. 38⅛ × 57½″
121 T. 1954–4. 38⅛ × 57½″
122 T. 1956–9. 70⅞ × 53⅞″
123 T. 1956–8. 70⅞ × 53⅞″
124 T. 1956–19. 70⅞ × 53⅞″
125 T. 1955–17. 63¾ × 44⅞″
126 T. 1956–20. 55⅞ × 76¾″
127 T. 1957–12. 51⅛ × 38⅛″
128 T. 1955–23. 63¾ × 48″
128 T. 1955–23. 63¾ × 48″
129 T. 1956–21. 70⅞ × 44⅞″
130 T. 1956–10. 55⅞ × 76¾″
131 T. 1955–24. 63¾ × 48″
132 T. 1957–10. 63¾ × 48″
133 T. 1957–11. 57½ × 38⅛″
134 T. 1959–2. 36¼ × 23⅝″
135 T. 1956–18. 63¾ × 41″
136 T. 1958–3. 36¼ × 28¾″
137 T. 1958–15. 21¼ × 28¾″
138 T. 1958–14. 23⅝ × 36¼″
139 T. 1957–8. 57½ × 44⅞″
140 T. 1960–20. 11¼ × 17¾″
141 T. 1961–H43. 19⅝ × 51⅛″
142 T. 1961–66. 21¼ × 57⅛″
143 T. 1962–H9. 39⅜ × 63¾″
144 T. 1961–H48. 36¼ × 59″
145 T. 1961–H23. 31⅞ × 23⅝″
146 T. 1962–R33. 31⅞″ × 25⅝″
147 T. 1962–R12. 70⅞ × 43¾″
148 T. 1962–R16. 70⅞ × 55⅞″
149 T. 1962–E1. 39⅜ × 63¾″
150 T. 1962–E8. 31⅞ × 51⅛″
151 T. 1962–U4. 70⅞ × 43¾″
152 T. 1963–H37. 70⅞ × 55⅞″
153 T. 1962–U50. 25⅝ × 36¼″
154 T. 1962–U47. 18⅛ × 24″
155 T. 1962–L33. 70⅞ × 55⅞″
156 T. 1963–R38. 70⅞ × 55⅞″
157 T. 1962–L49. 63¾ × 51⅛″
158 T. 1963–E45. 70⅞ × 55⅞″
159 T. 1963–U28. 21⅝ × 13″
160 T. 1963–H48. 39⅜ × 31⅞″
161 T. 1962–L46. 18⅛ × 13″
162 T. 1963–U17. 28¾ × 36¼″
163 T. 1962–A10. 21⅝ × 13″
164 T. 1962–A20. 13 × 21⅝″
165 T. 1963–U40. 24 × 18⅛″
166 T. 1963–U18. 36¼ × 28¾″
167 T. 1964–E12. 44⅞ × 57½″
168 T. 1963–R23. 40⅛ × 51⅛″
169 T. 1963–U44. 19⅝ × 25⅝″
170 T. 1963–U45. 19⅝ × 25⅝″
171 T. 1964–E31. 28¾ × 36¼″
172 T. 1964–E27. 28¾ × 36¼″
173 T. 1963–E7. 41⅜ × 25⅝″
174 T. 1963–E6. 41⅜ × 25⅝″
175 T. 1963–H21. 25⅝ × 19⅝″
176 T. 1963–E40. 39⅜ × 63¾″
177 T. 1962–K10. 36¼ × 59″
178 T. 1965–H9. 27⅛ × 70⅞″
179 T. 1963–H26. 39⅜ × 31⅞″
180 T. 1963–H24. 31⅞ × 39⅜″
181 T. 1965–H19. 13¾ × 8⅝″
182 T. 1965–E9. 8⅝ × 13¾″
183 T. 1964–H45. 70⅞ × 43¾″
184 T. 1964–H44. 70⅞ × 55⅞″
185 a) T. 1963–R18. 70⅞ × 27⅛″
b) T. 1963–R19. 70⅞ × 27⅛″
c) T. 1963–R20. 70⅞ × 27⅛″
d) T. 1963–R21. 70⅞ × 27⅛″
186 T. 1963–K45. 31⅞ × 23⅝″
187 T. 1963–K33. 25⅝ × 18⅛″
188 T. 1964–H35. 59 × 36¼″
189 T. 1964–H40. 51⅛ × 40⅛″
190 T. 1964–H7. 25⅝ × 31⅞″
191 T. 1964–R2. 25⅝ × 19⅝″
192 T. 1964–R15. 51⅛ × 40⅛″
193 T. 1964–R1. 25⅝ × 19⅝″
194 T. 1964–R3. 23⅝ × 28¾″
195 E. C. 1964
196 E. C. 1964
197 E. C. 1964
198 E. C. 1964
199 T. 1965–E32. 60⅝ × 98⅜″
200 T. 1964–R24. 60⅝ × 98⅜″
201 T. 1965–E34. 60⅝ × 98⅜″
202 T. 1966–H1. 15¾ × 41⅜″

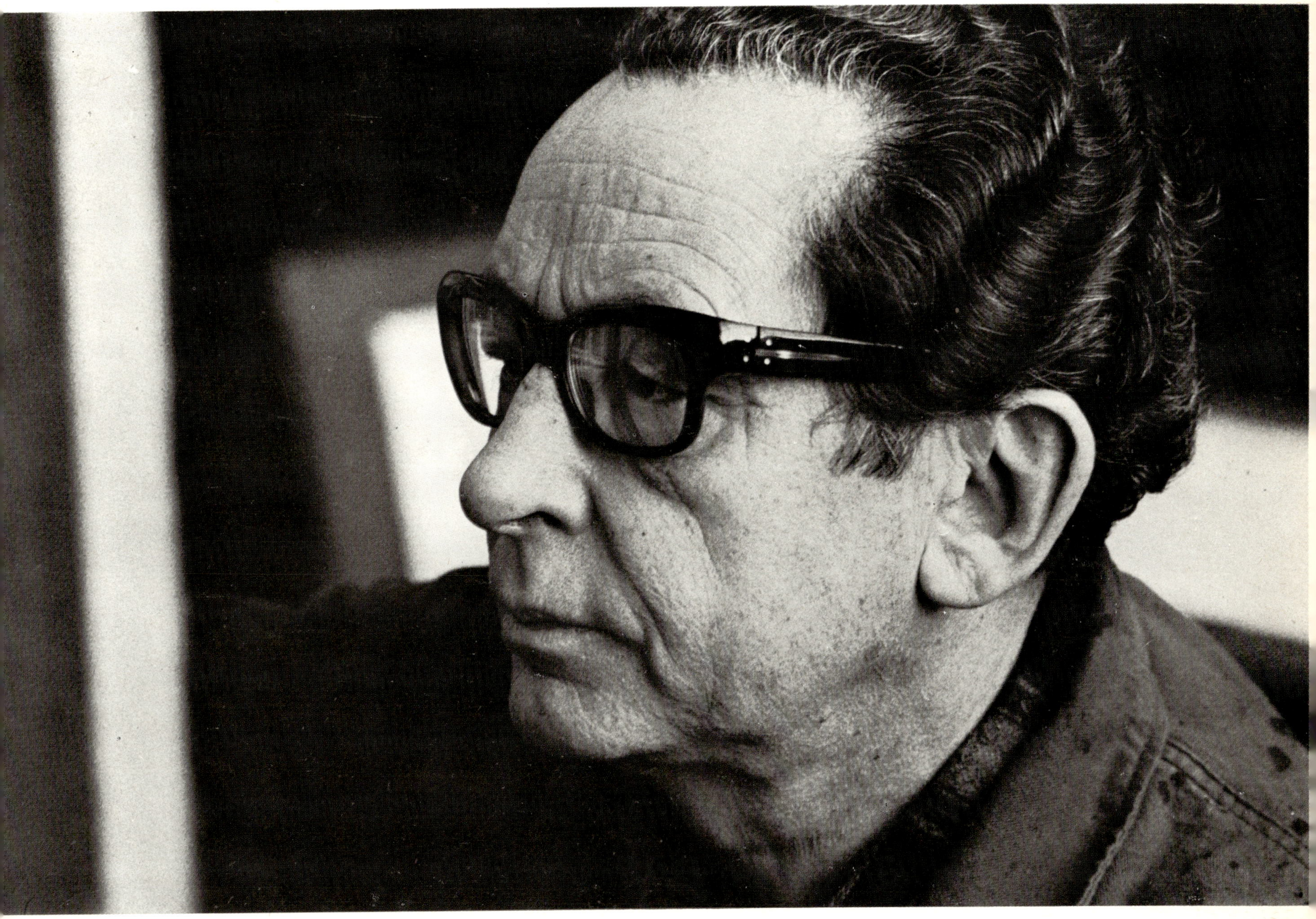

LEGENDA

		Abréviations	Abbreviations	Abkürzungen	Abbreviazioni
A.	=	*aquarelle*	aquarelle	*Aquarell*	acquerello
C.	=	*crayon*	crayon	*Bleistift*	matita
C.N.	=	*craie noire*	black chalk	*schwarze Kreide*	creta nera
E.	=	*encre*	ink	*Tinte*	inchiostro
E.C.	=	*encre de Chine*	Chinese ink	*Tusche*	inchiostro di China
F.	=	*fusain*	charcoal	*Kohle*	carboncino
G.	=	*gouache*	gouache	*Gouache*	guazzo
P.	=	*pastel*	pastel	*Pastell*	pastello
S.	=	*sanguine*	sanguine	*Rötel*	sanguigna
Sc.	=	*sculpture*	sculpture	*Skulptur*	scultura
T.	=	*peinture sur toile*	painting on canvas	*Bild auf Leinewand*	pittura su tela

1 S. 1922

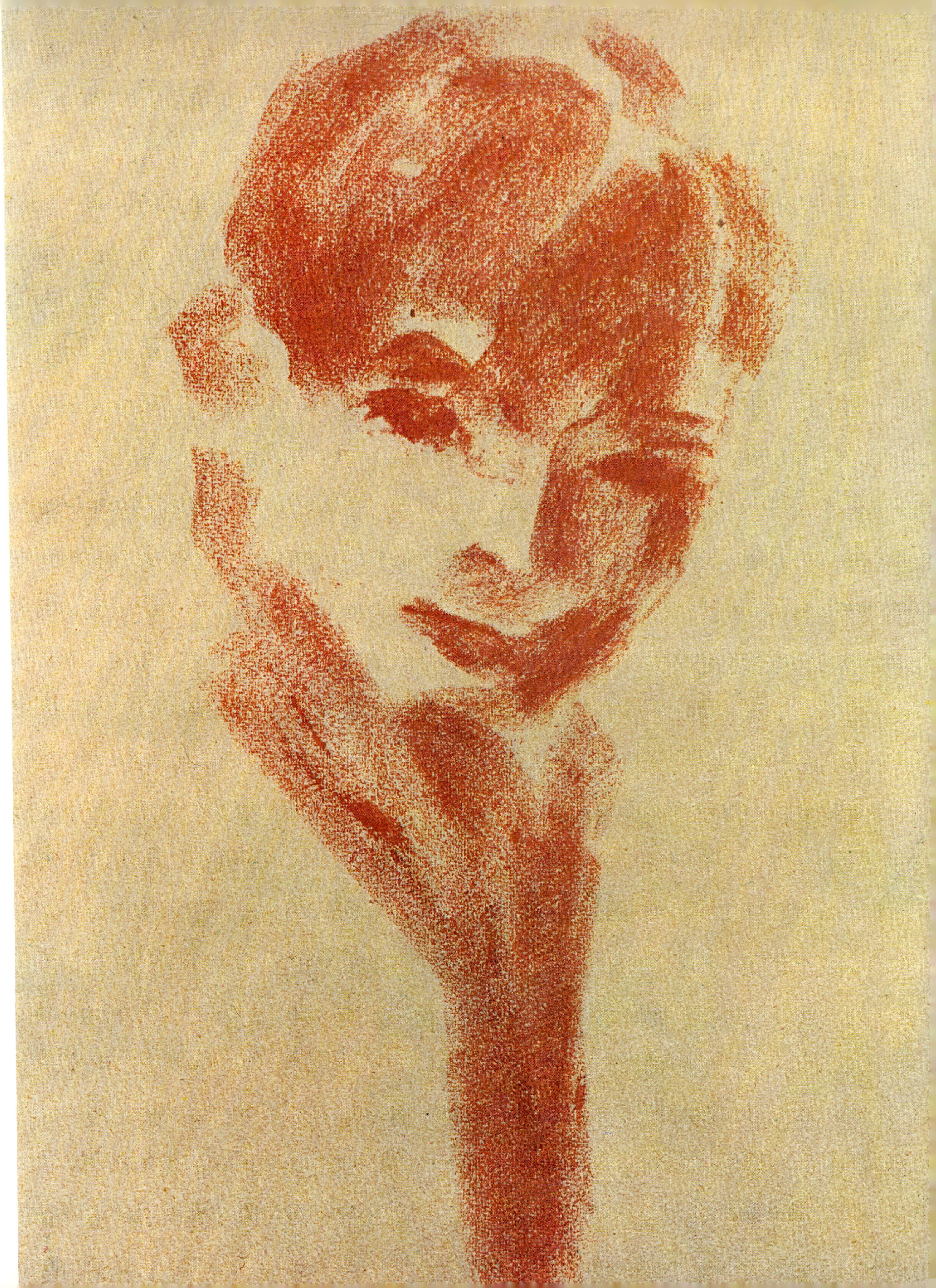

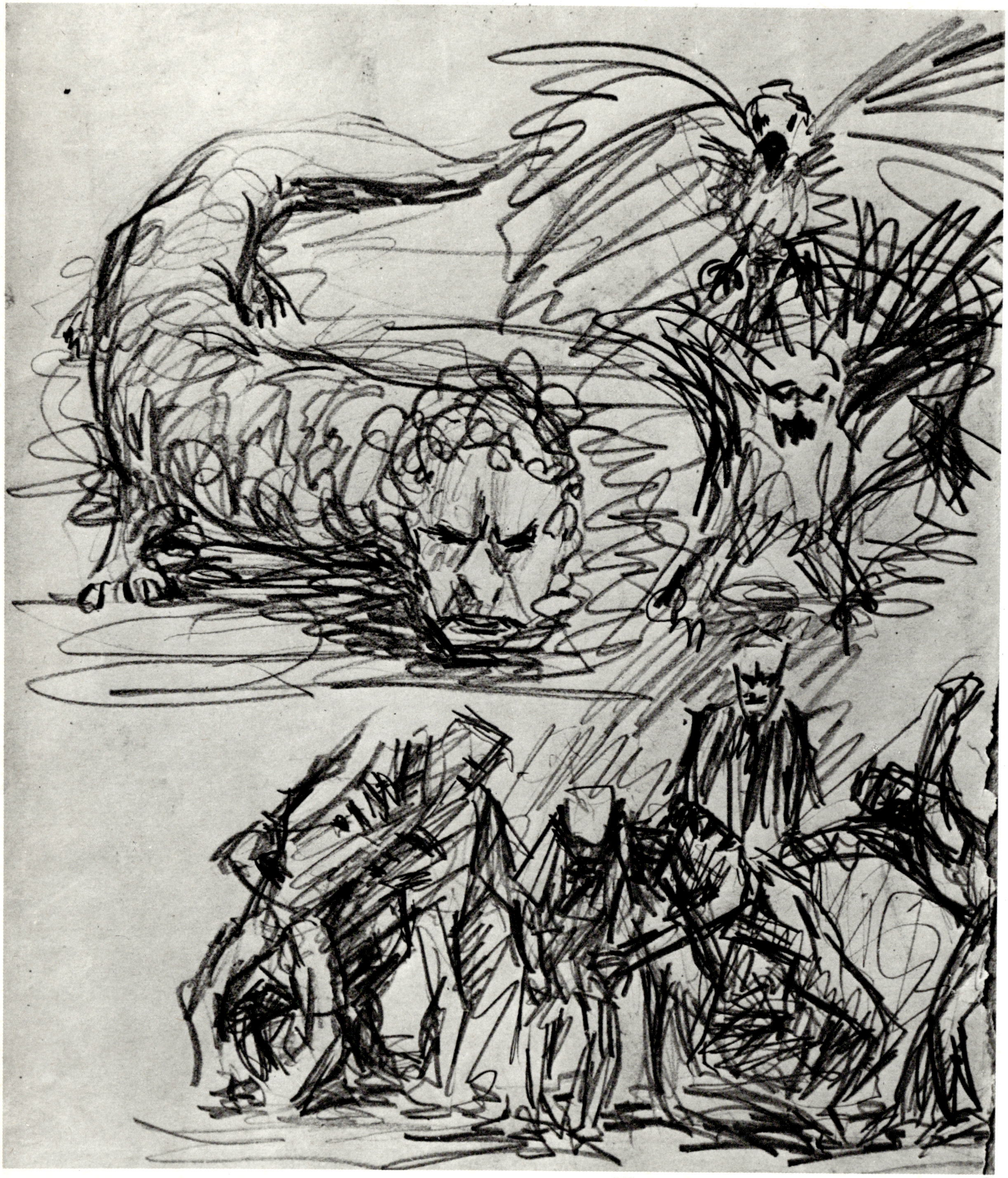

2 C. 1922

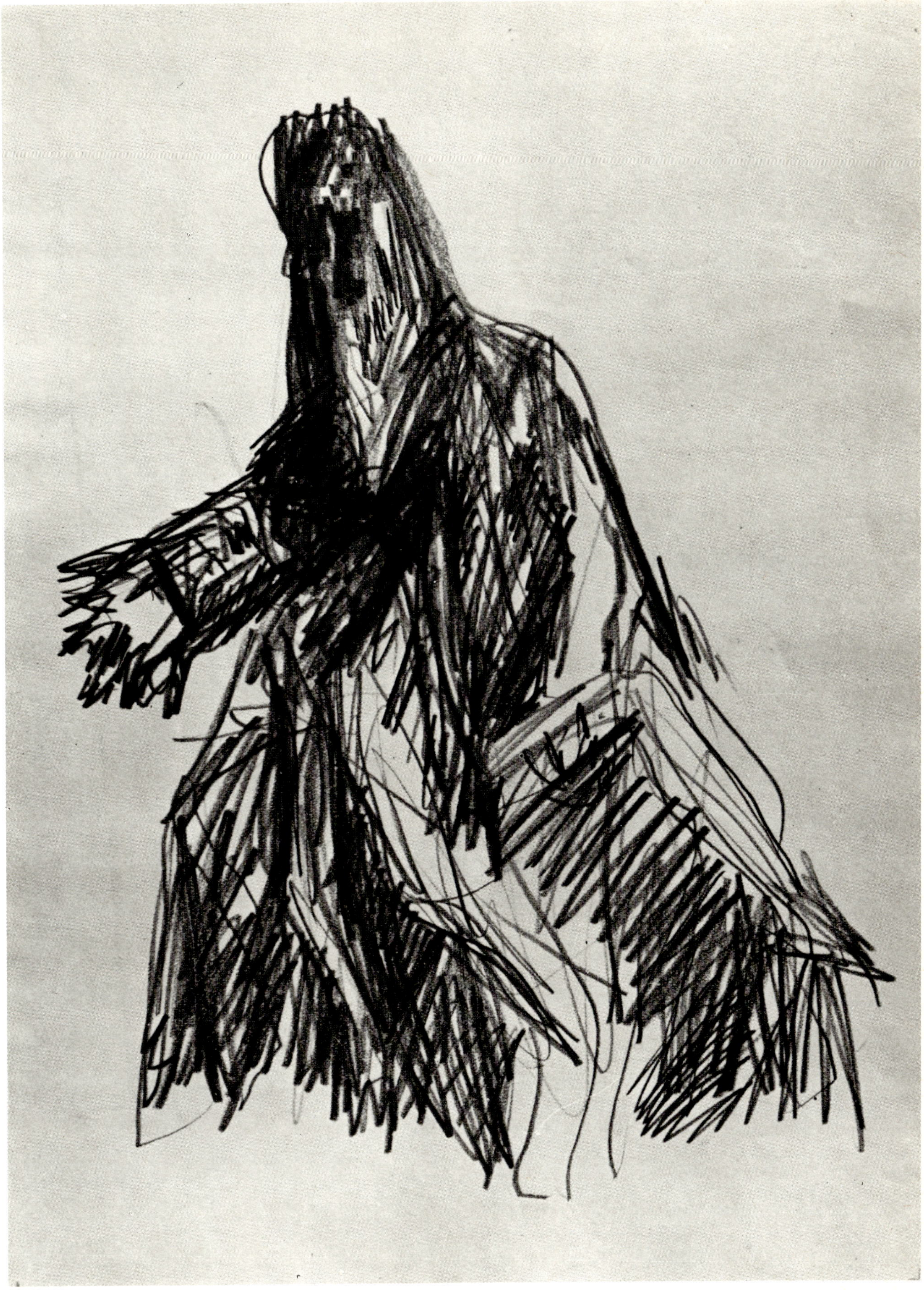

3 C. 1922

4 C. 1921

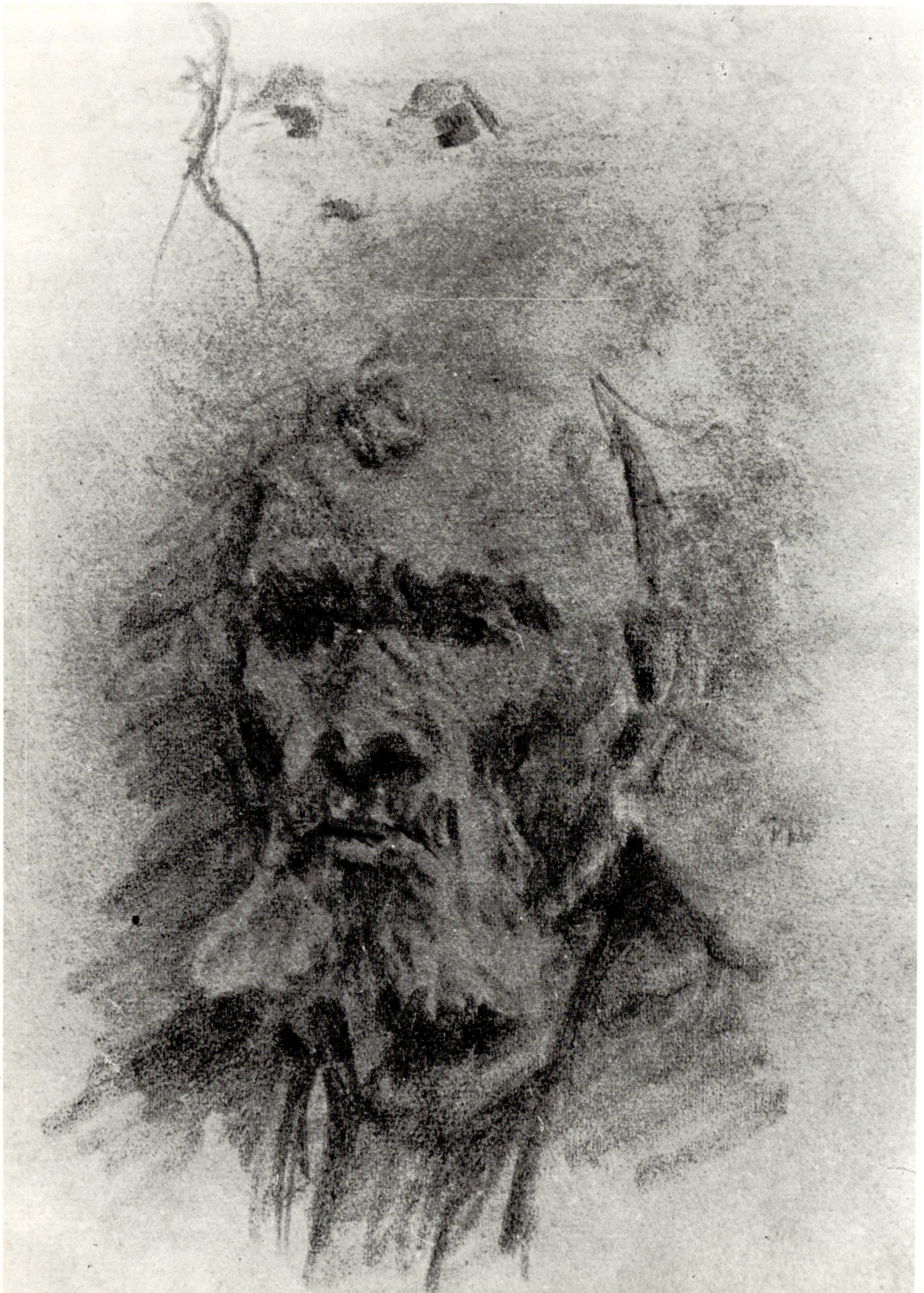

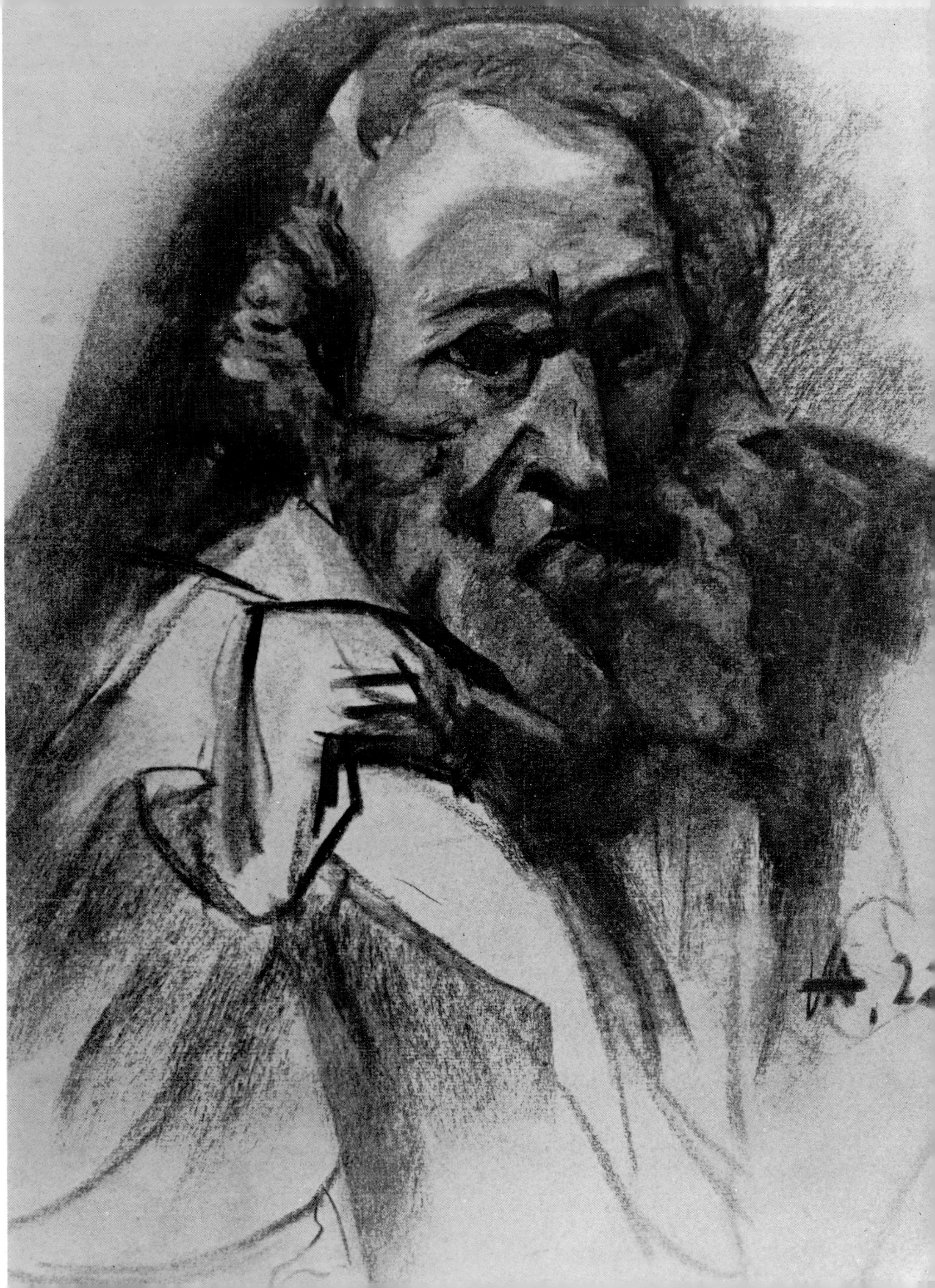

F. 1922

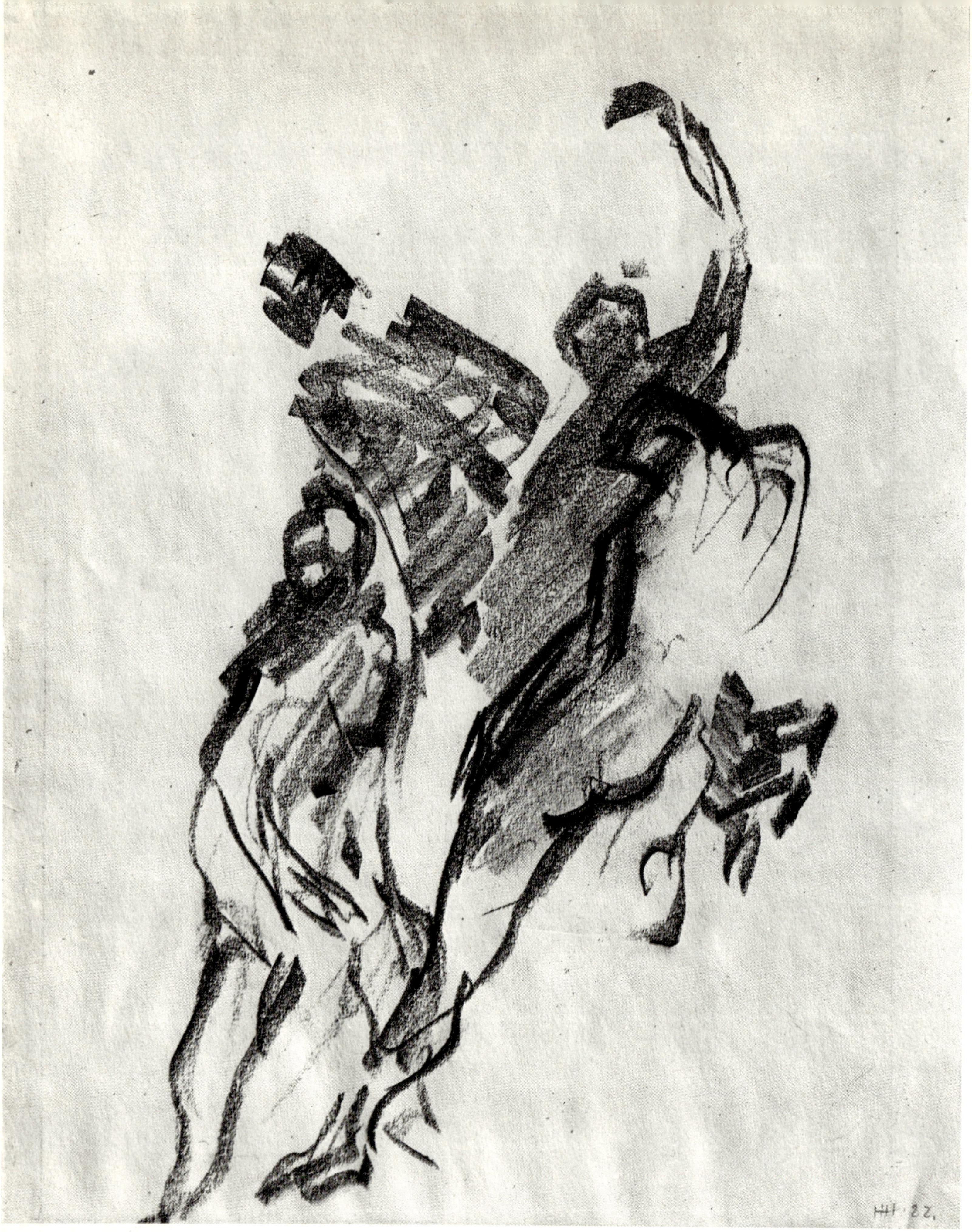

6 C. 1922

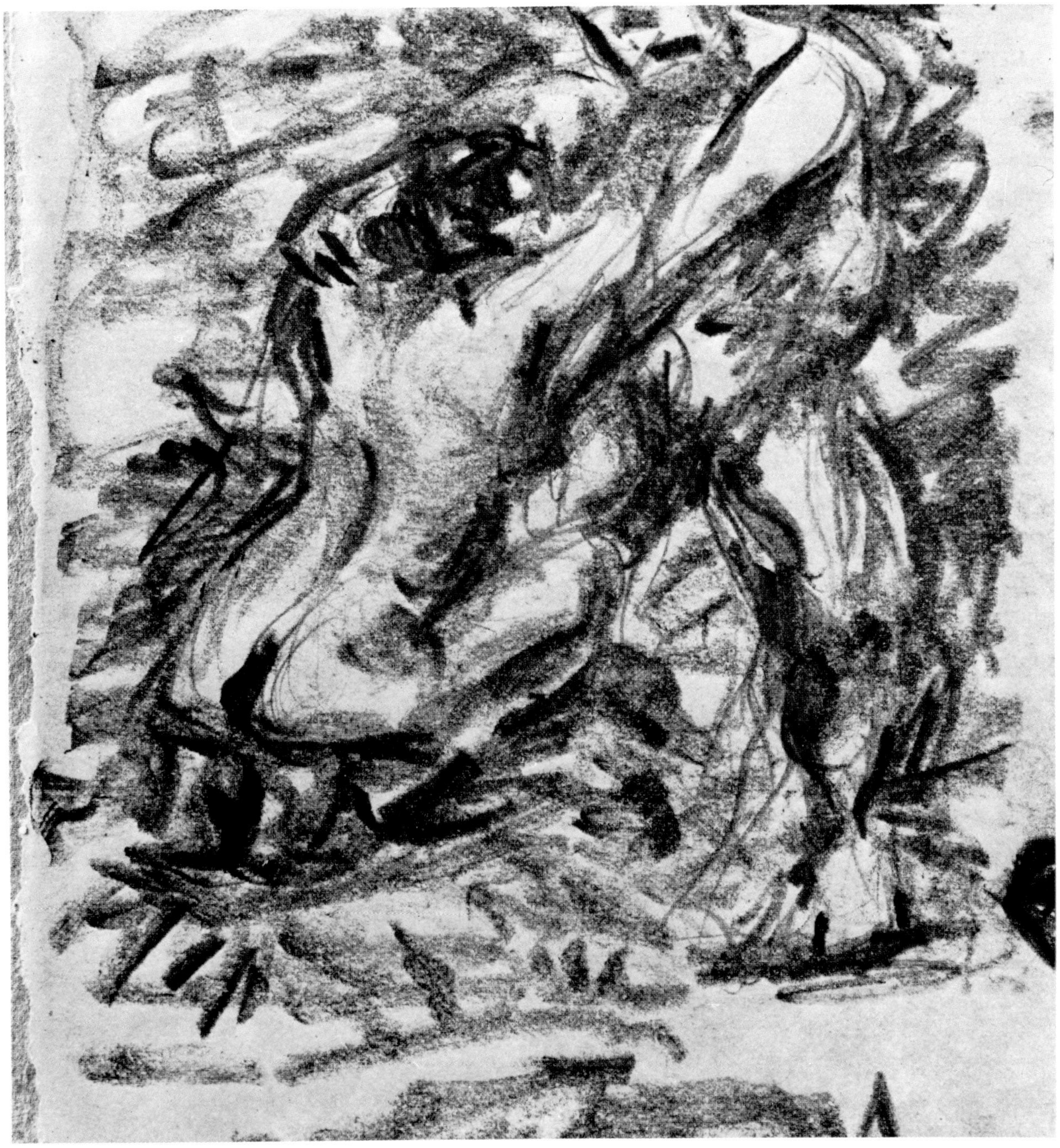

7 C. 1922

8 C. 1922

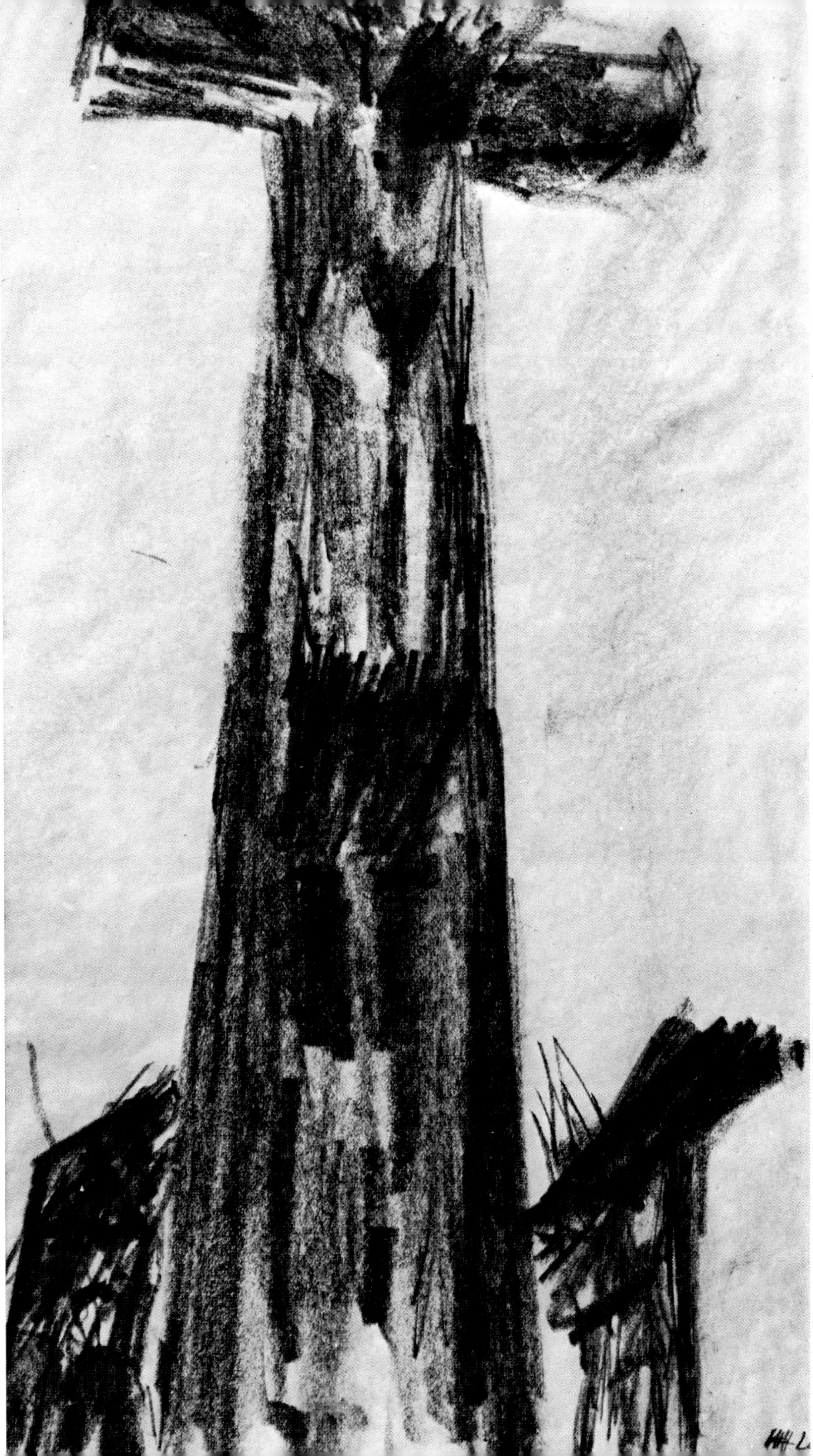

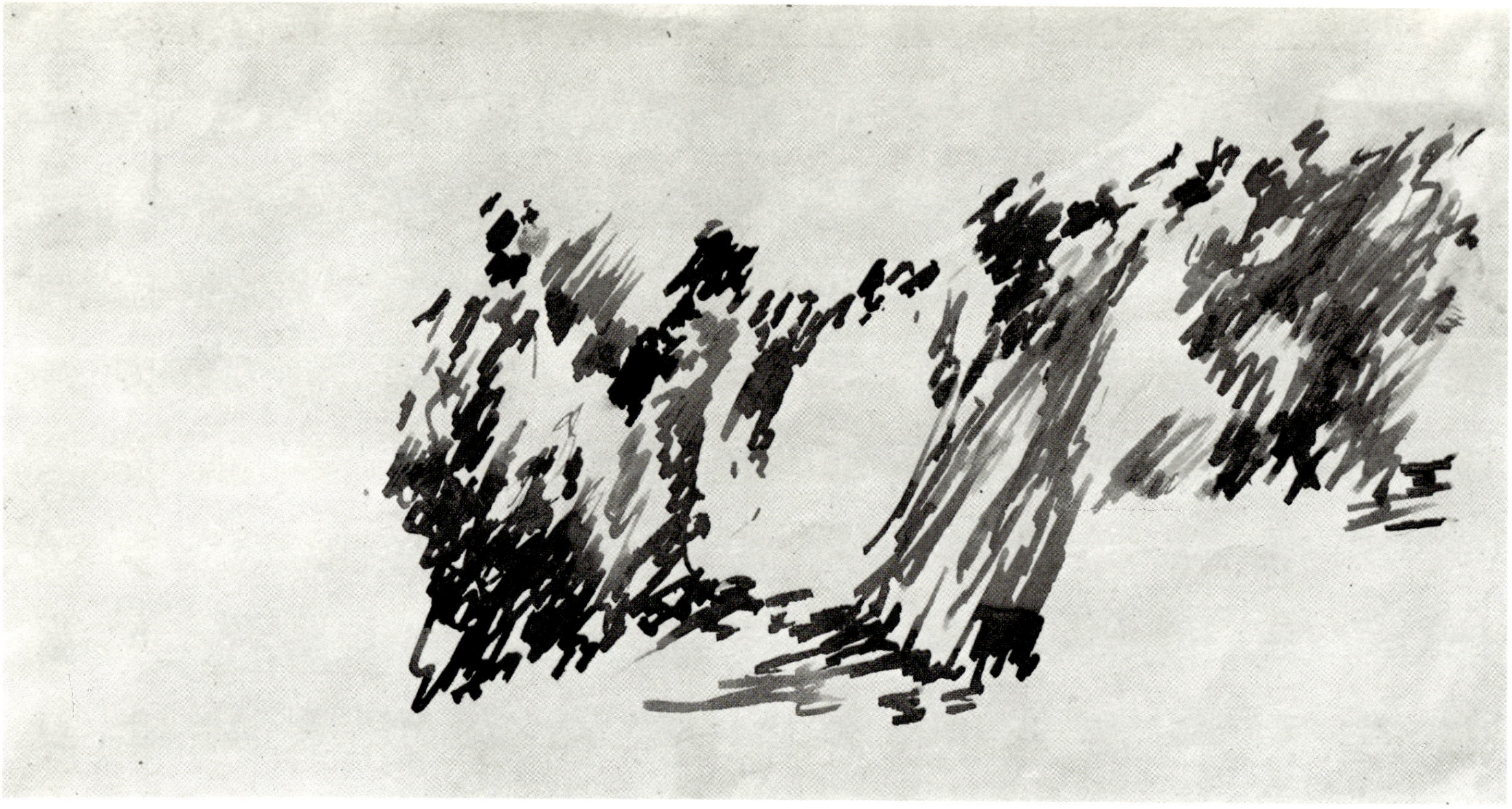

9 E. 1922

10 E. 1922

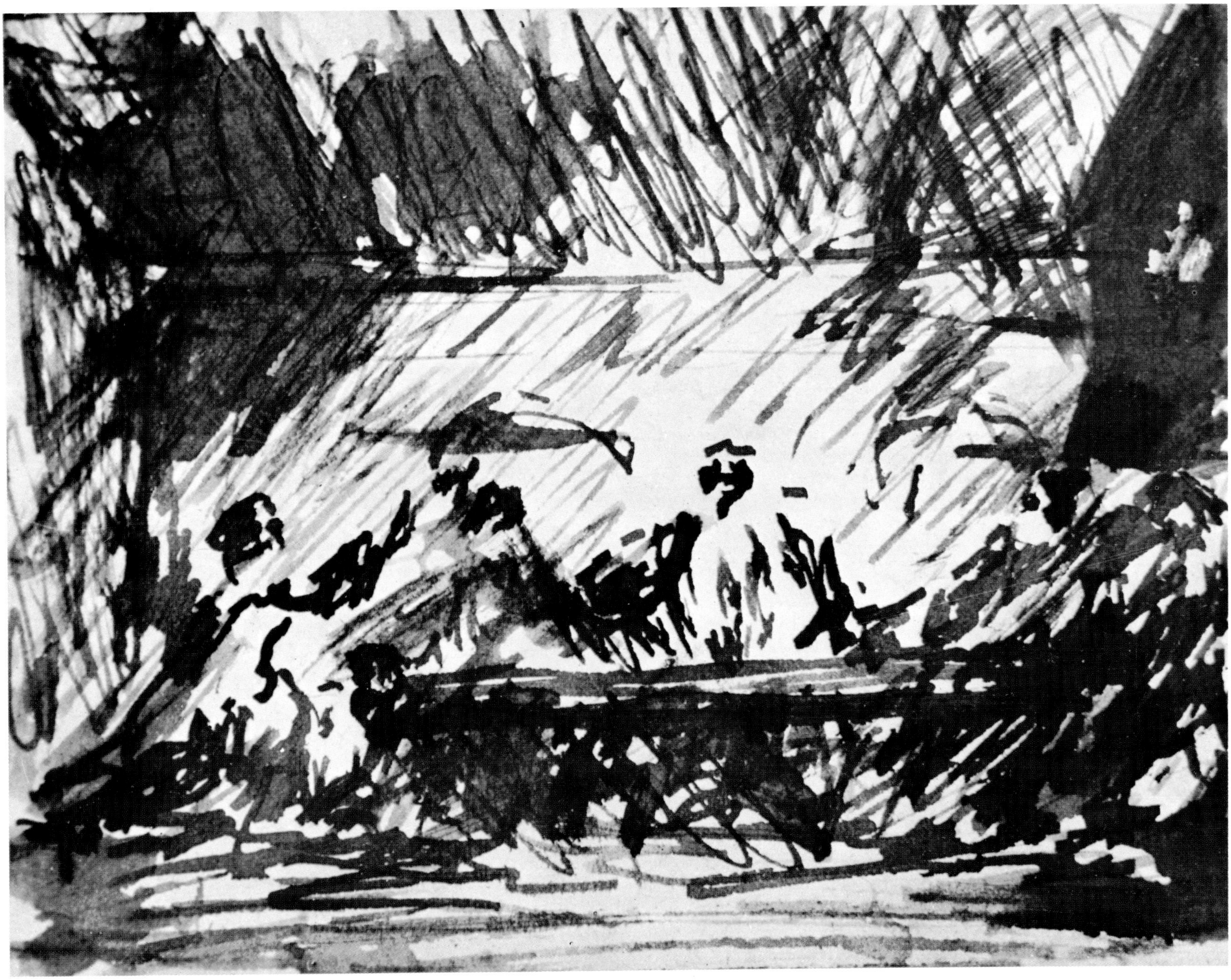

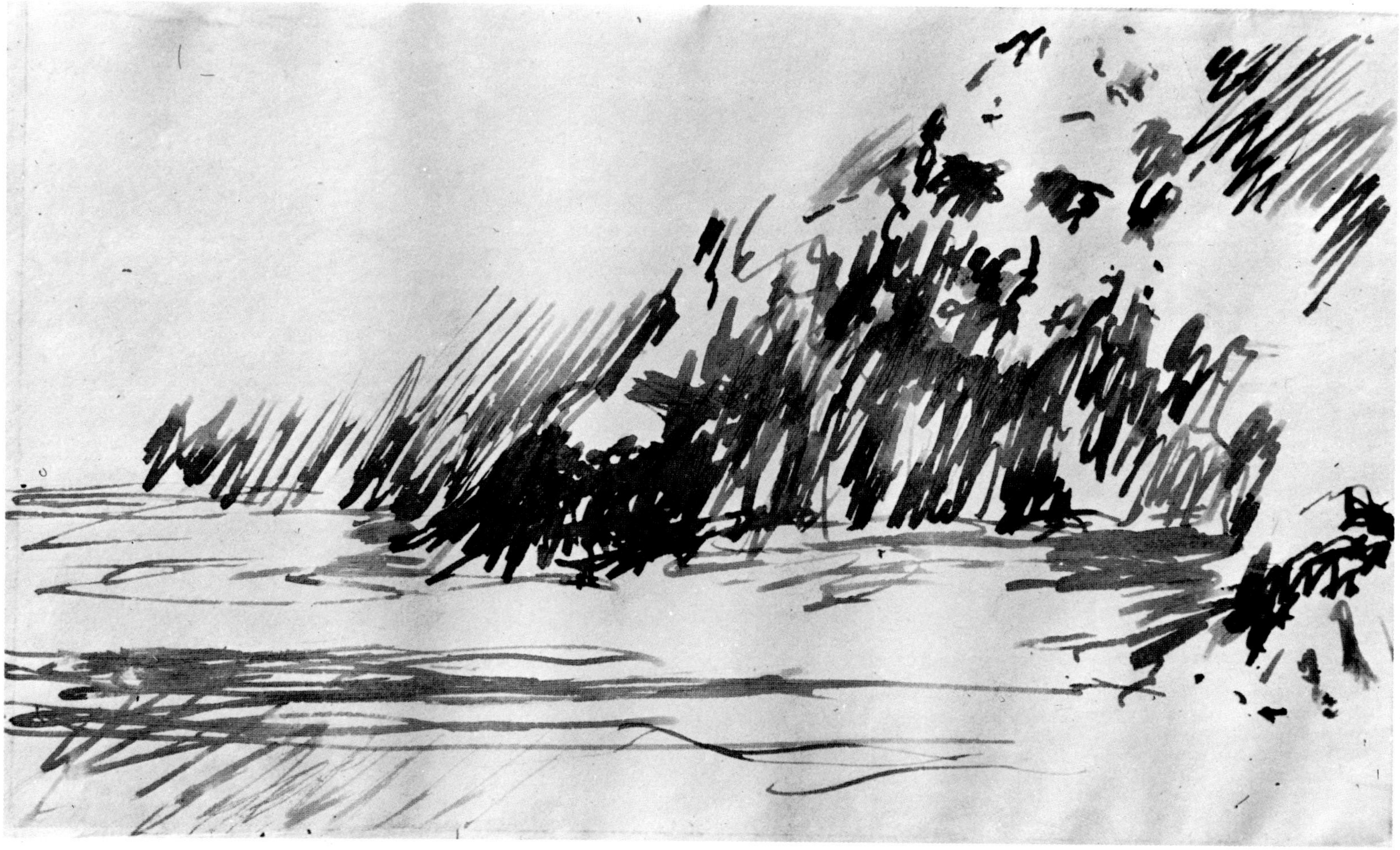

11 E. 1922

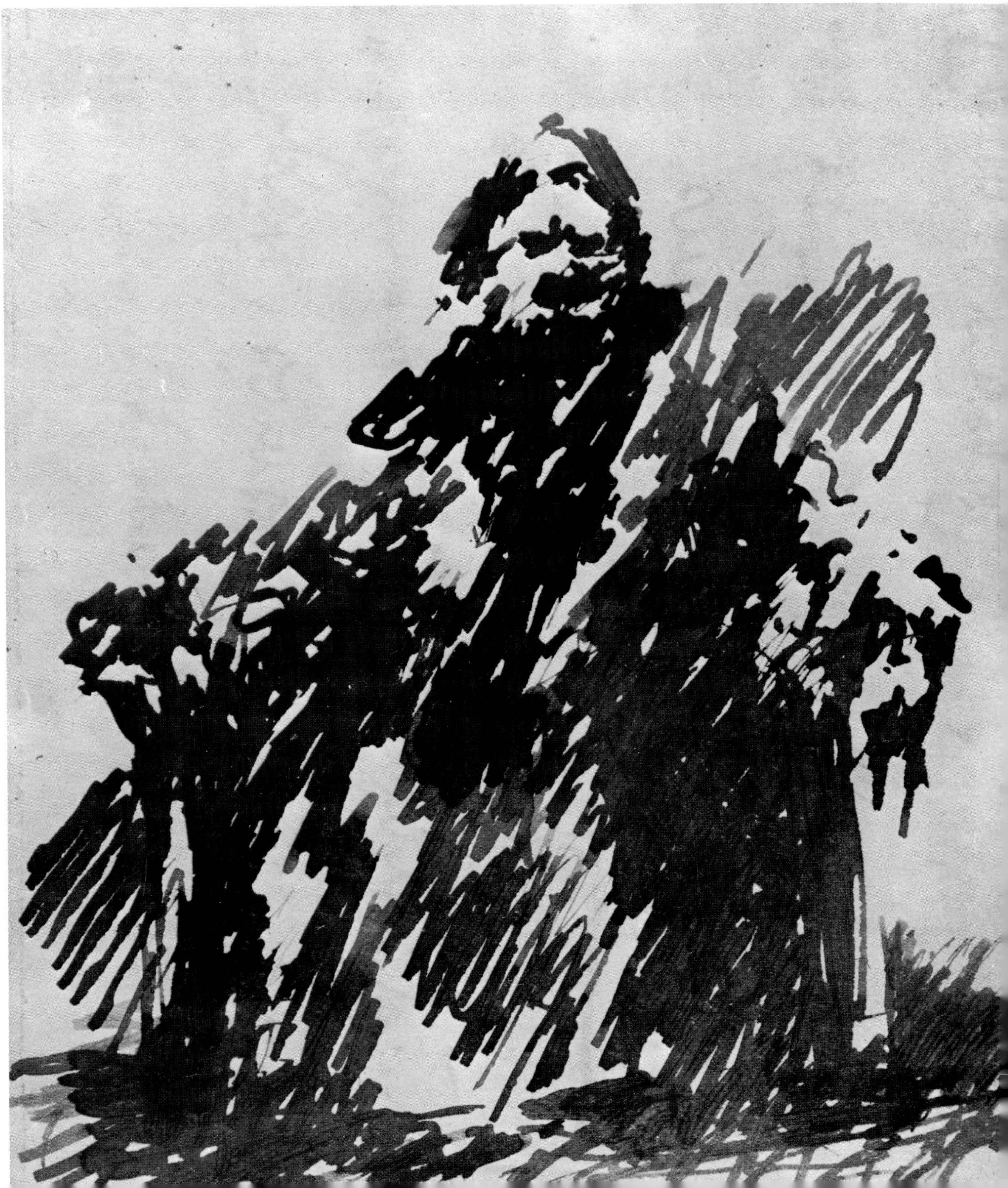

12 E. 1922

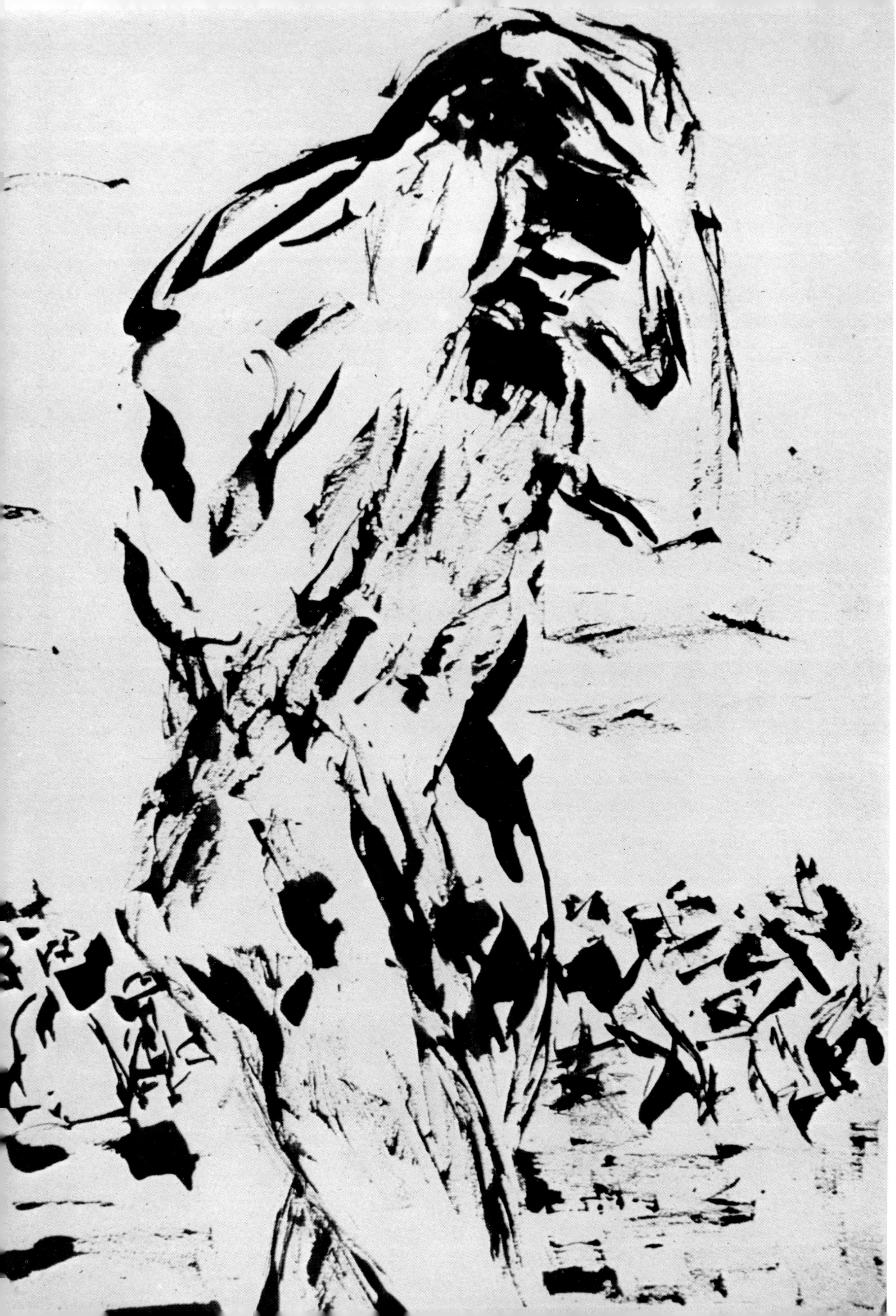

13 E. C. 192

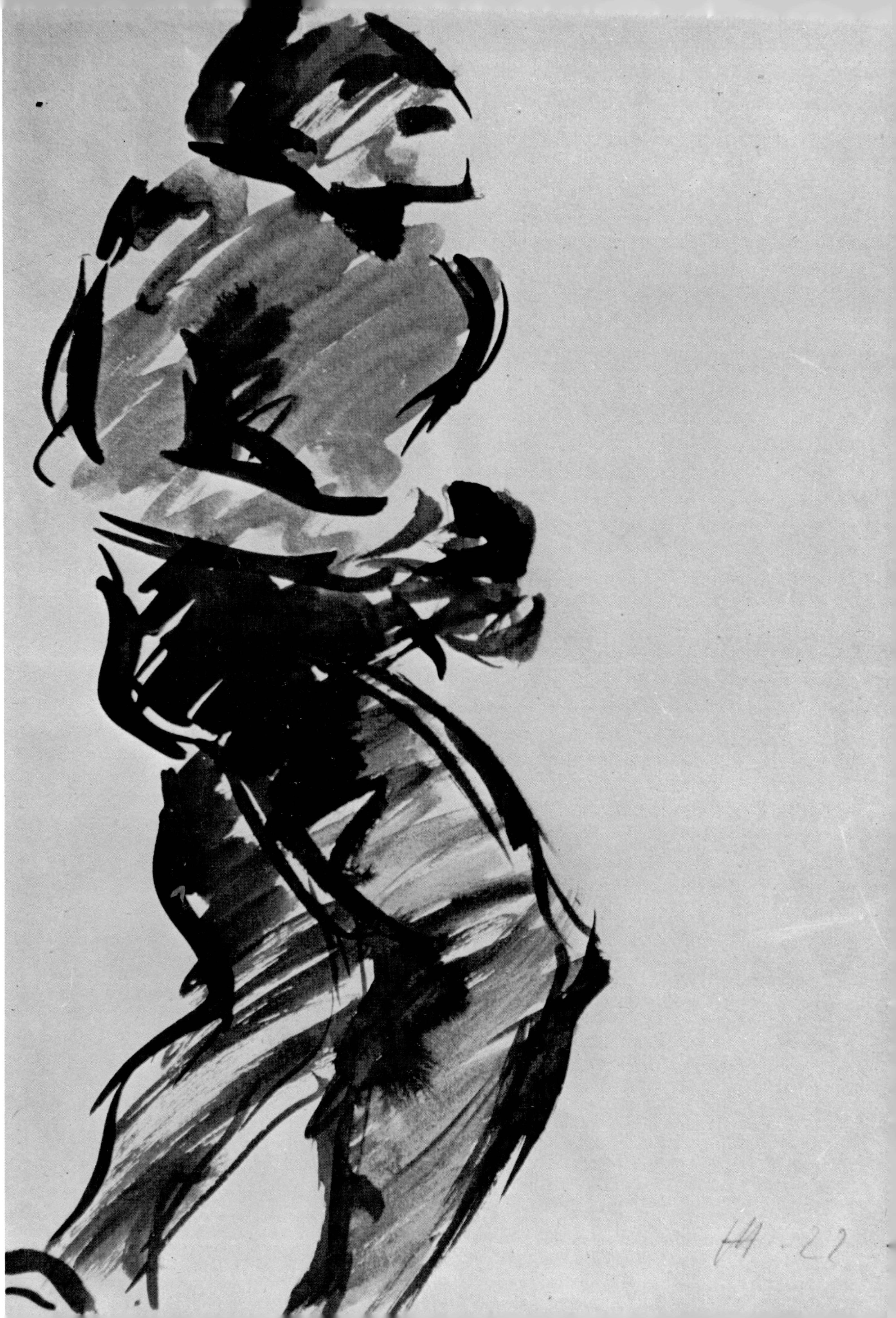

14 E. C. 1922

15 E. 1922

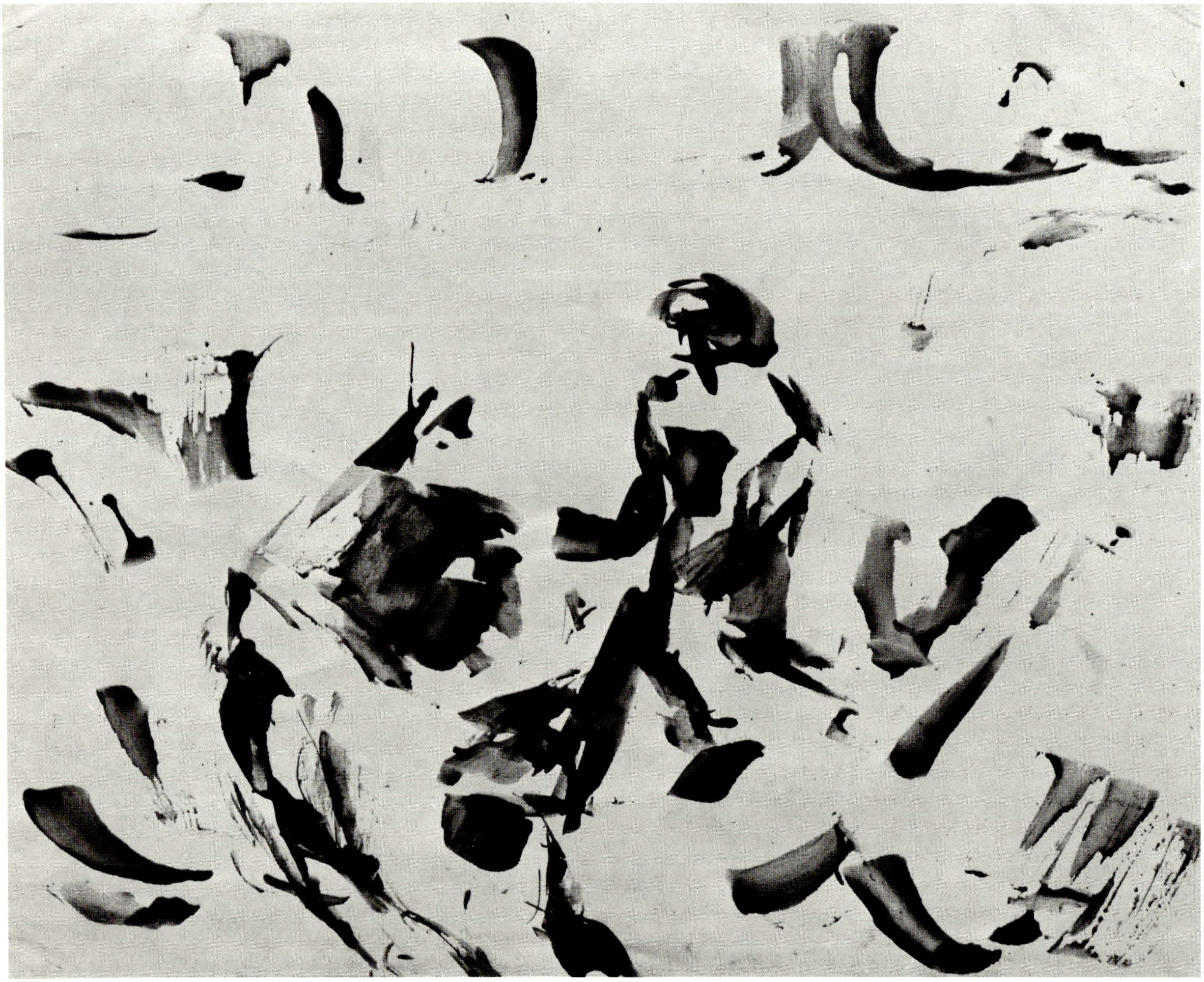

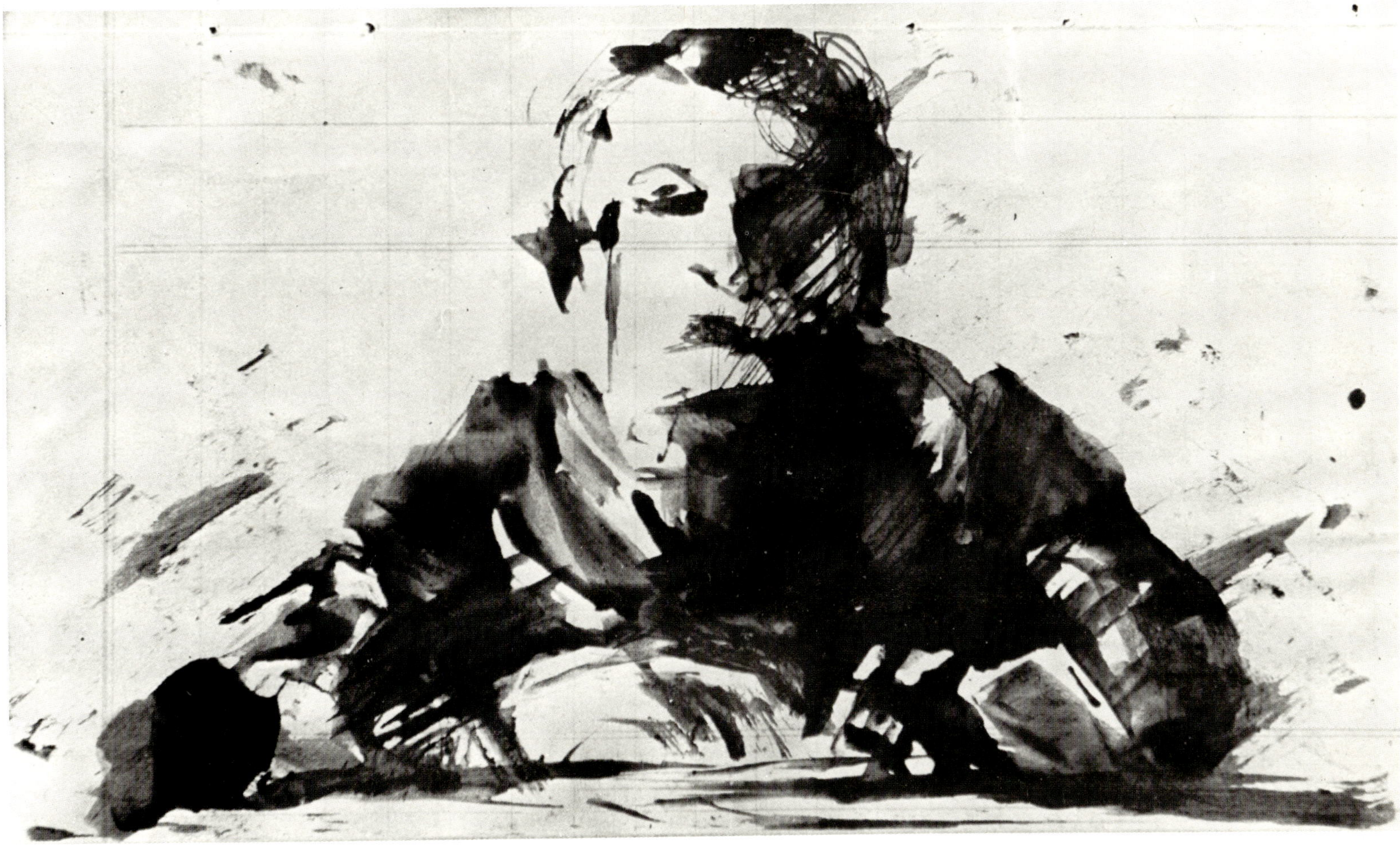

16 E. 1922

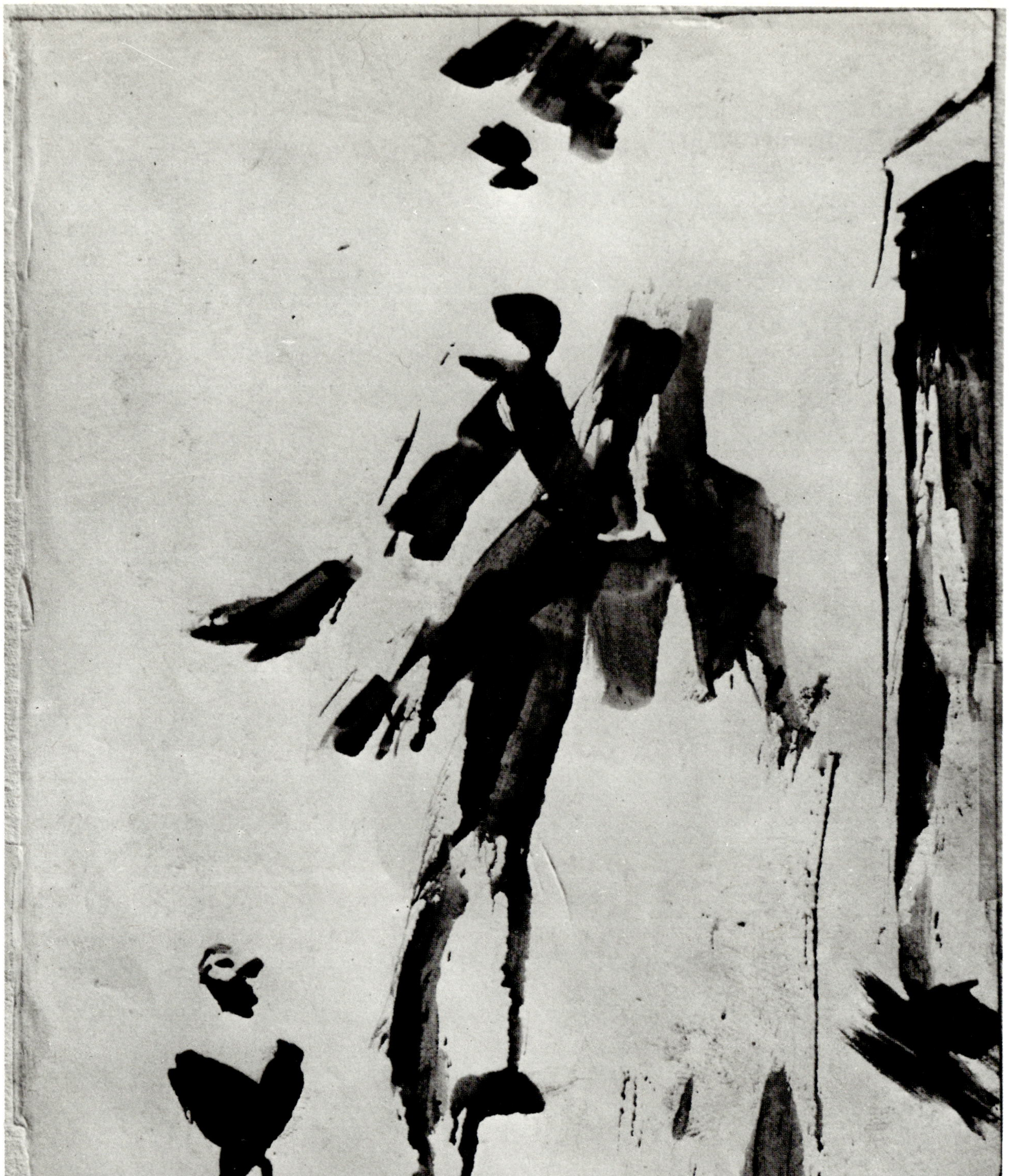

17 E. 1922

18 E. 1923

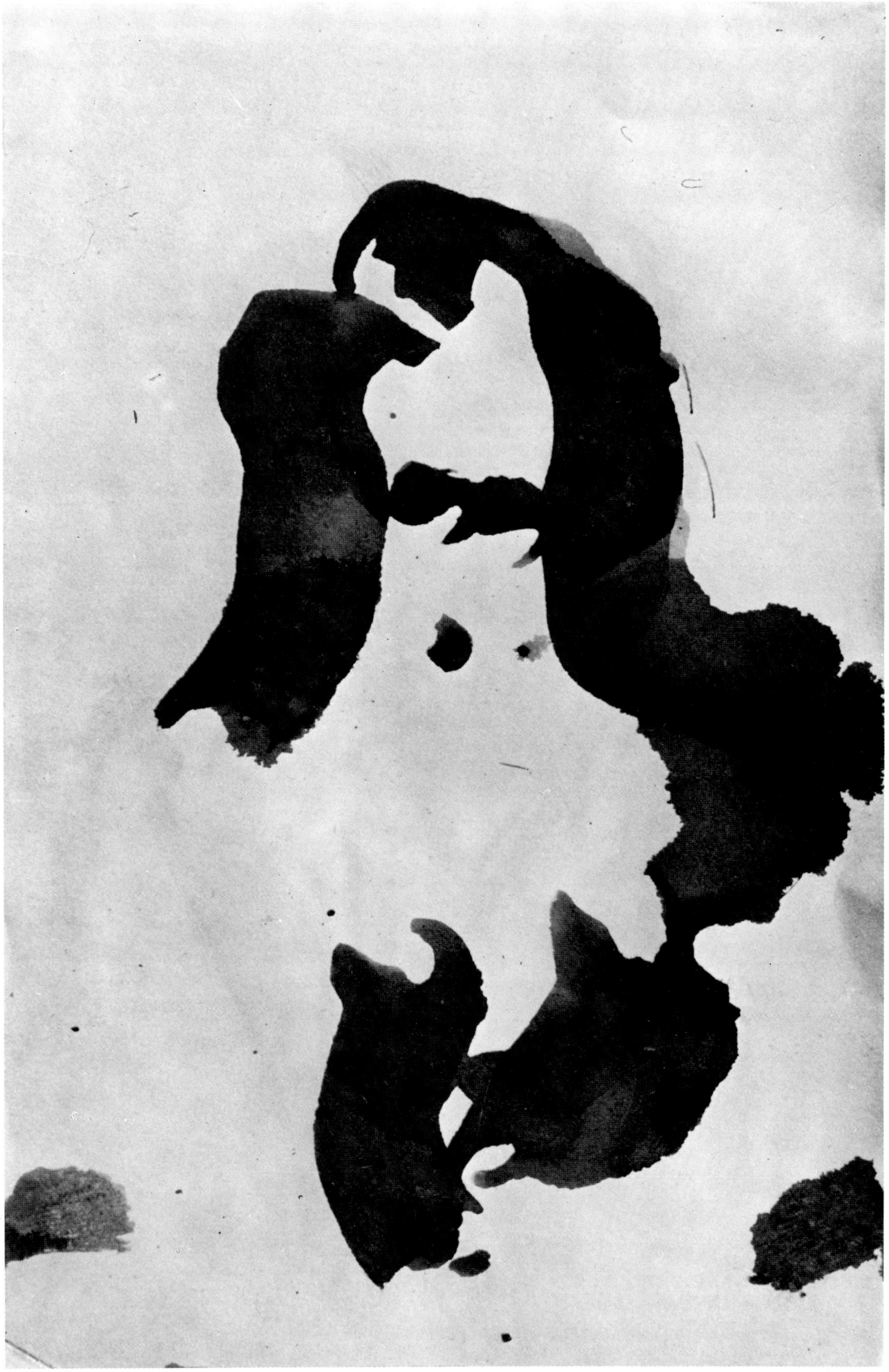

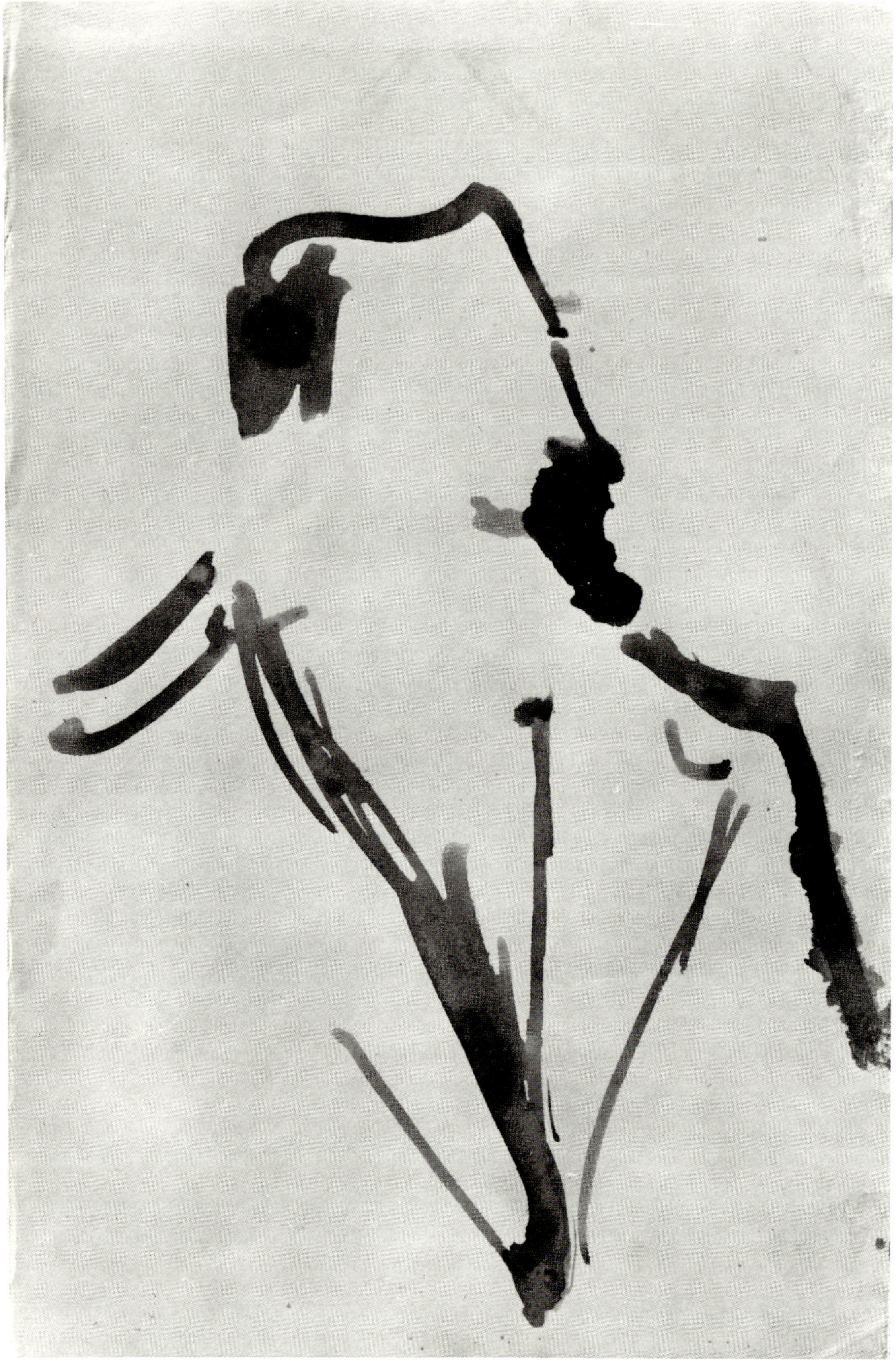

19 E. 1922

20 E. 1923

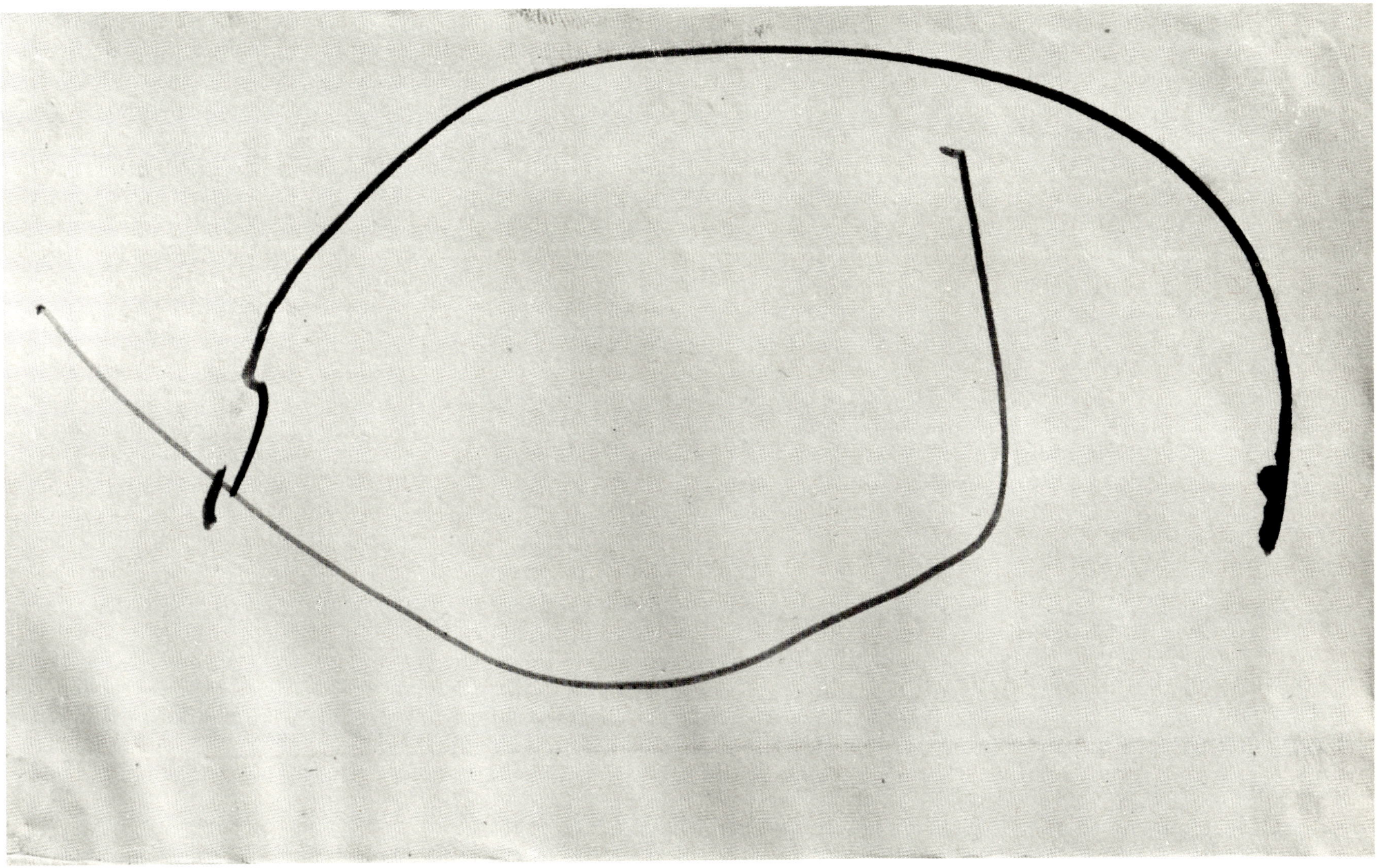

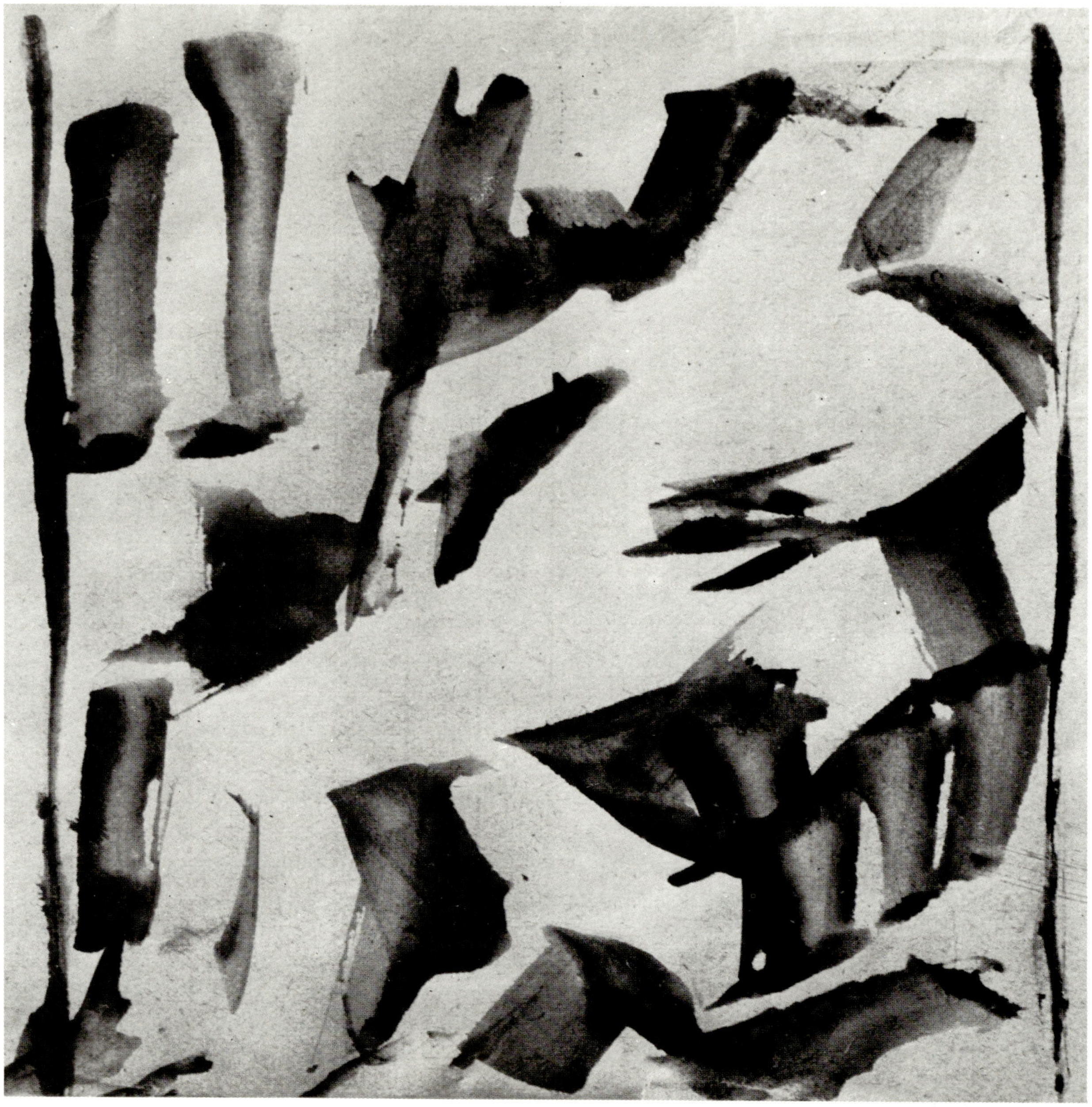

21 E. 1922

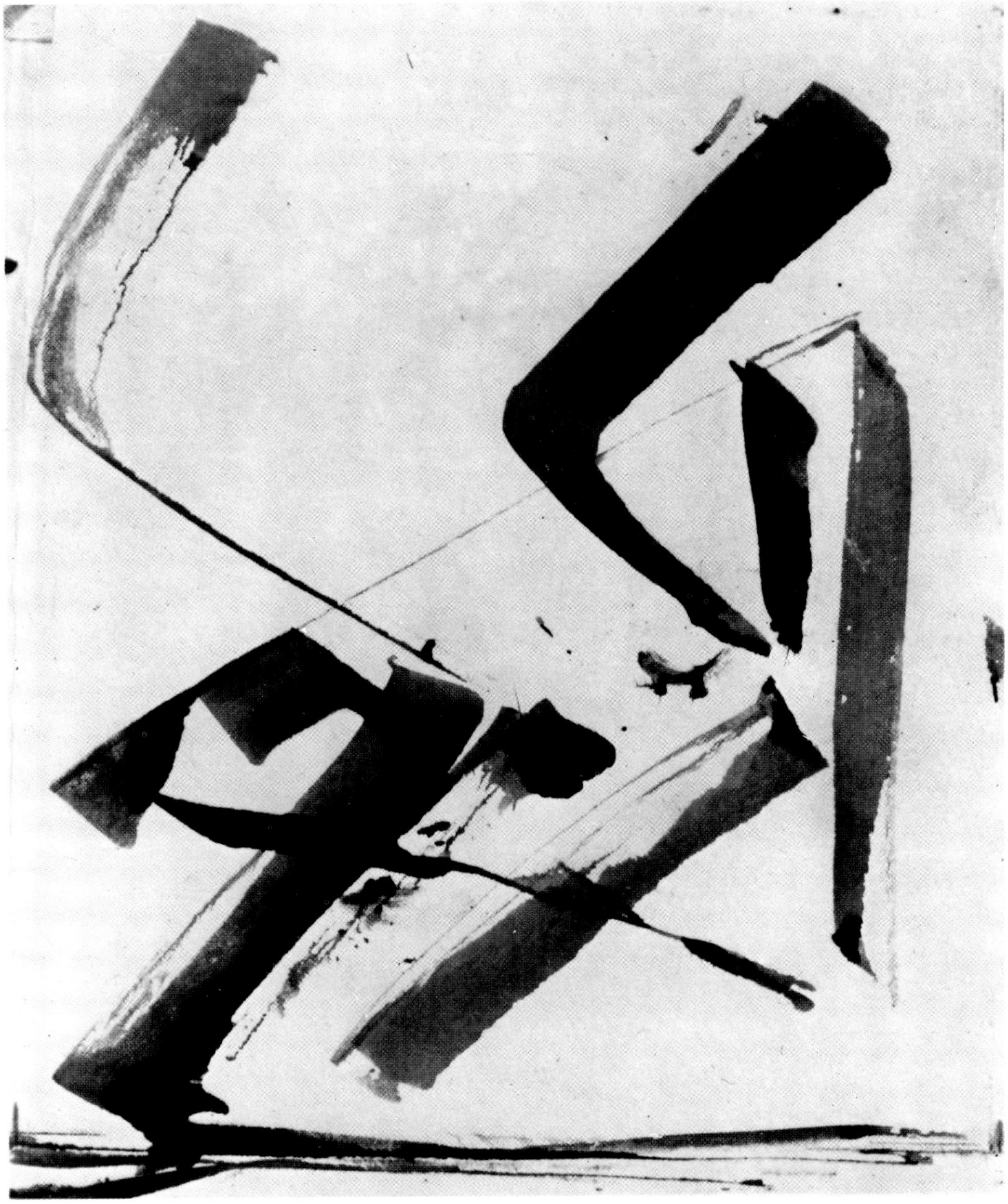

22 E. 1923

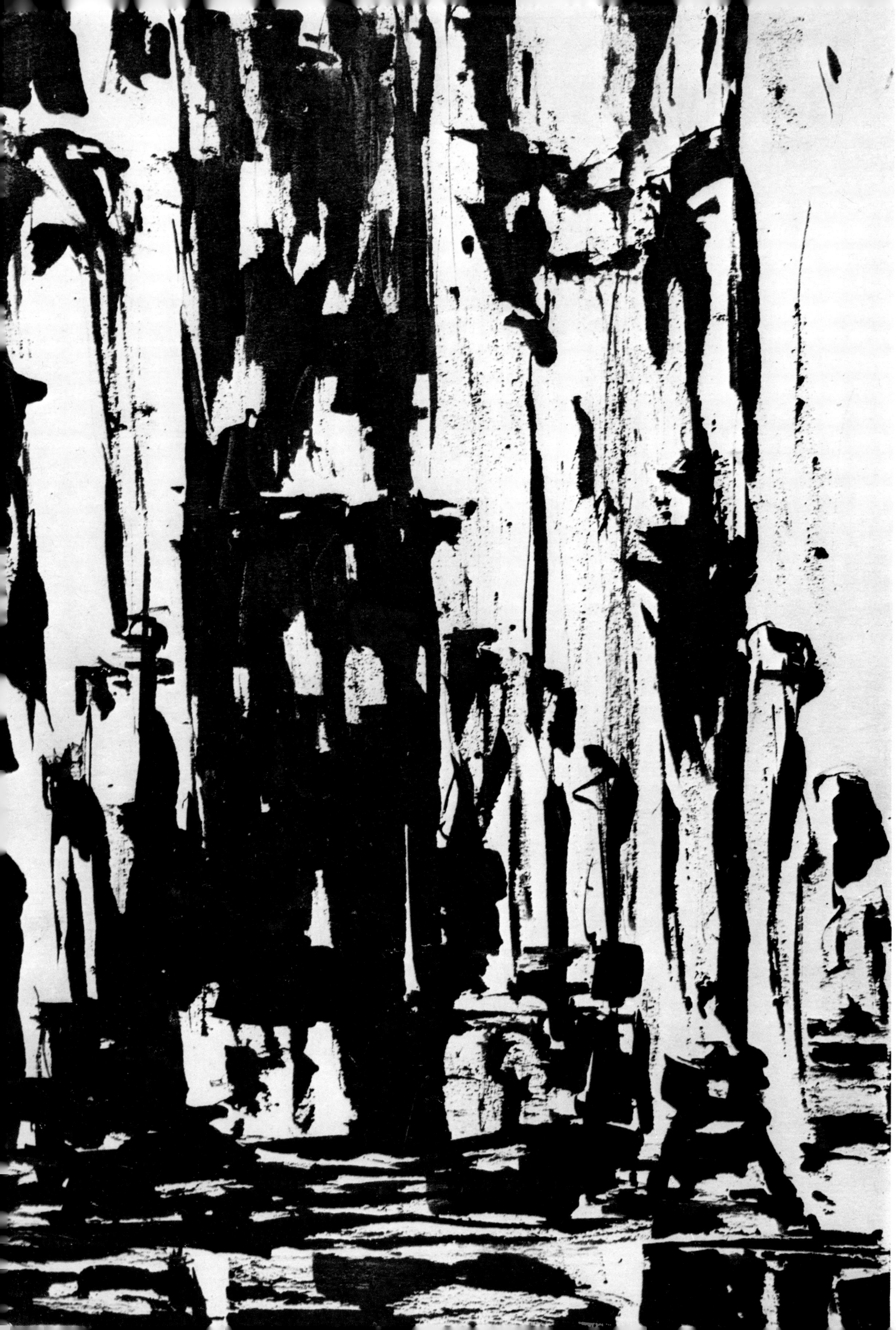

23 E. C. 1922

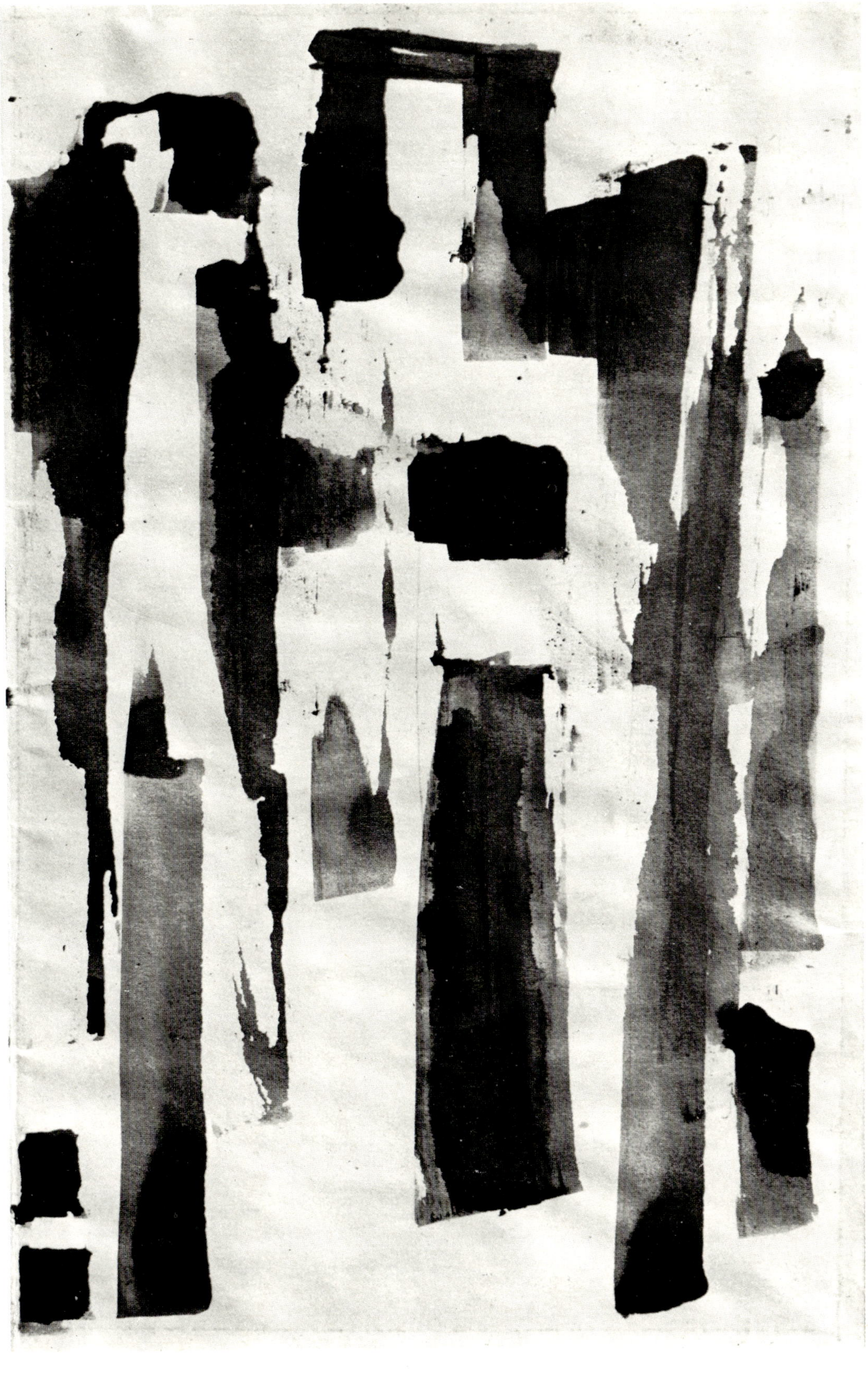

24 E. 1922

25 E. 1922

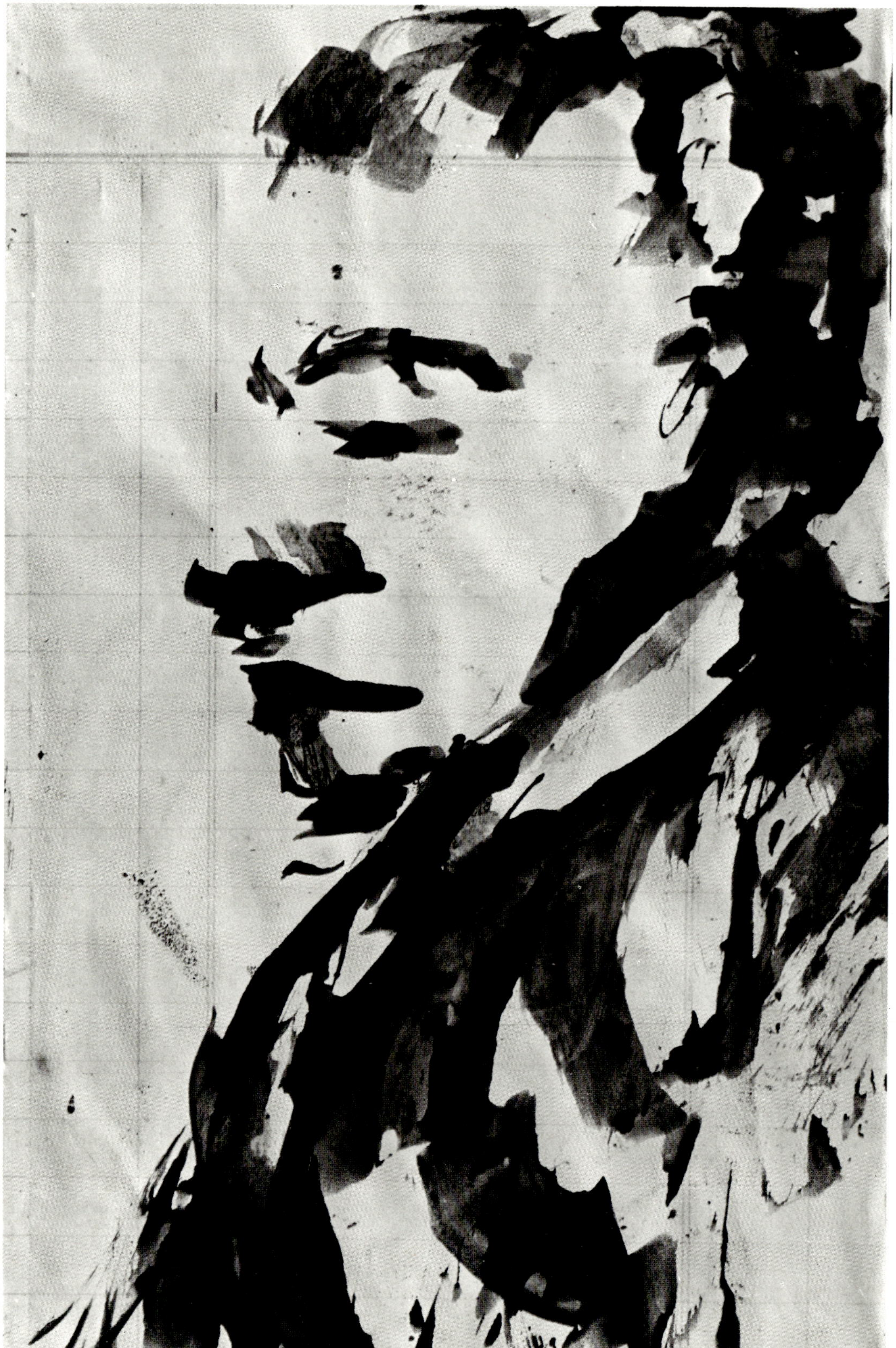

26 E. 1922

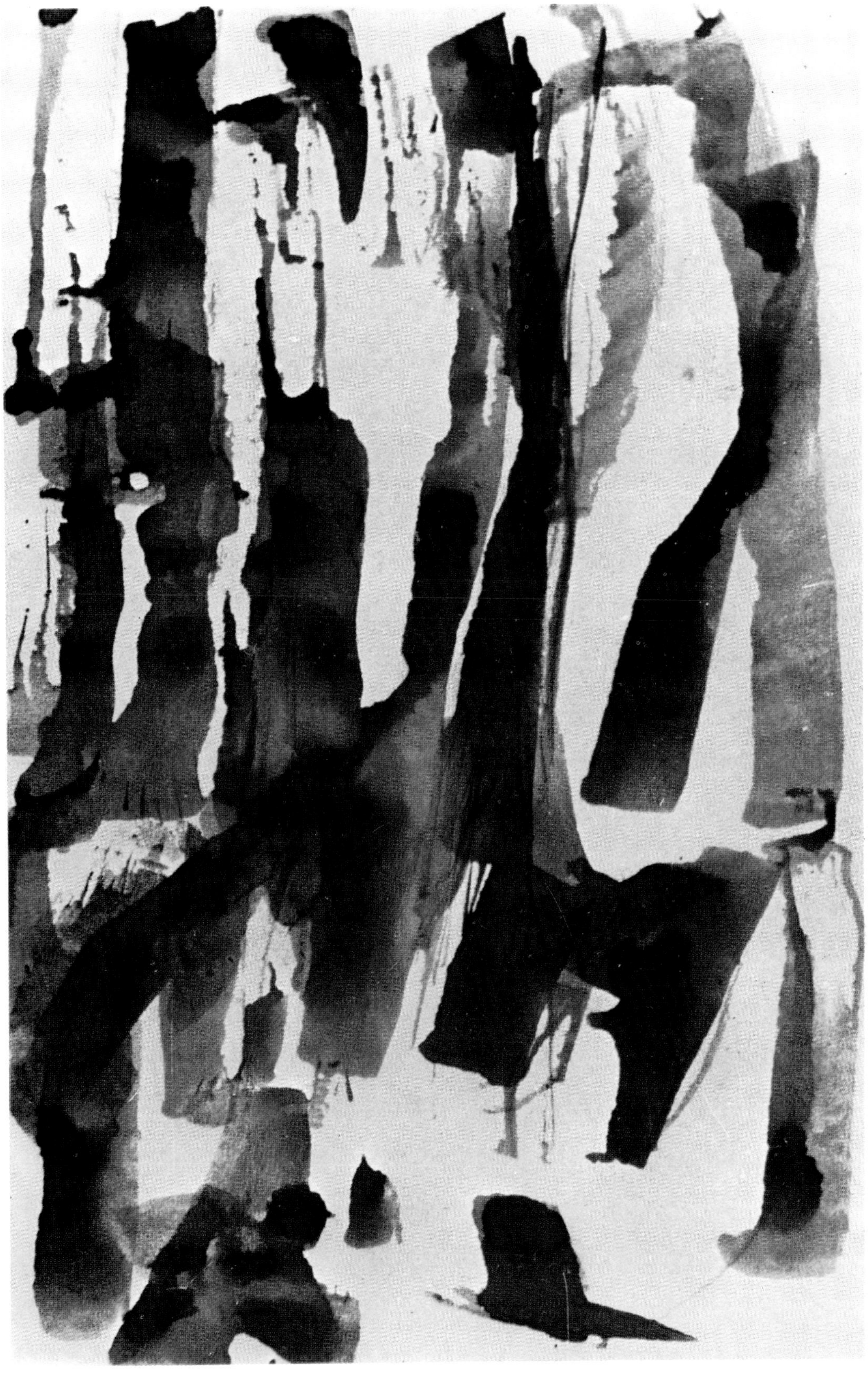

27 E. 1923

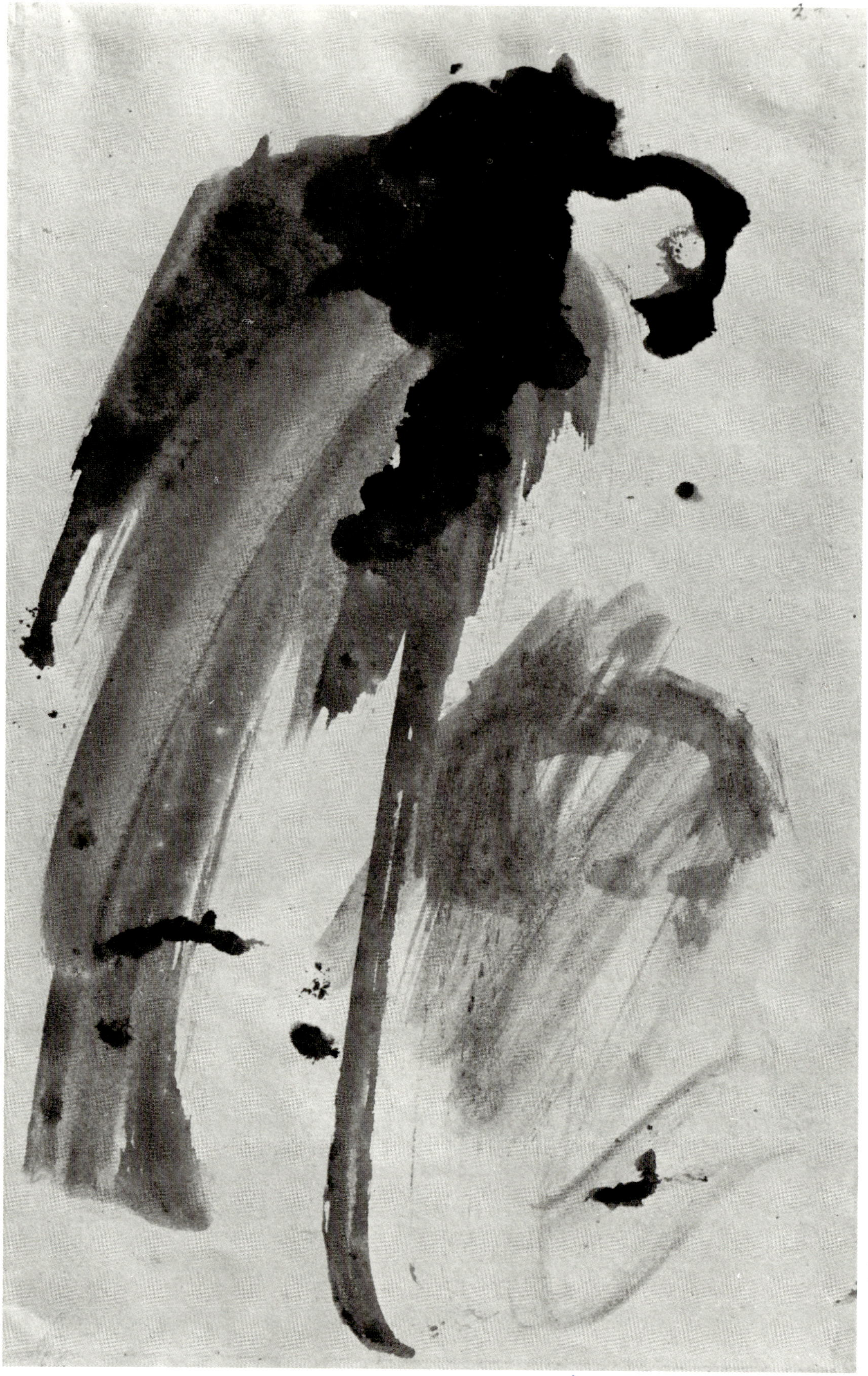

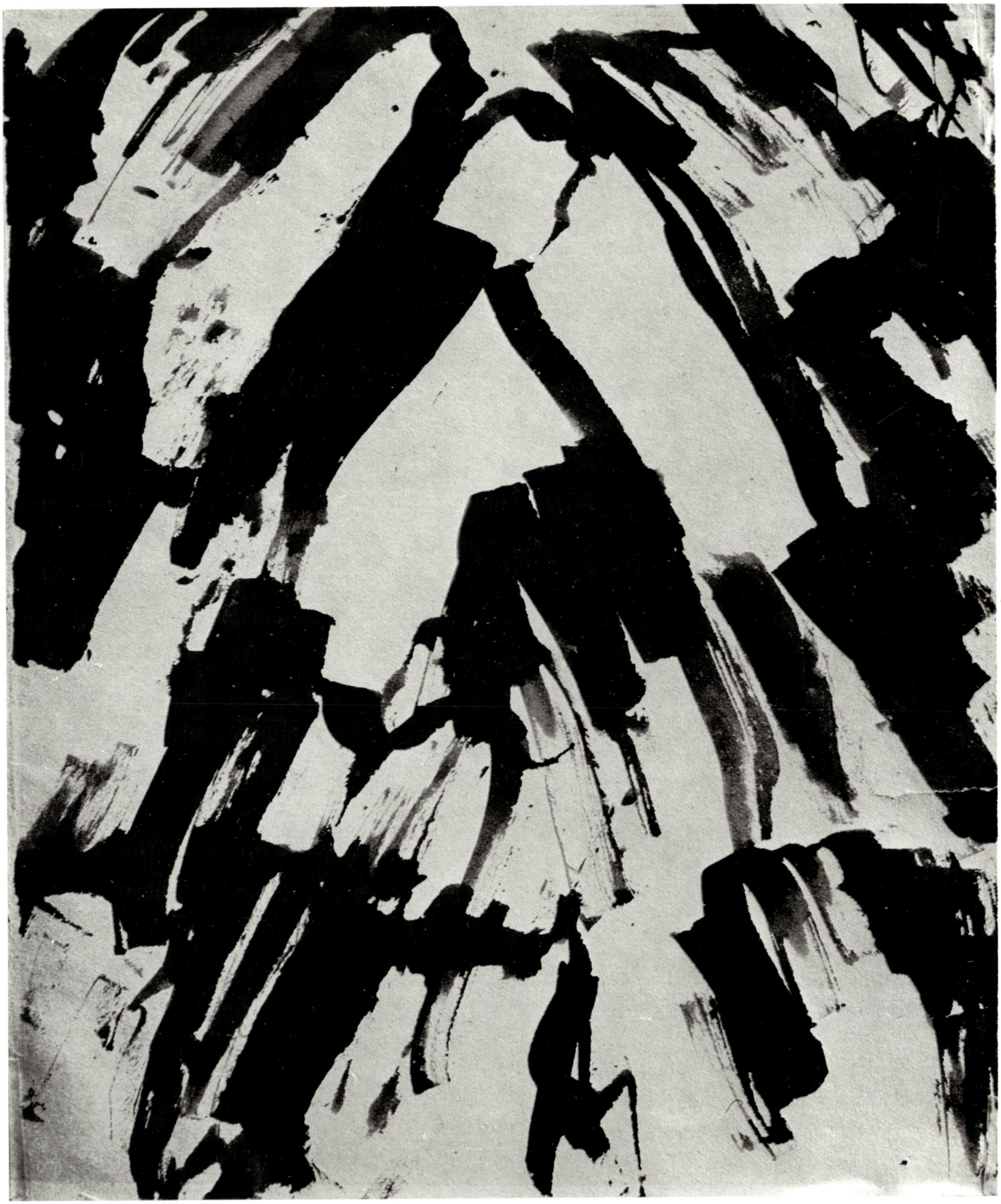

28 E. 1922

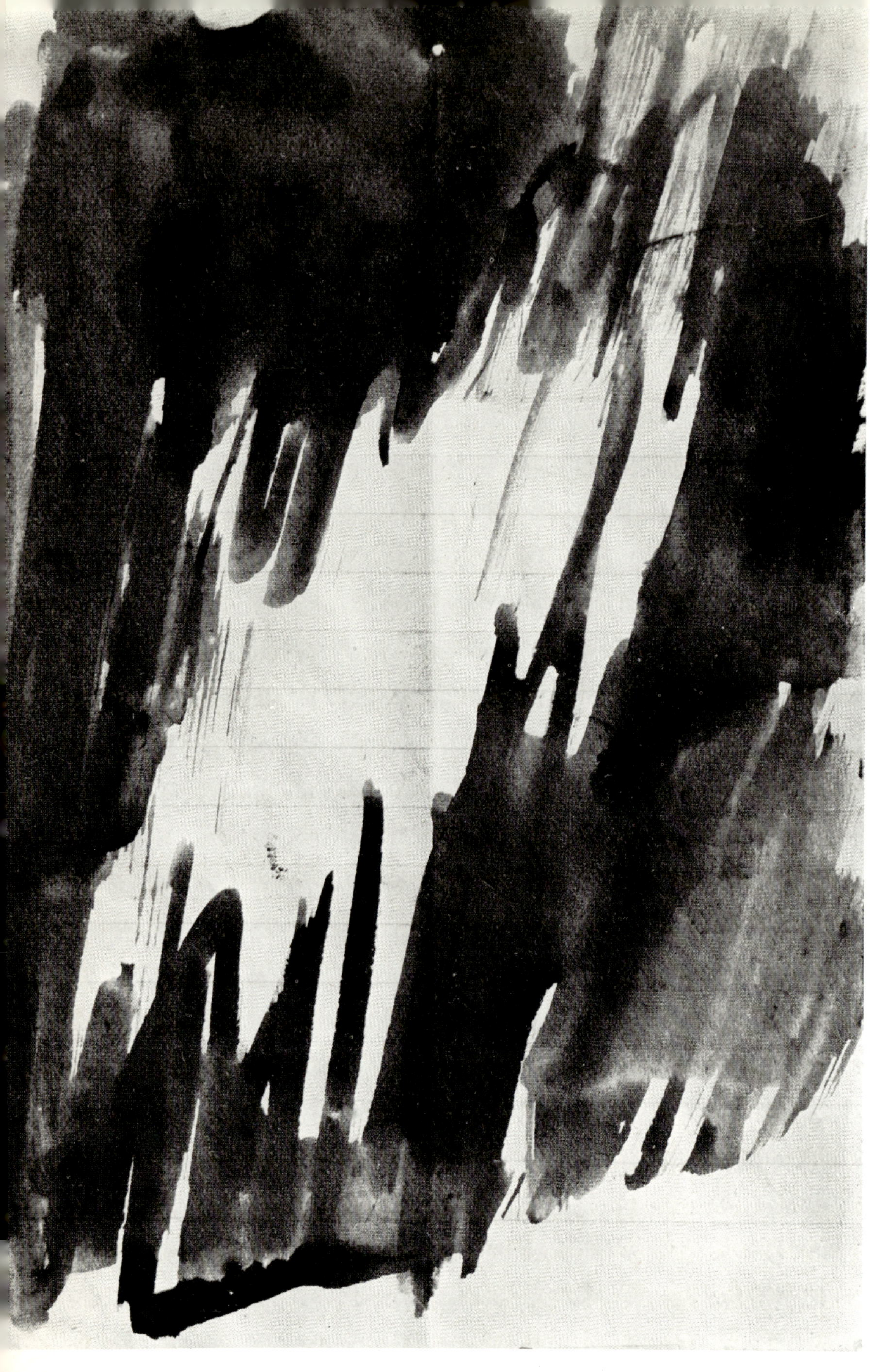

29 E. 1923

0 E. 1923

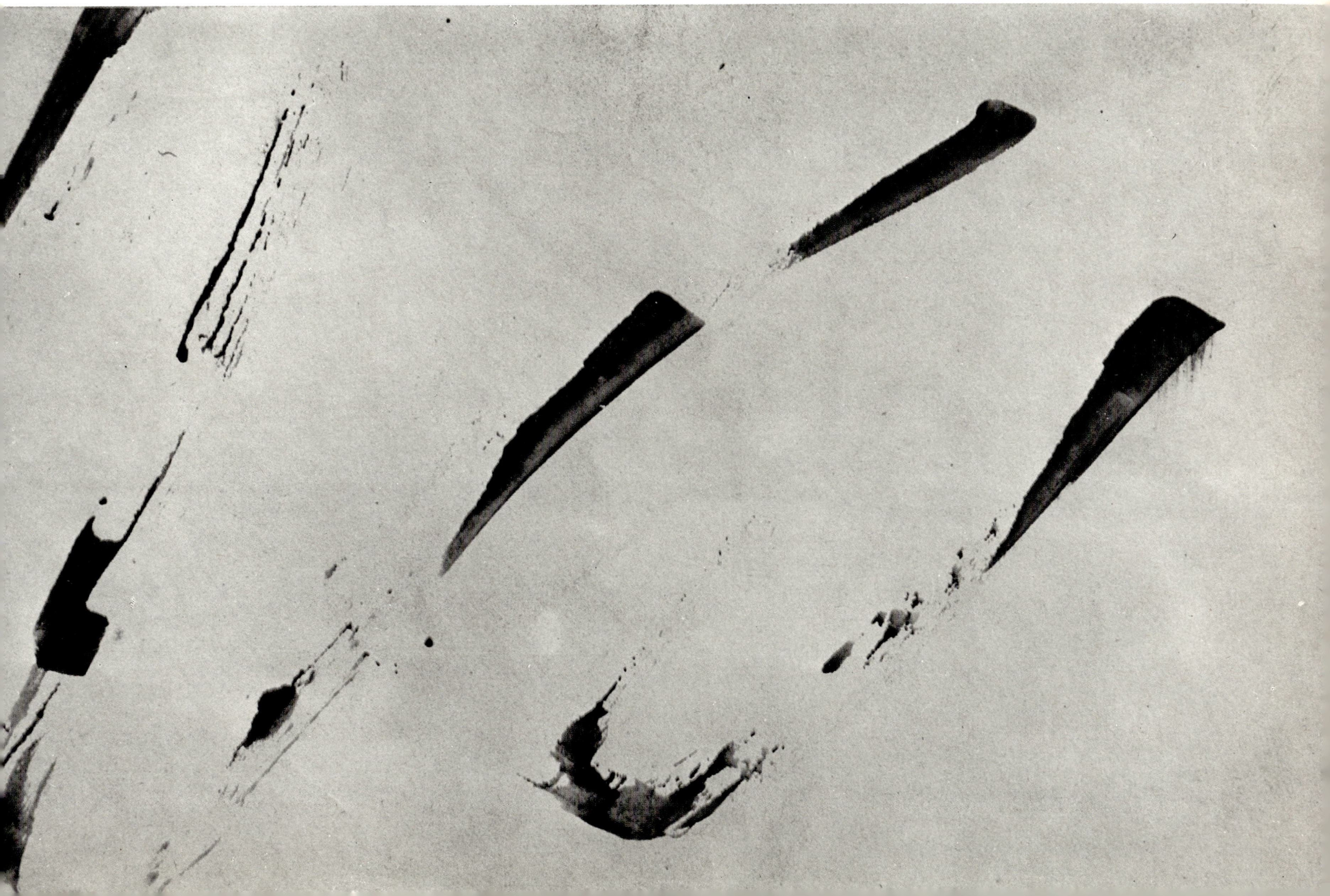

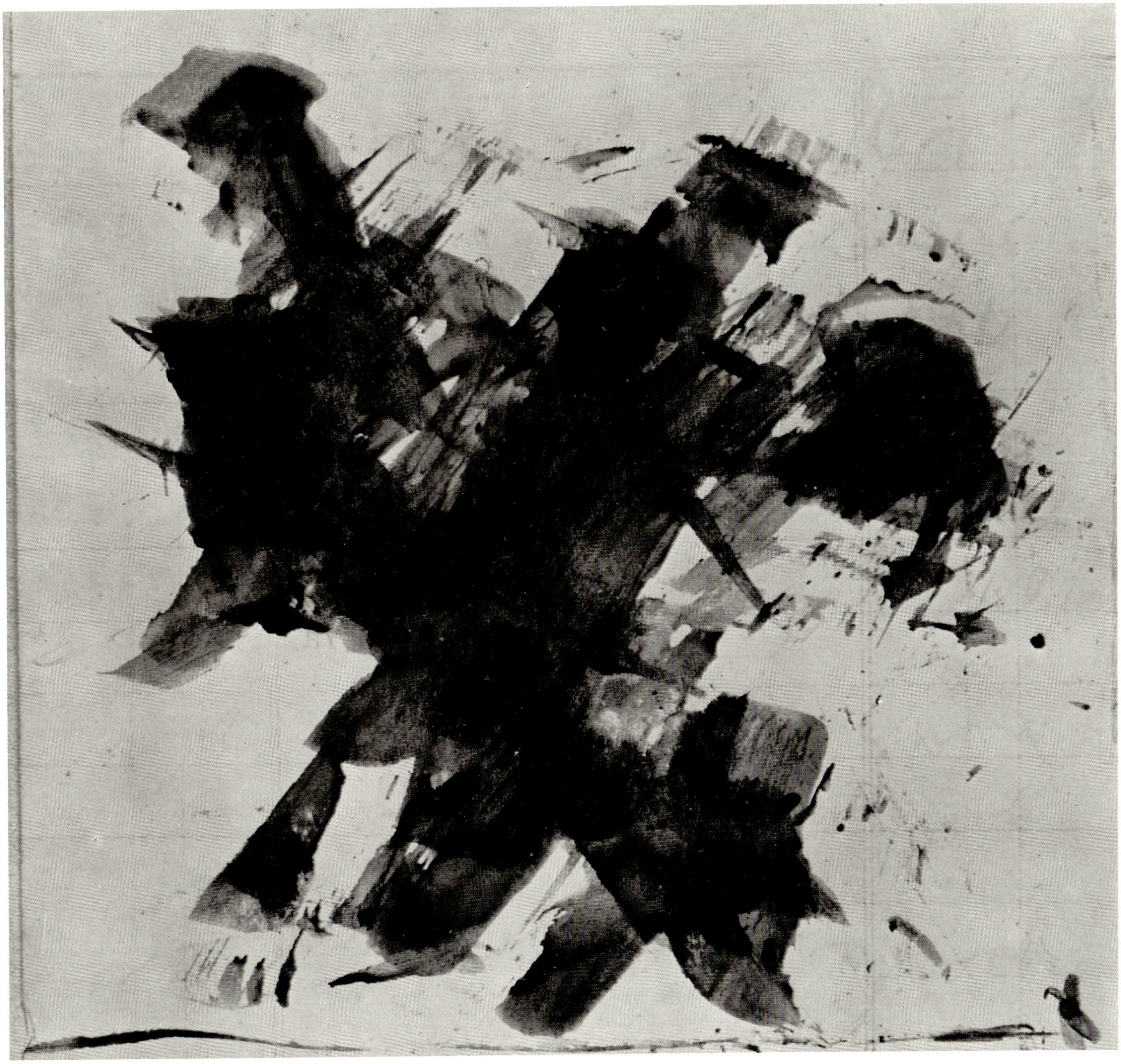

31 E. 1923

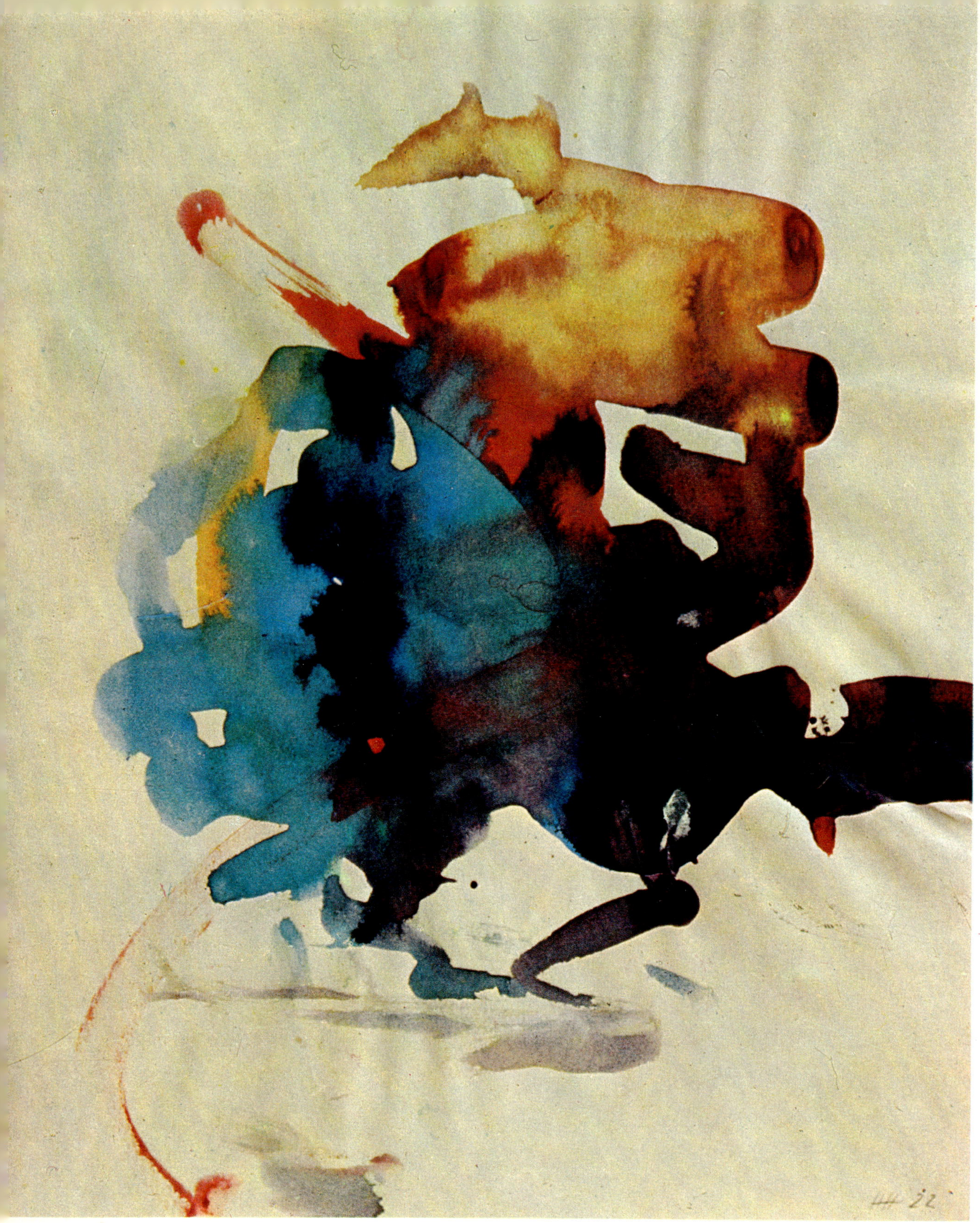

32 A. 1922

3 A. 1922

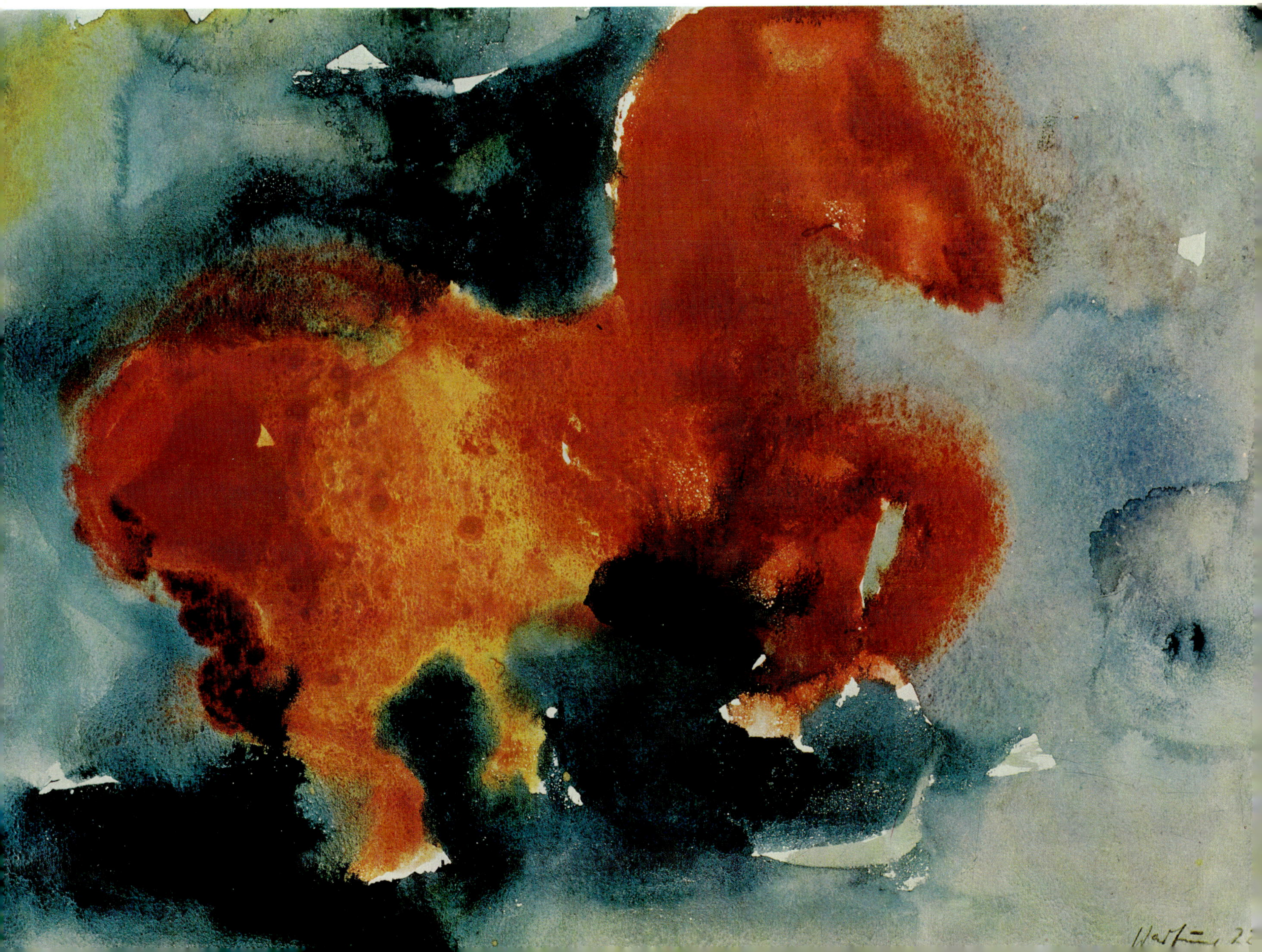

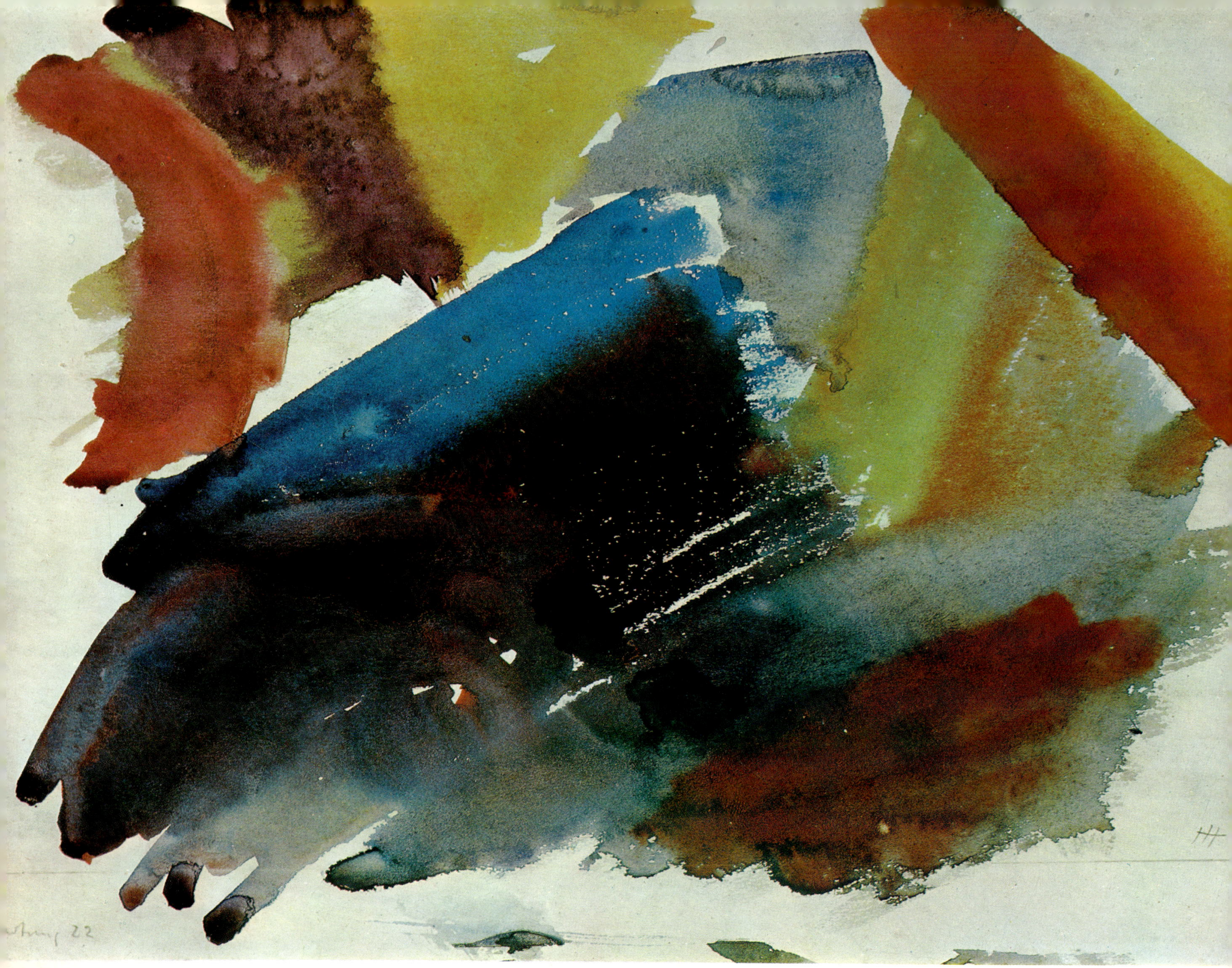

34 A. 192

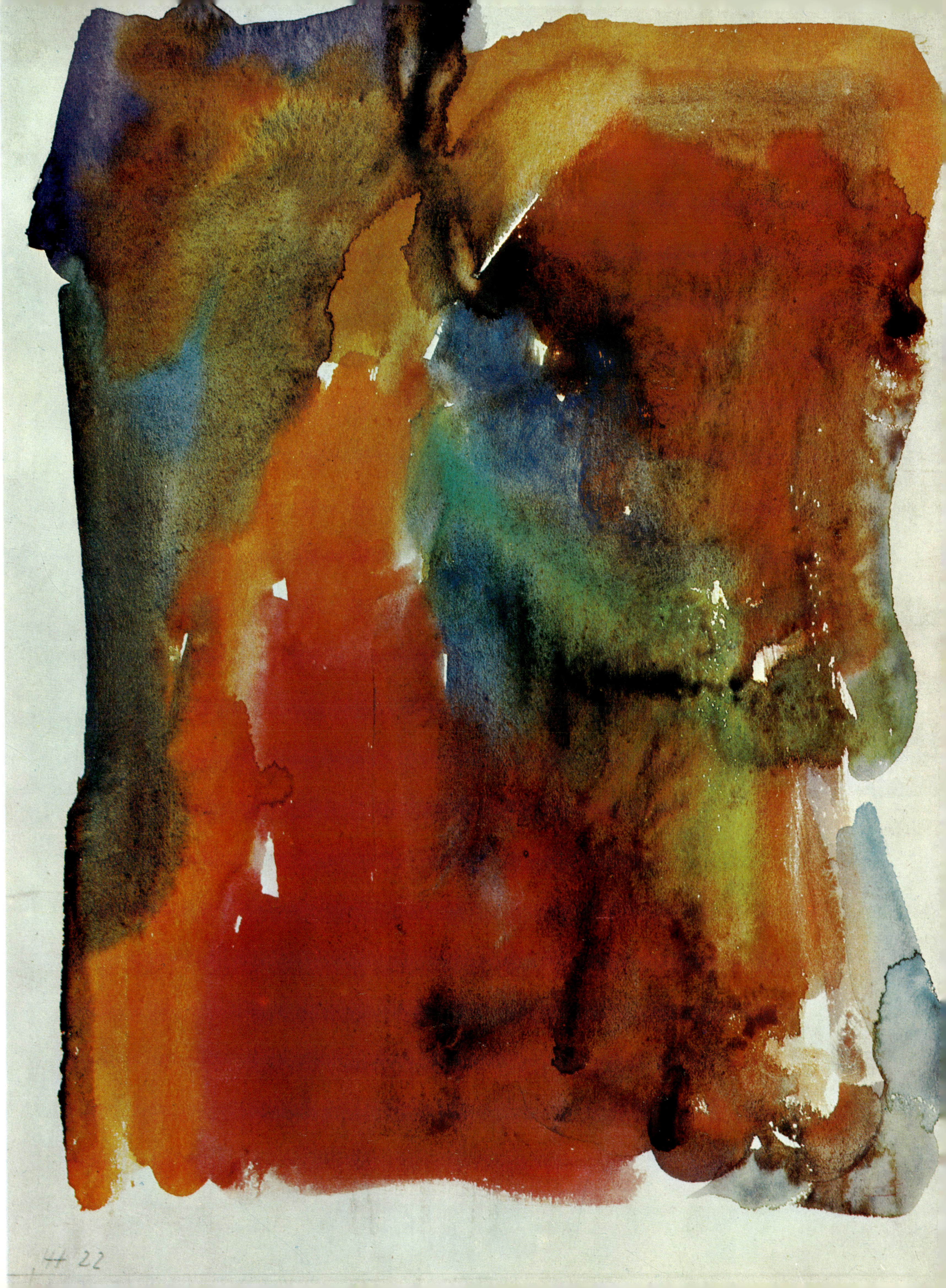

A. 1922

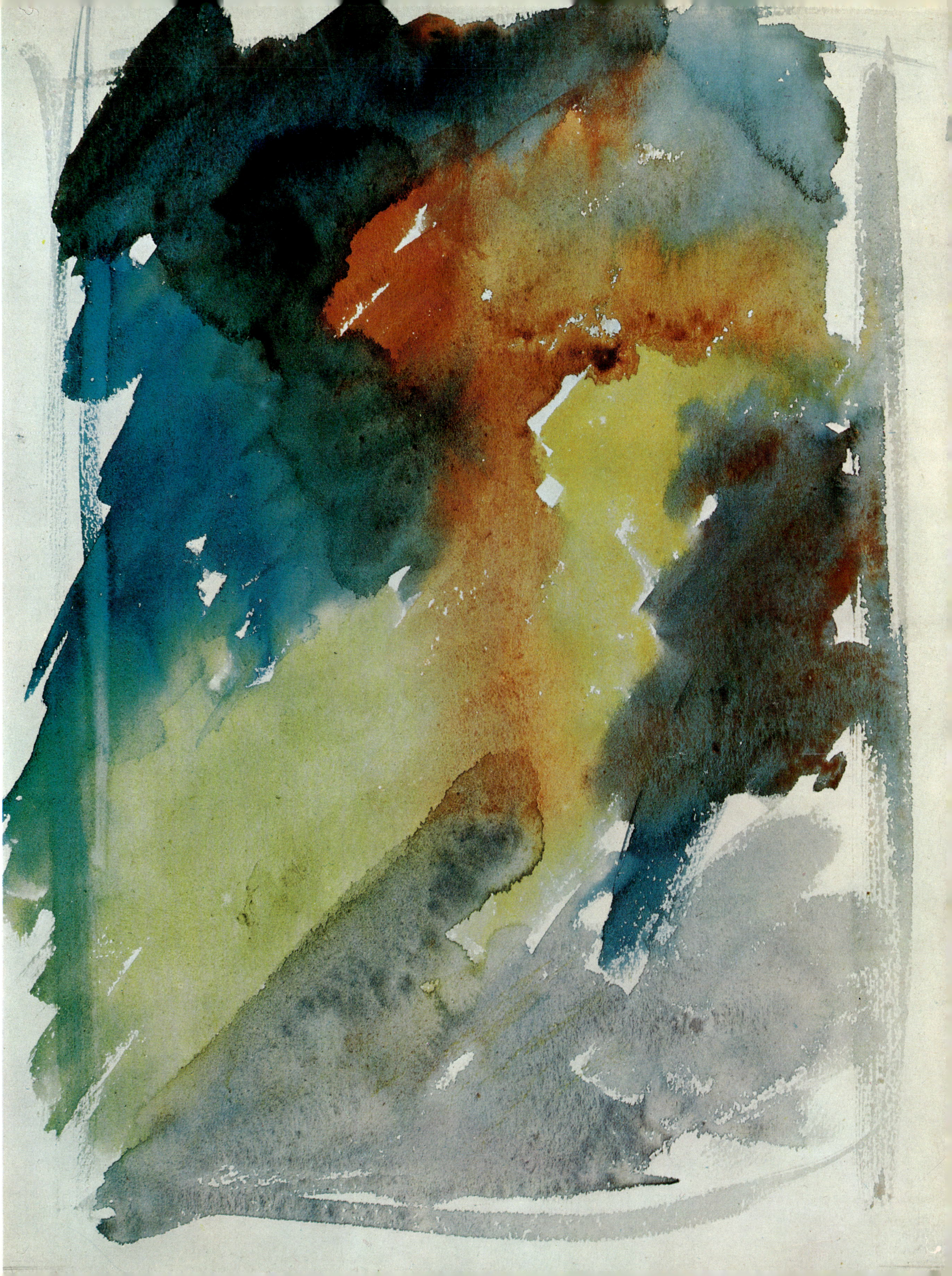

36

. 1922

37 C. N. 1924

38 S. 192

39 C. N. 1924

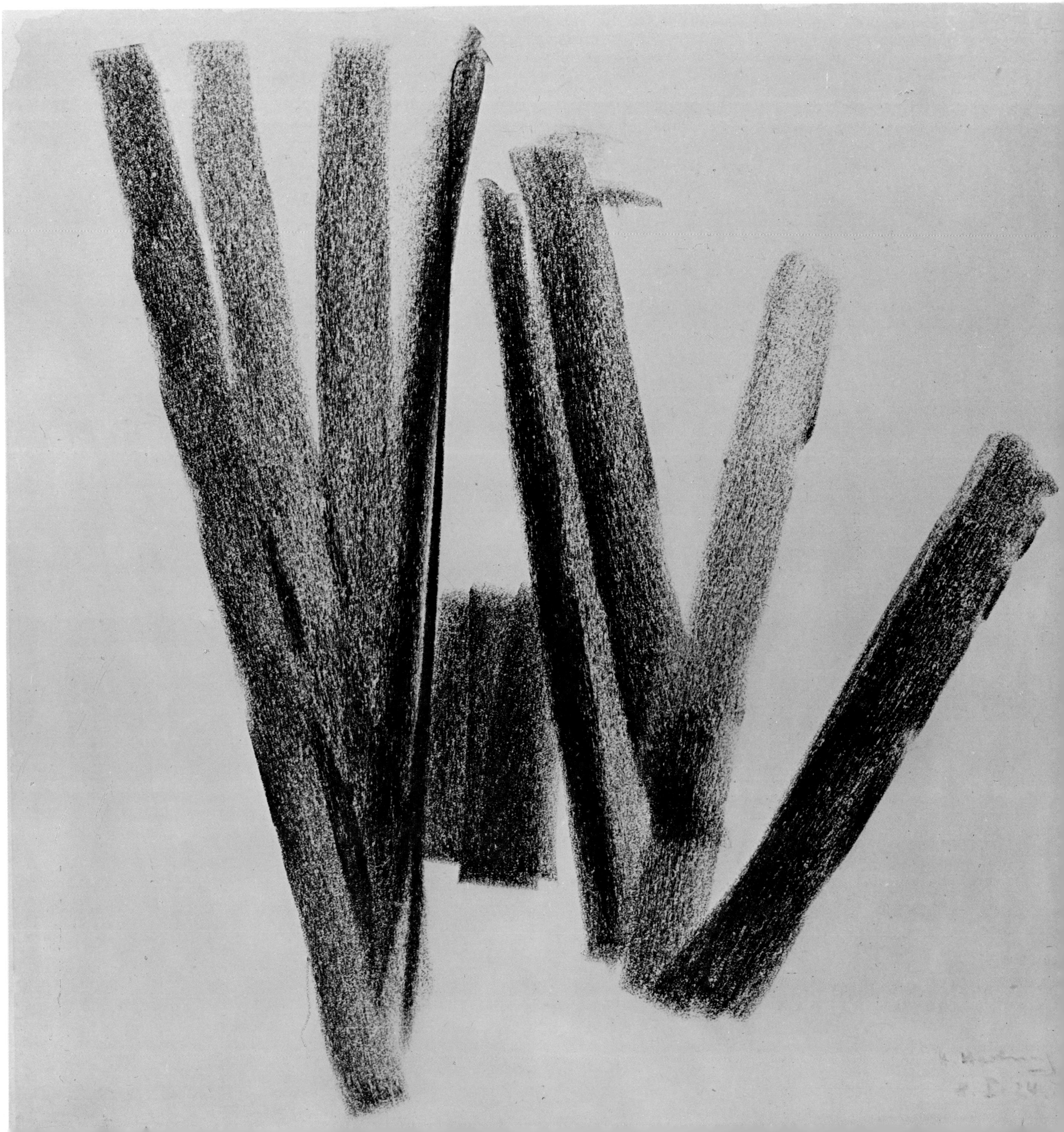

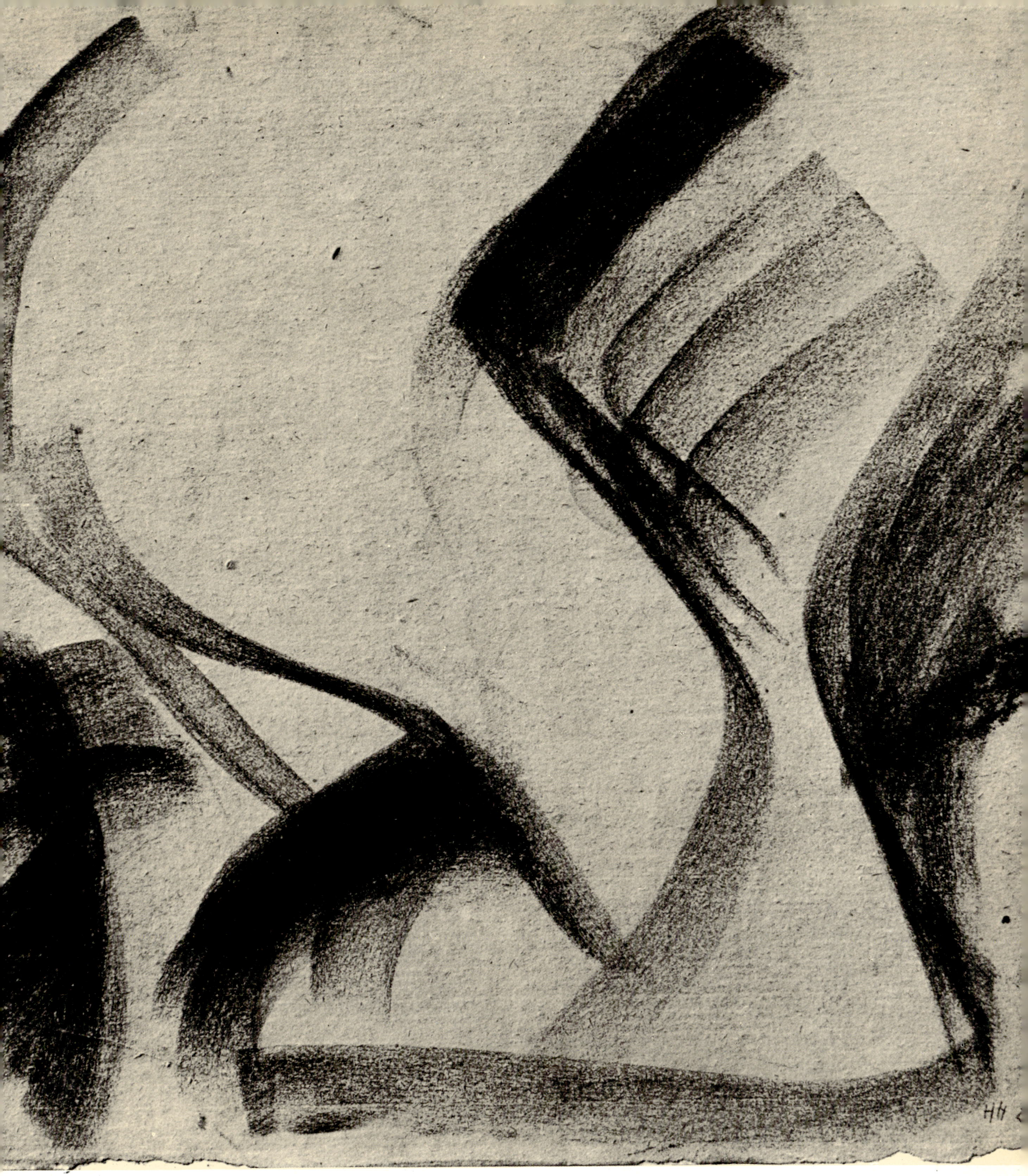

40 S. 1923

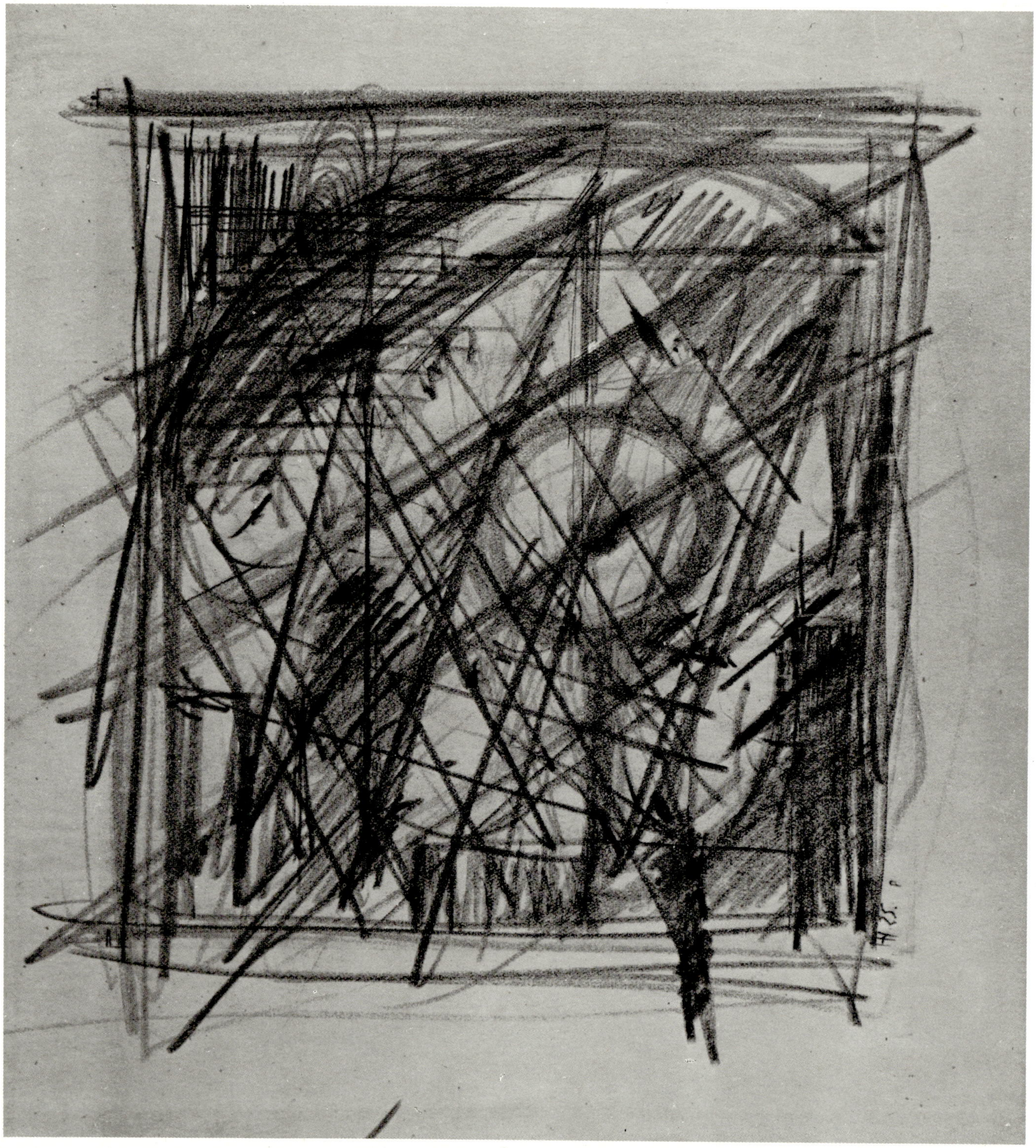

41 C. 1925

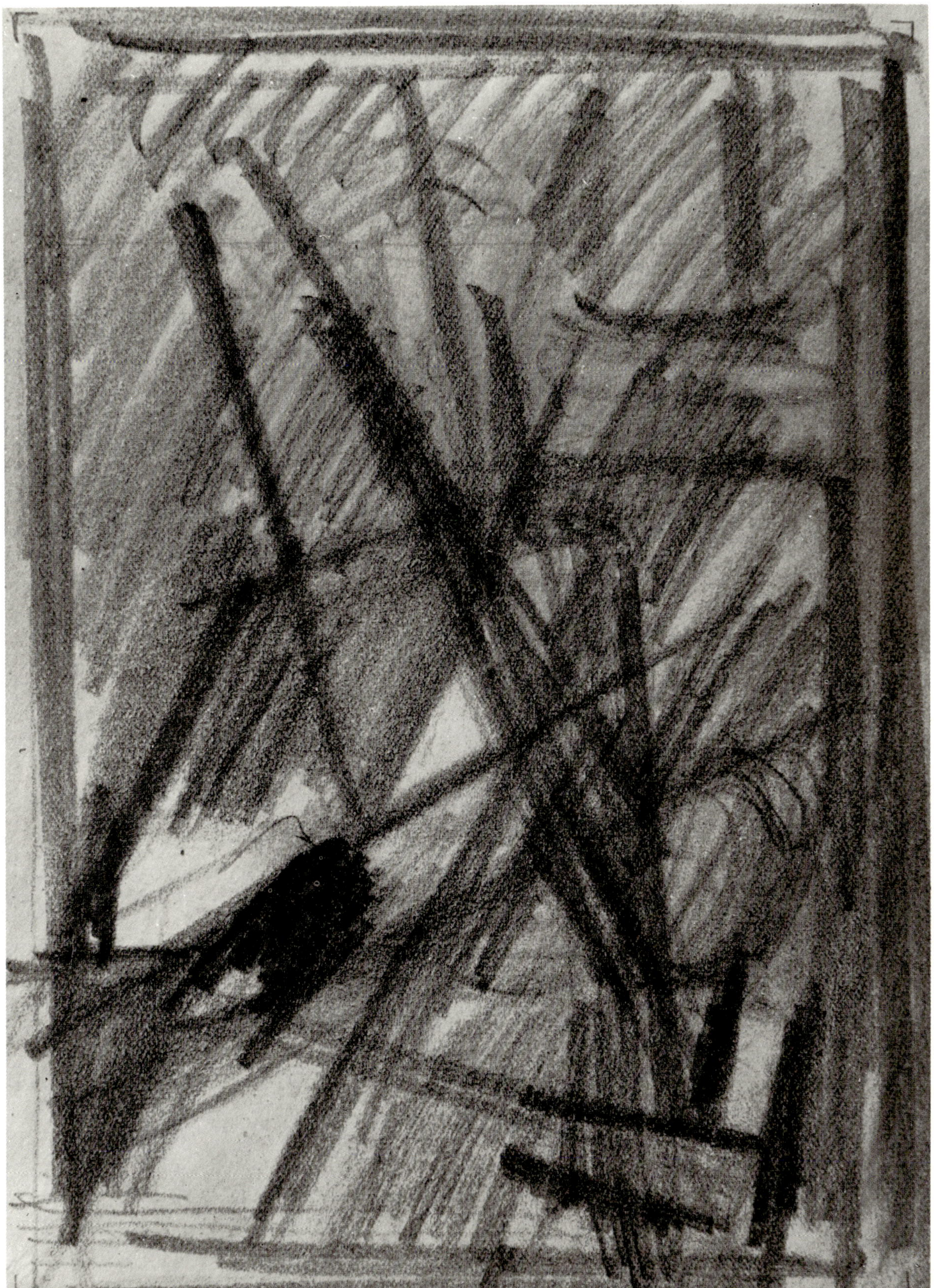

42 C. 1926

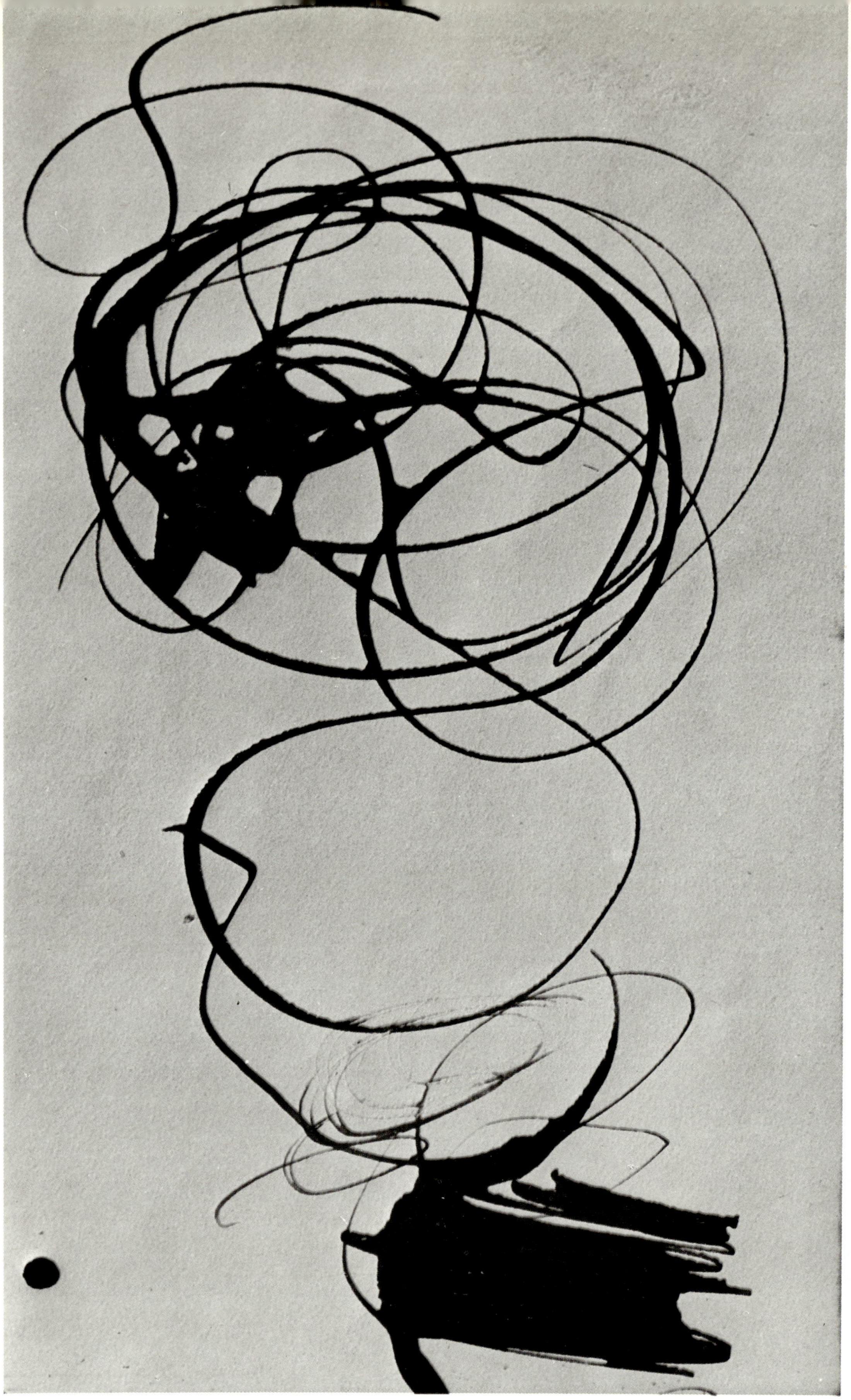

43 E. C. 1927

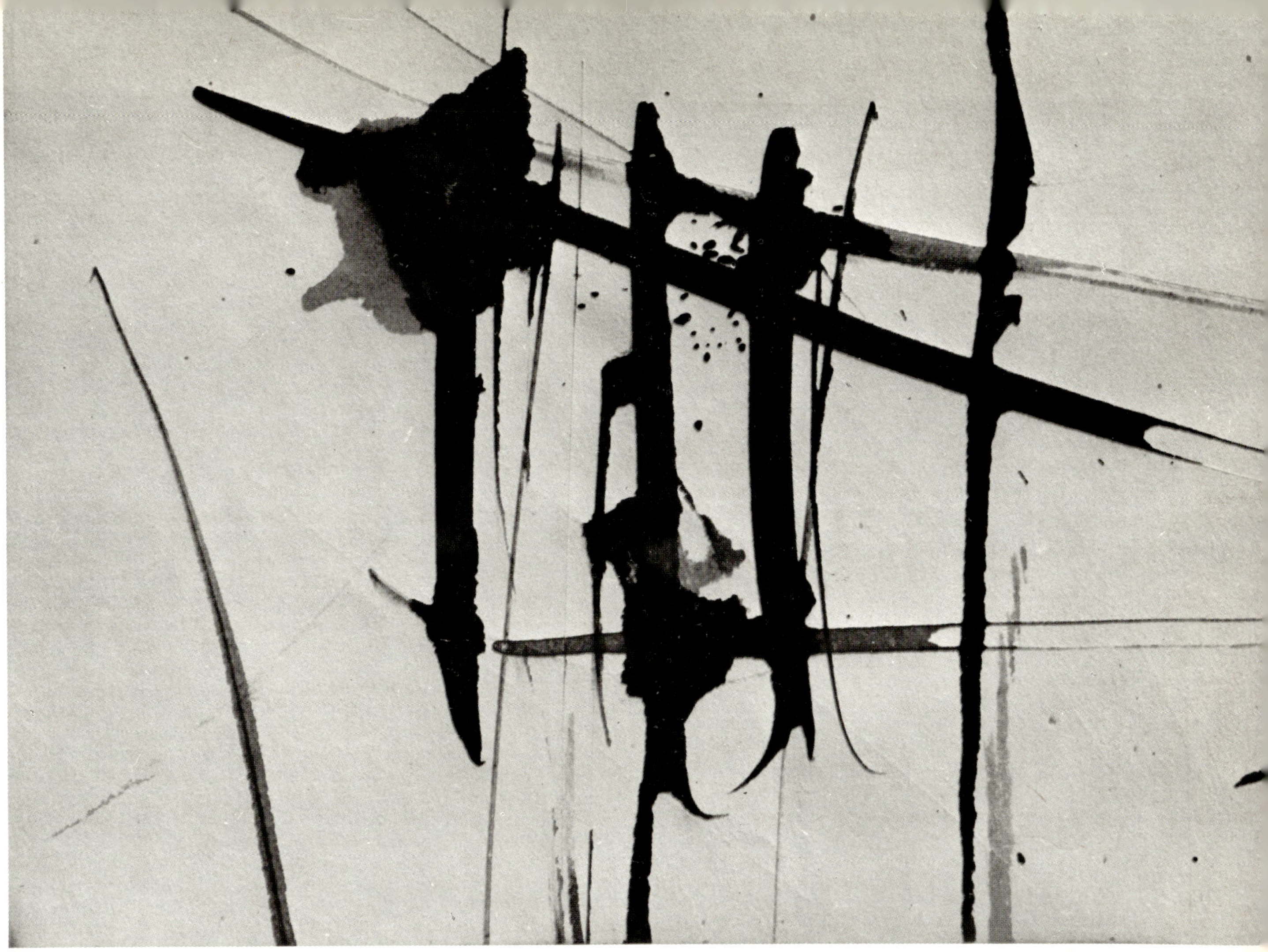

44 E. C. 1927

45 E. C. 1927

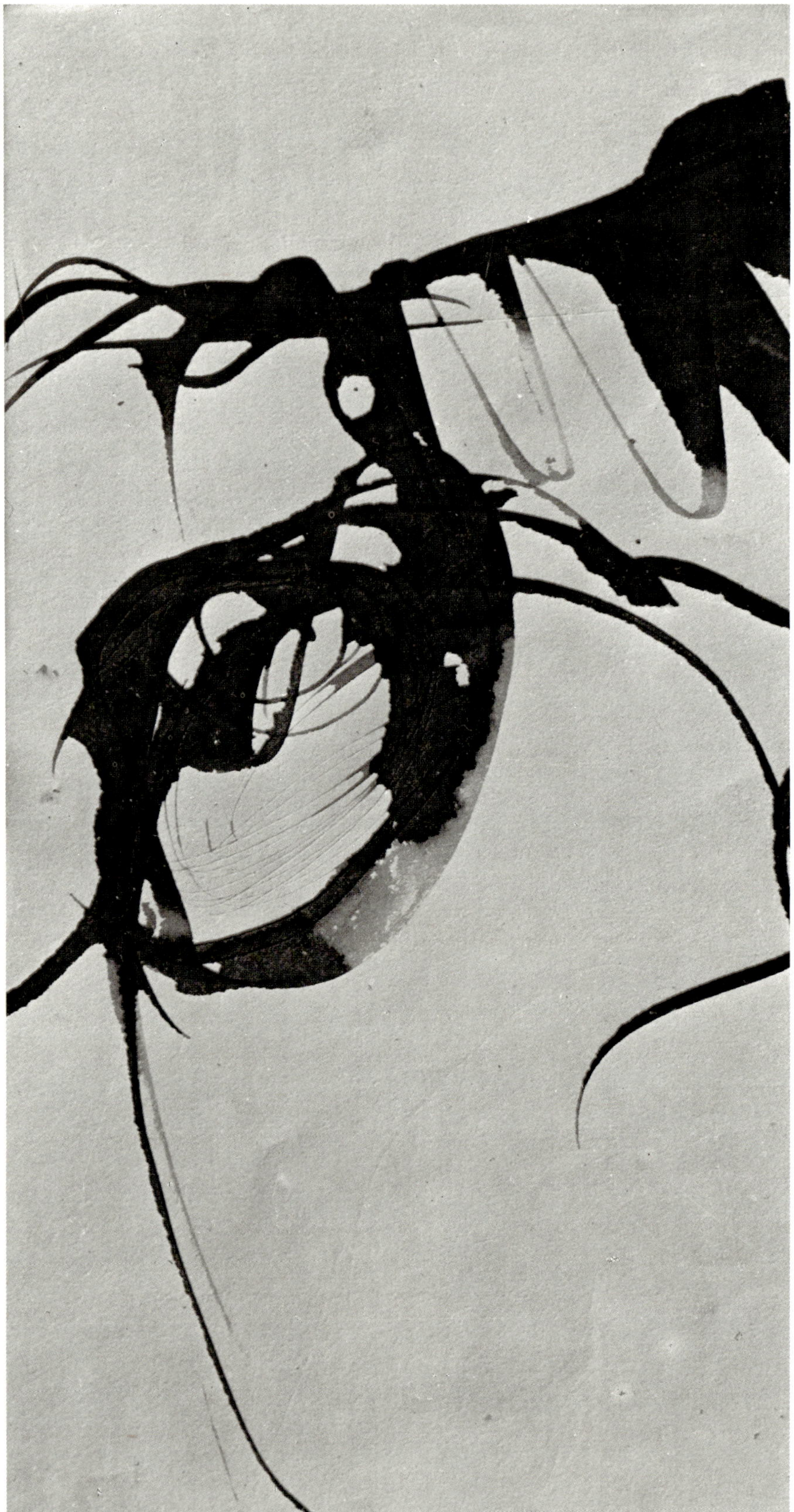

46 E. C. 1927

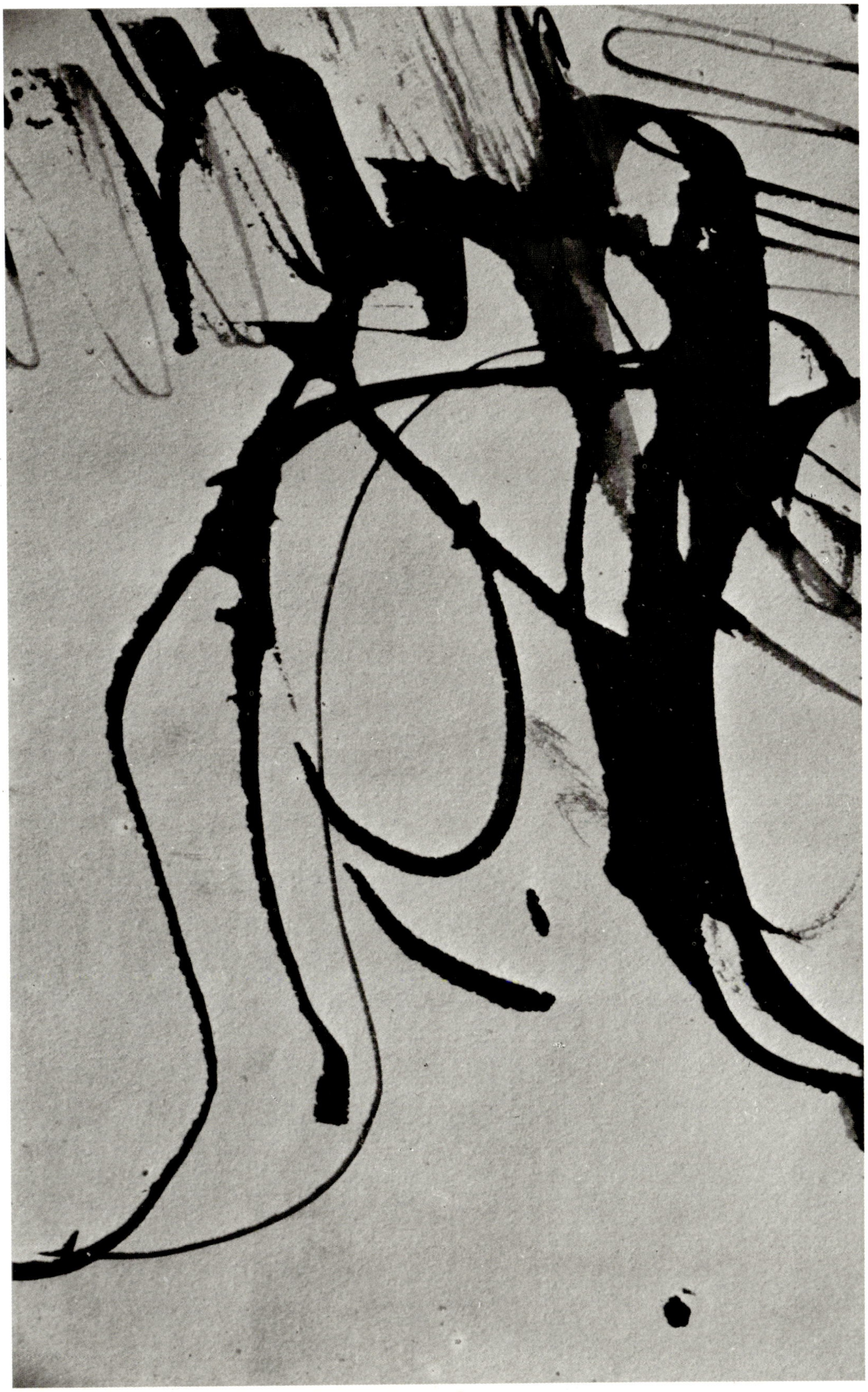

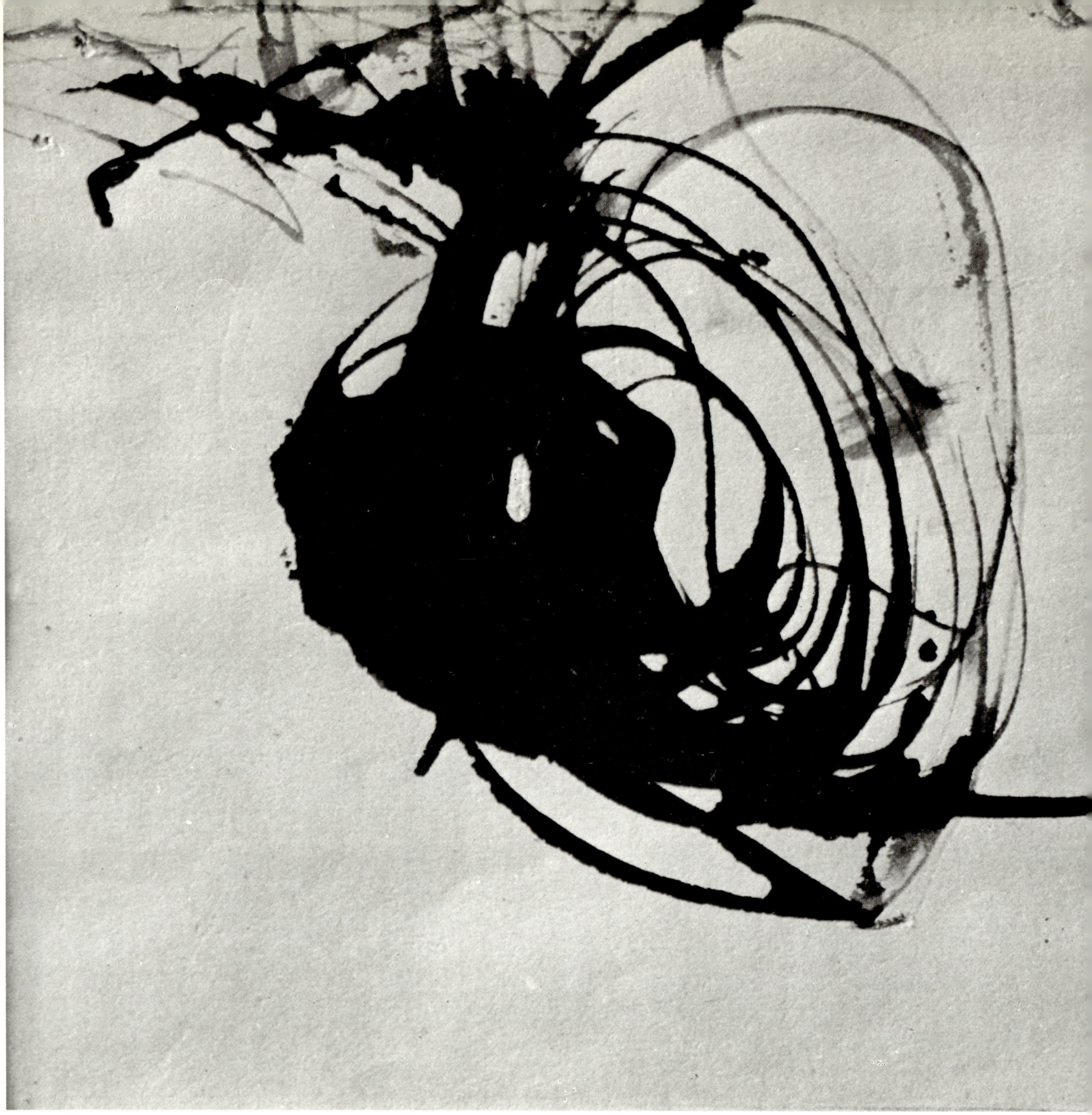

47 E. C. 1927

1921-1930

48 E. C. 192

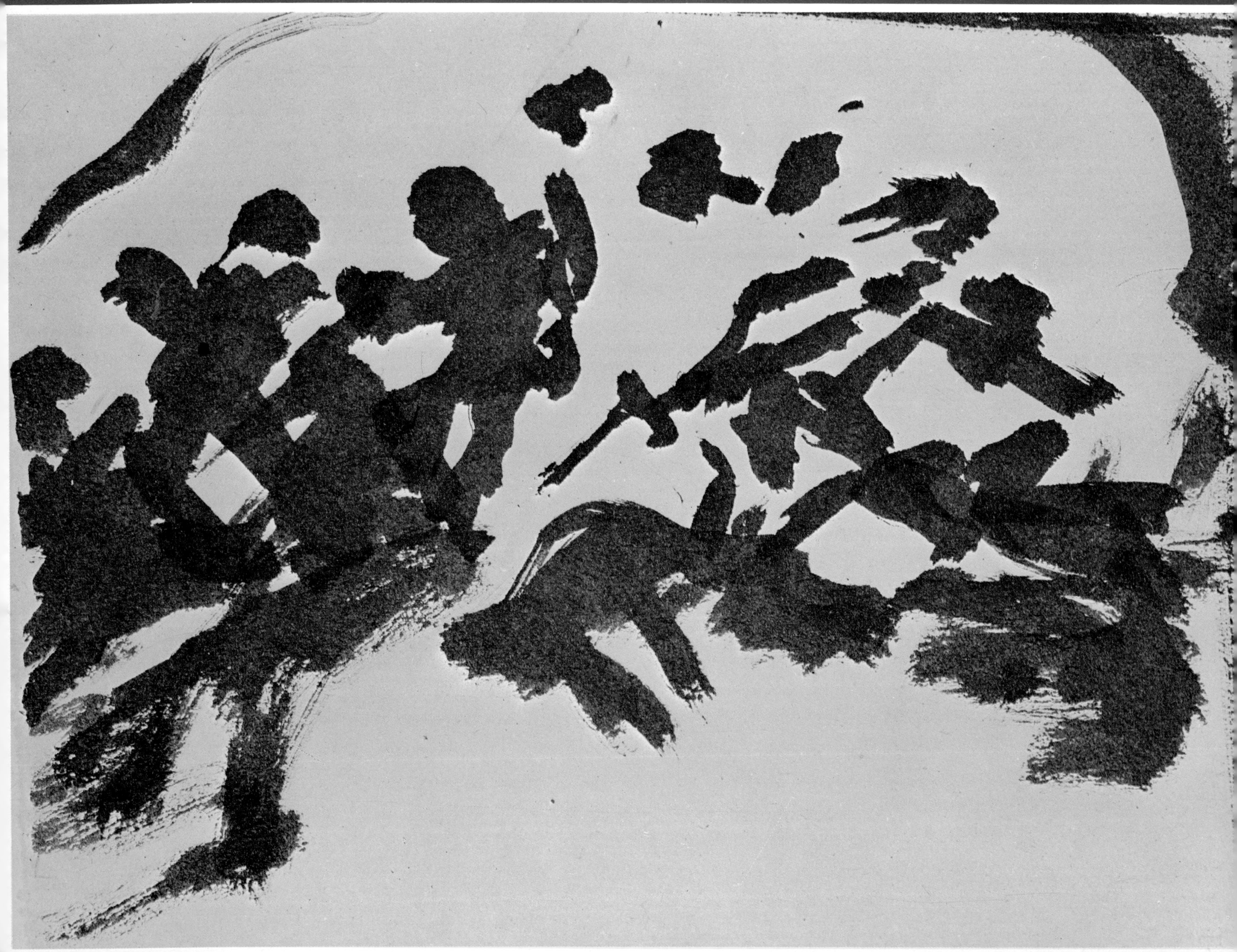

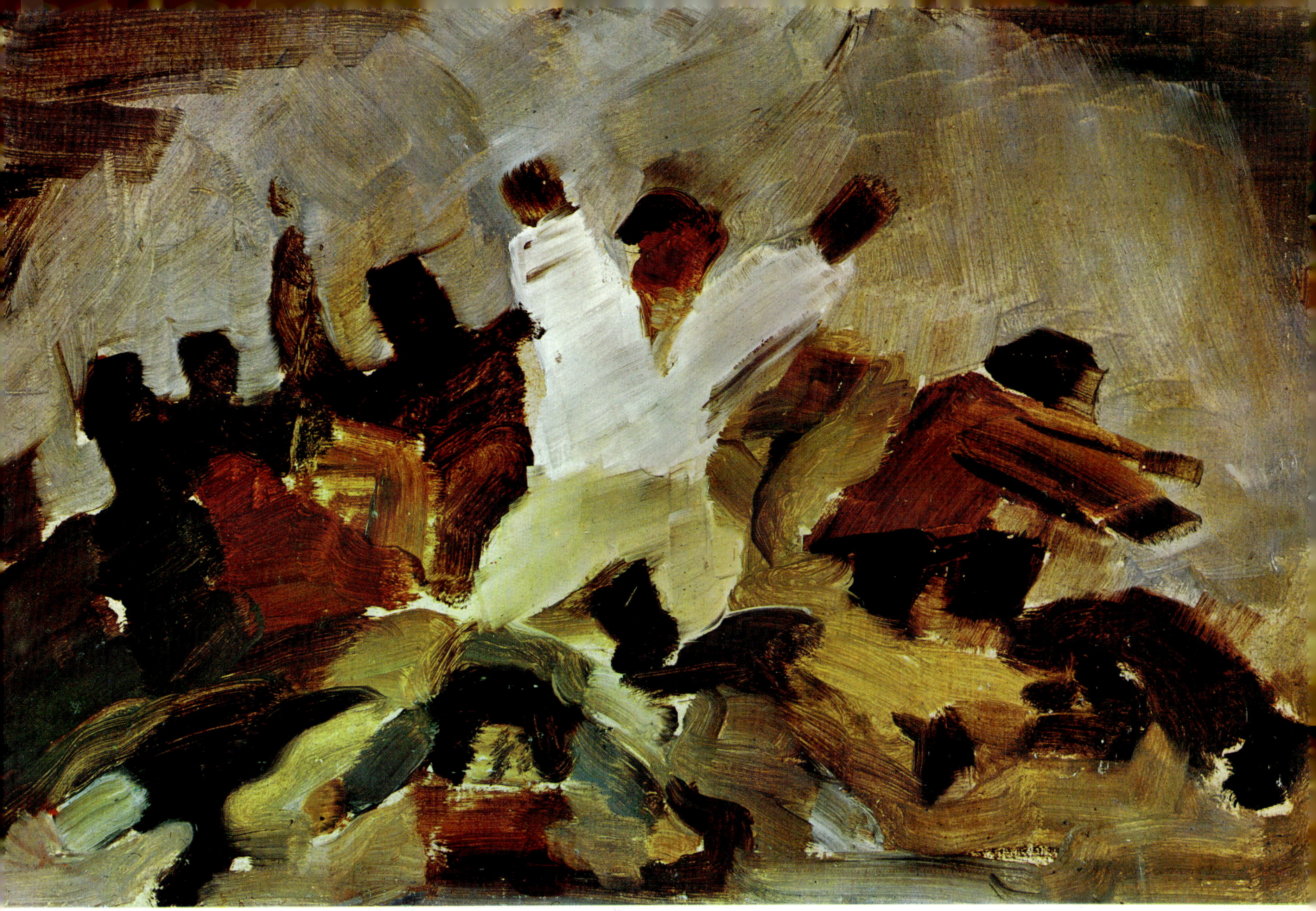

T. 1921-1

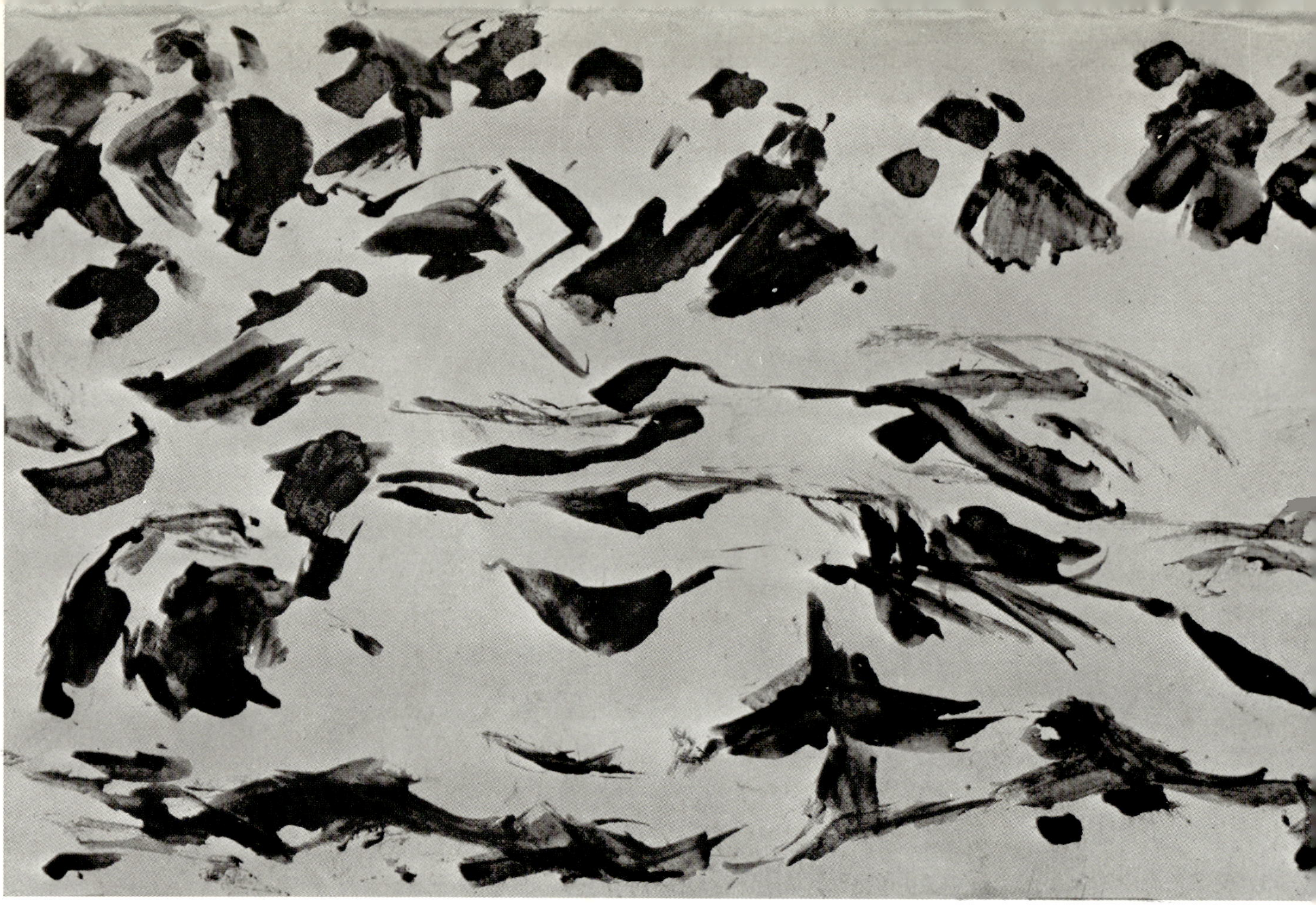

50 E. 1922

51 T. 1922-1

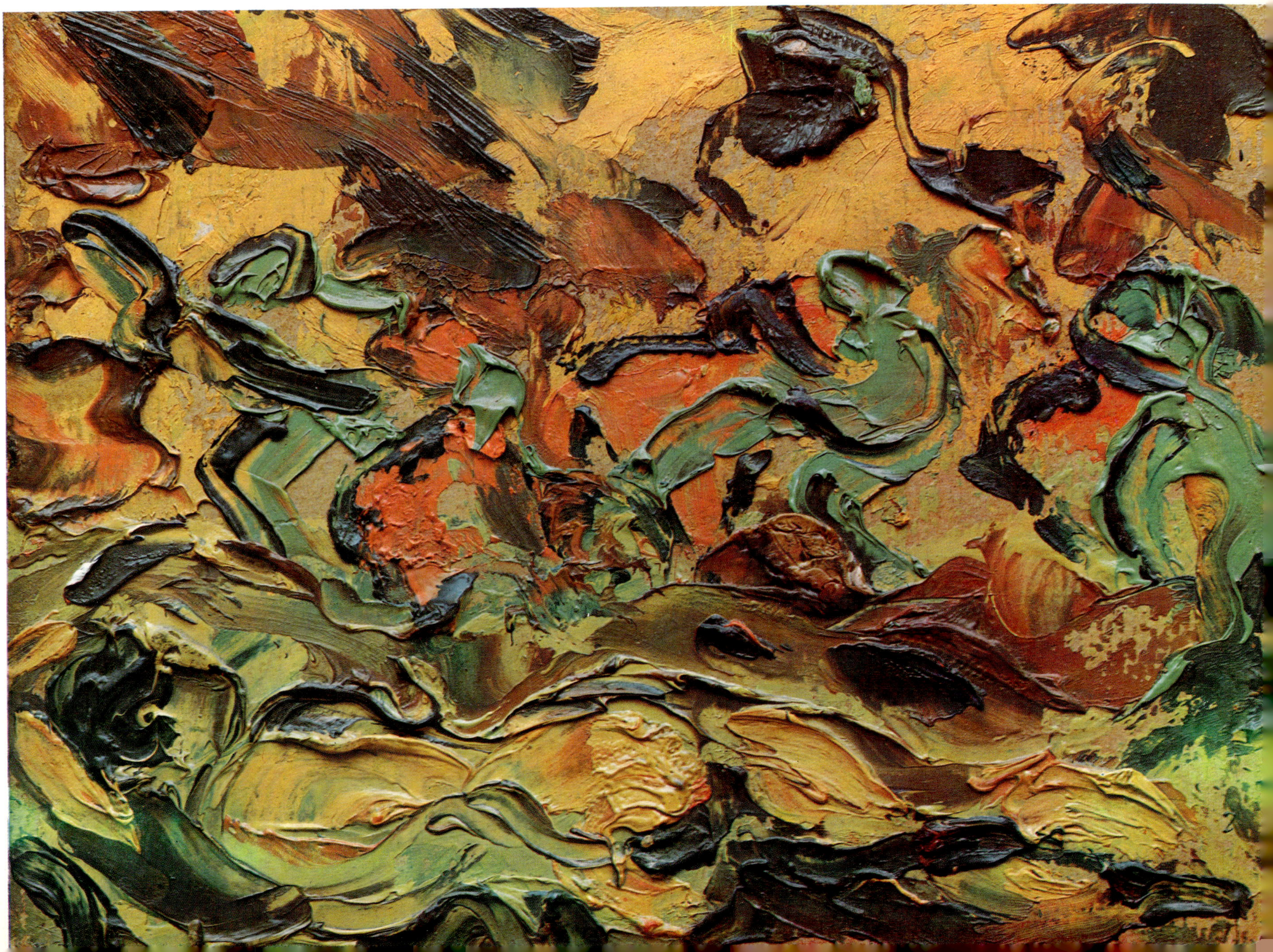

52 C. N. 1924

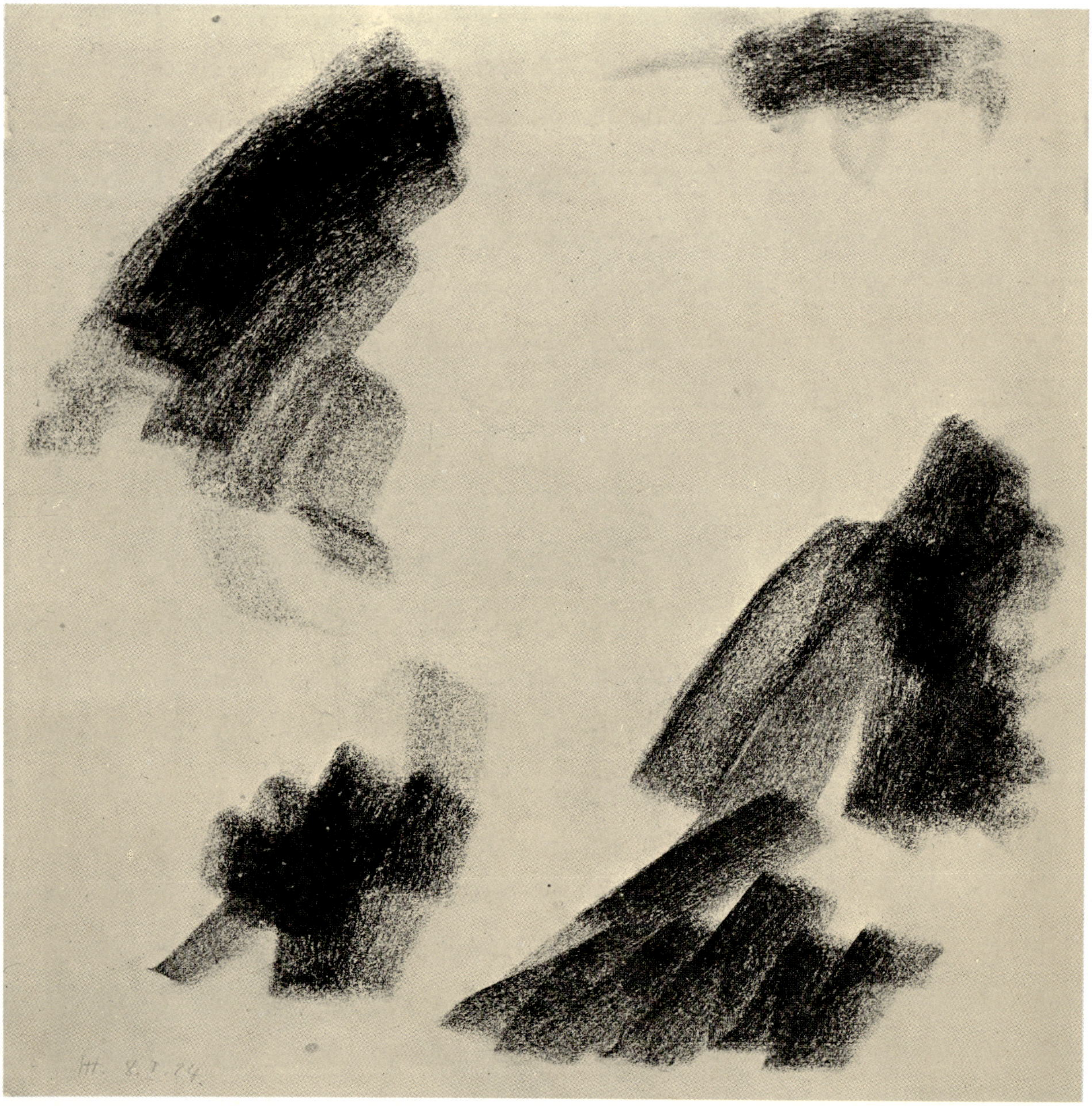

3 T. 1923-1

56 G. 1932-7

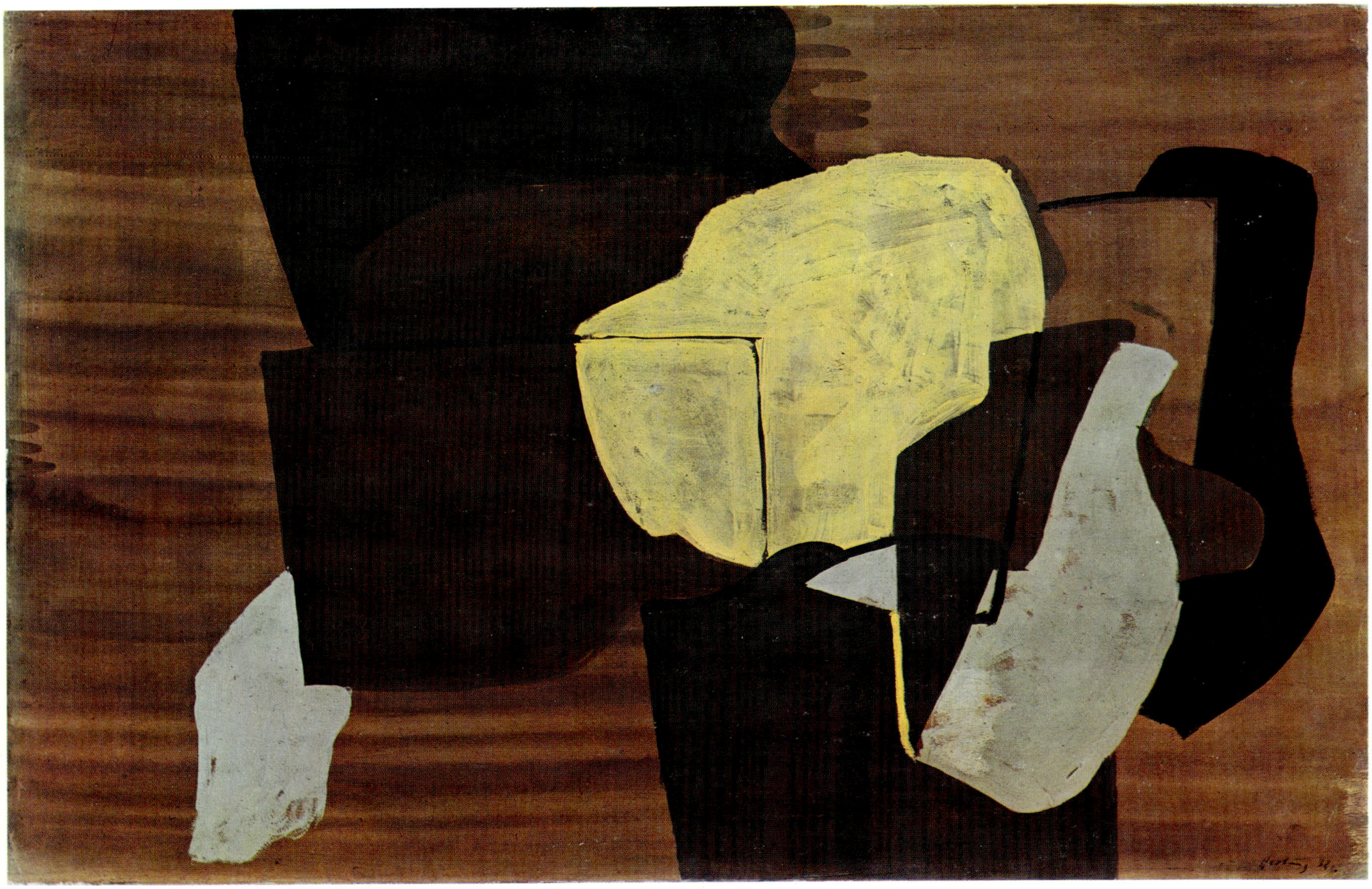

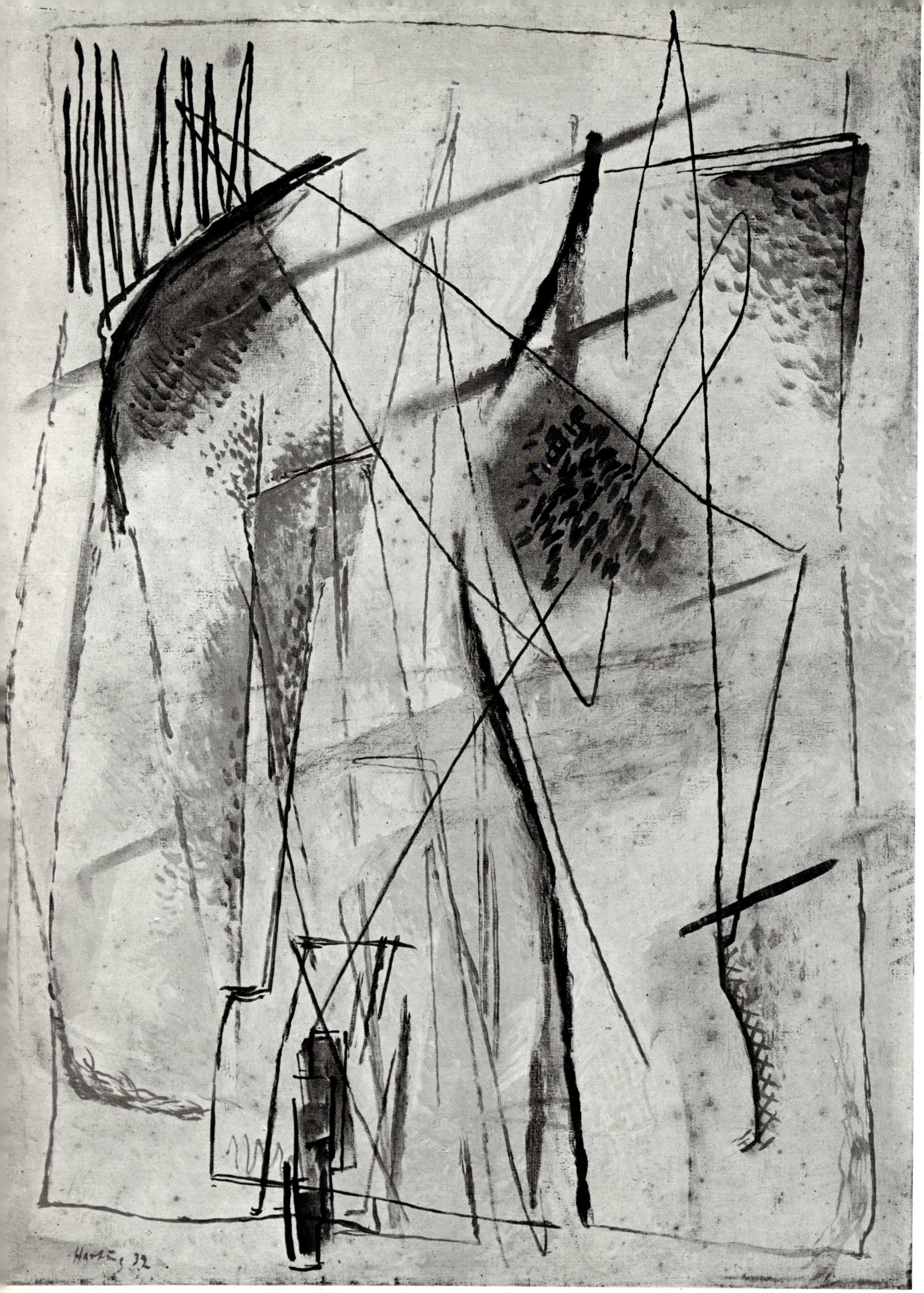

57 T. 1932-10

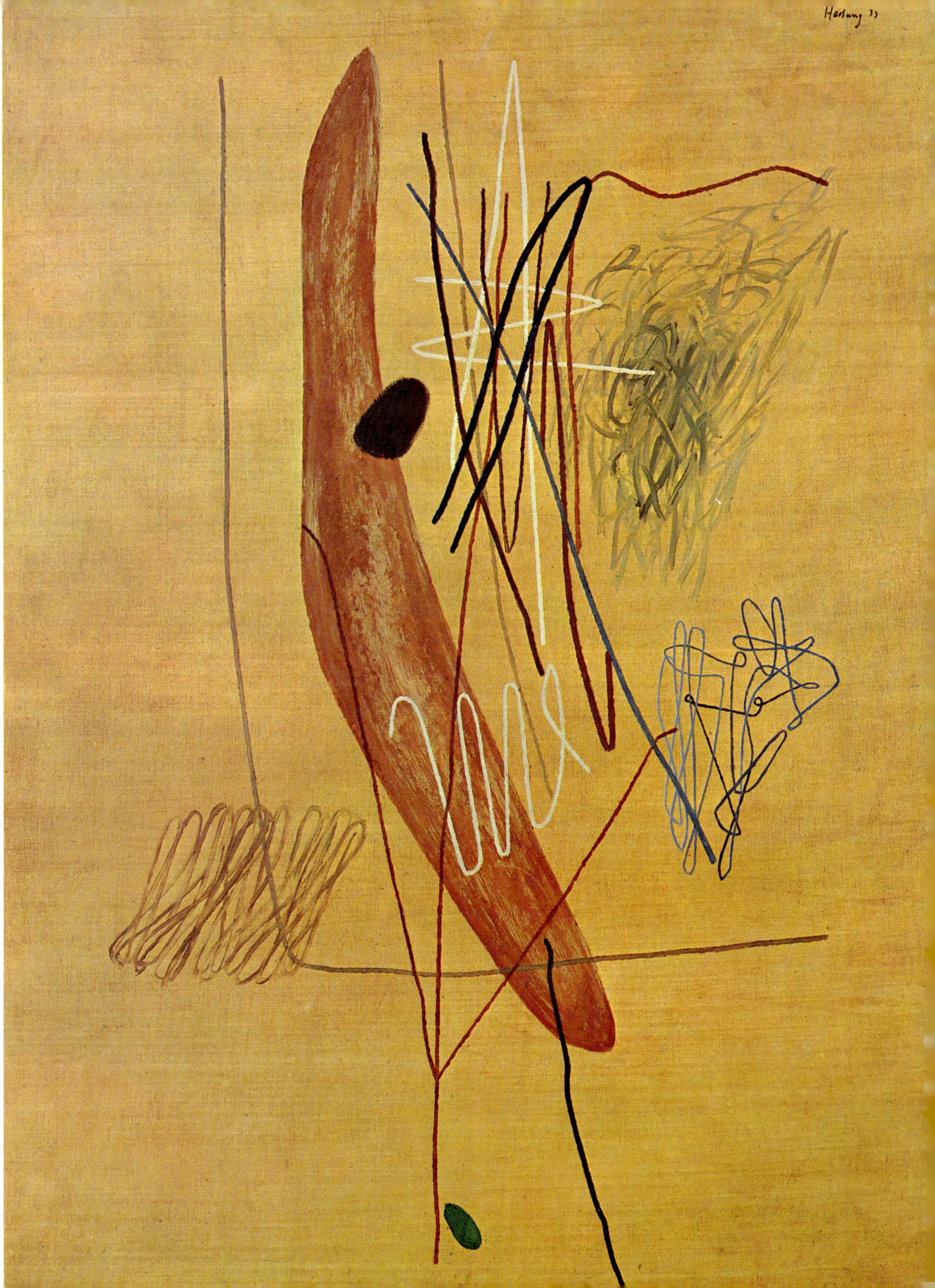

T. 1933-14

59 T. 1933-12

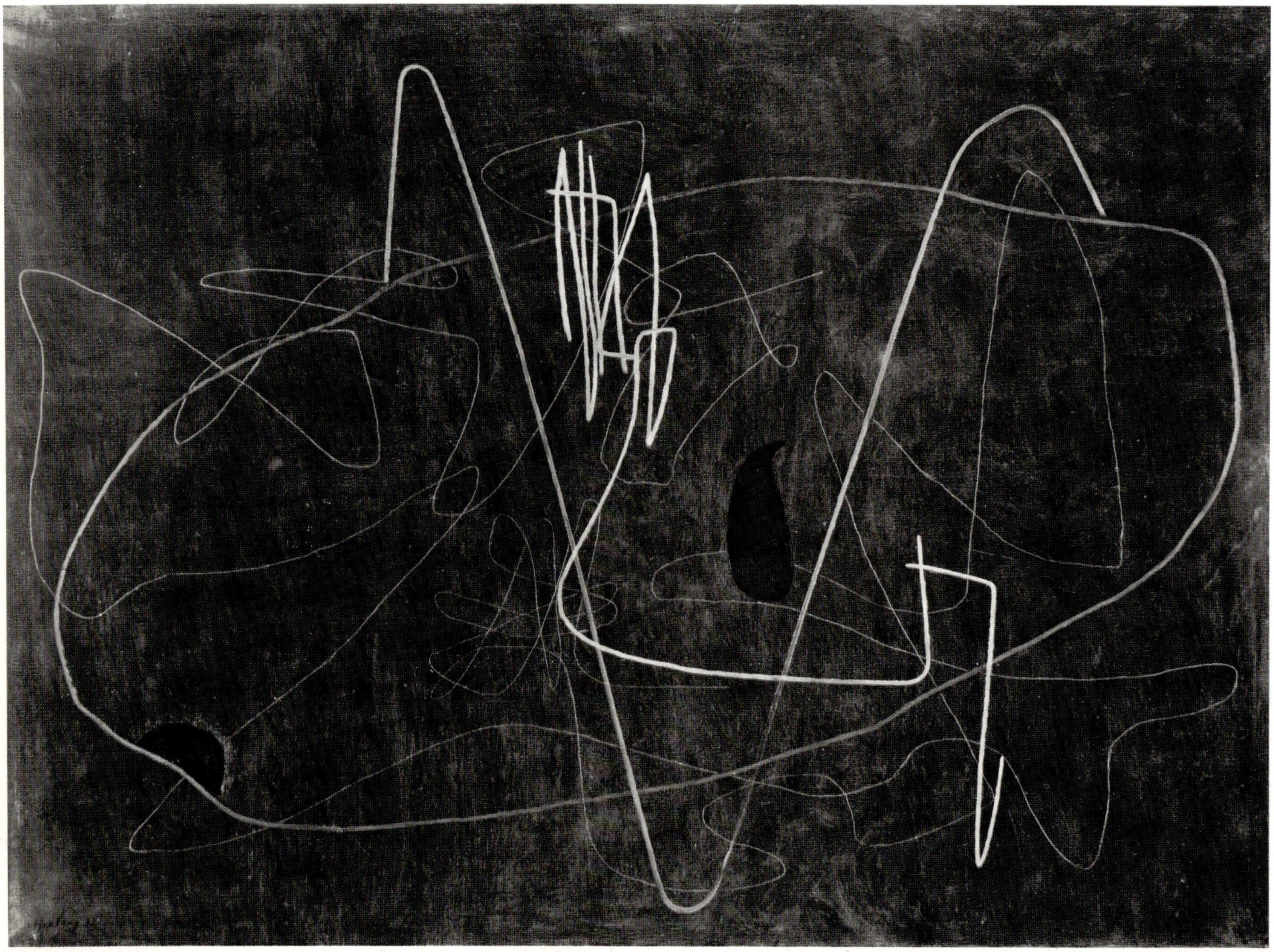

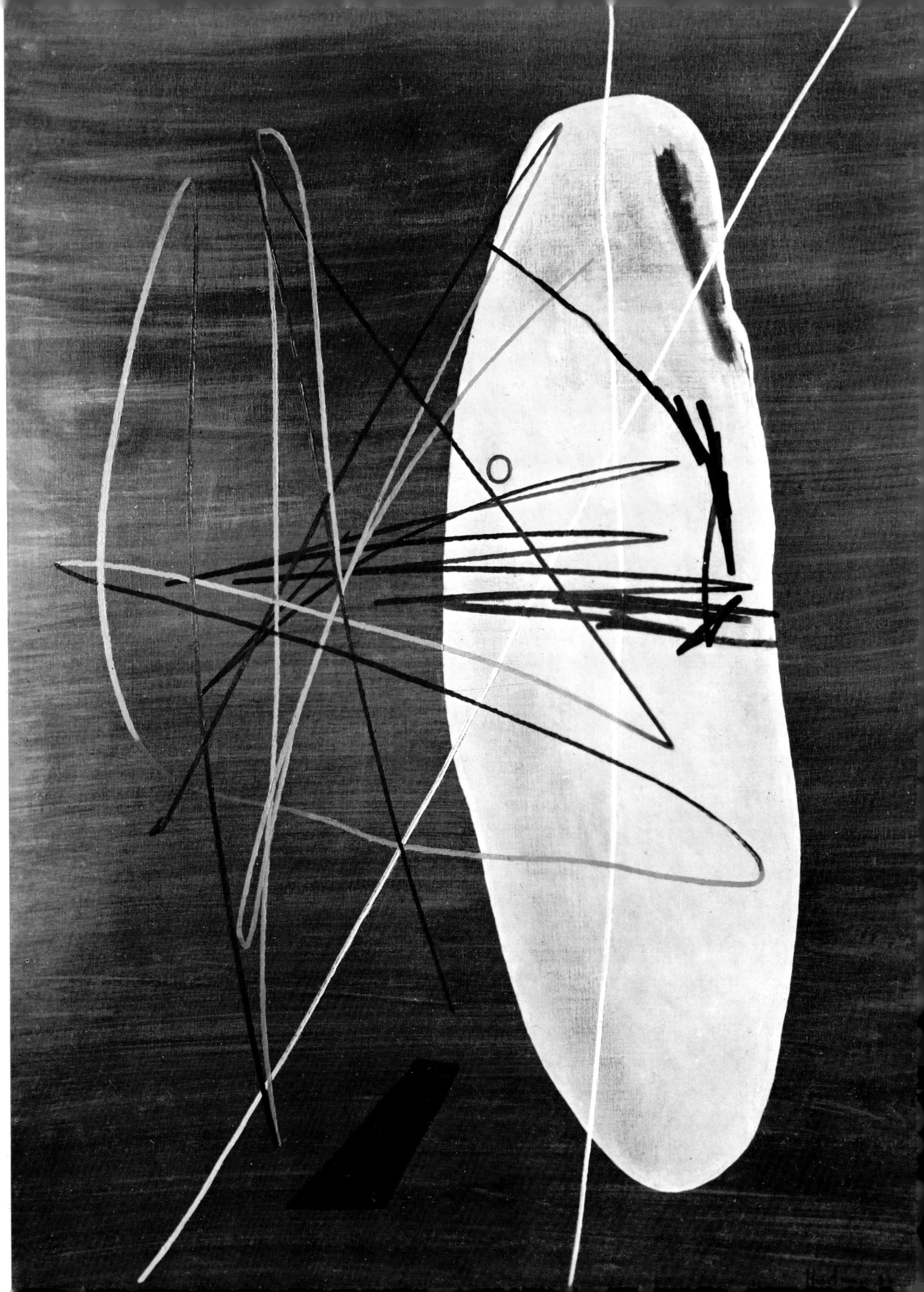

T. 1934-2

61 T. 1933-17

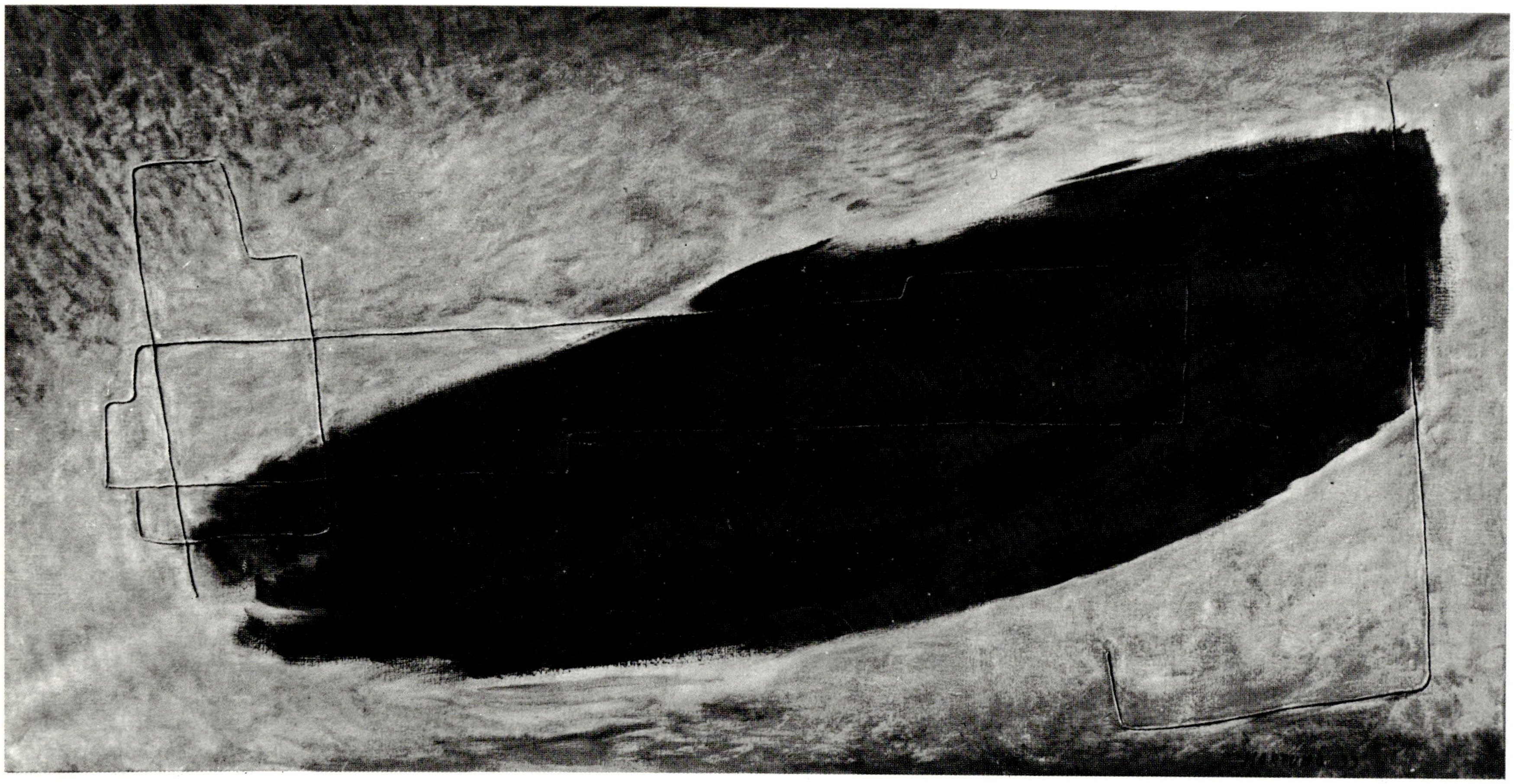

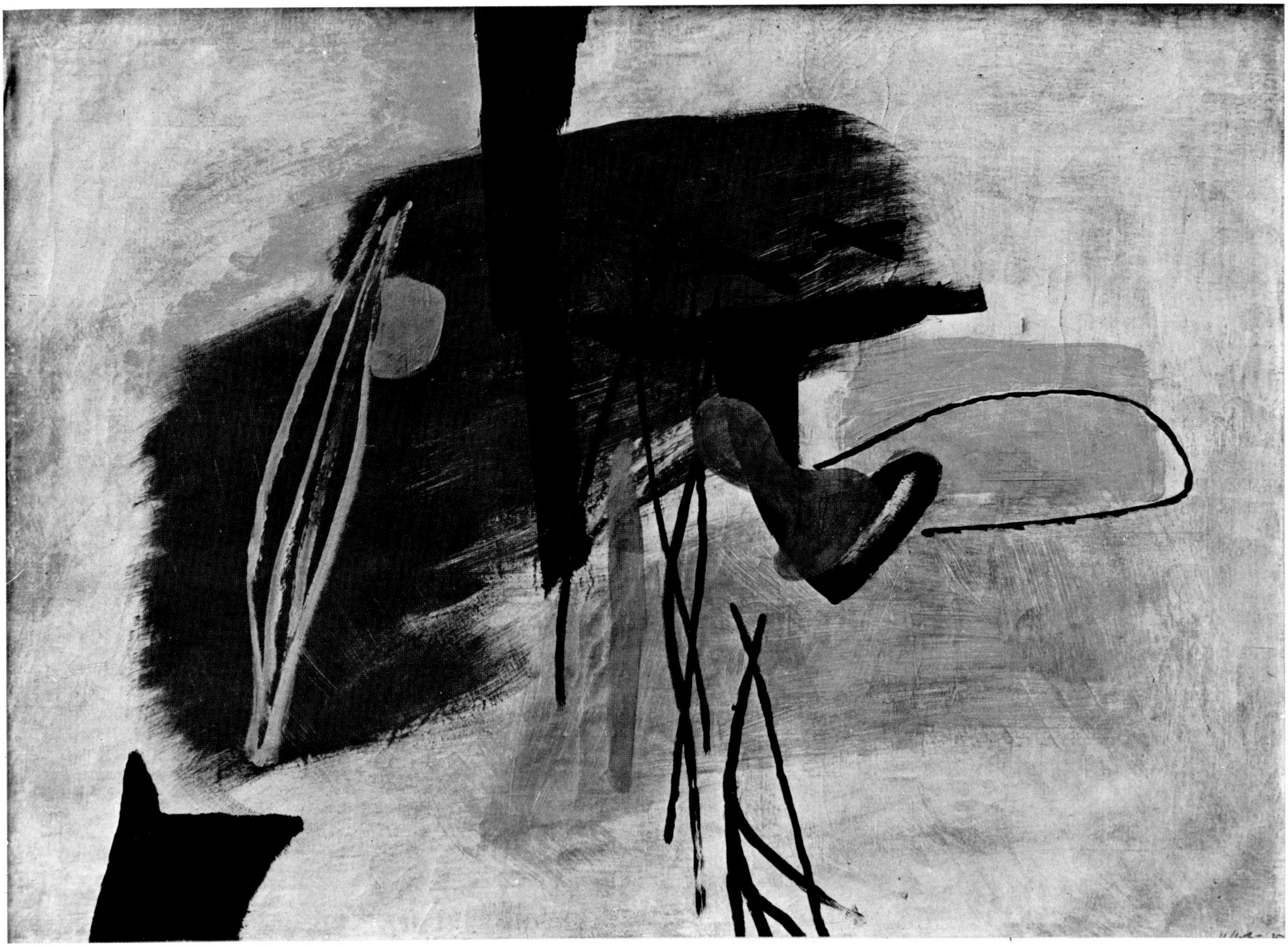

62 T. 1935-2

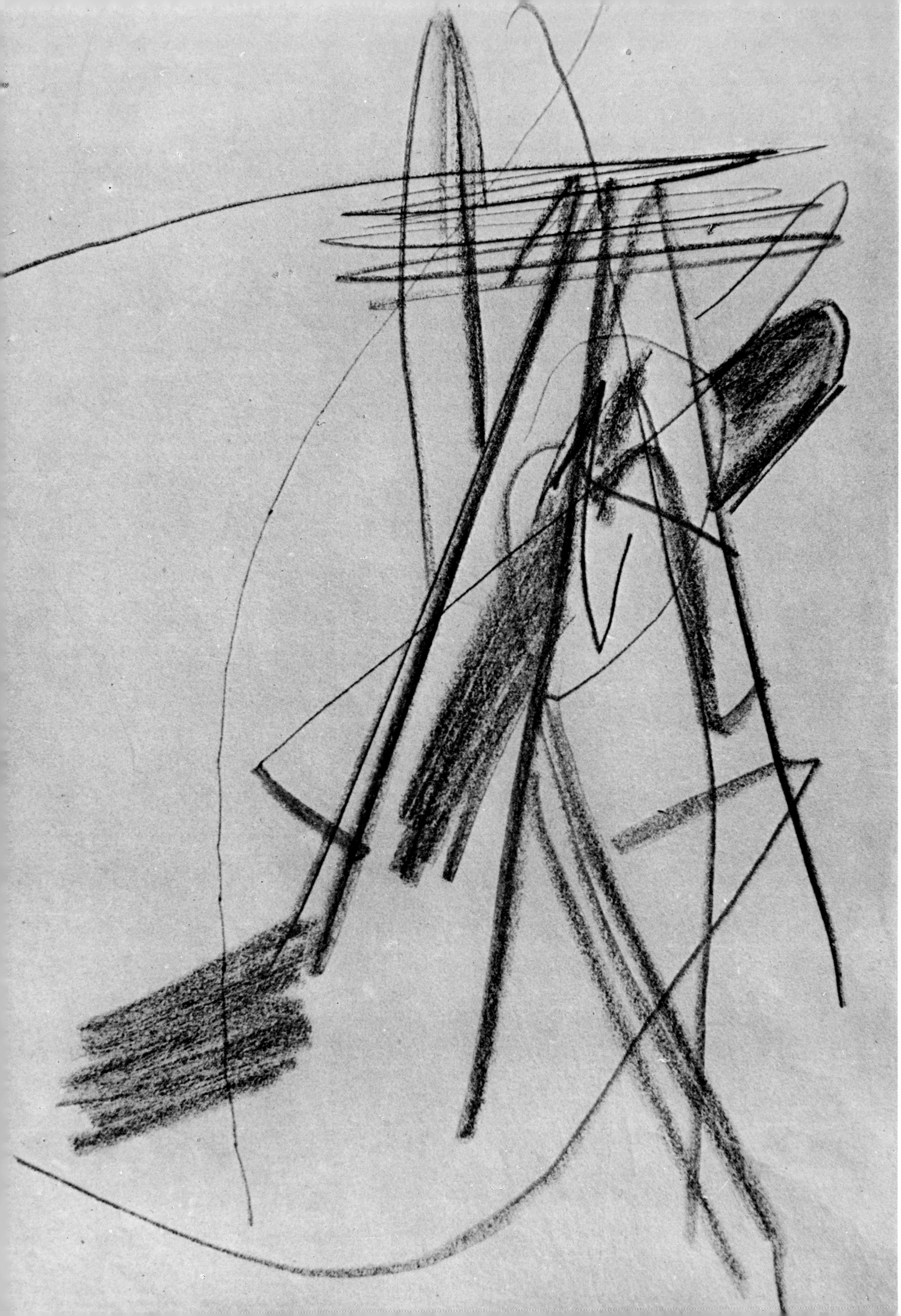

63 C. 1935

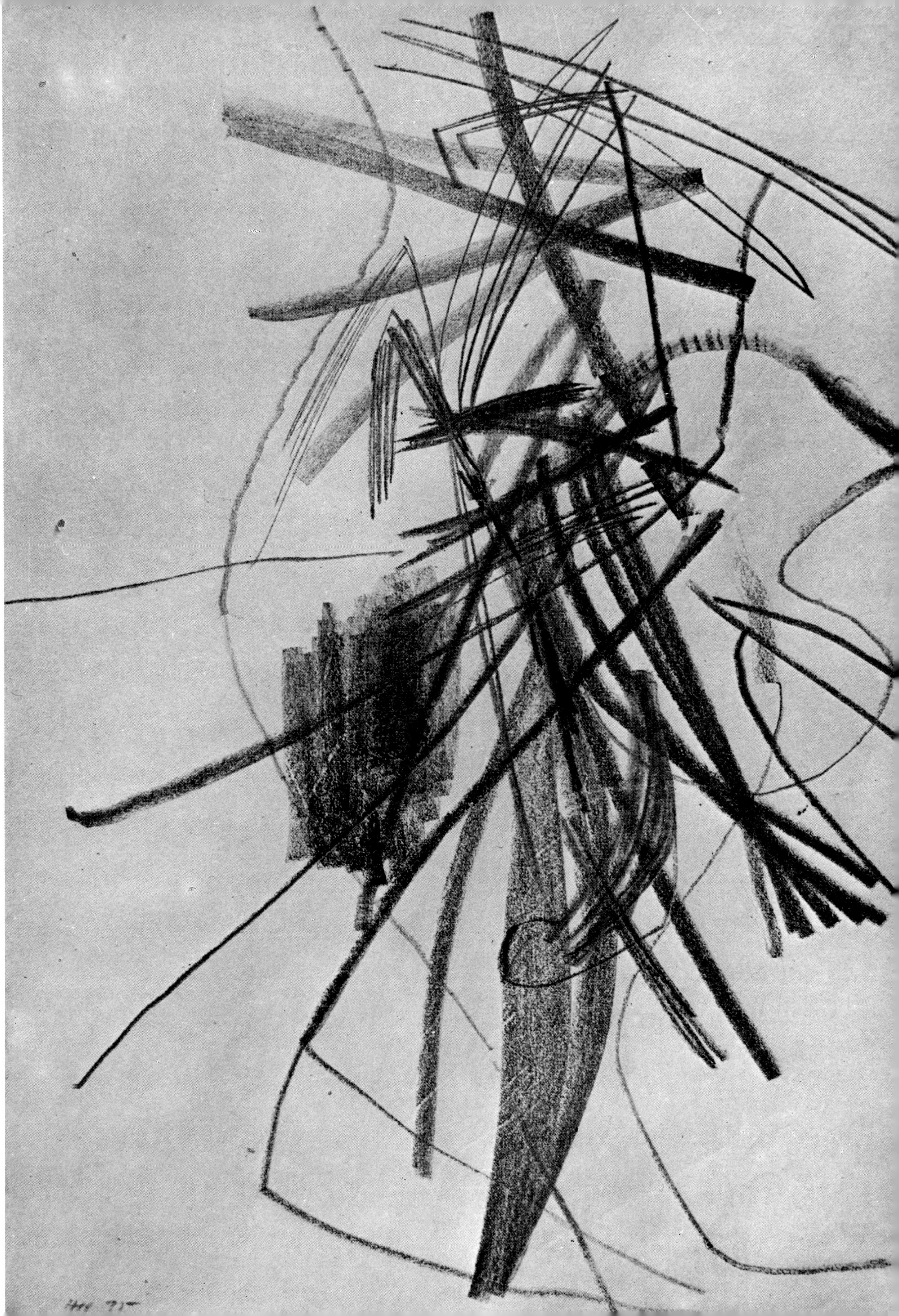

64 C. 1935

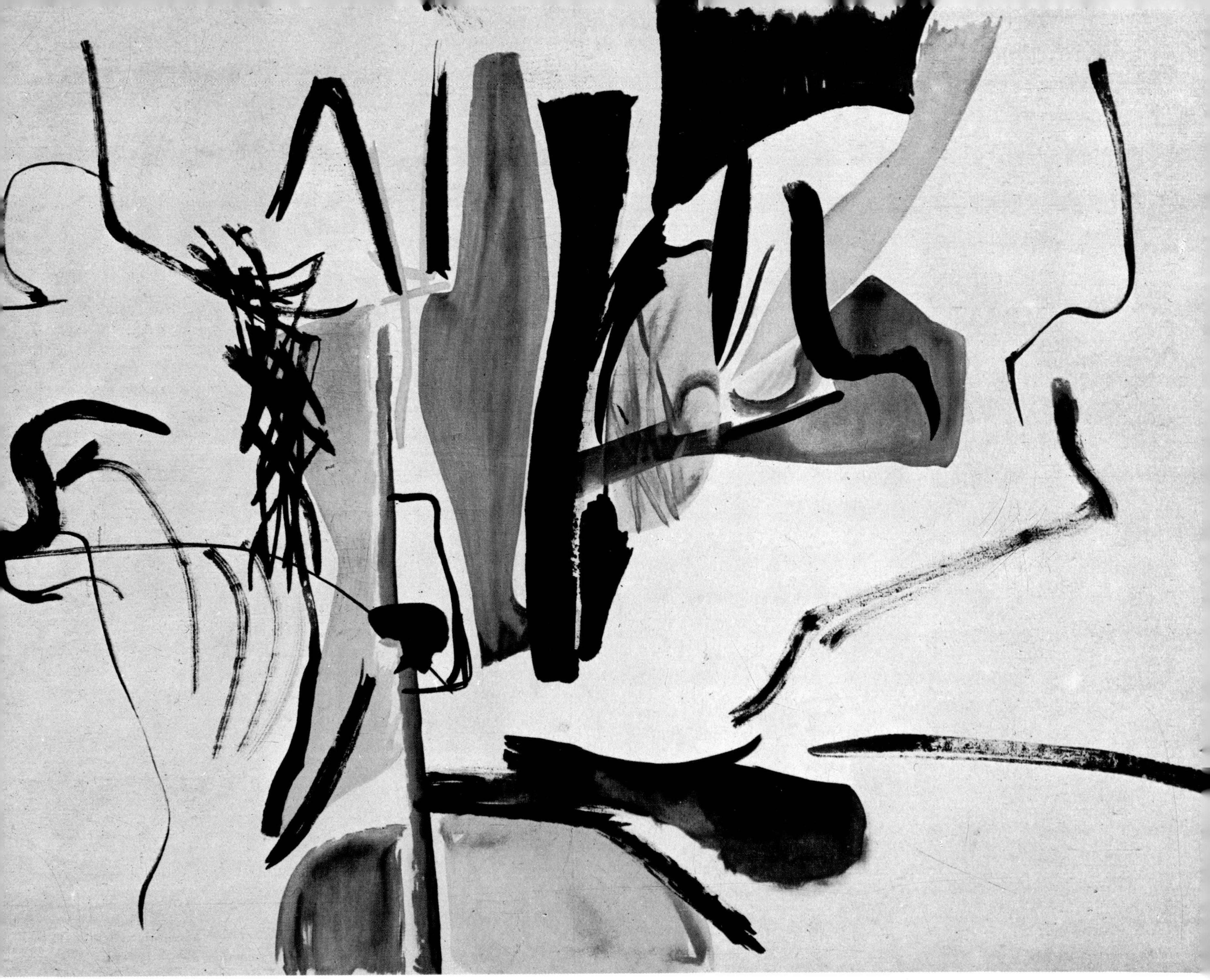

65 T. 1935-1

66 C. 1935

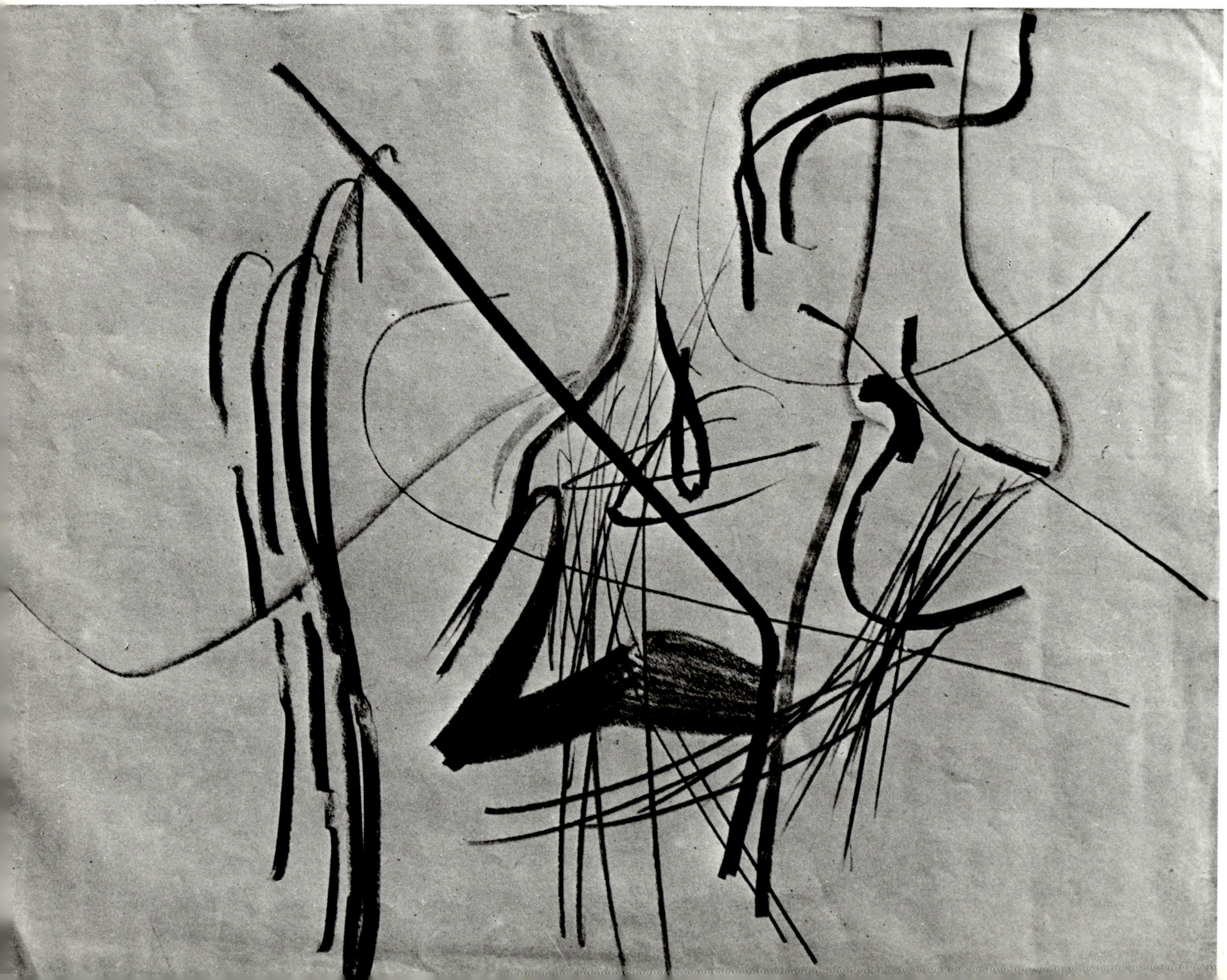

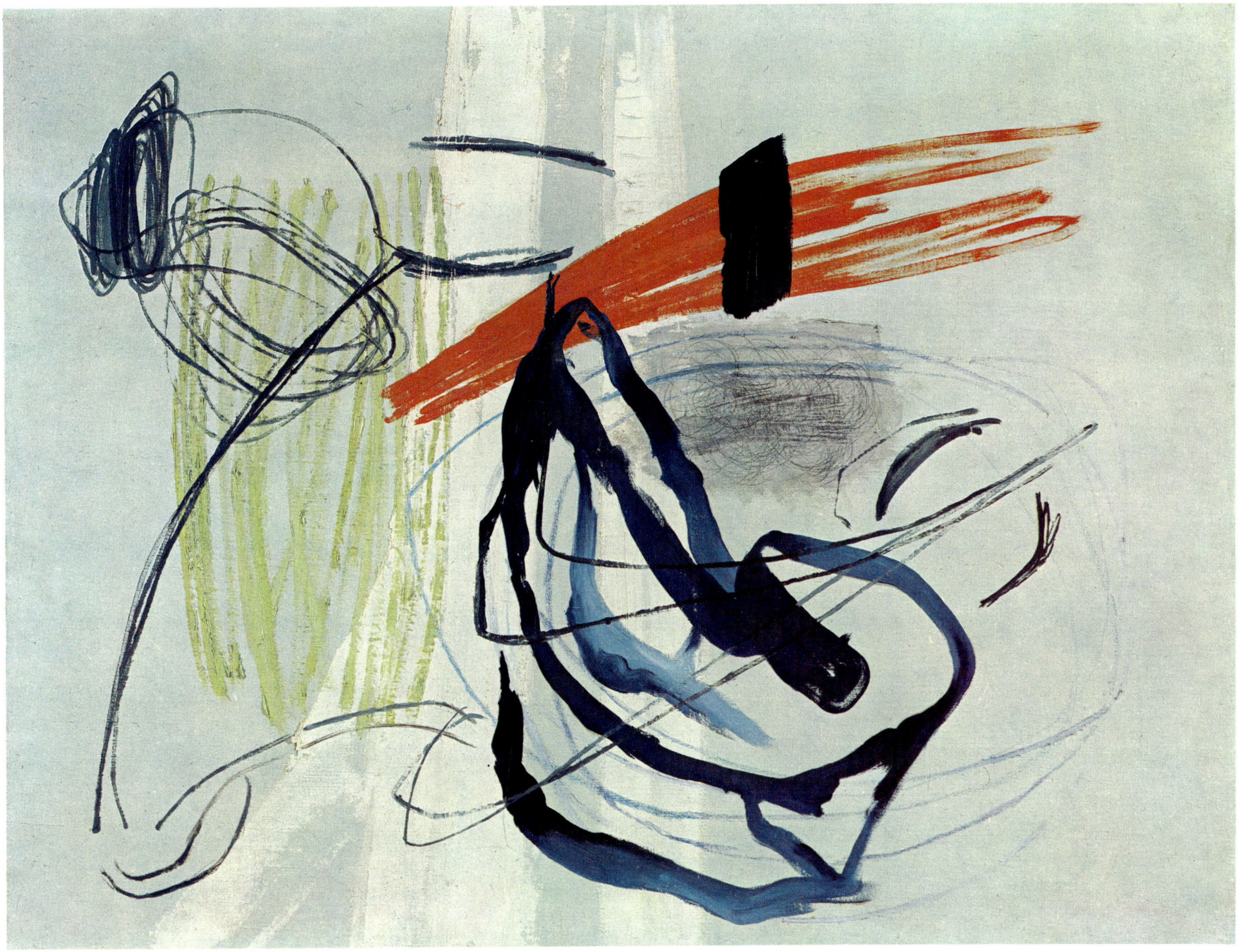

67 T. 1936-10

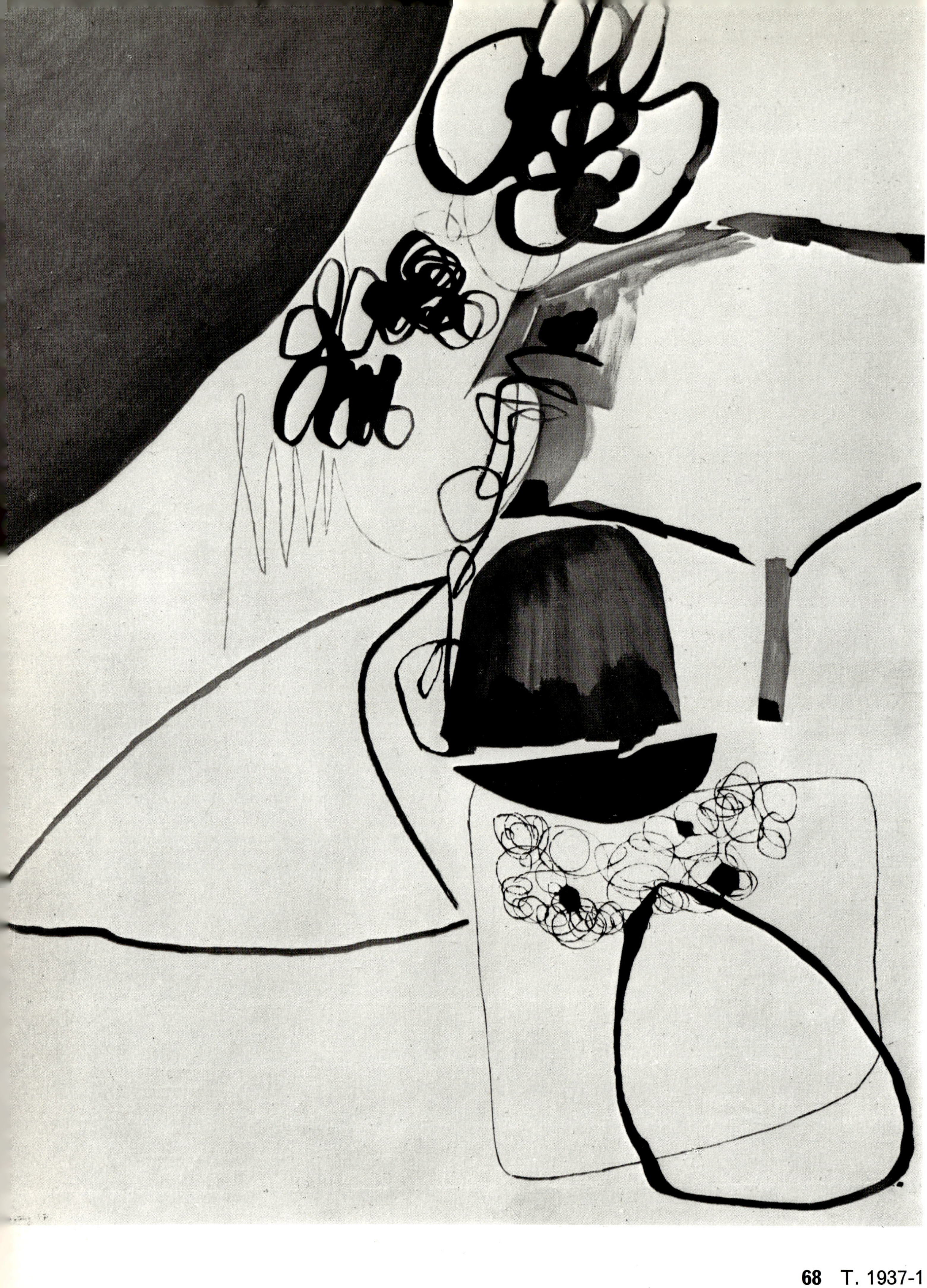

68 T. 1937-1

9 T. 1936-11

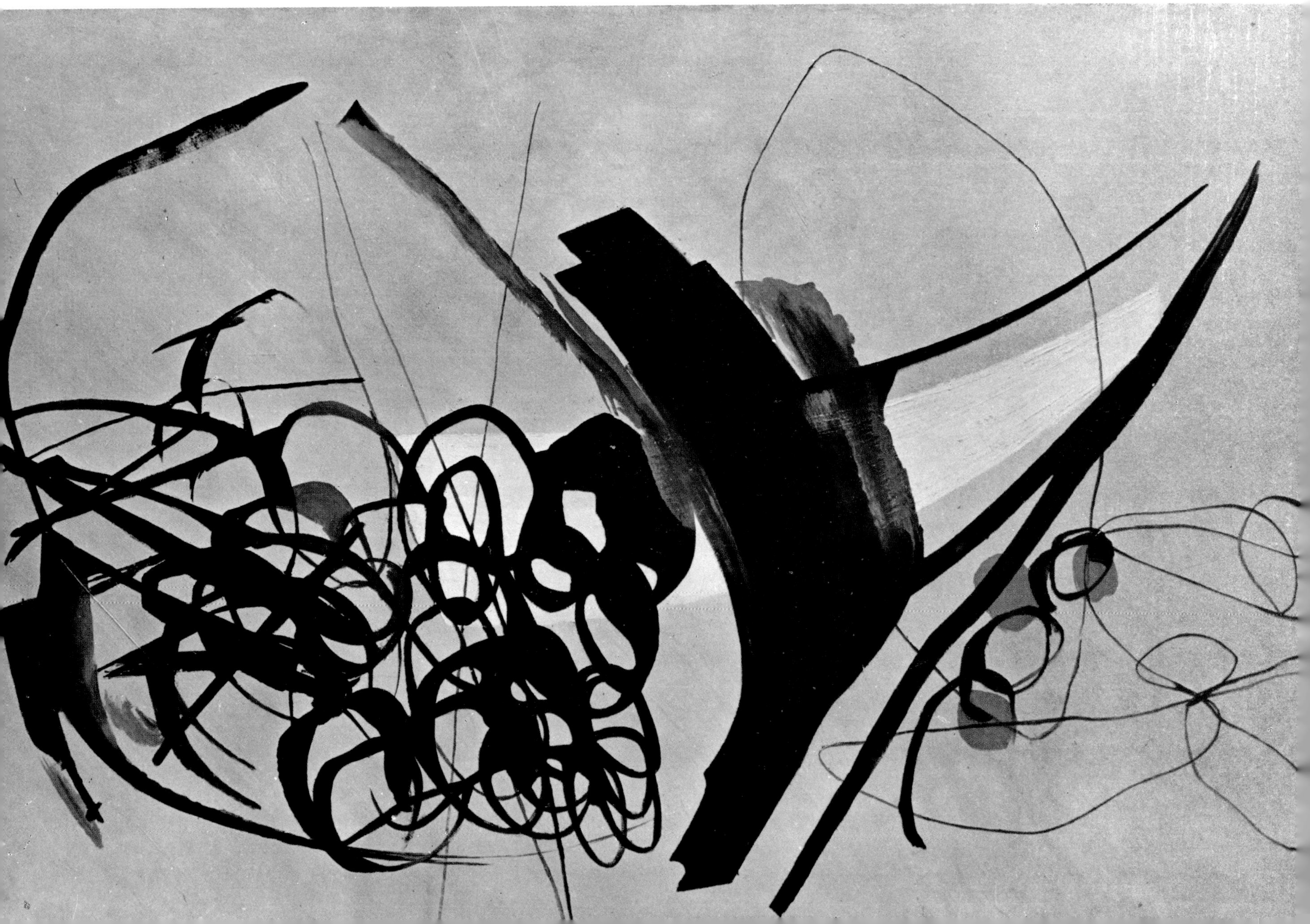

70 T. 1937-33

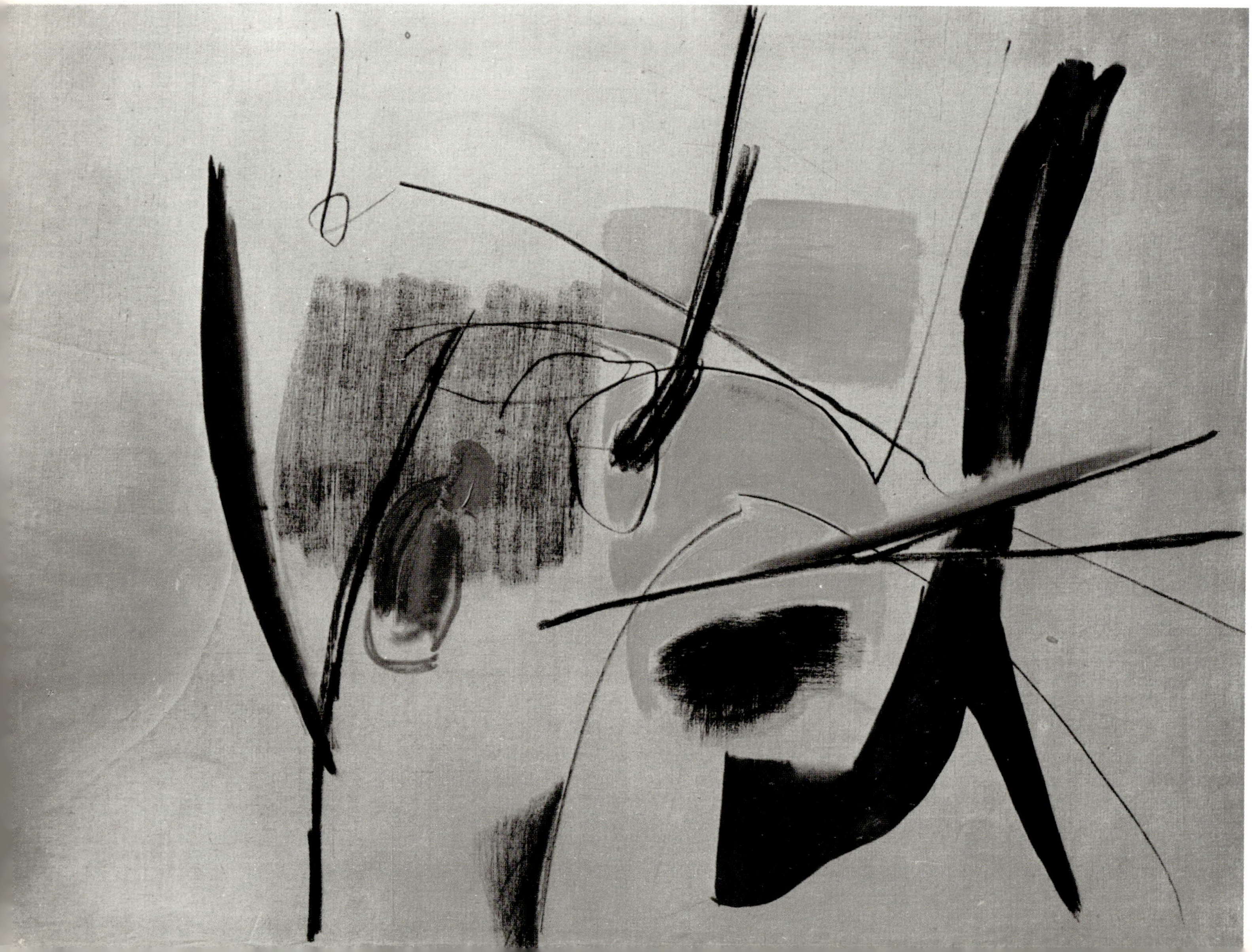

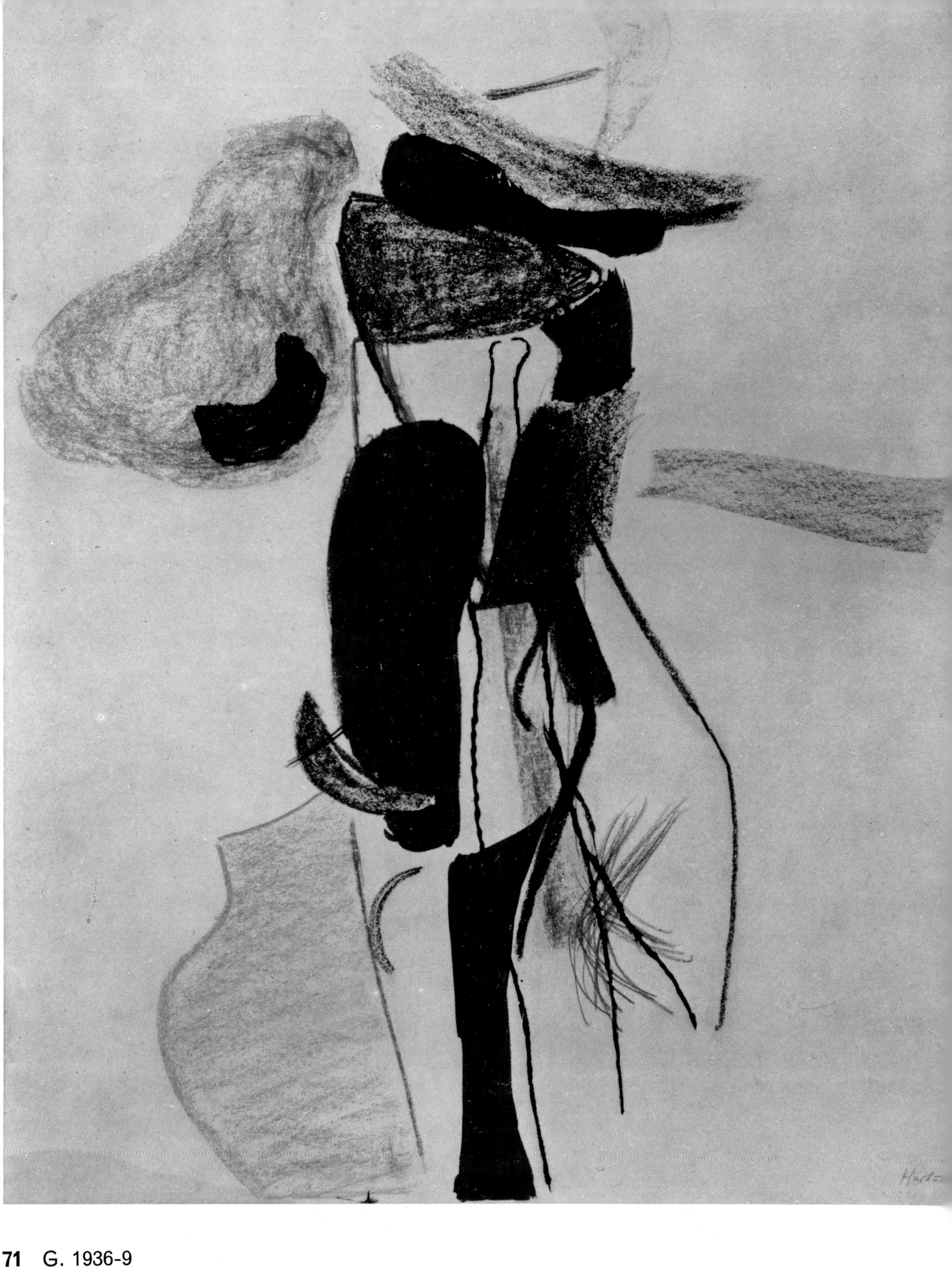

71 G. 1936-9

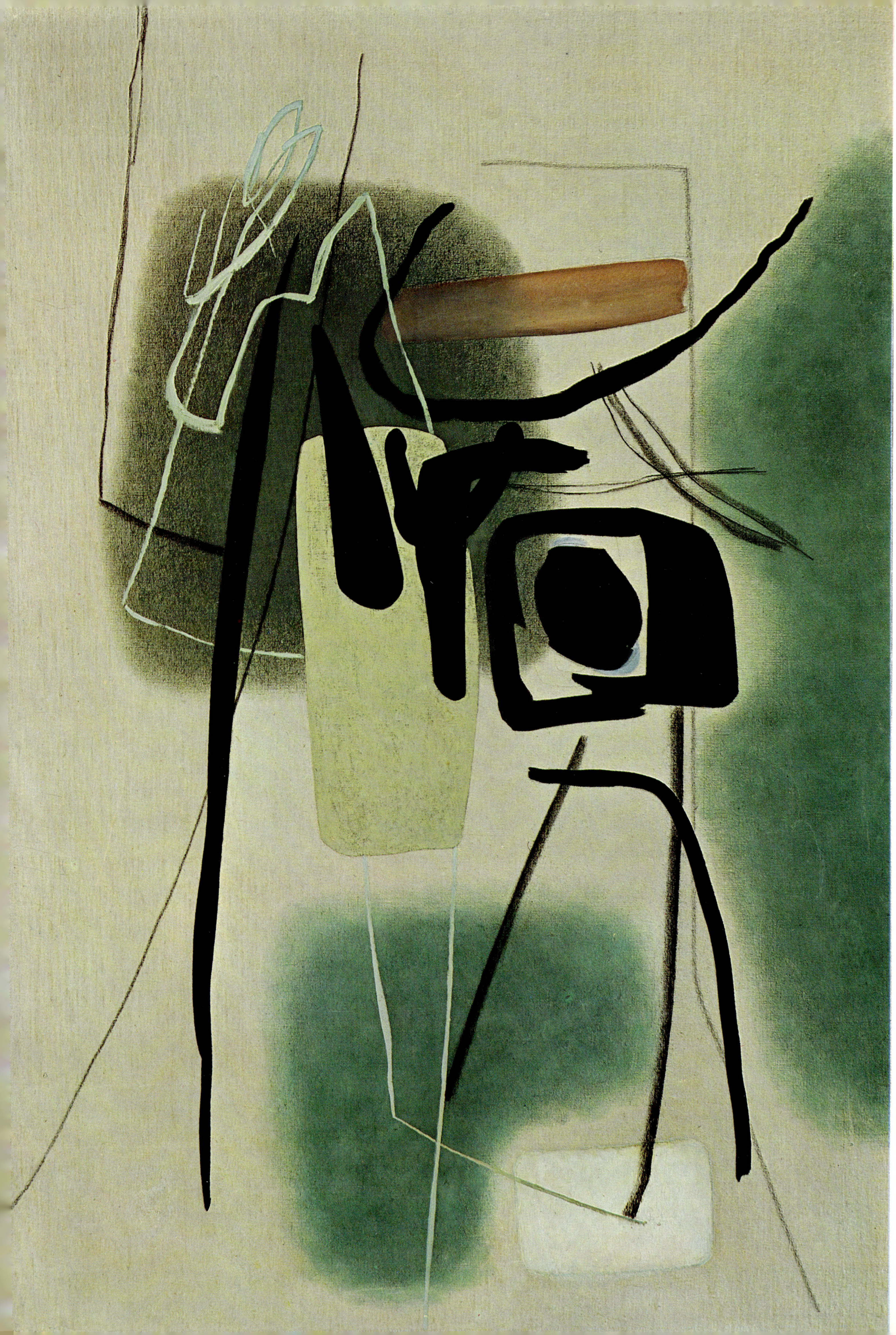

72 T. 1936-2

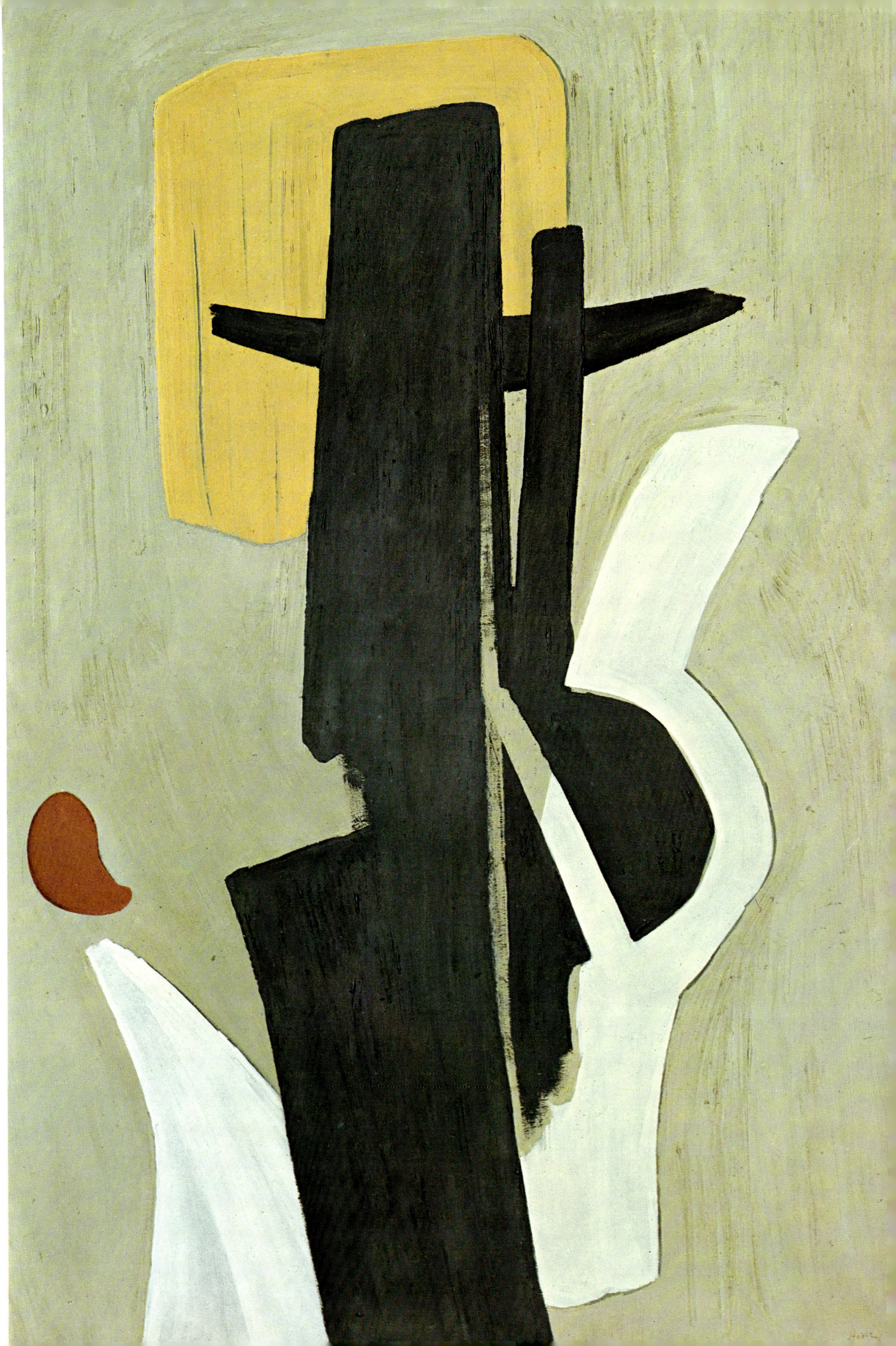

73 T. 1936-14

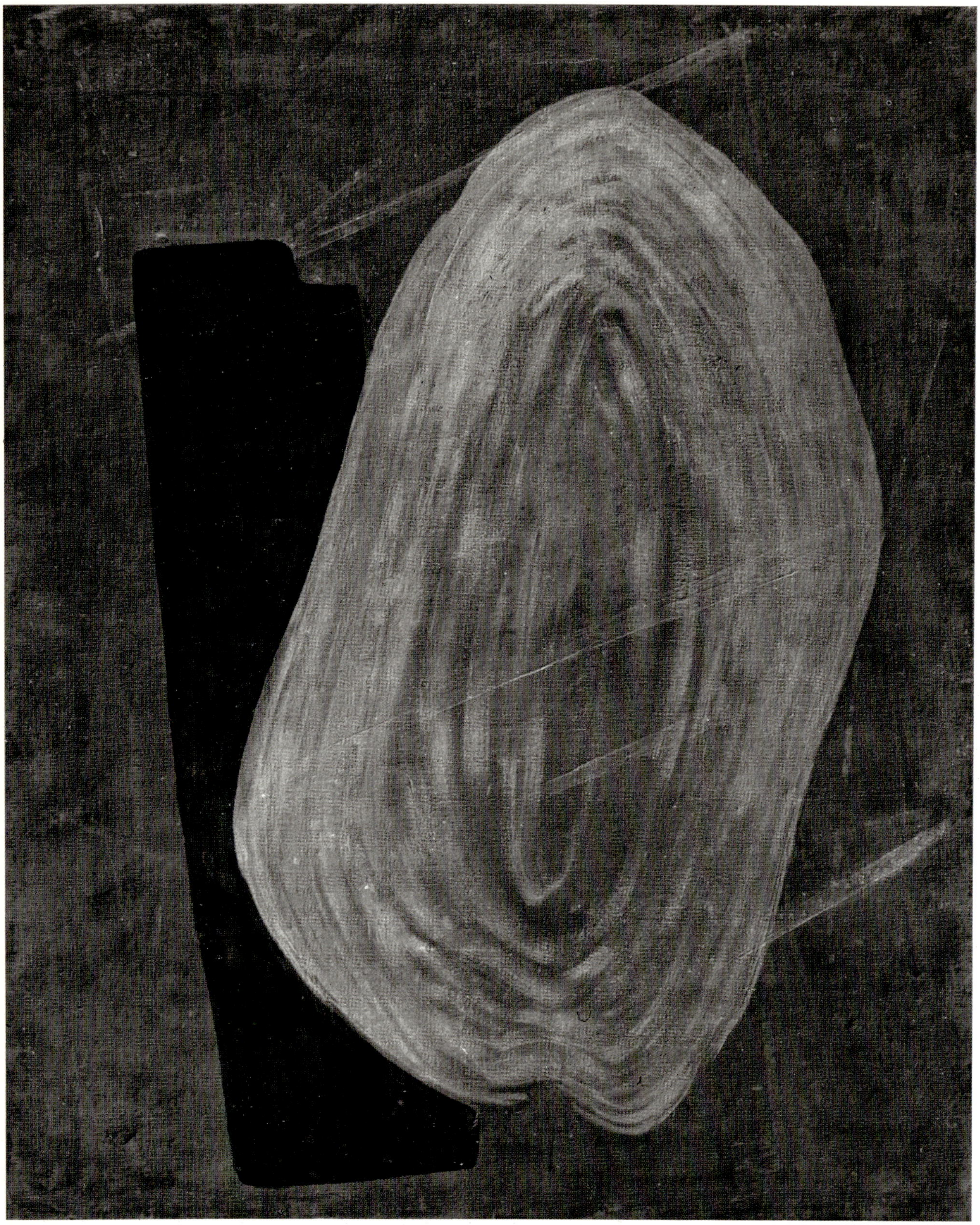

74 T. 1937-7

75 T. 1937-15

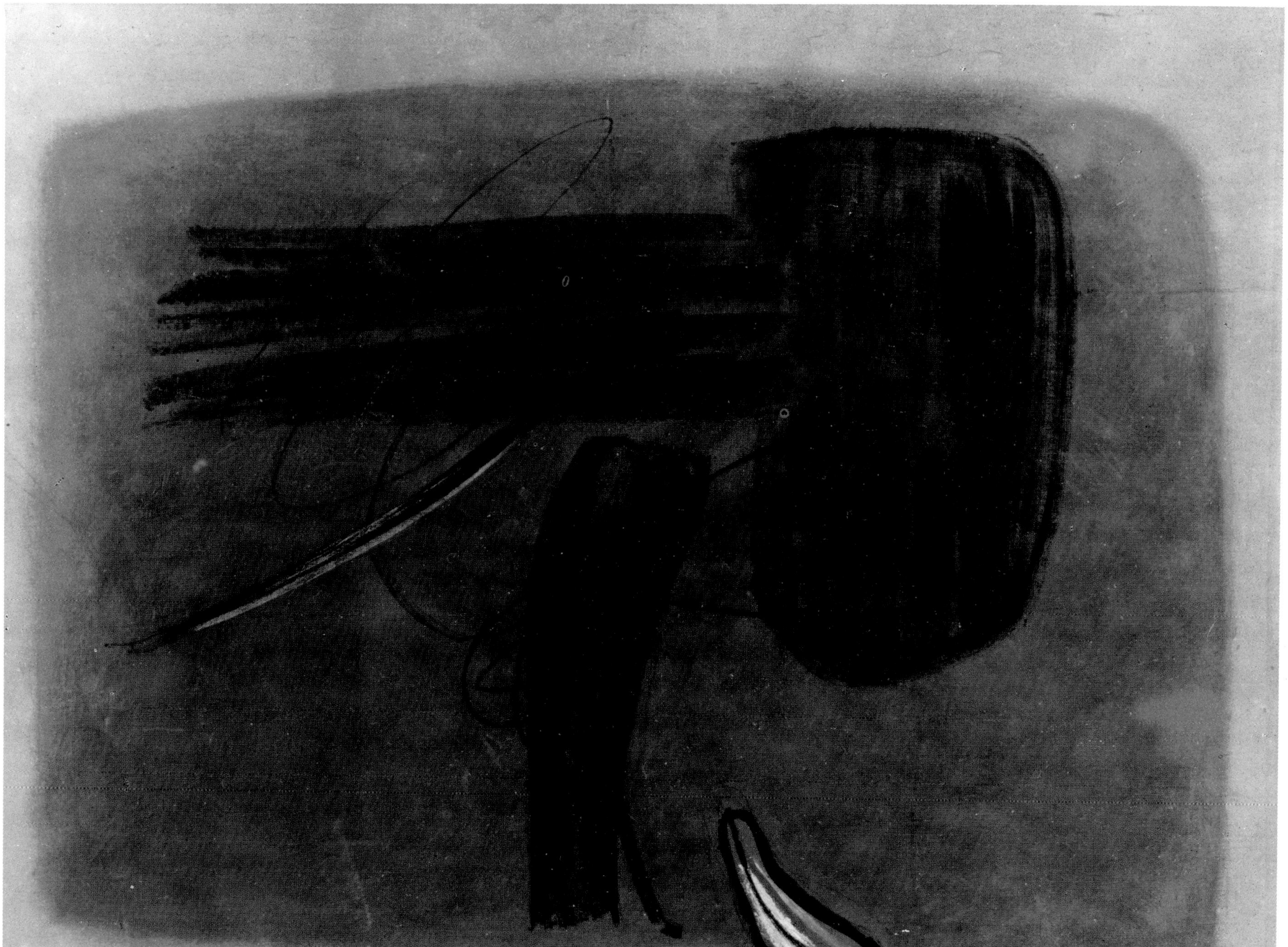

76 T. 1938-2

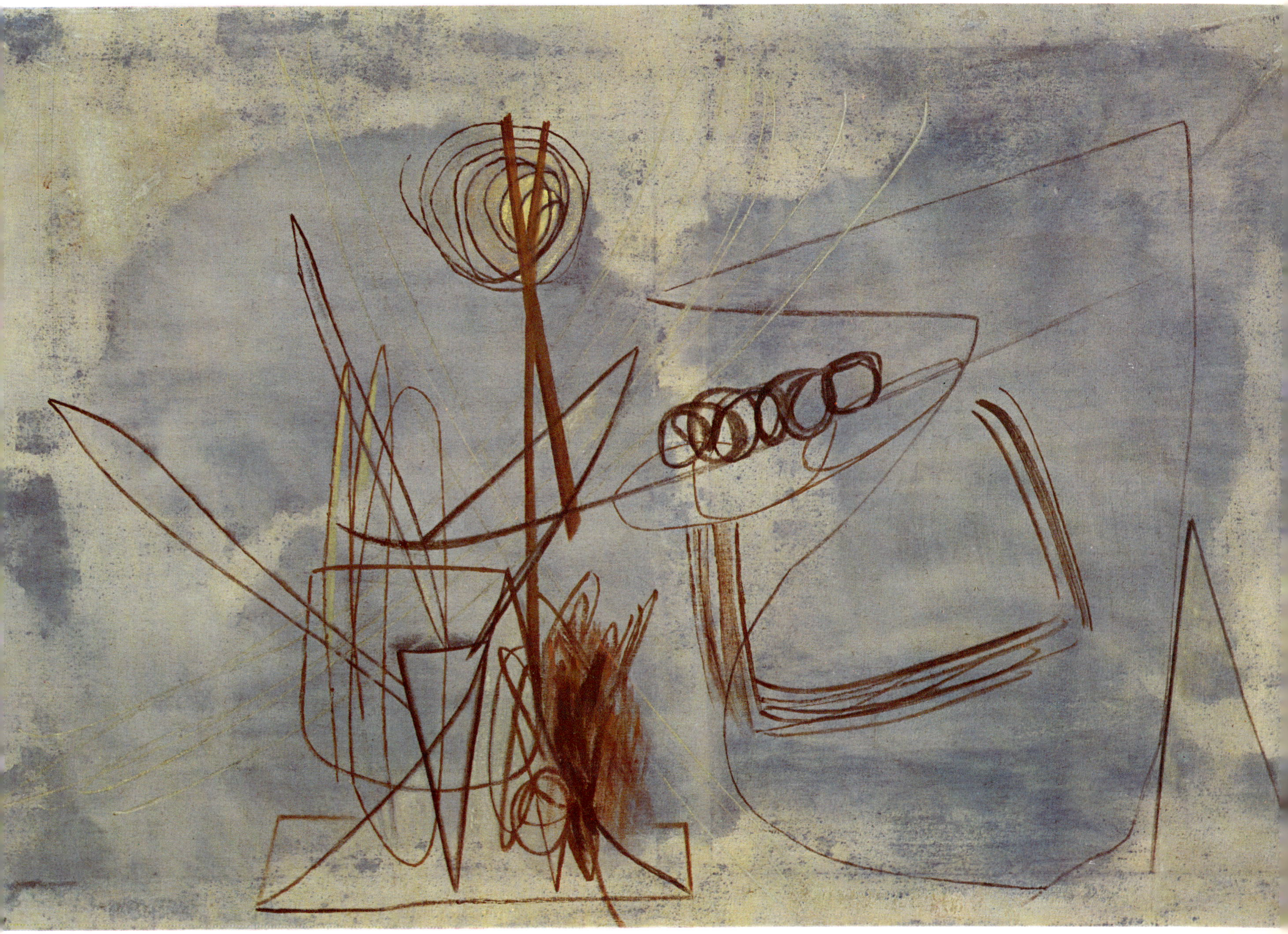

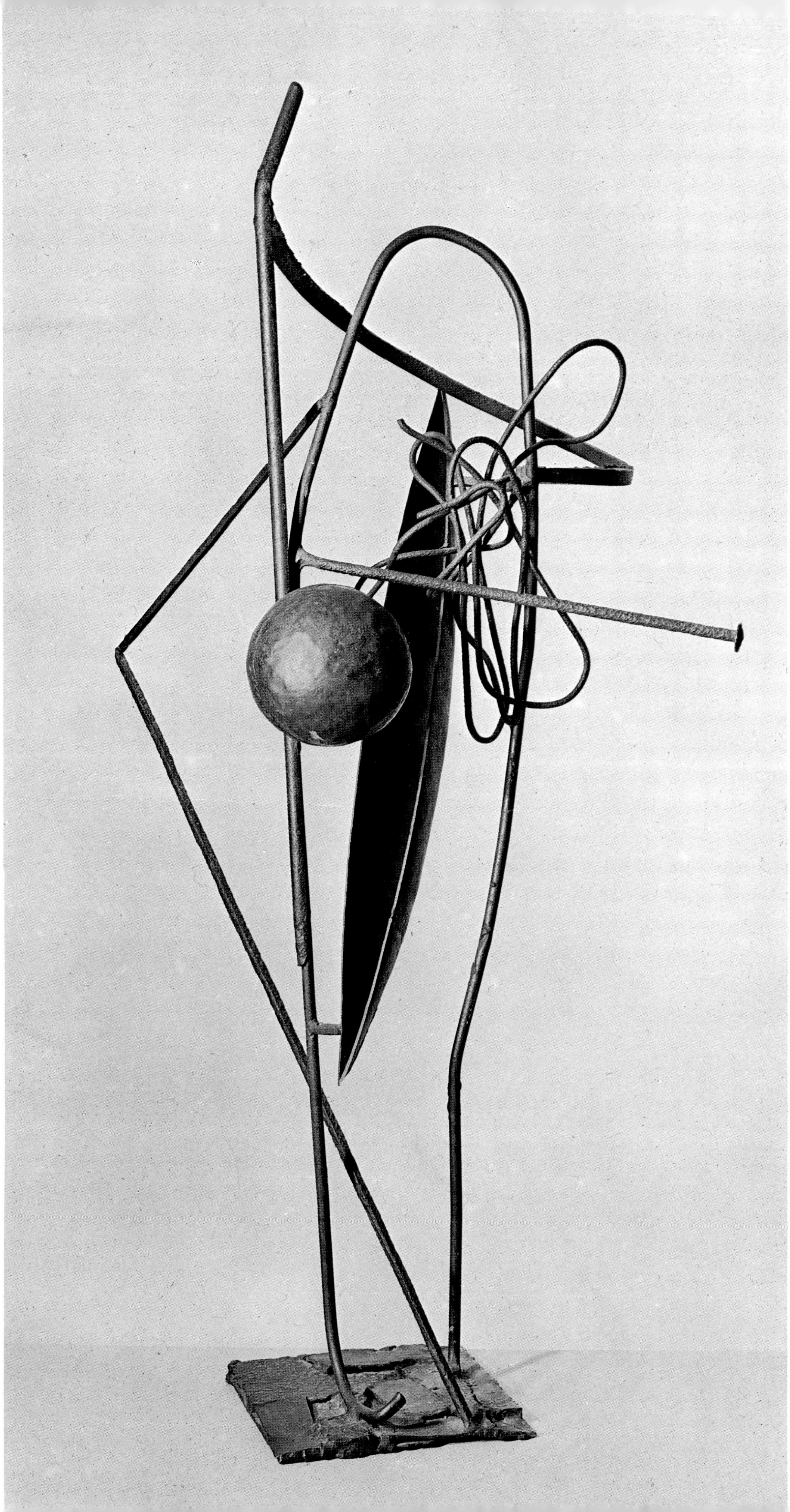

77 Sc. 1938

78 E. C. 1938

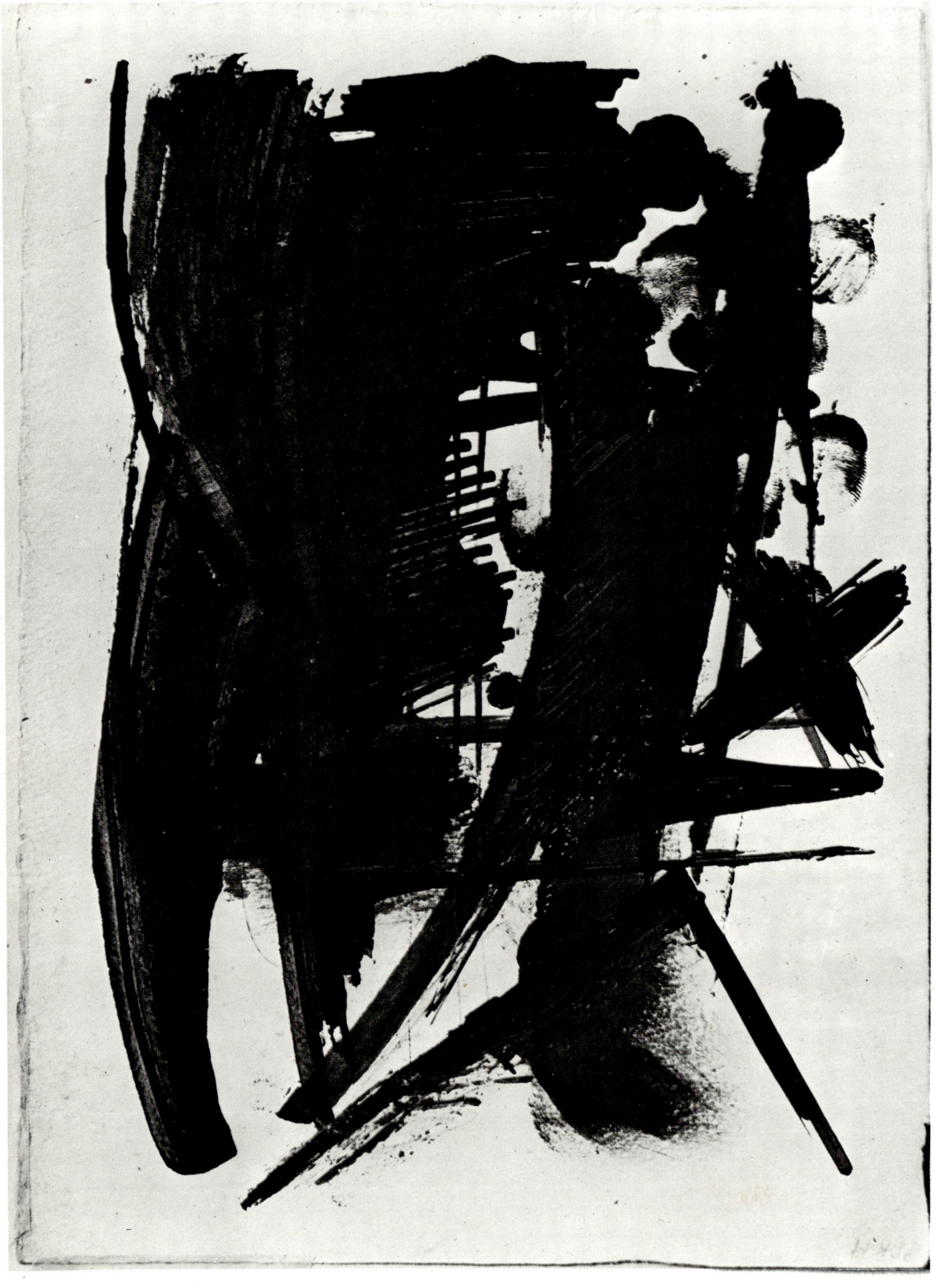

79 E. C. 1938

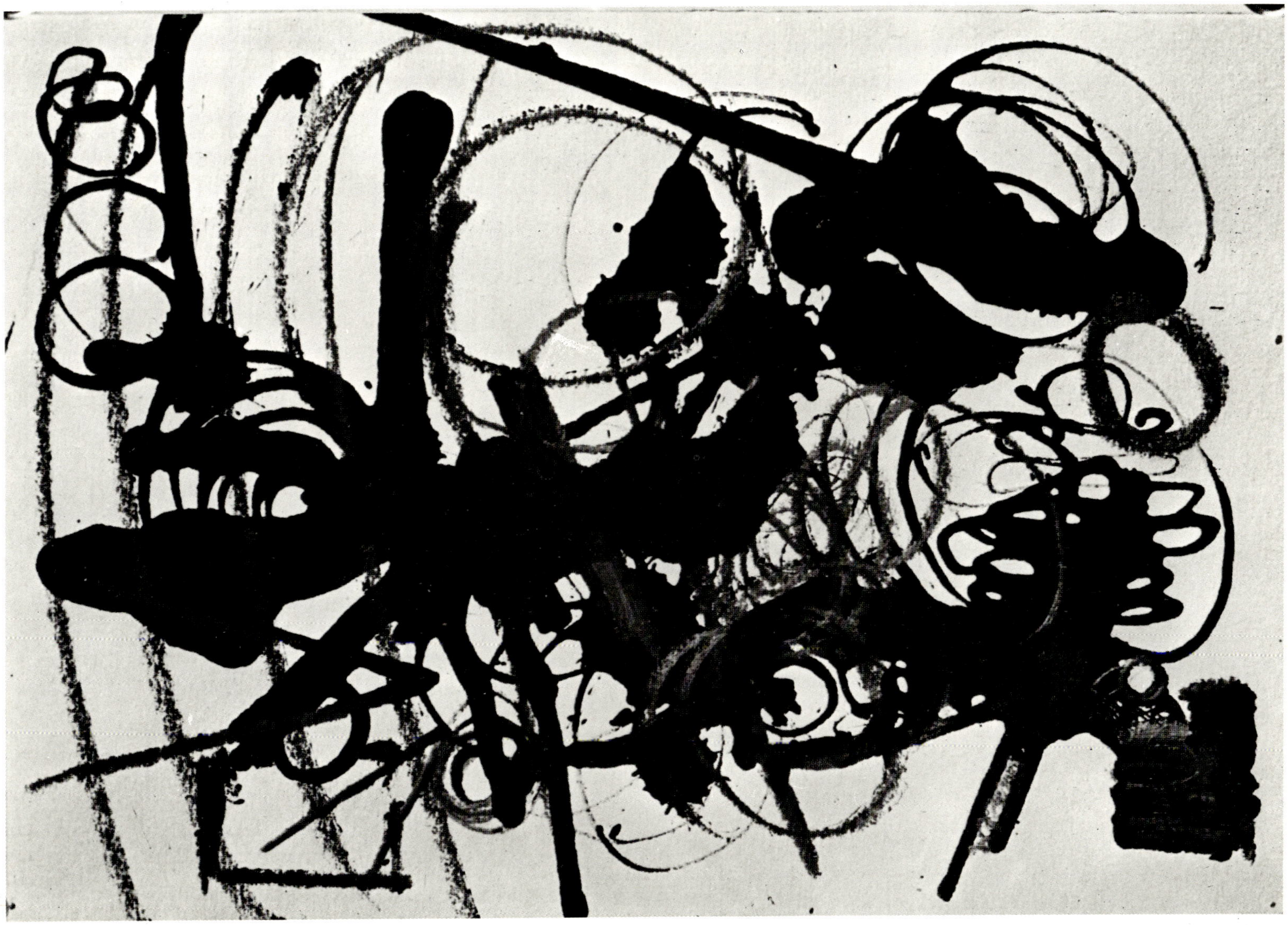

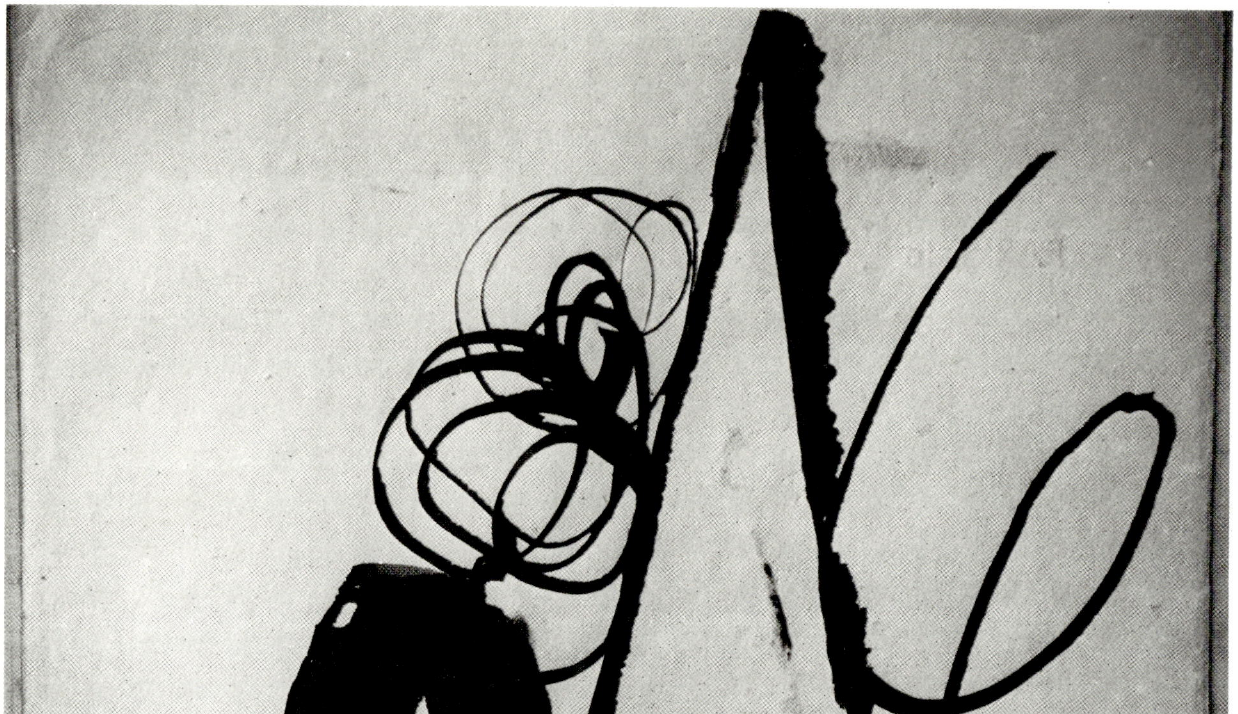

80 E. 1938

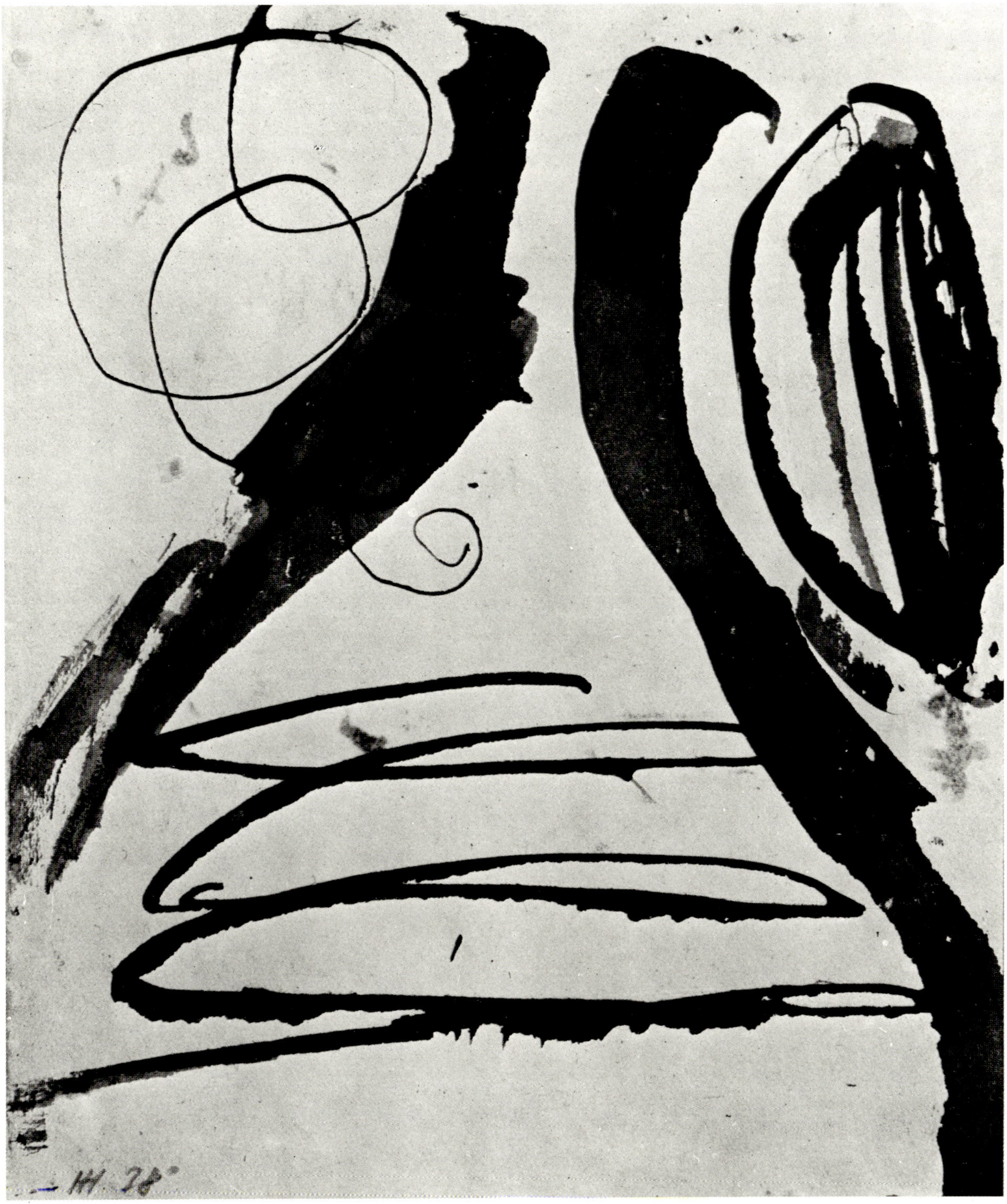

81 E. 1938

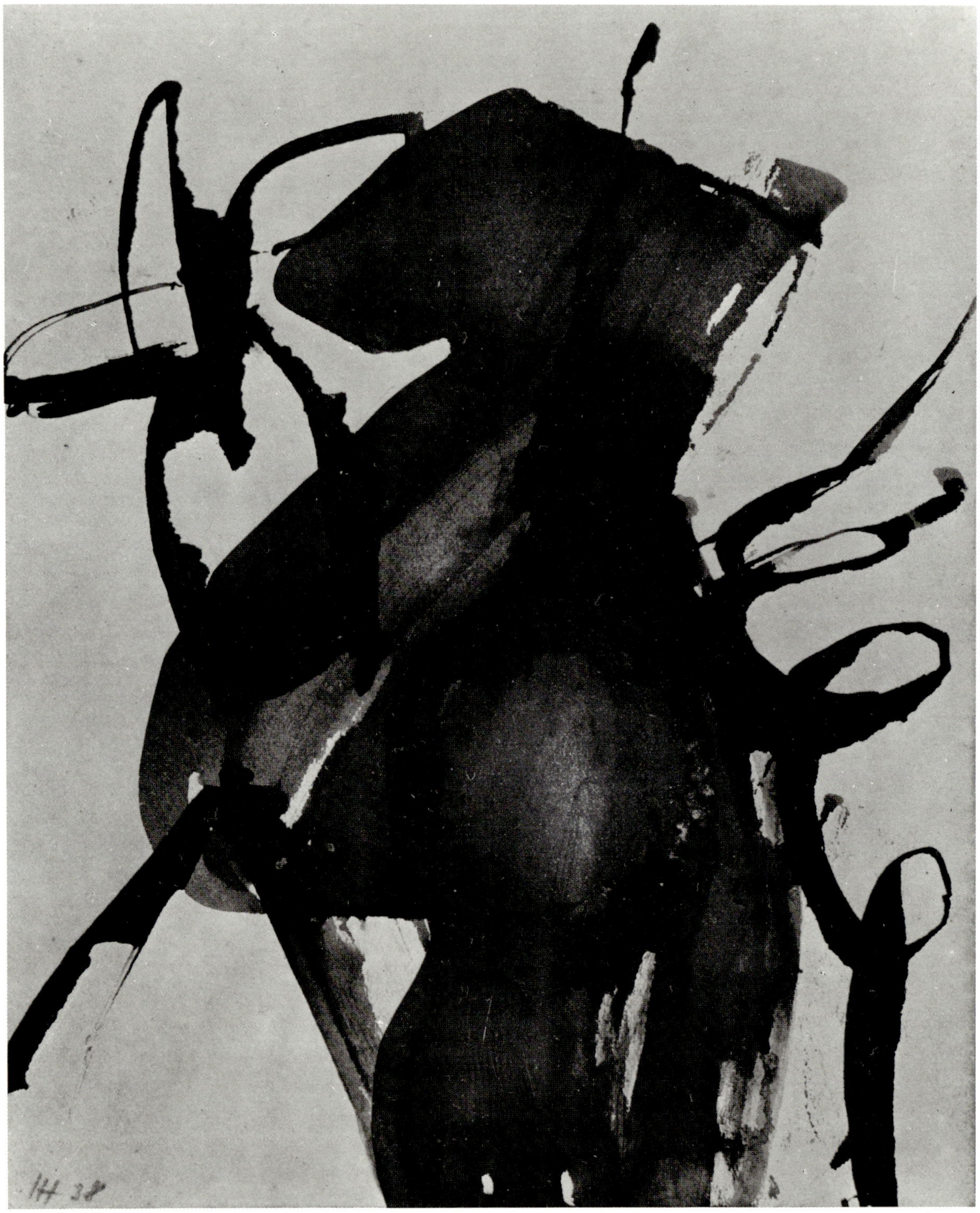

82 E. 1938

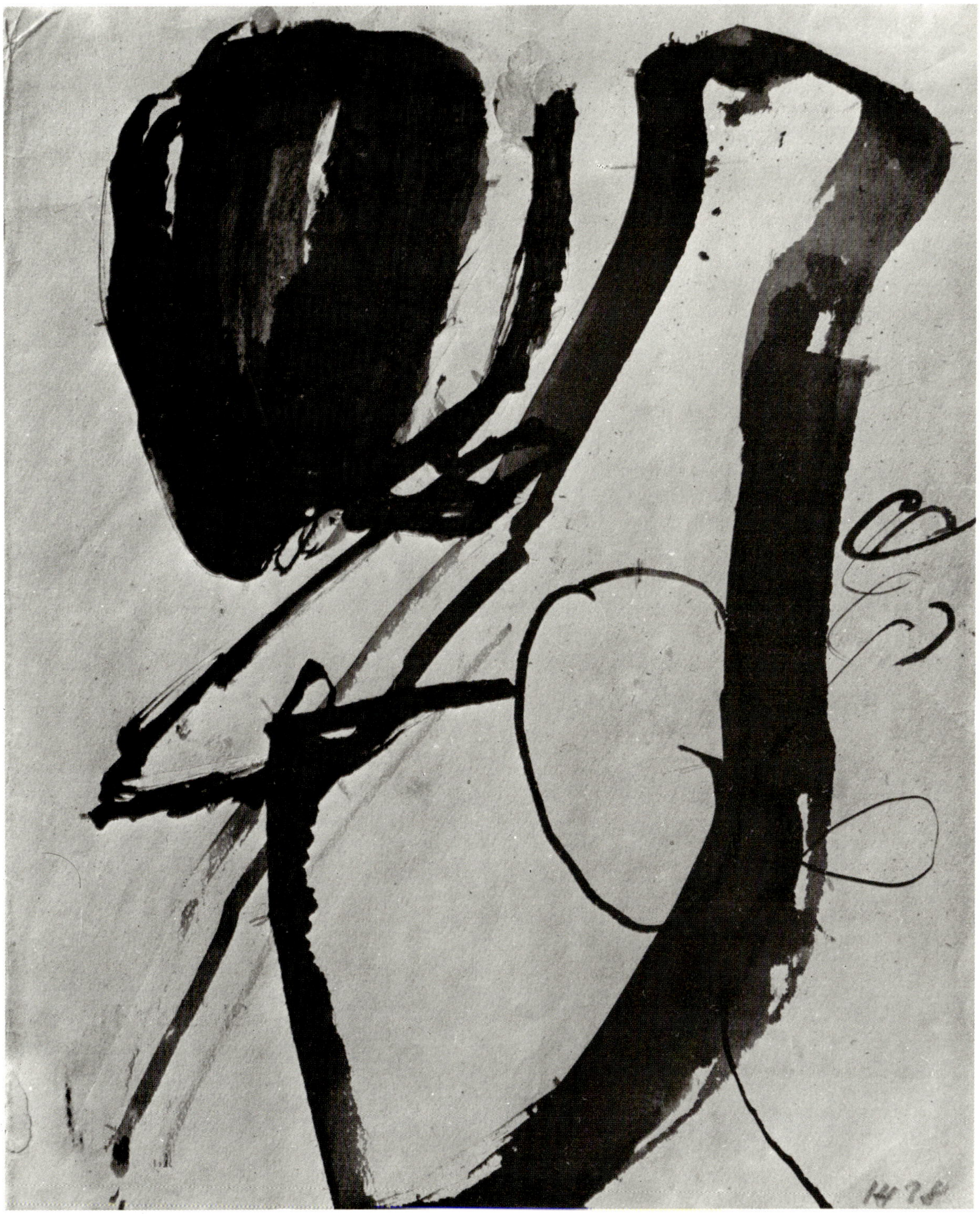

83 E. 1938

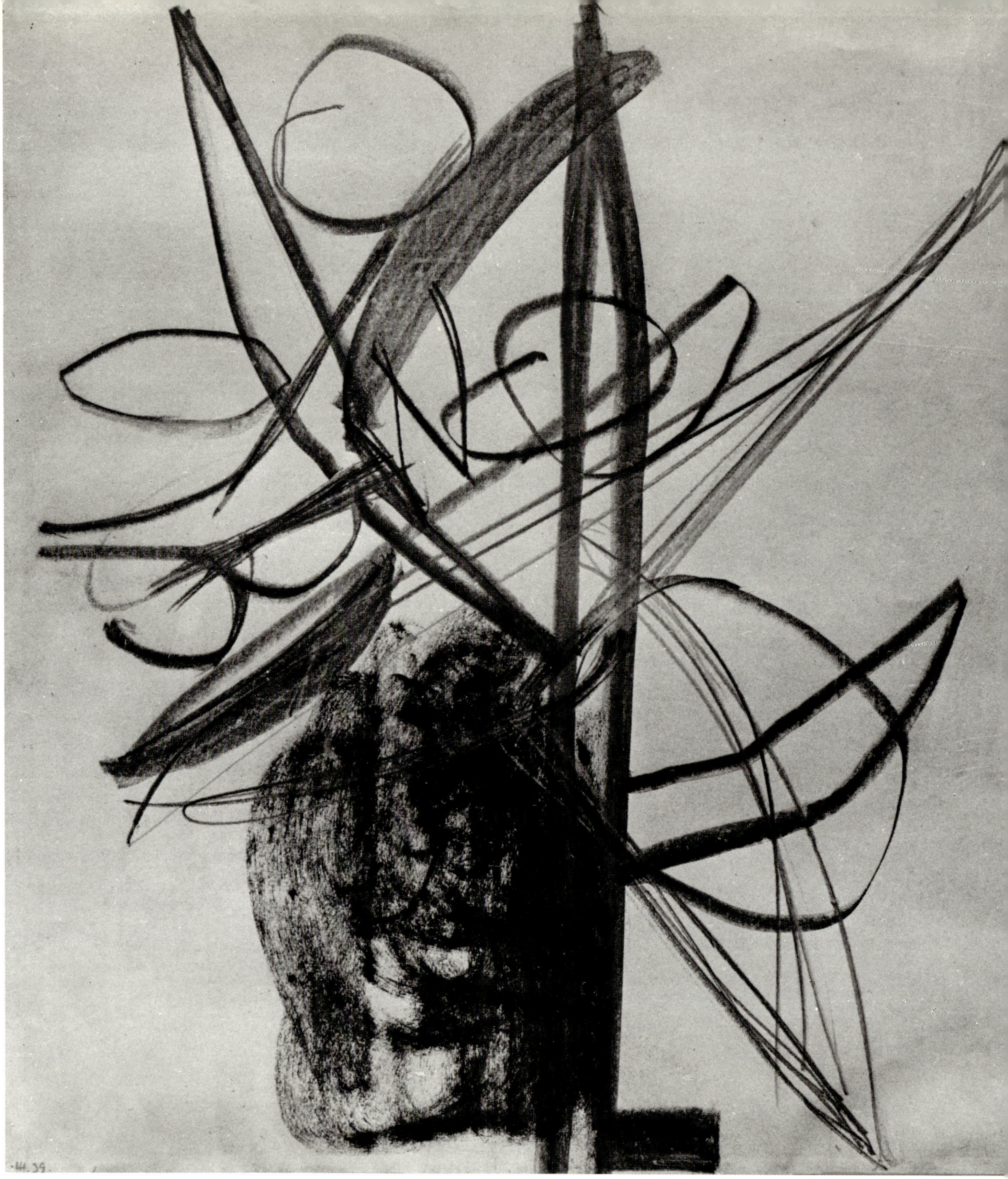

84 P. 1939

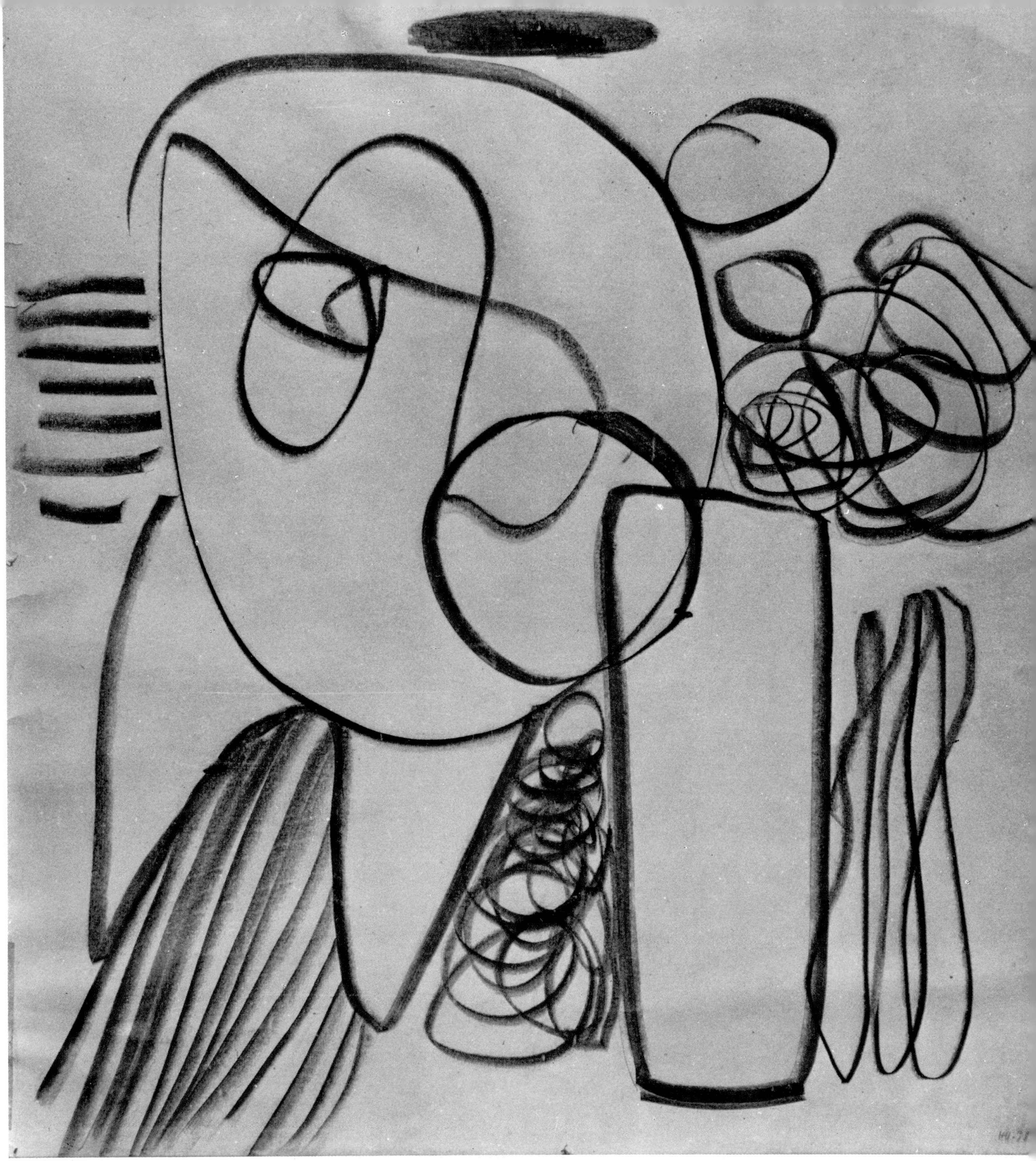

85 C. 1938

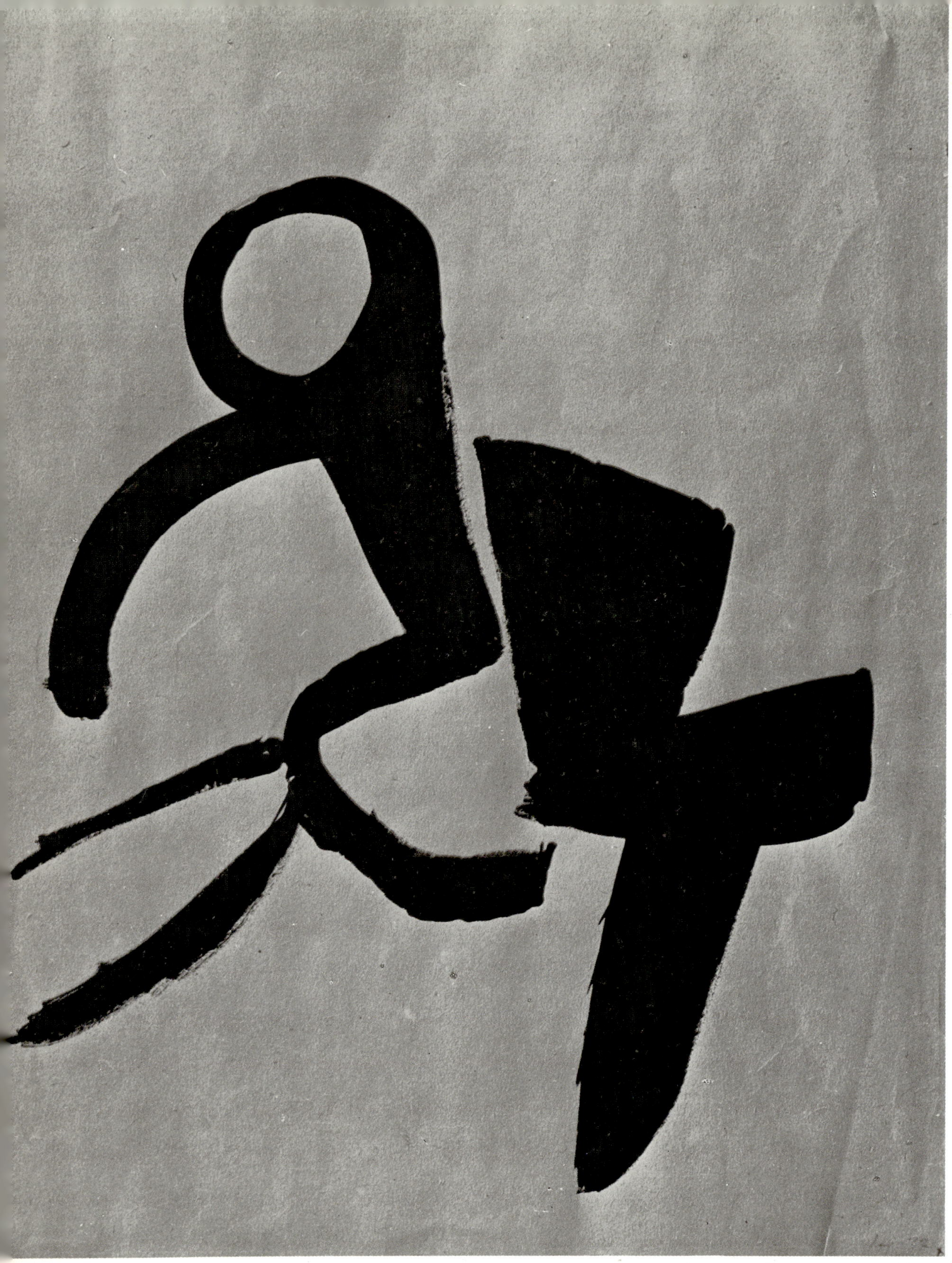

86 E. C. 1937

87 E. C. 1937

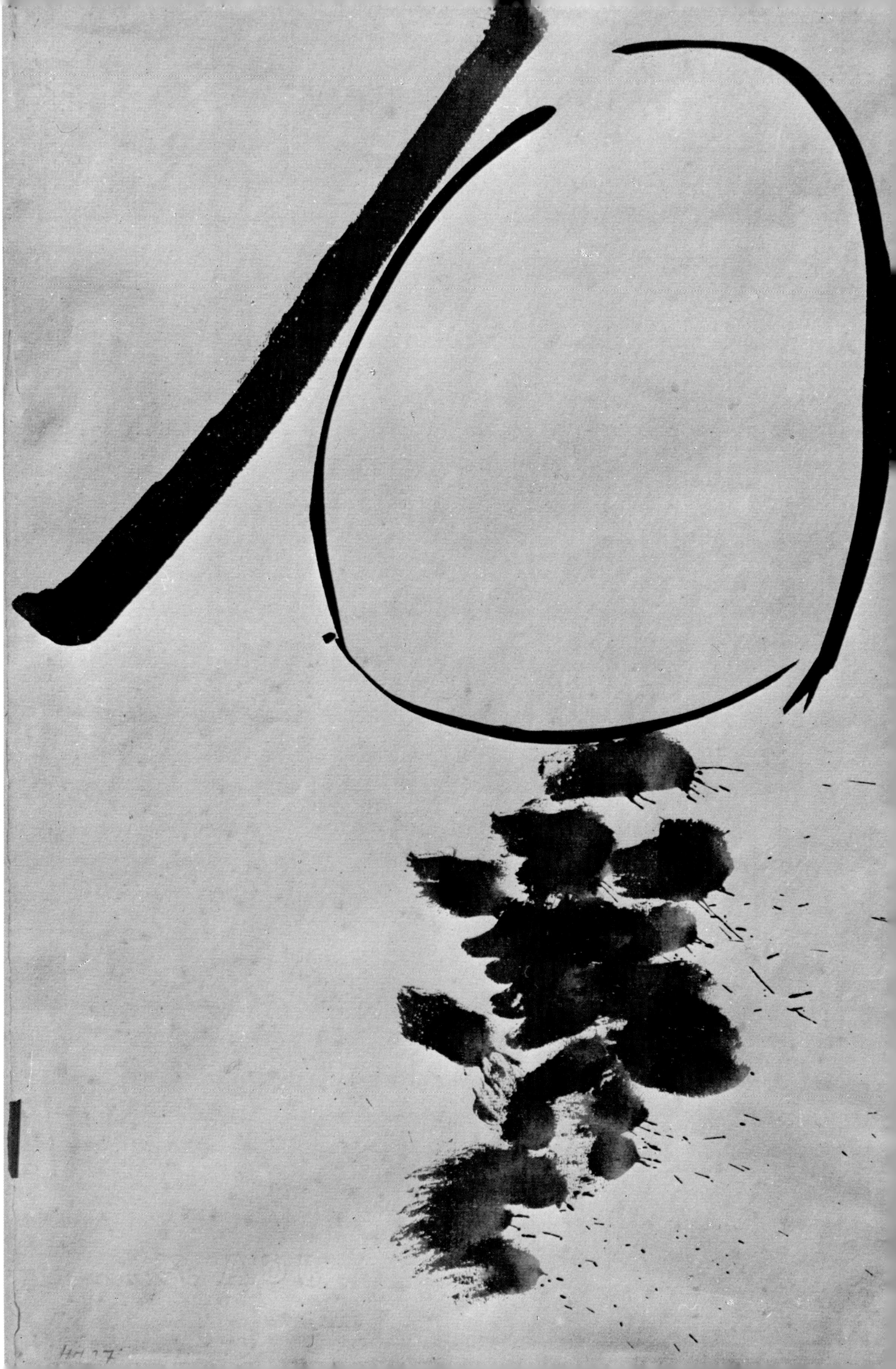

88 A. 1938

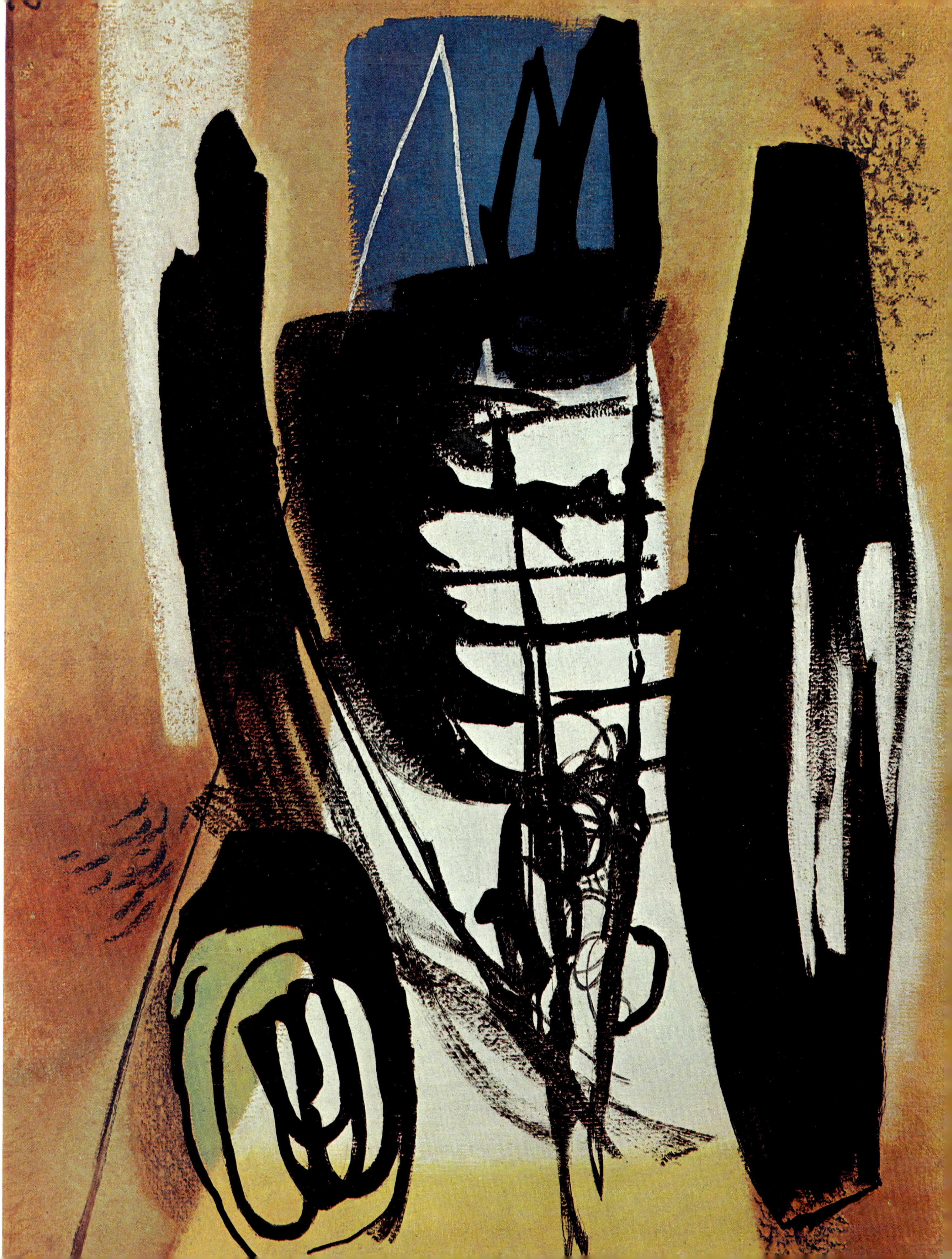

90 T. 1938-33

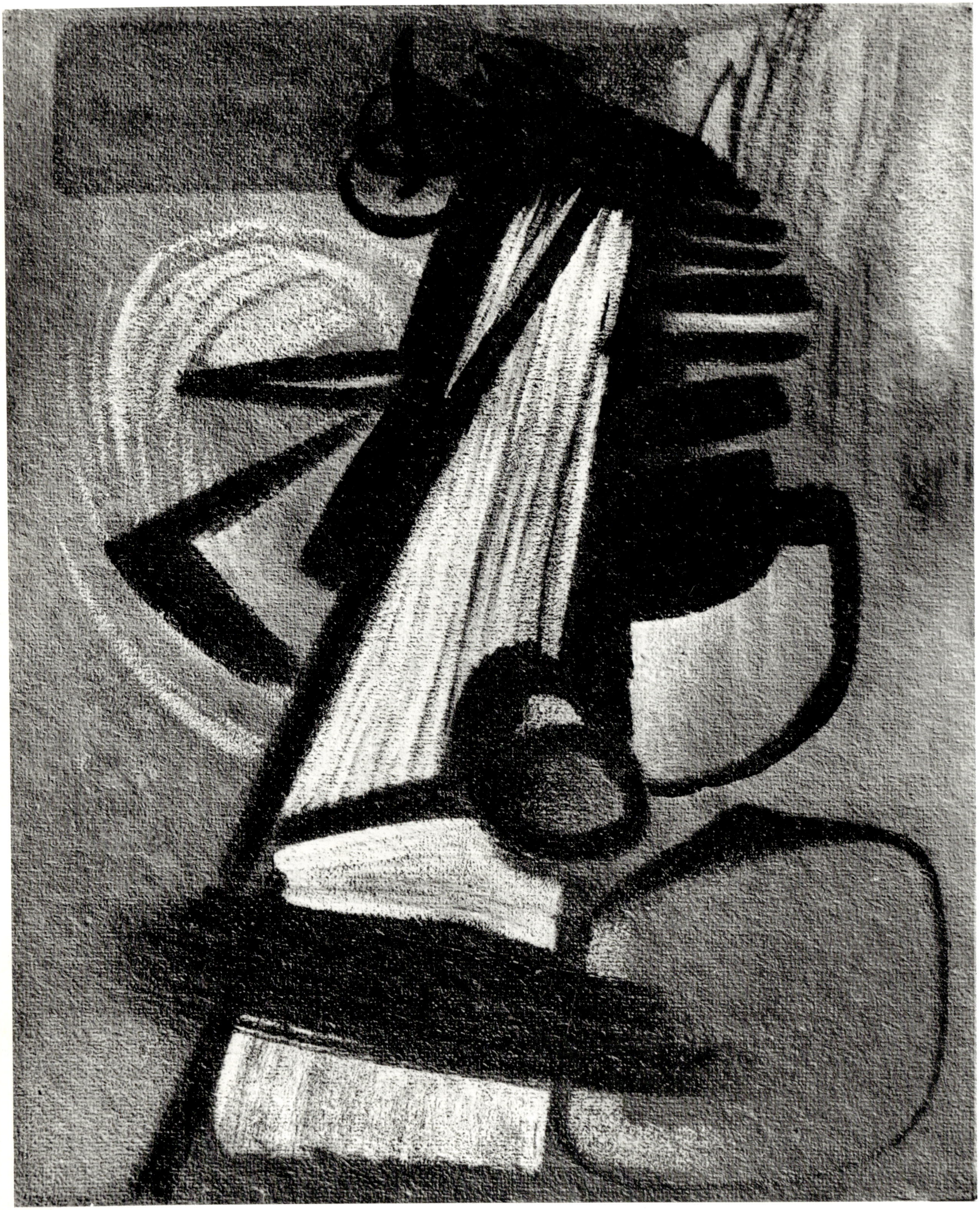

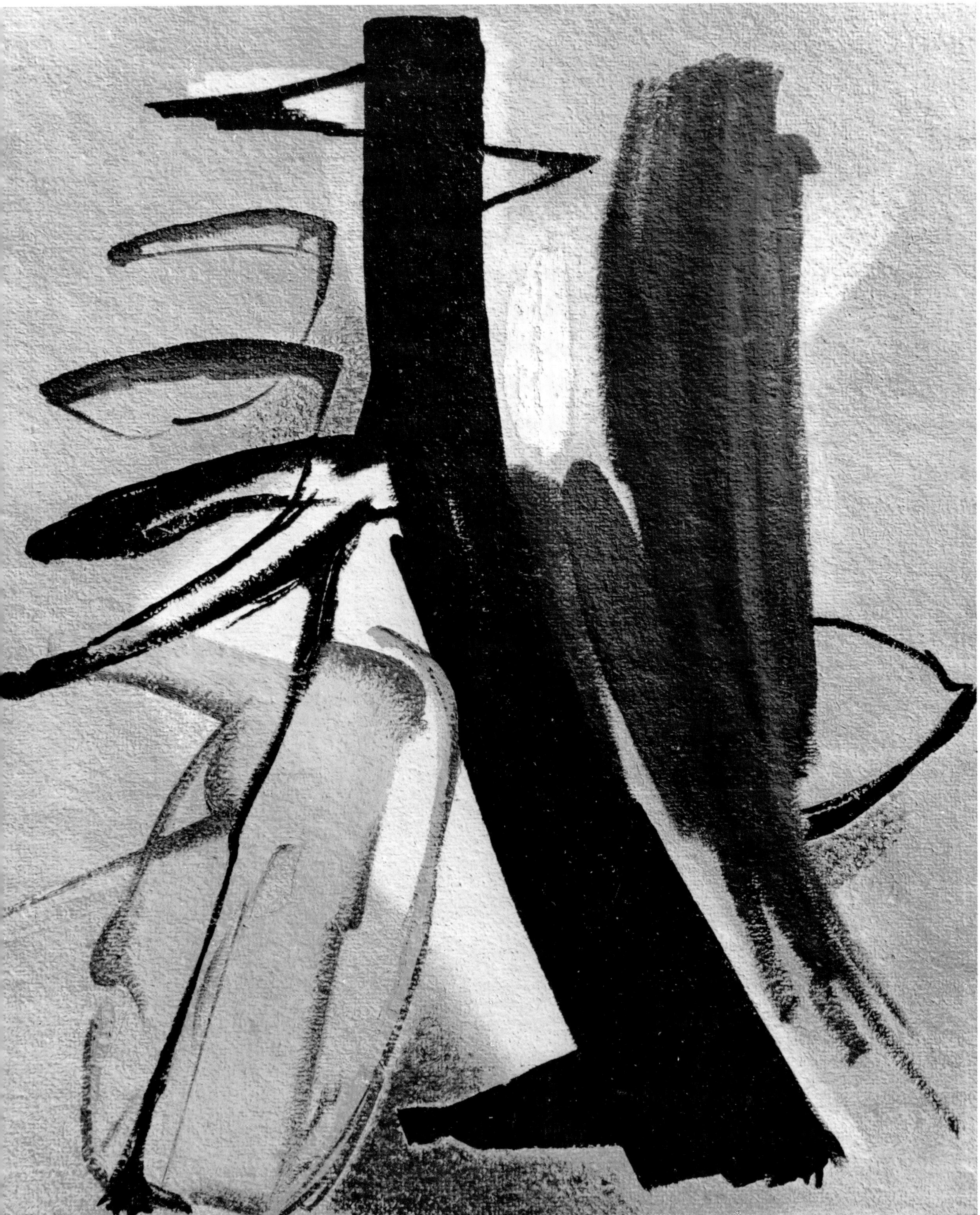

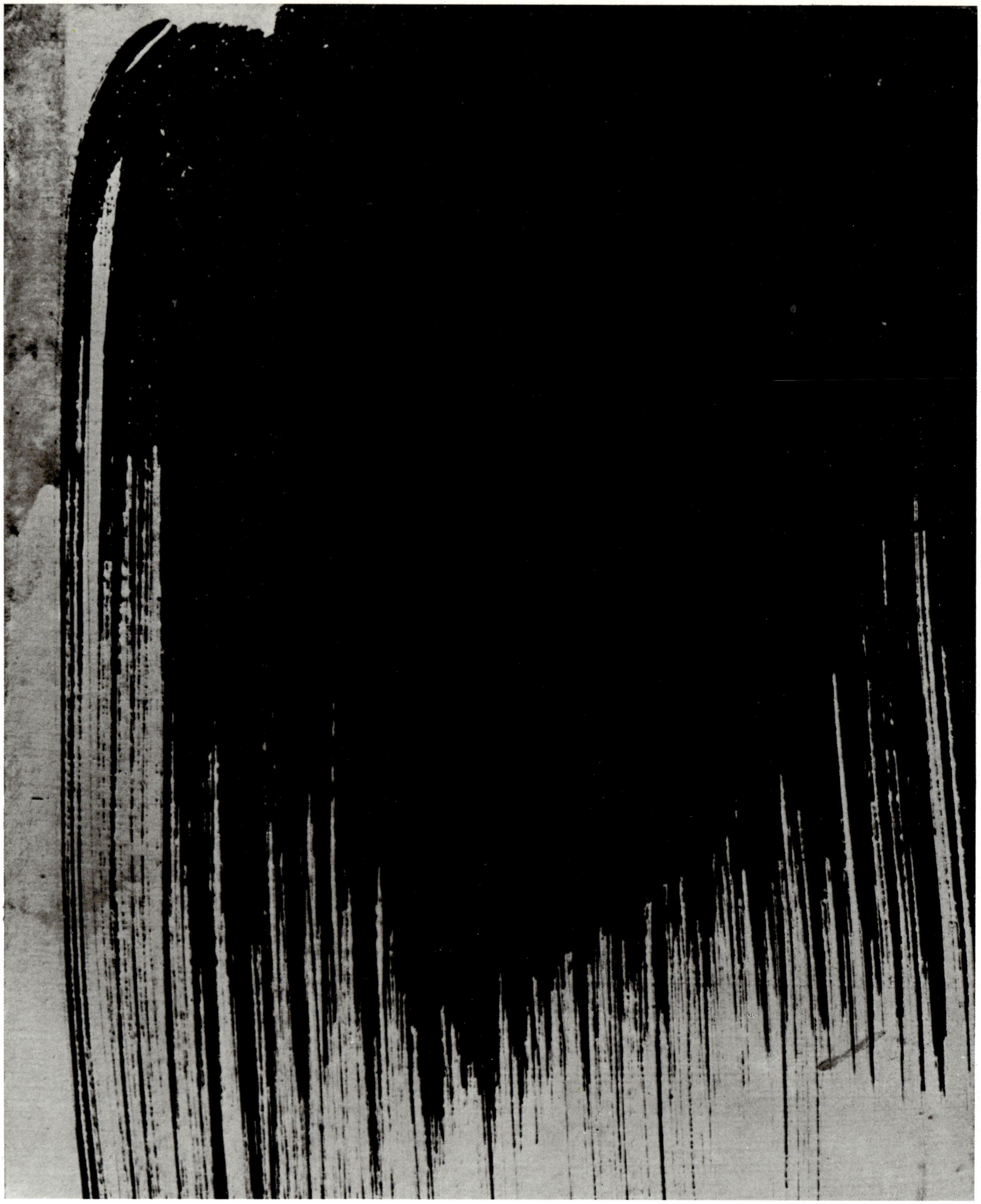

92 T. 1938-32

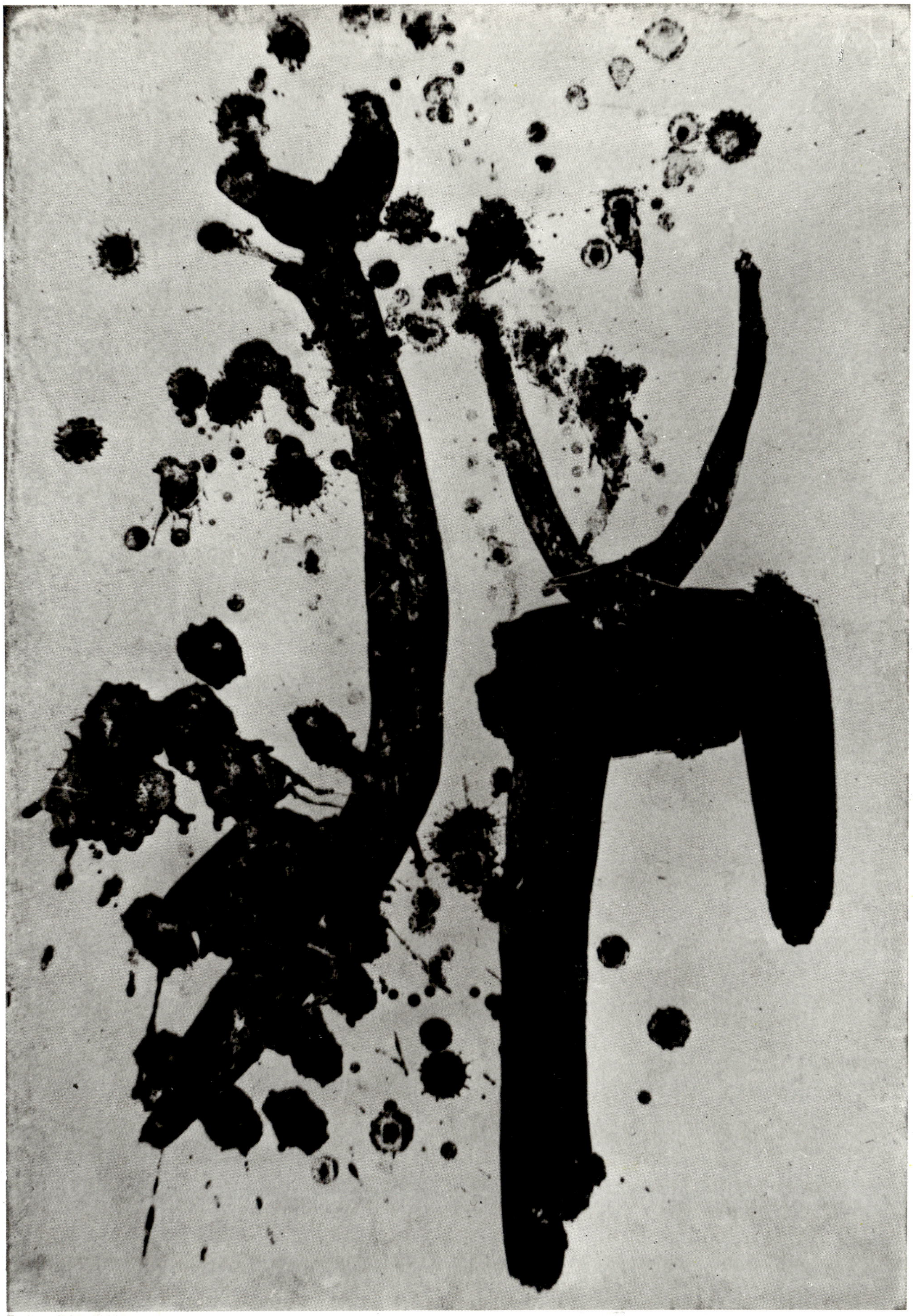

93 T. 1938-31

94 T. 1938-3

1945-1949

95 E. C. 1945

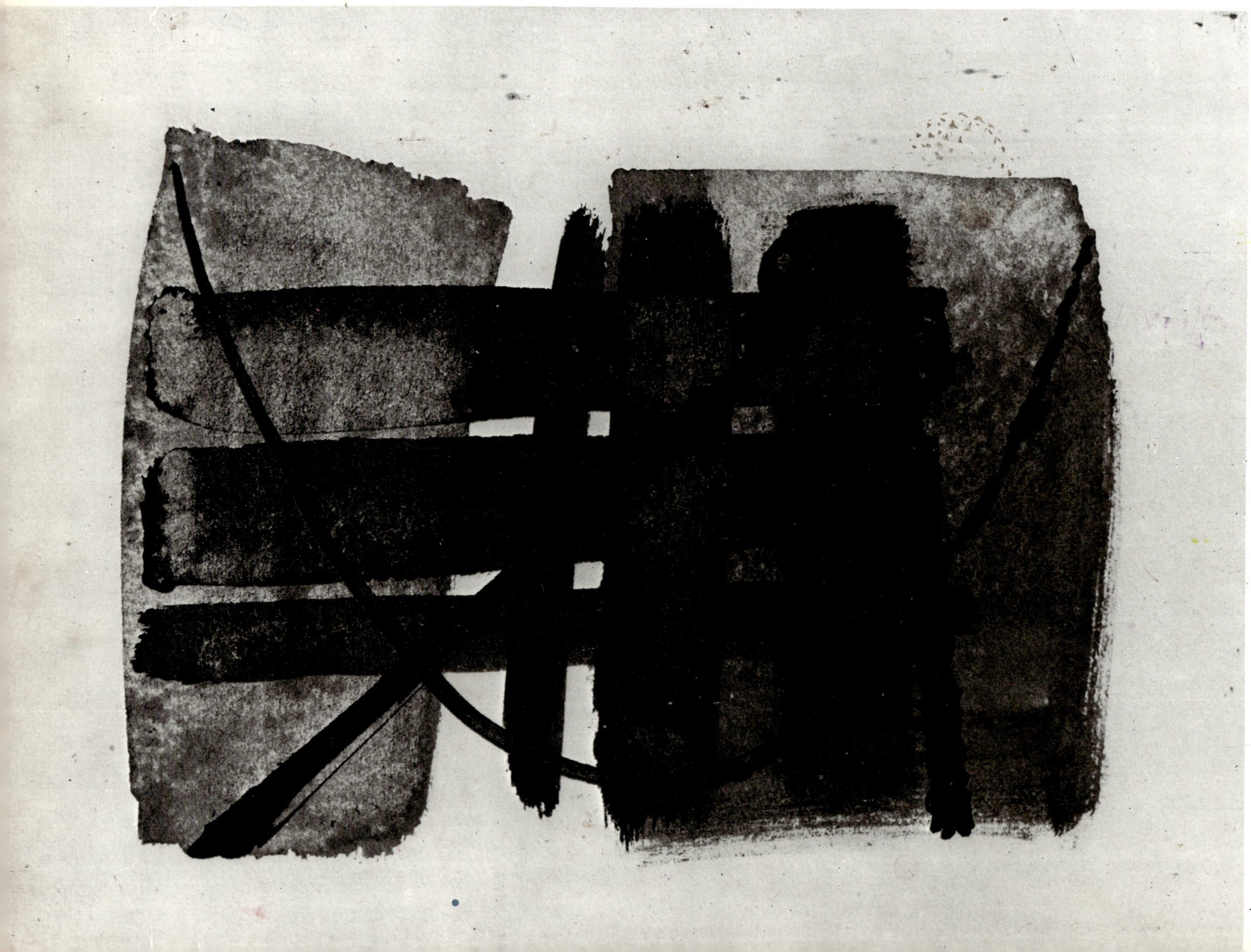

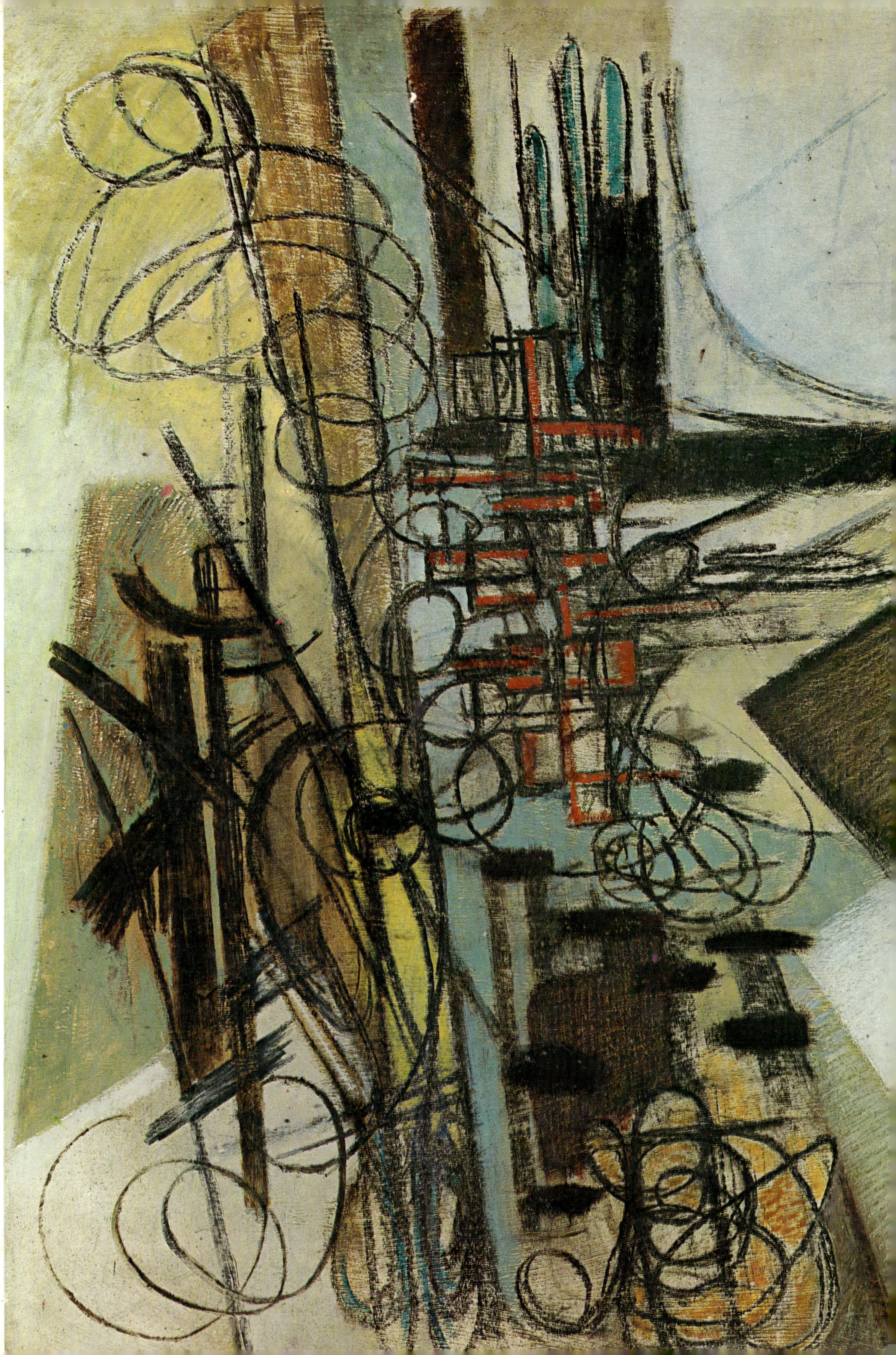

96 T. 1947-9

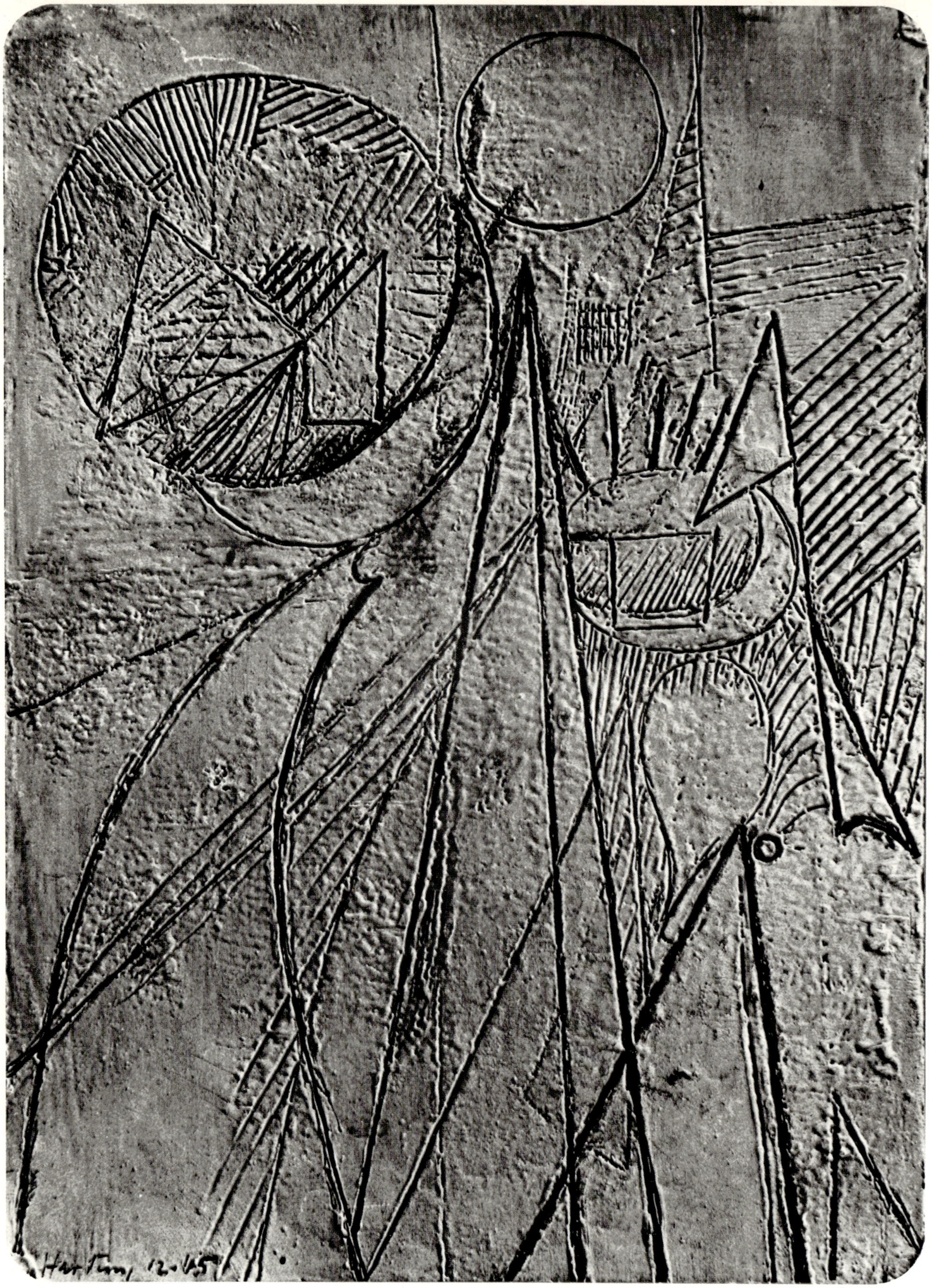

97 T. 1945-27

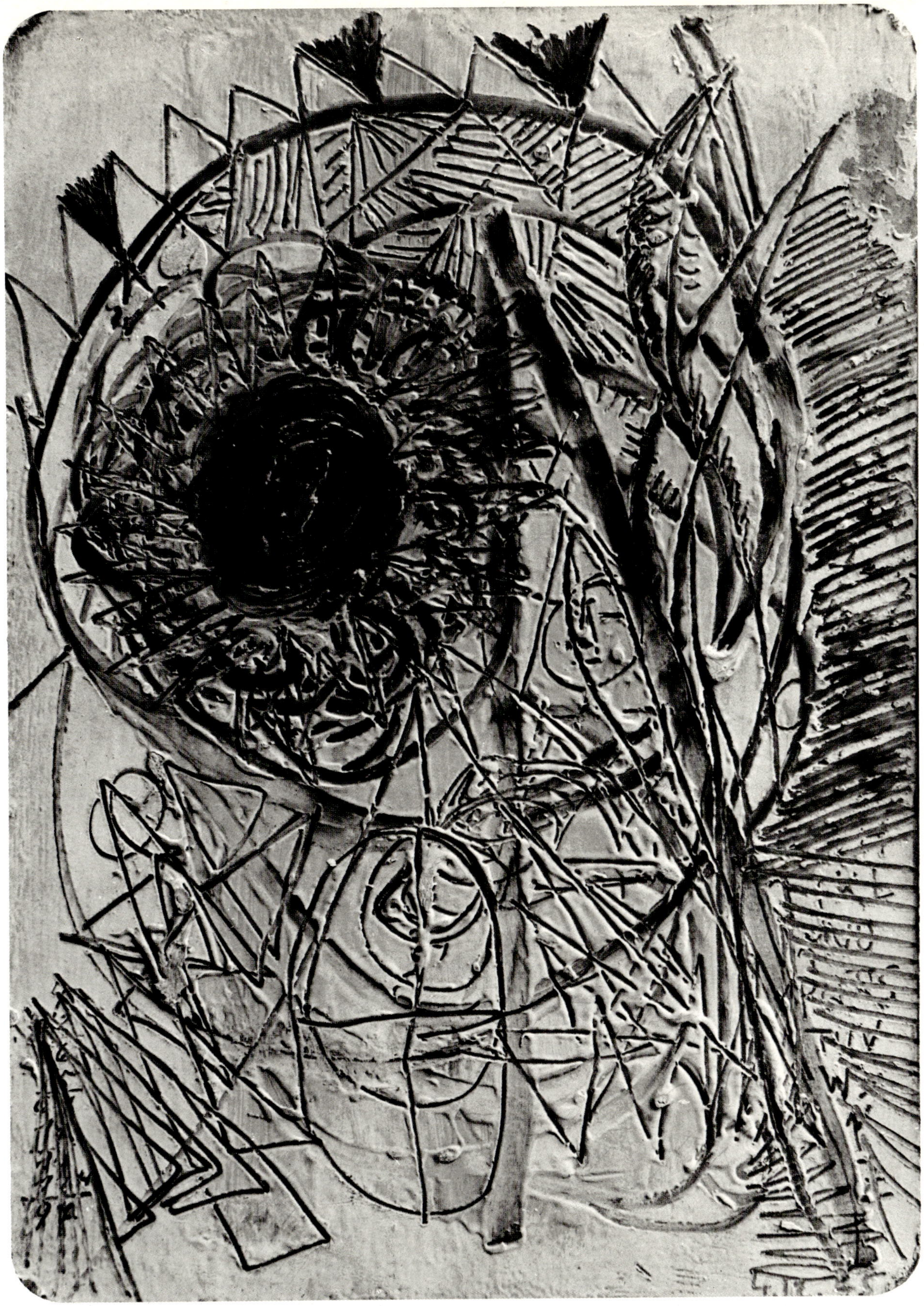

98 T. 1945-28

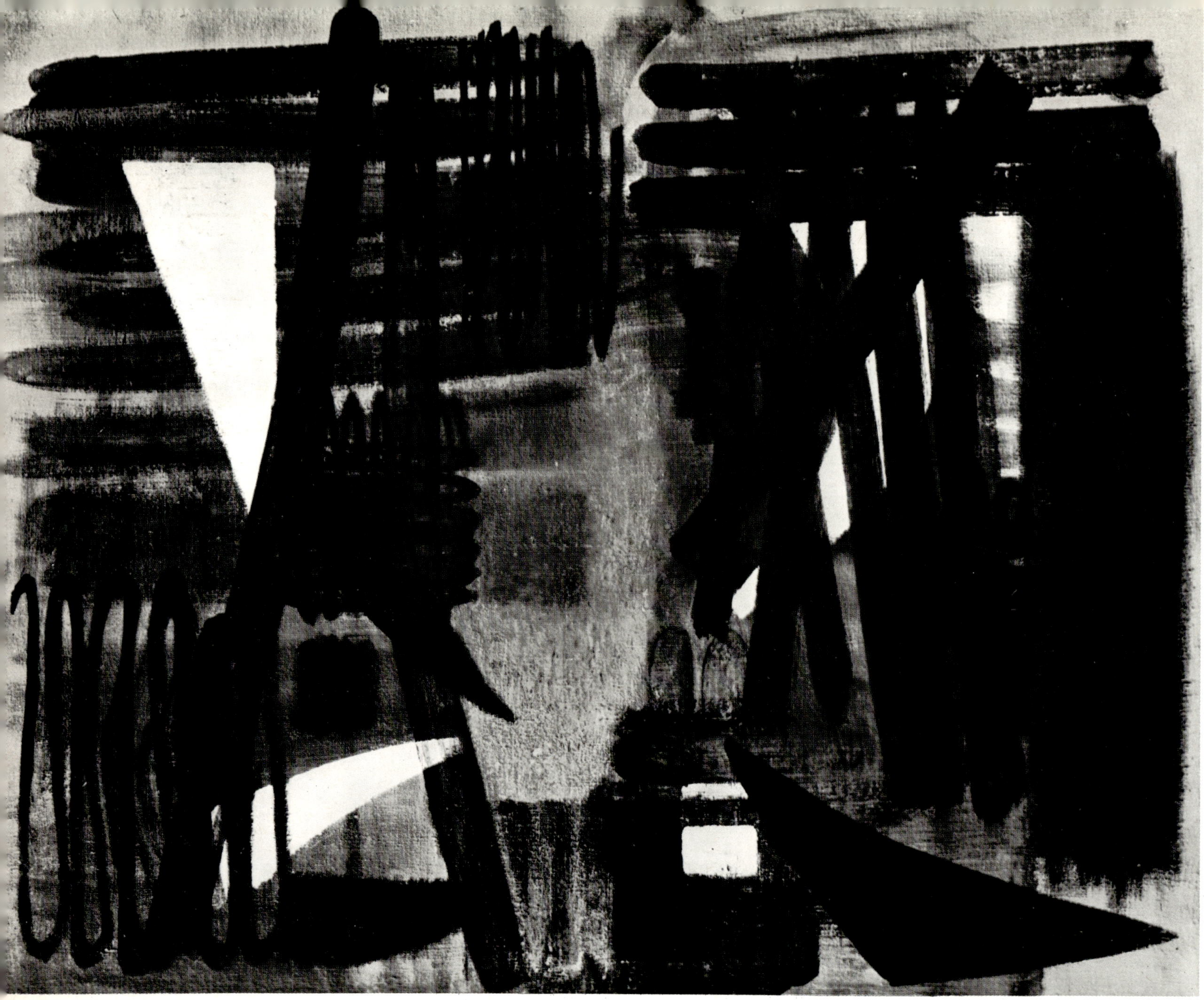

99 T. 1947-30

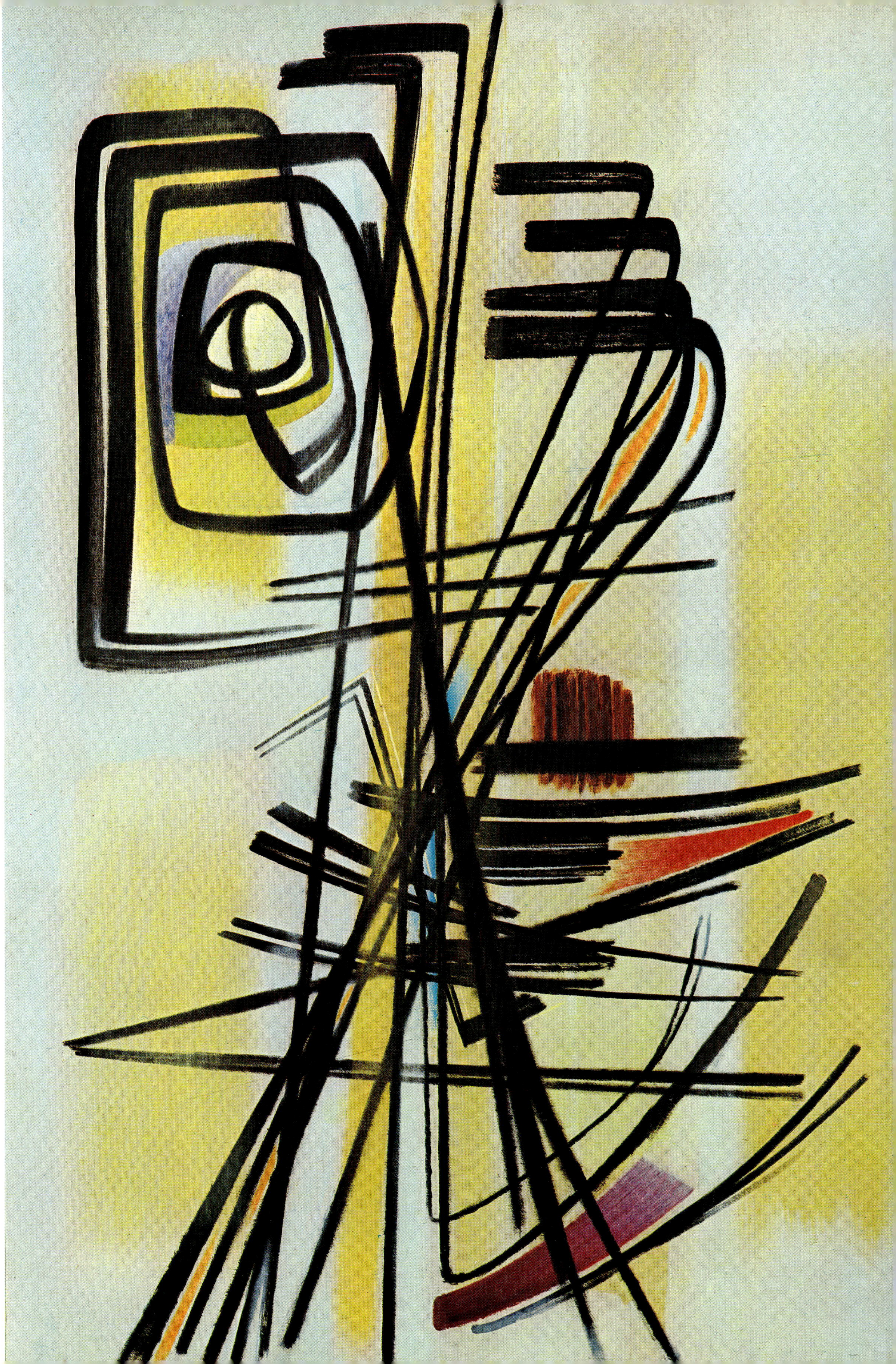

100 T. 1947-12

101 T. 1947-39

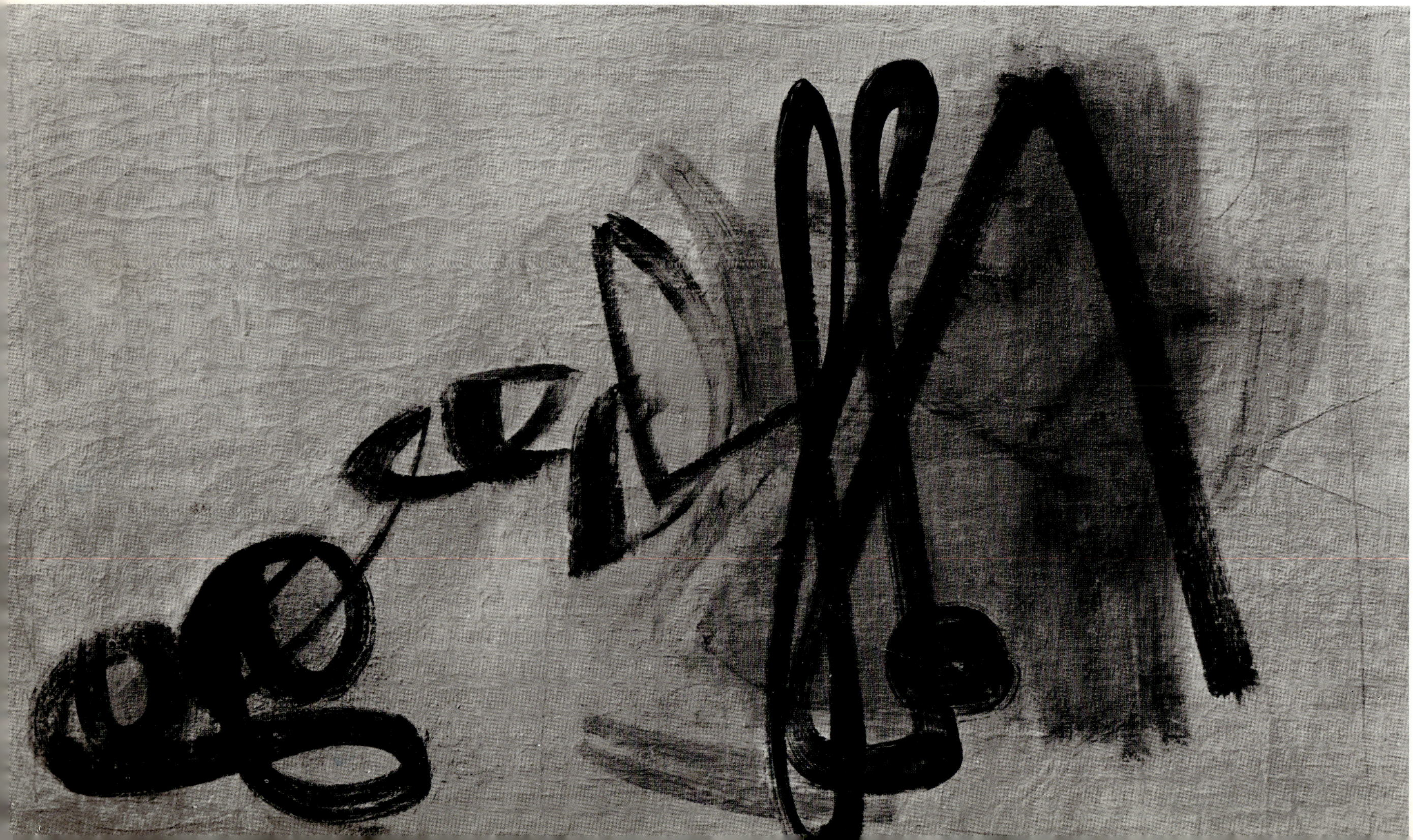

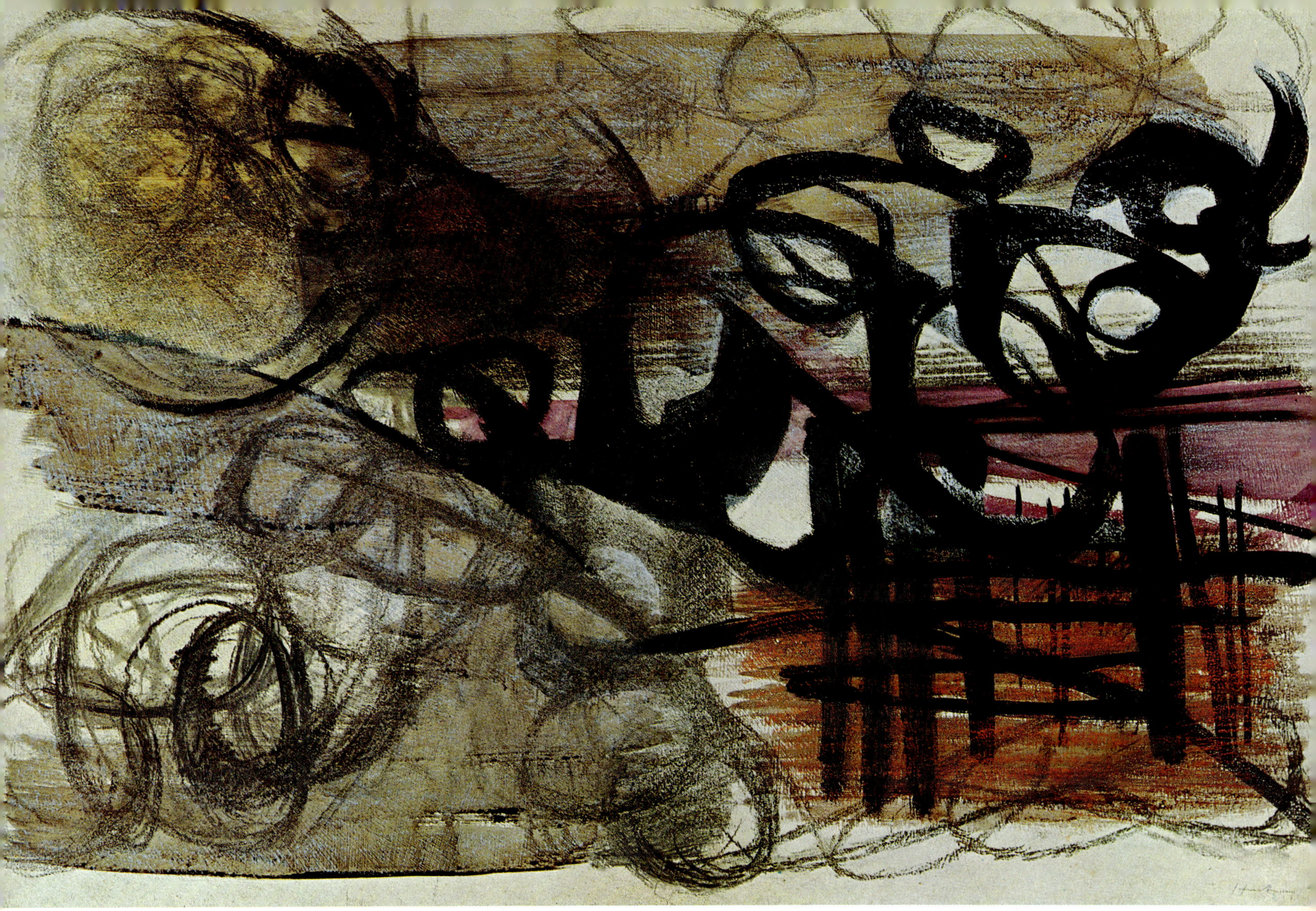

2 T. 1947-25

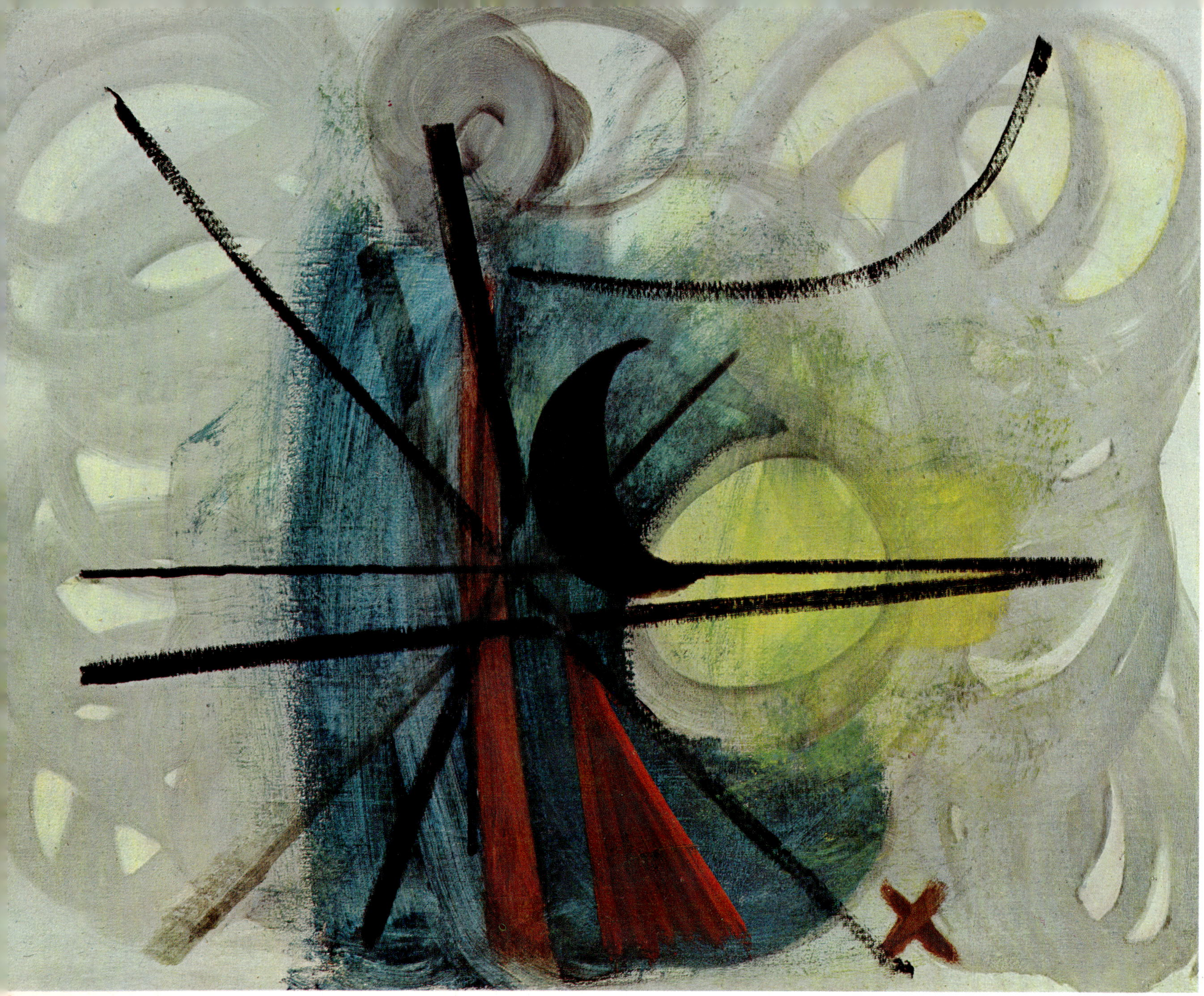

103 T. 1948-23

104 T. 1948-34

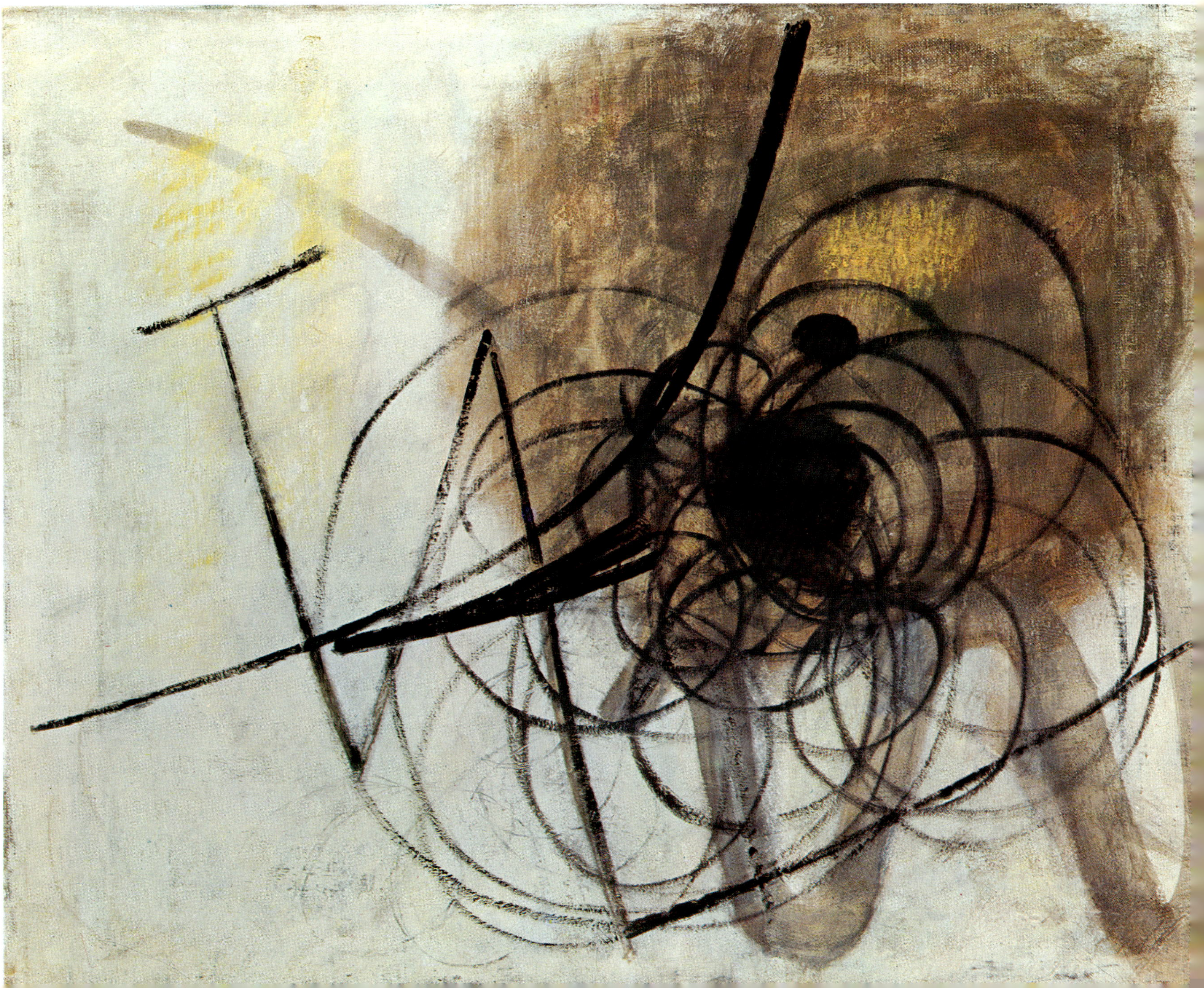

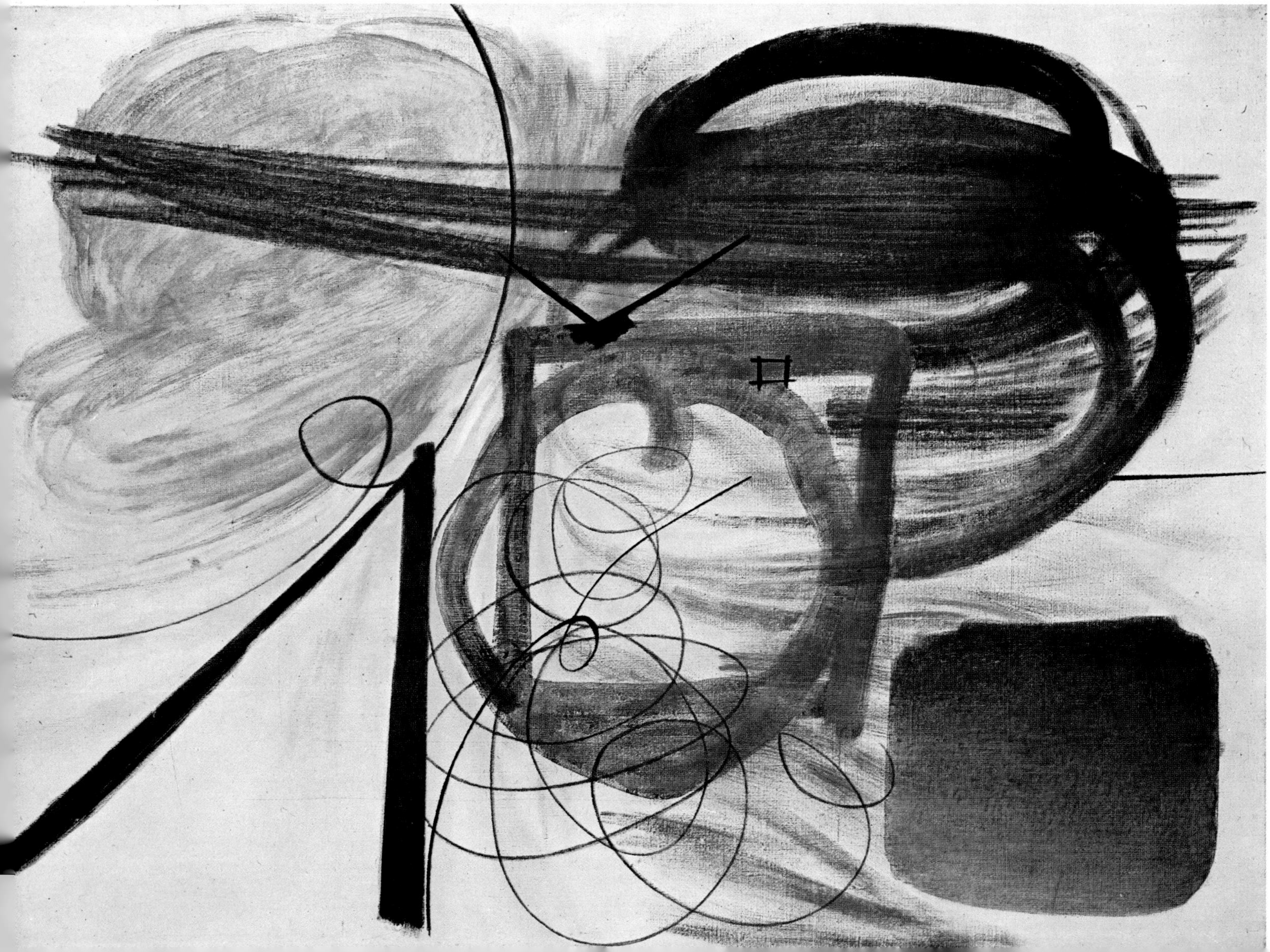

105 T. 1947-1

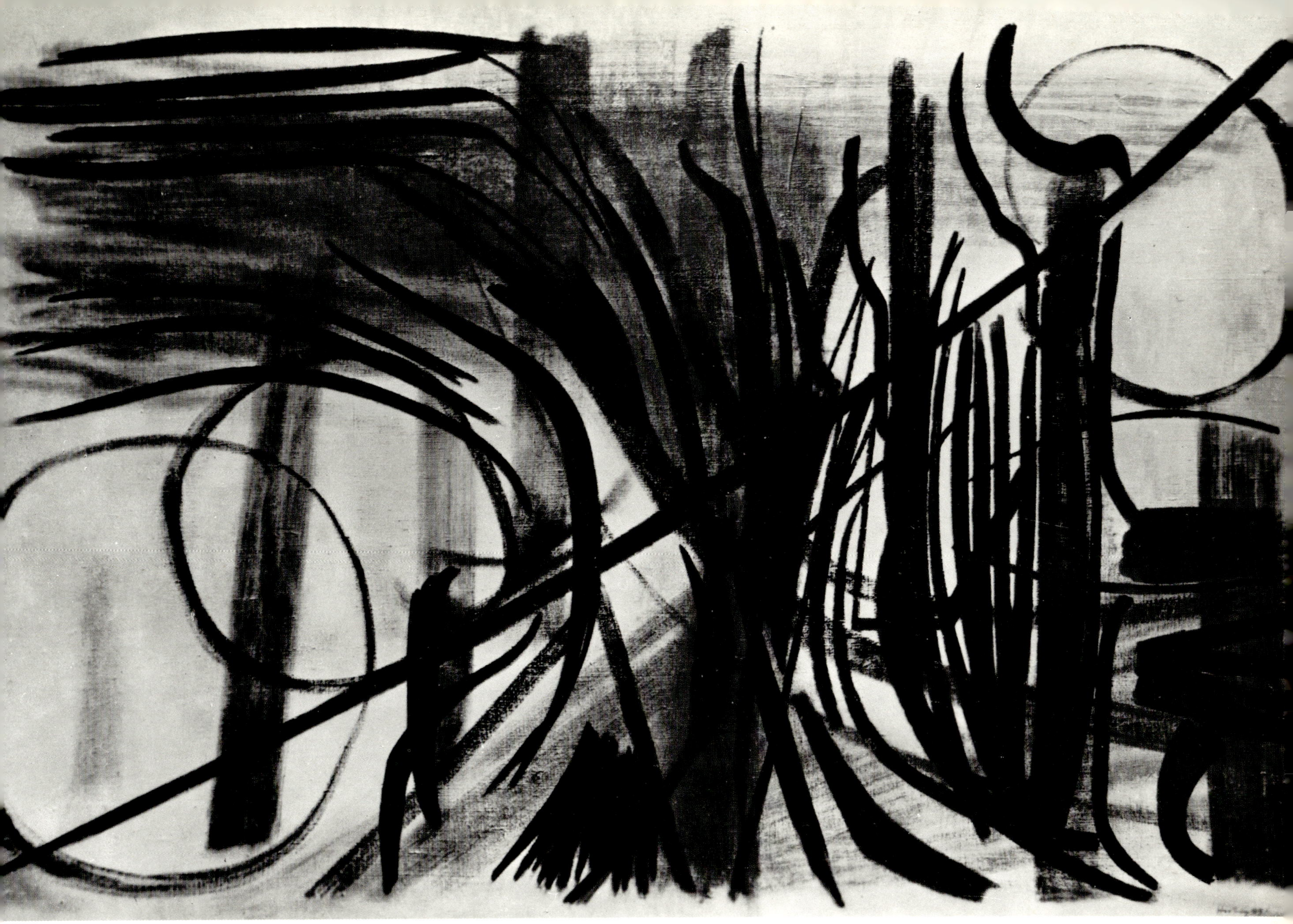

106 T. 1949-26

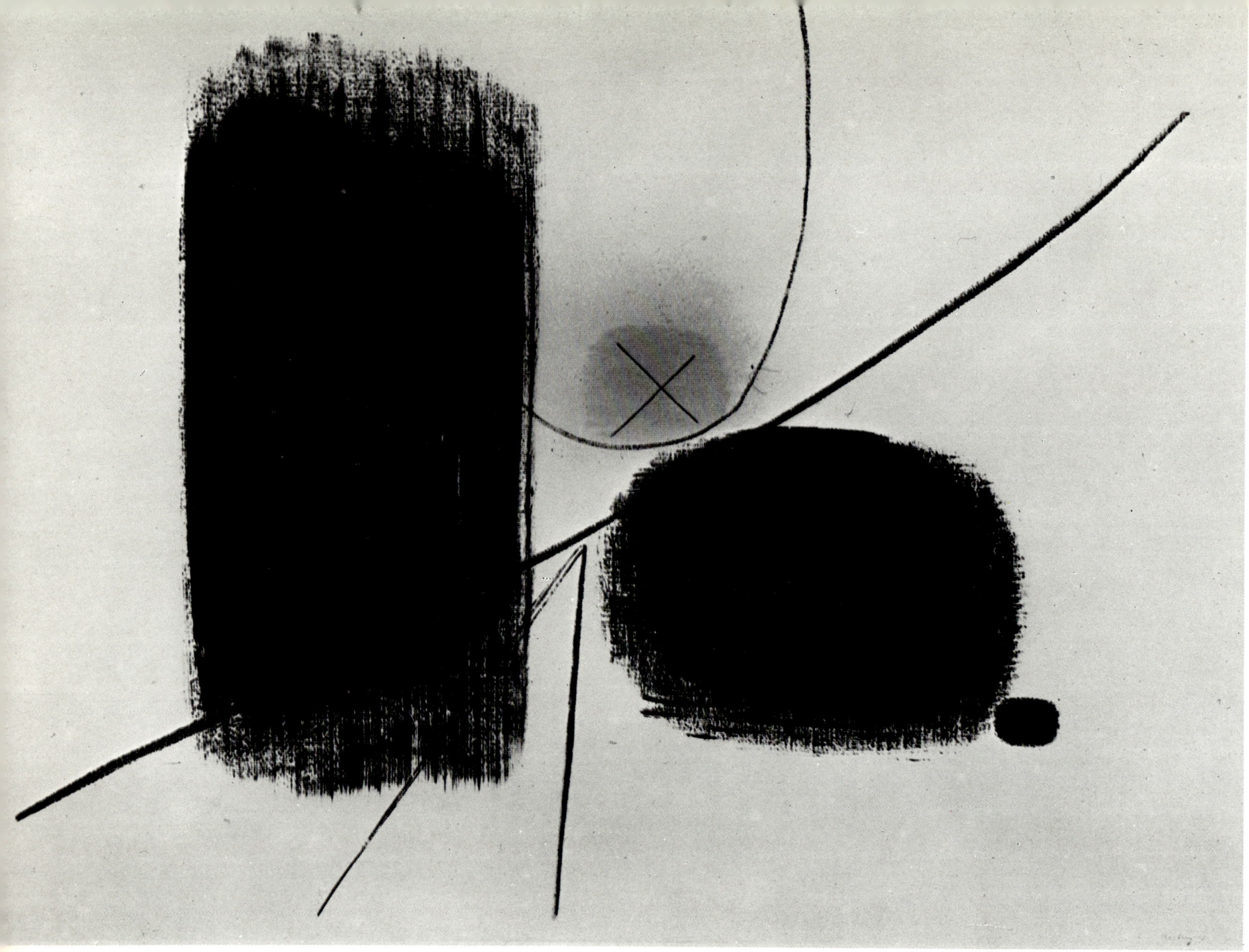

107 T. 1948-19

08 T. 1949-9

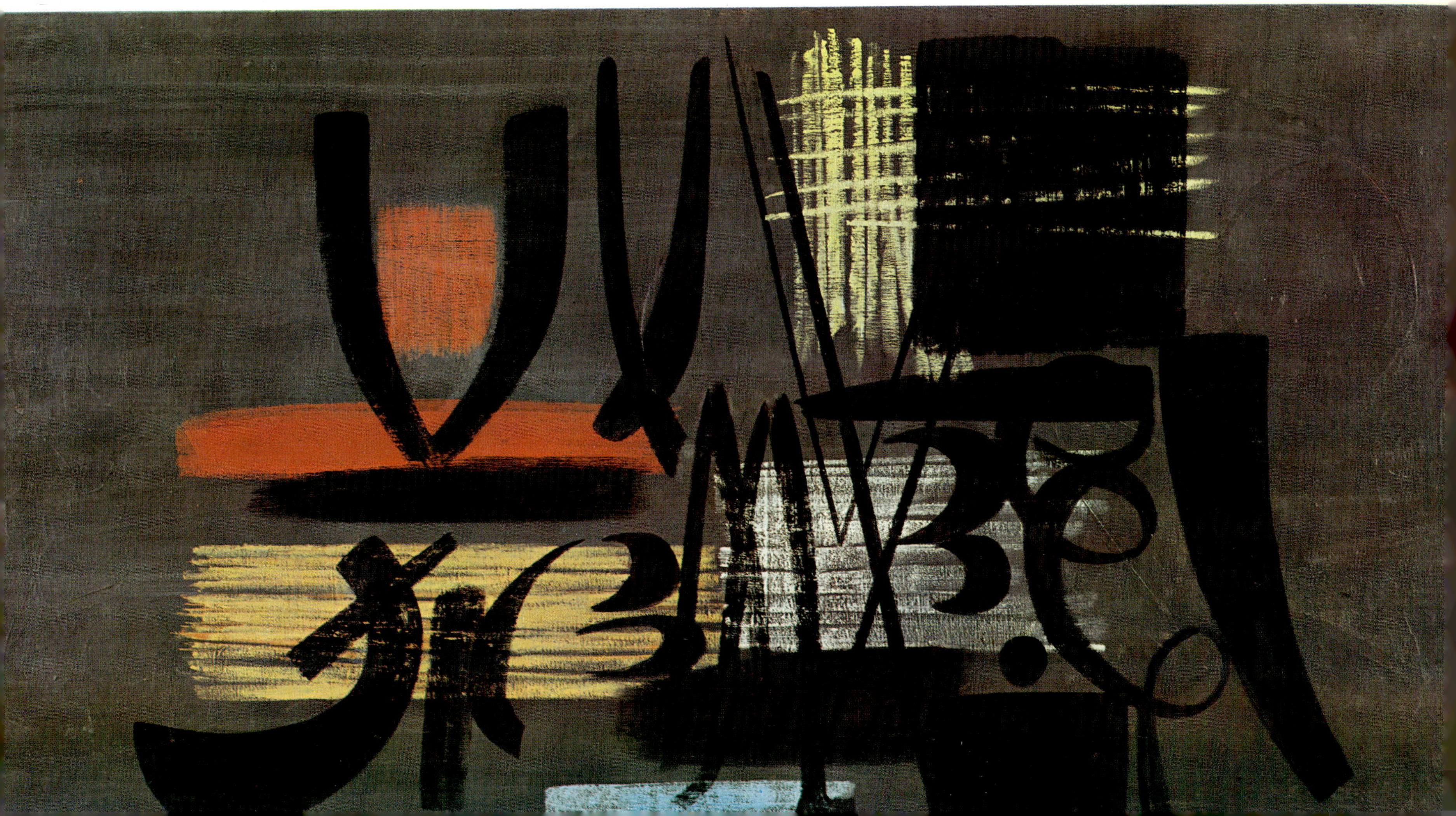

109 T. 1949-2

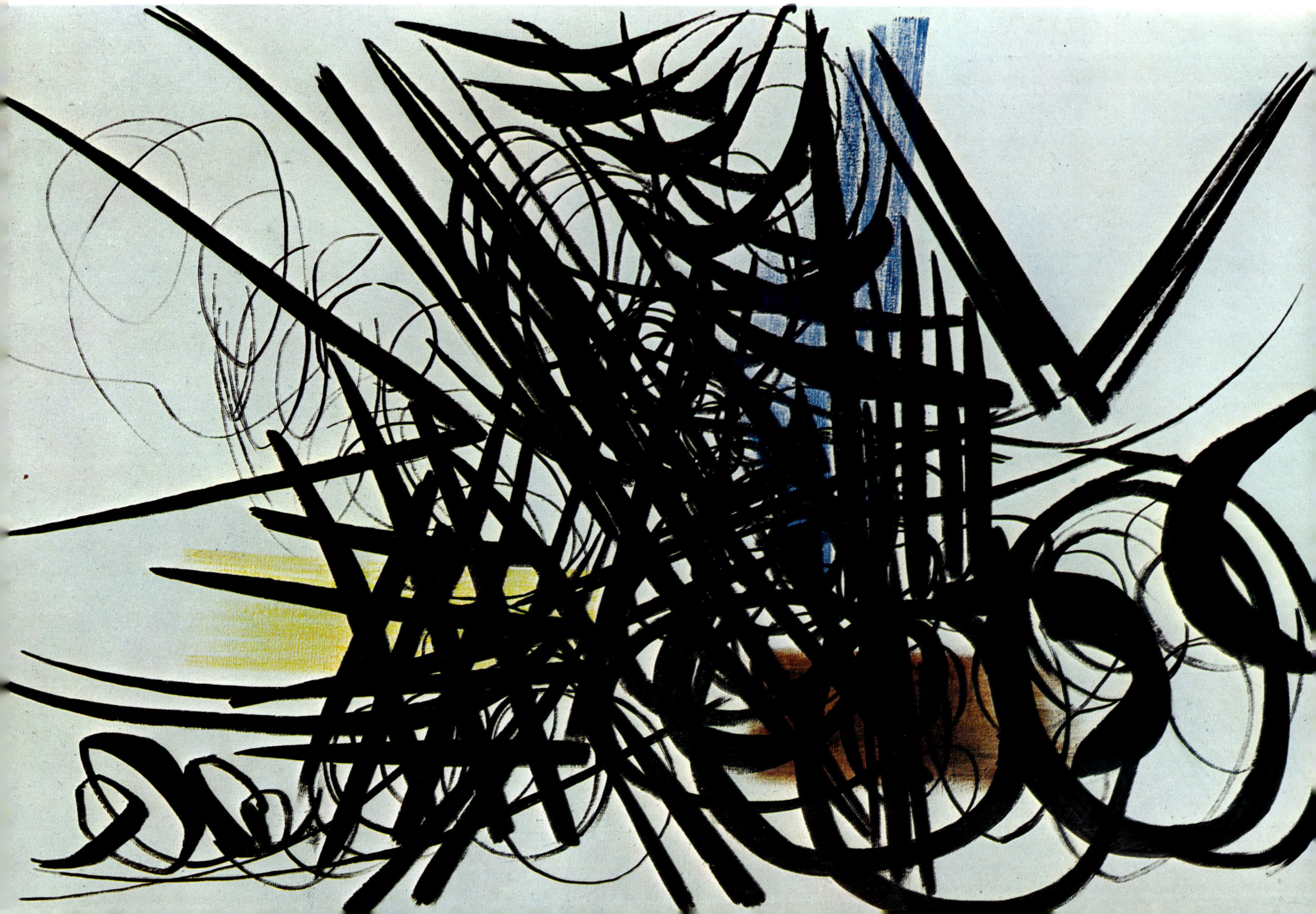

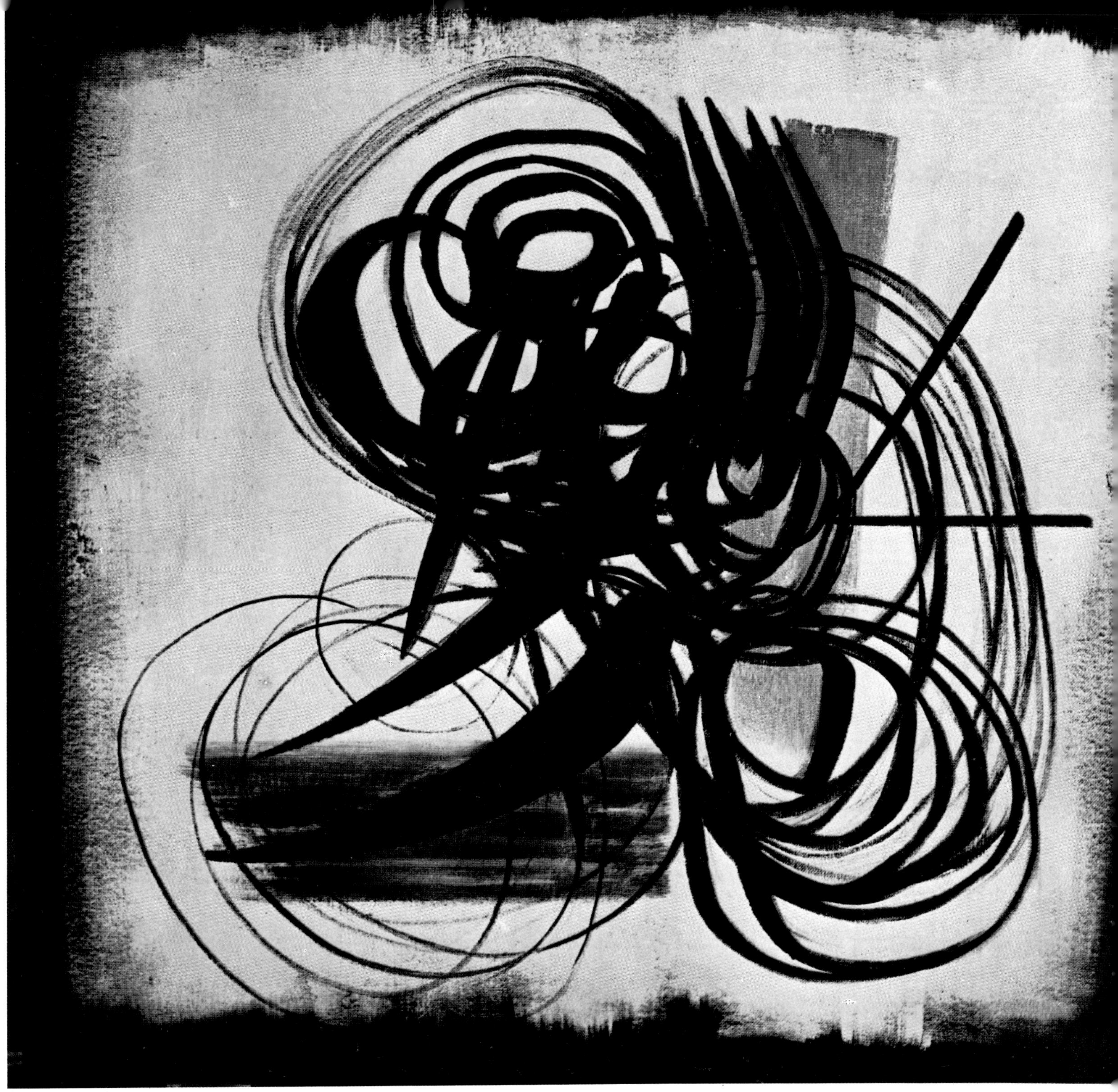

110 T. 1949-25

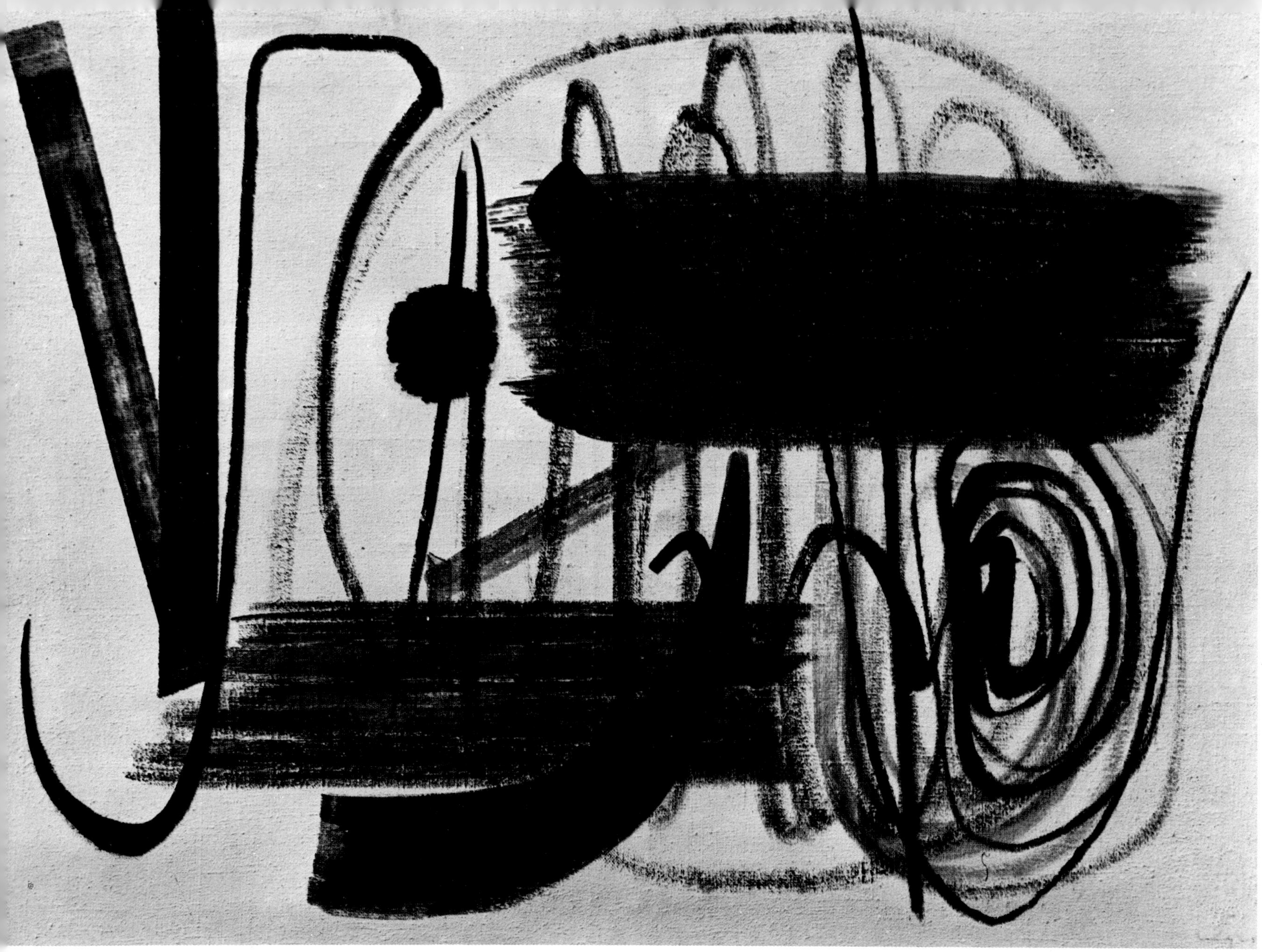

111 T. 1949-23

12 T. 1948-8

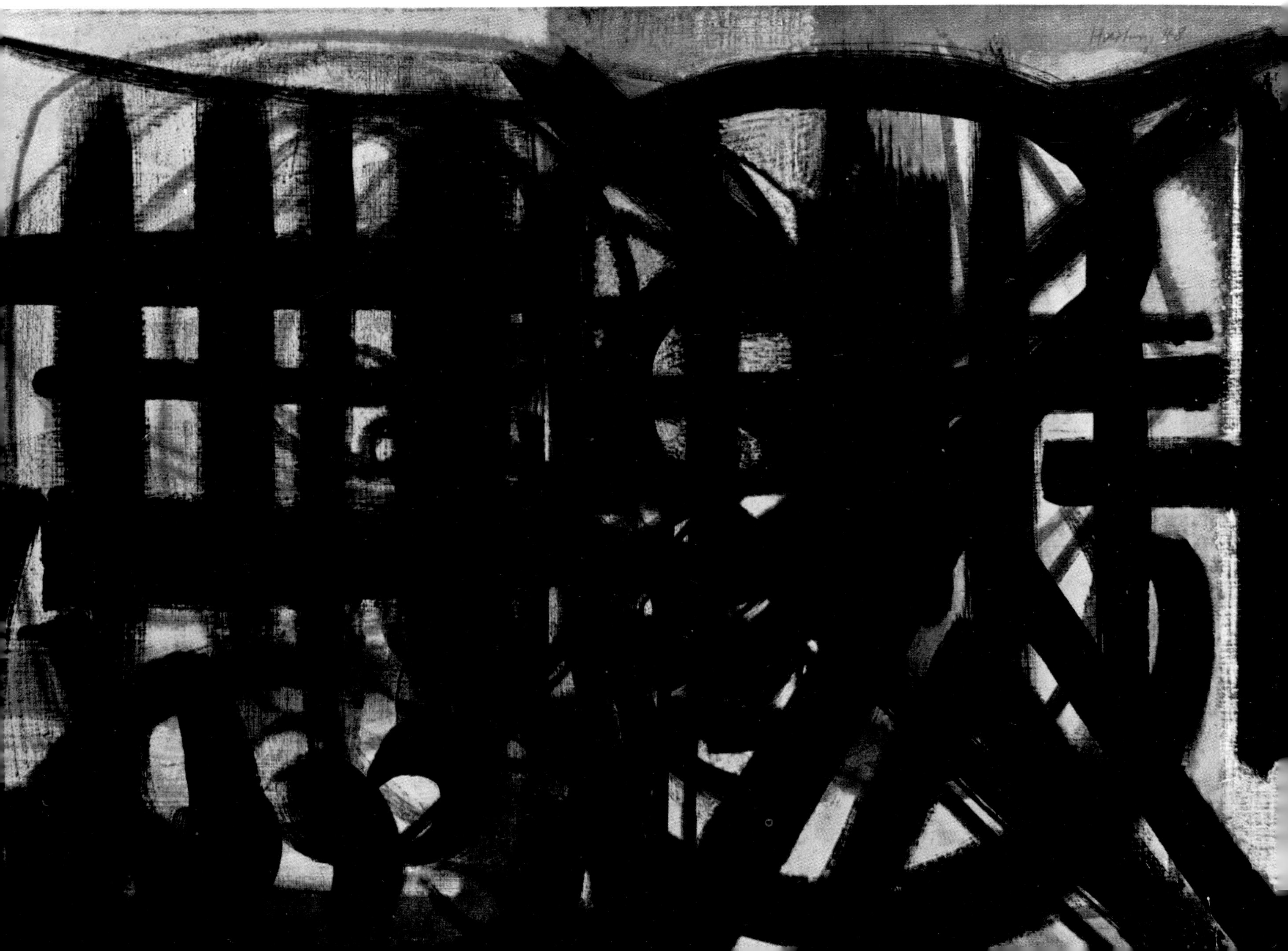

113 T. 1950-46

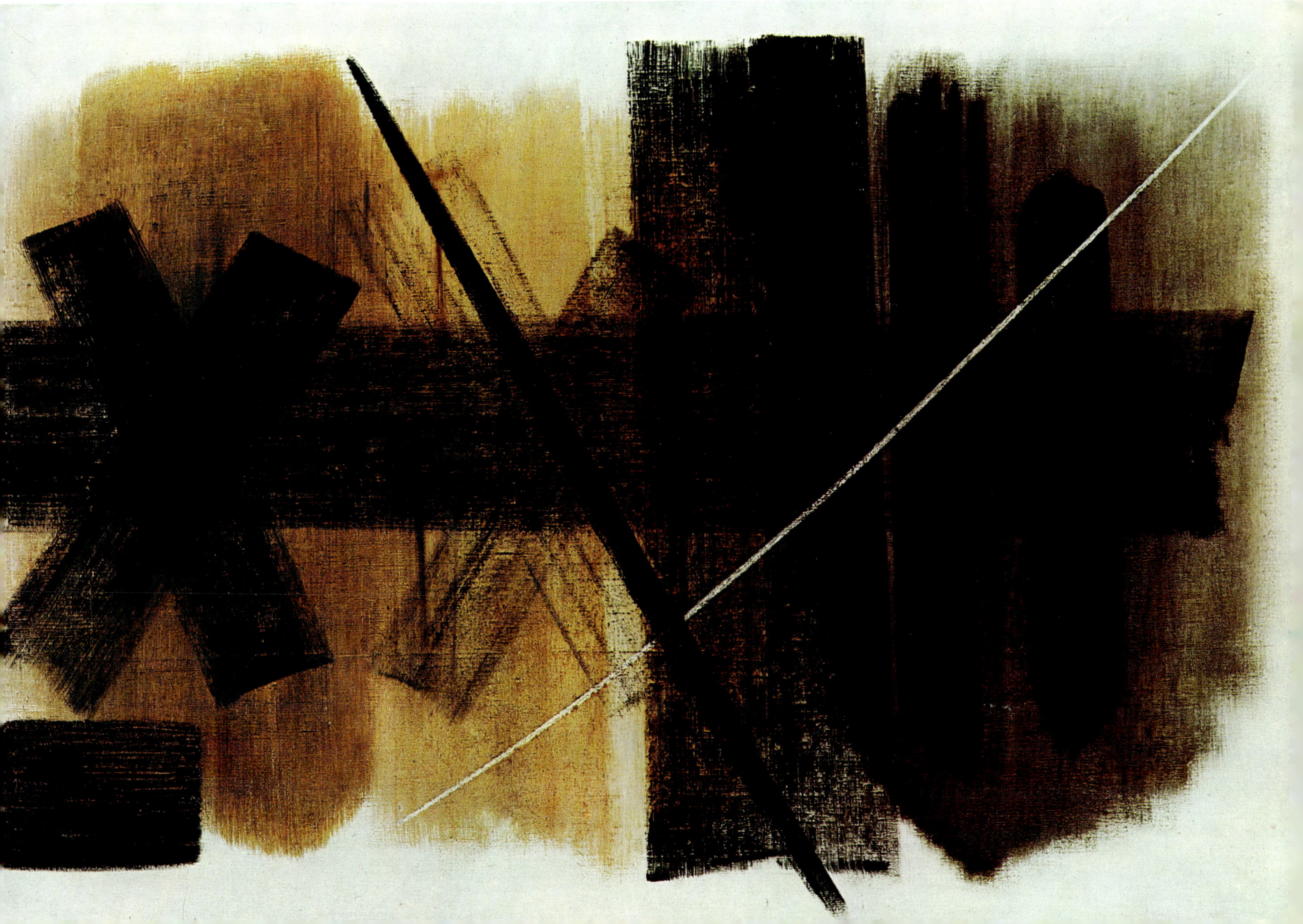

114 T. 1952-50

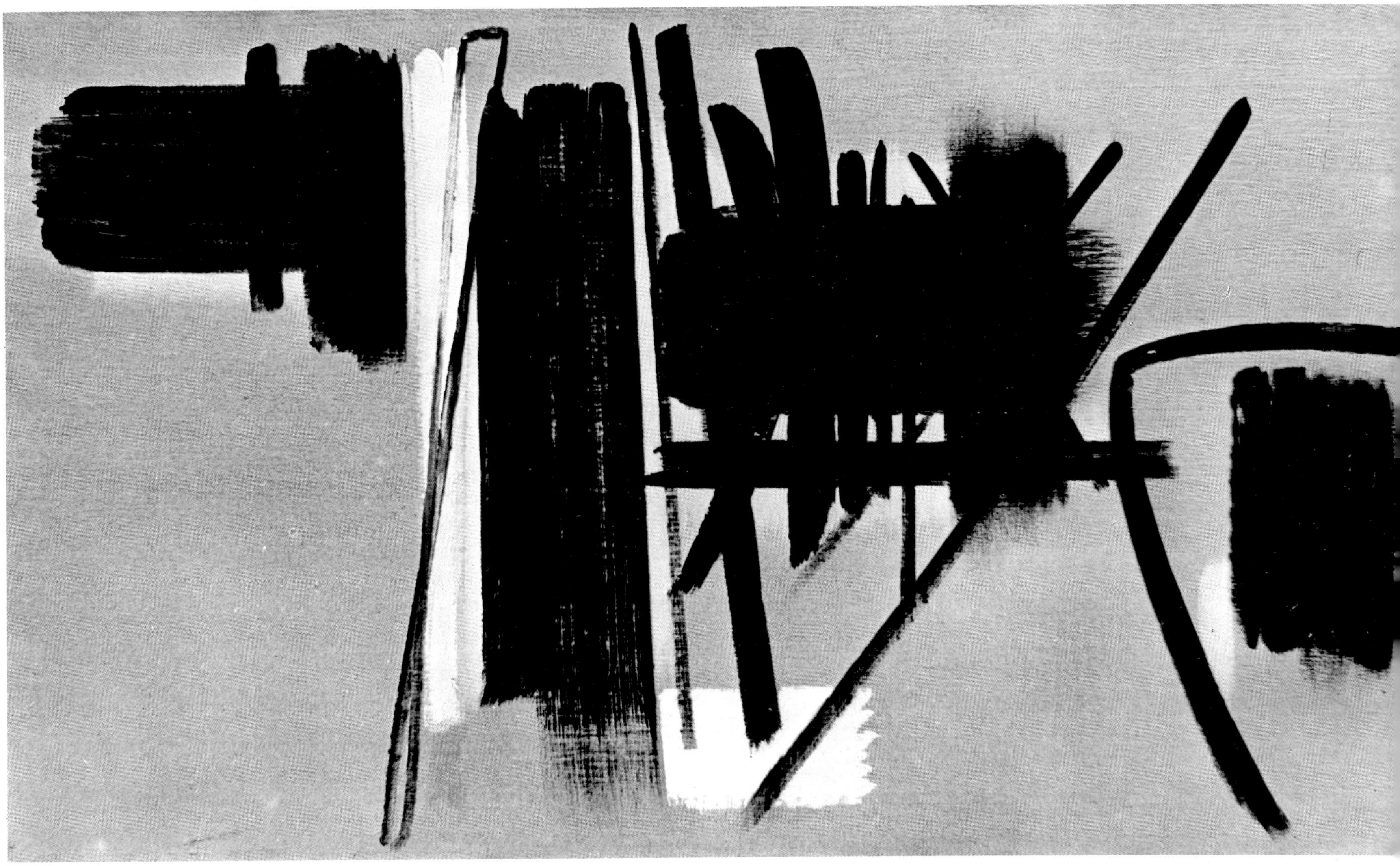

115 T. 1952-53

116 T. 1951-8

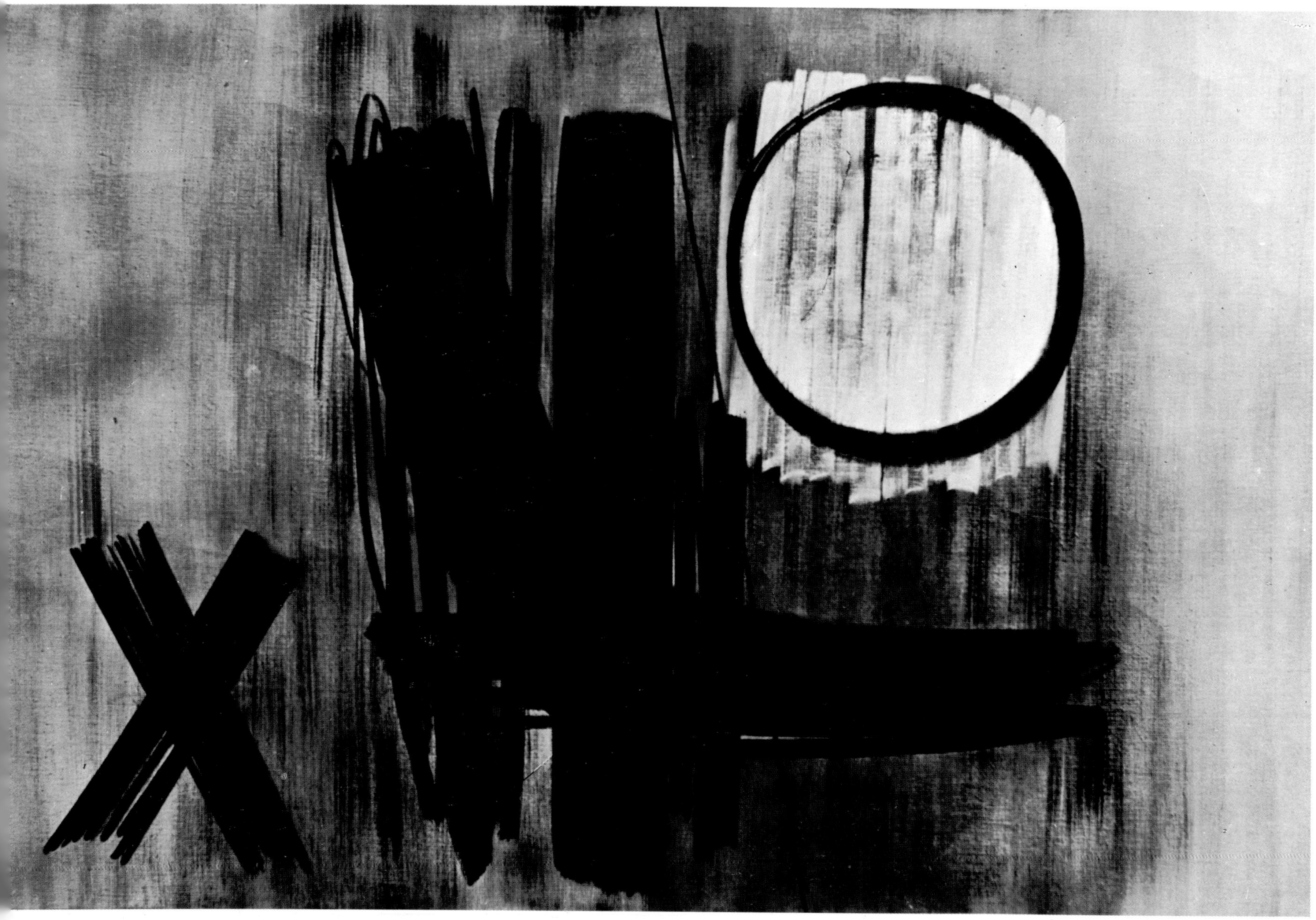

117 T. 1951-5

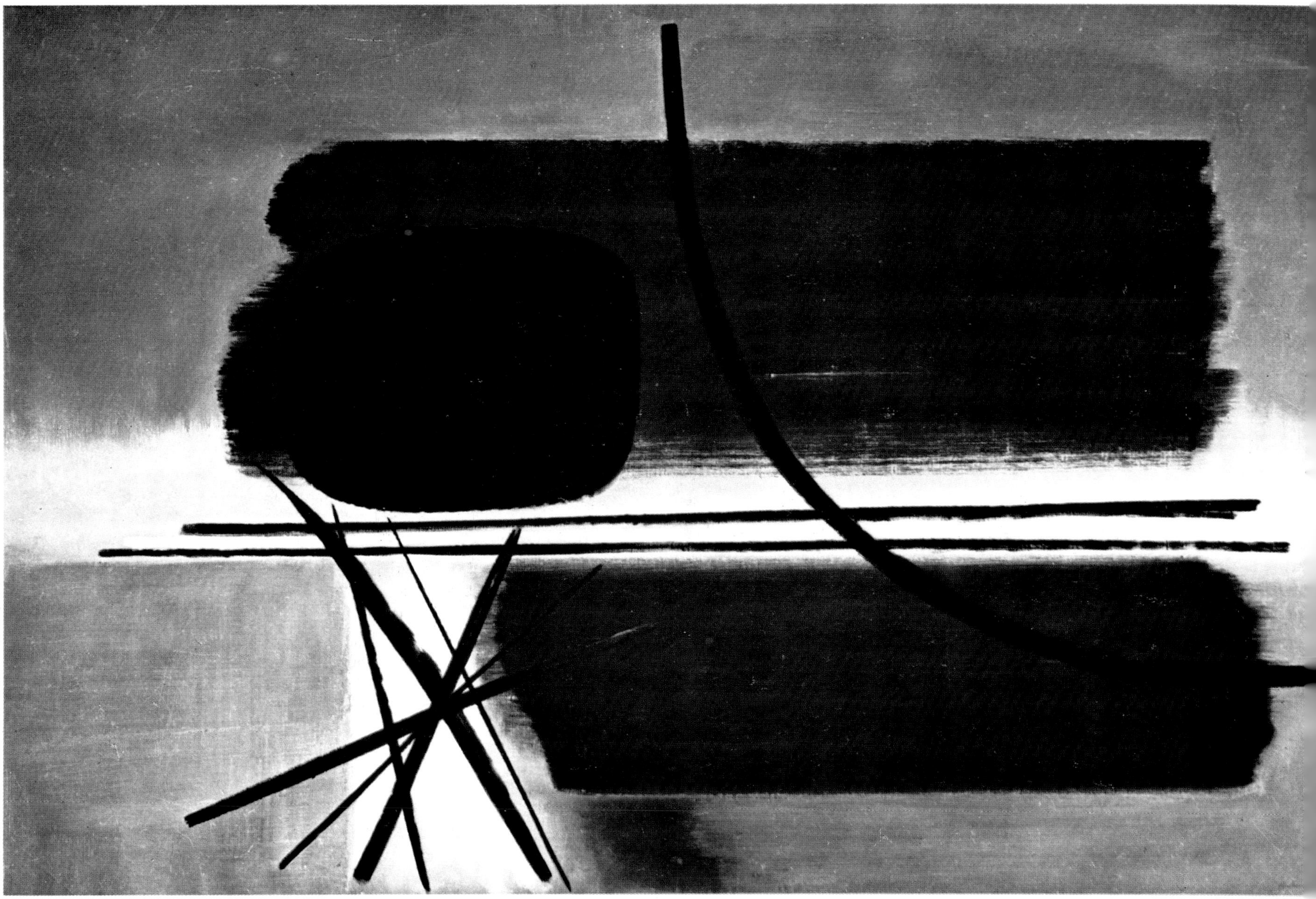

118 T. 1952-40

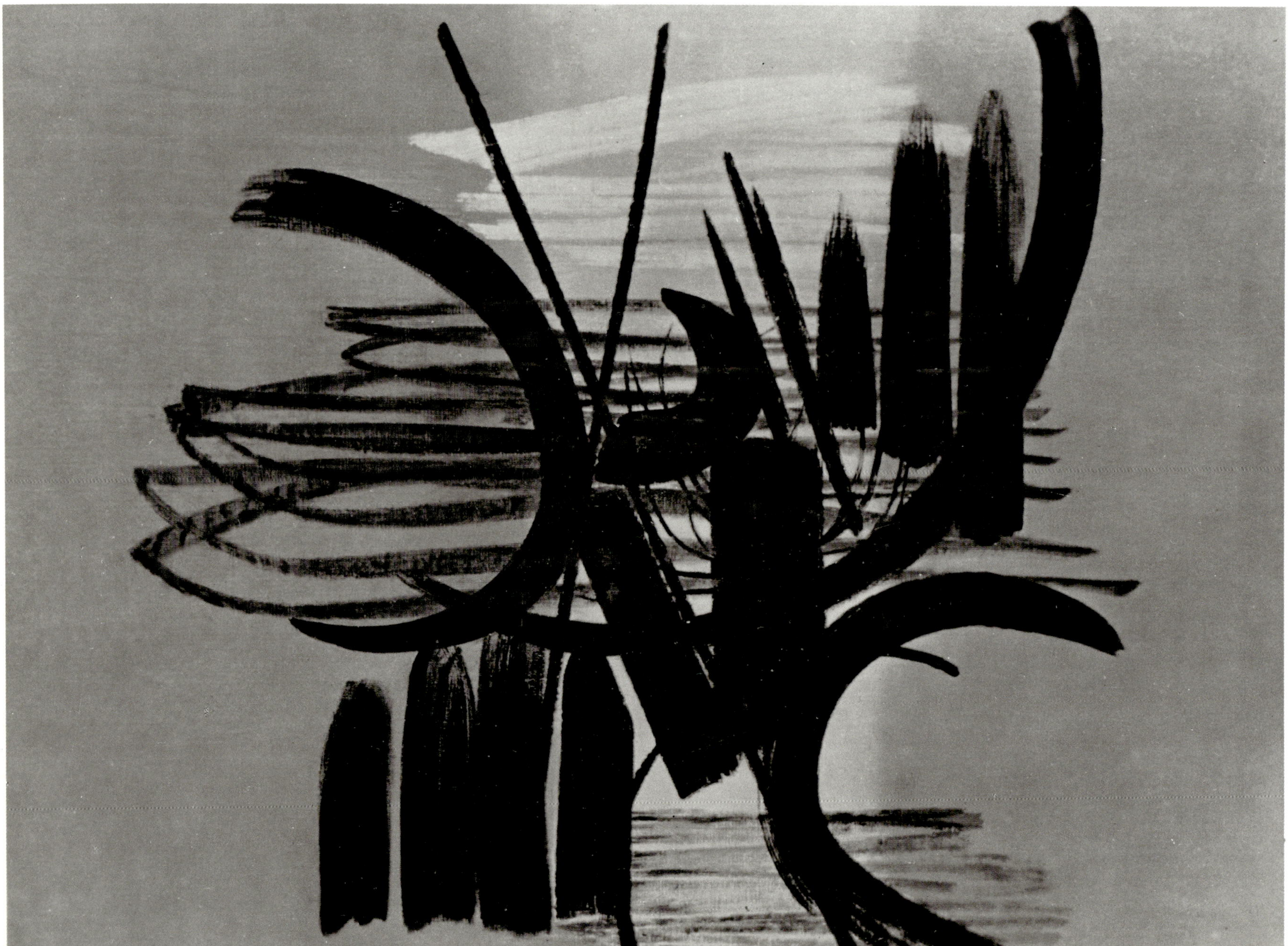

119 T. 1952-3

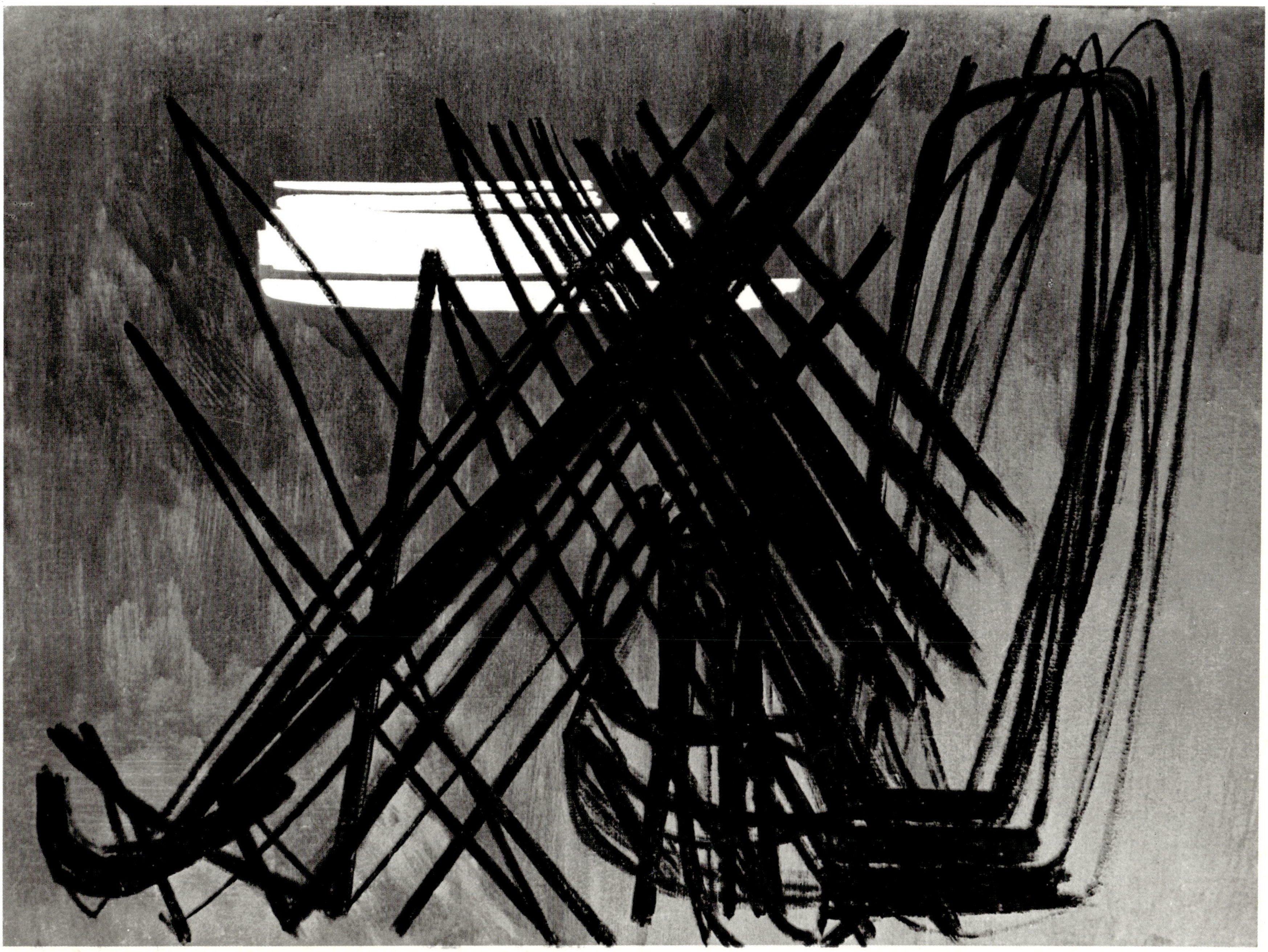

120 T. 1955-12

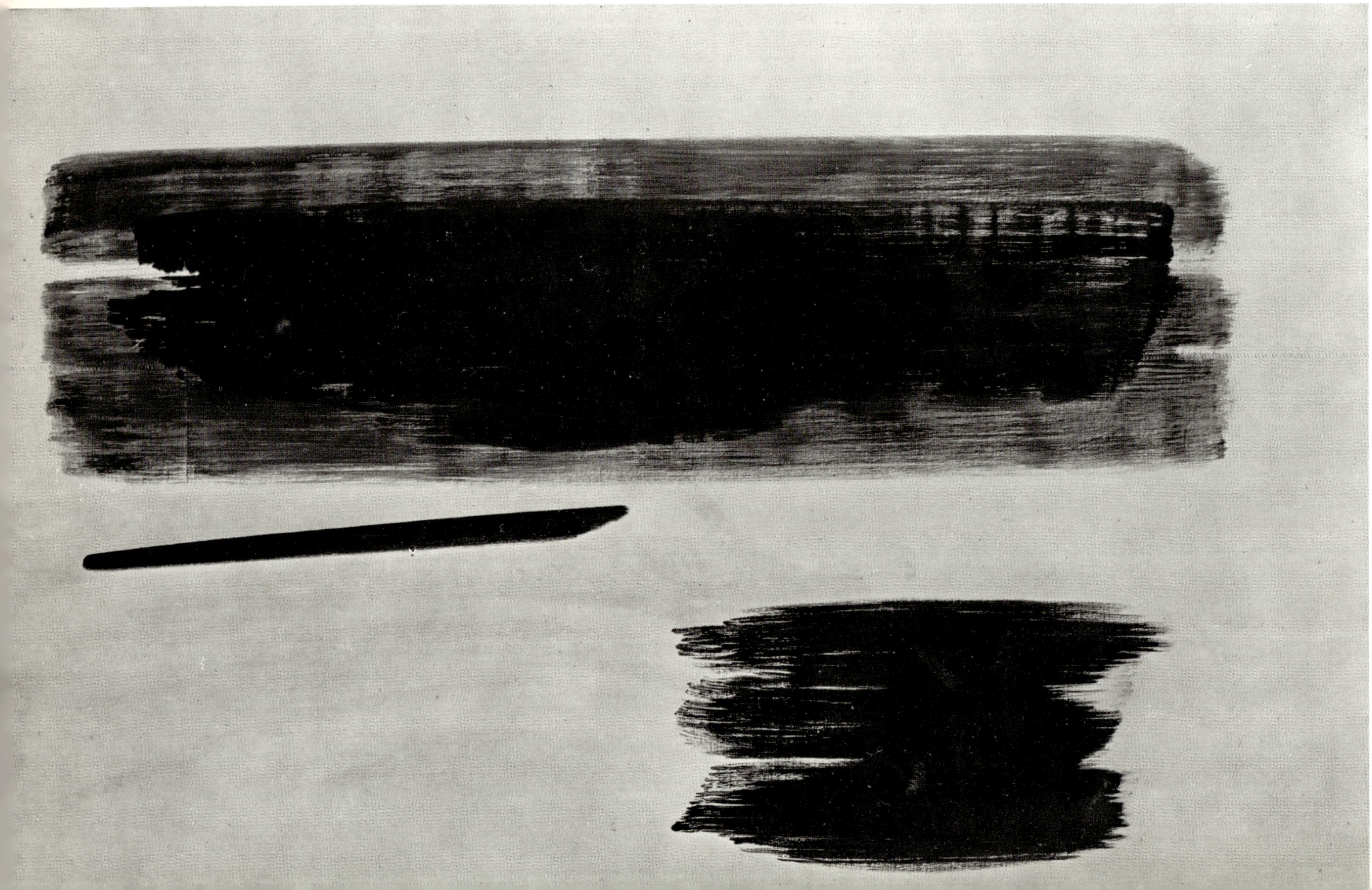

21 T. 1954-4

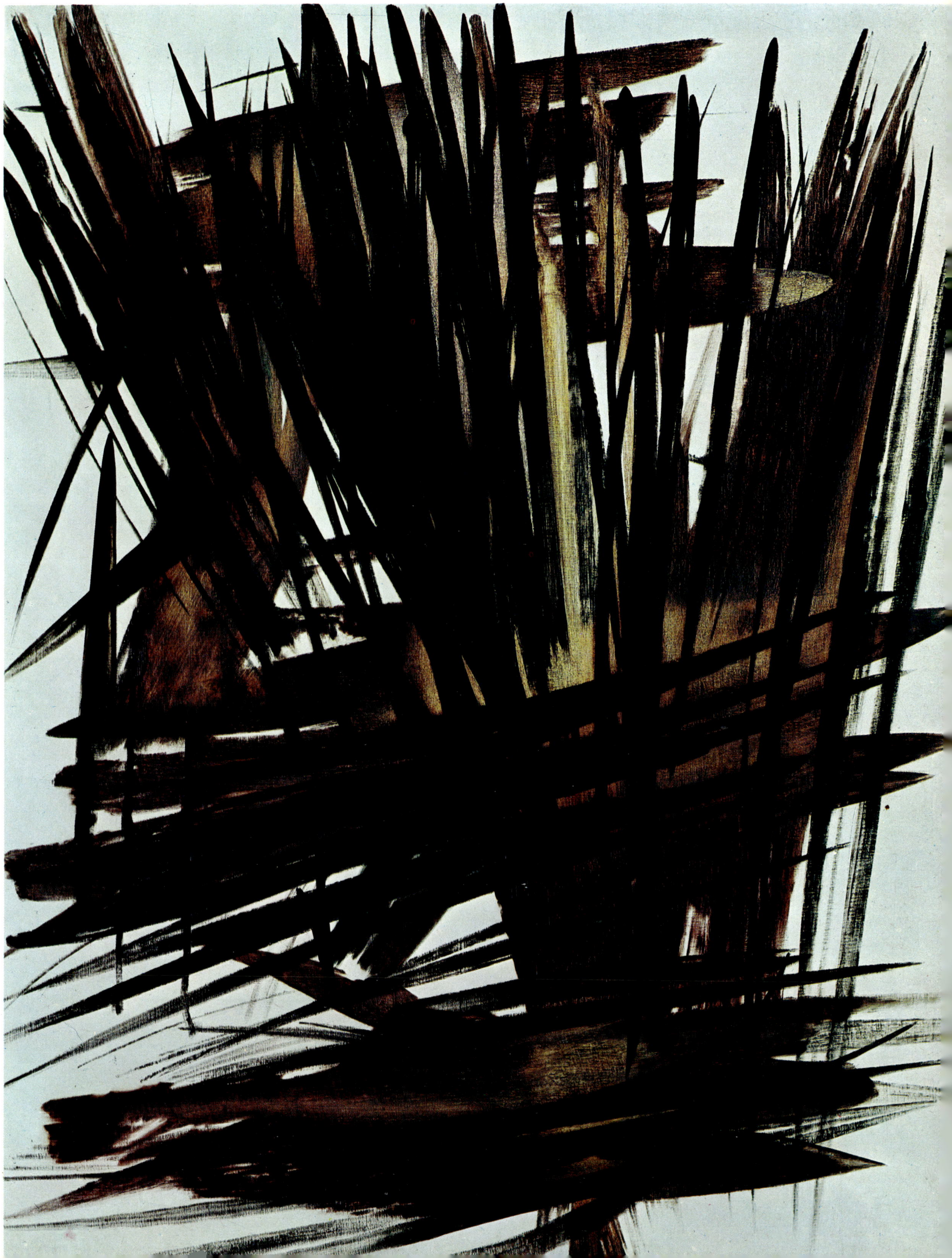

2 T. 1956-9

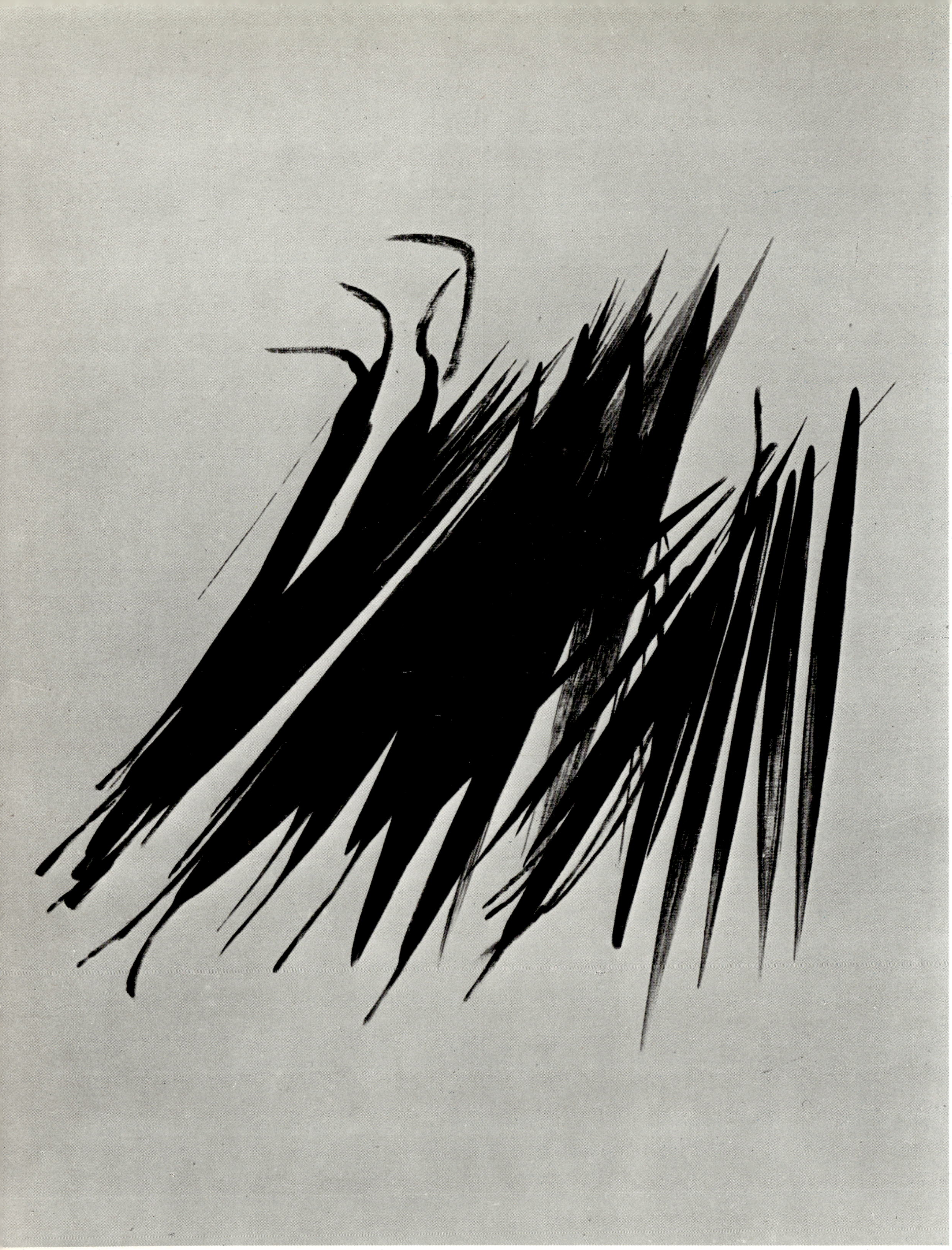

123 T. 1956-8

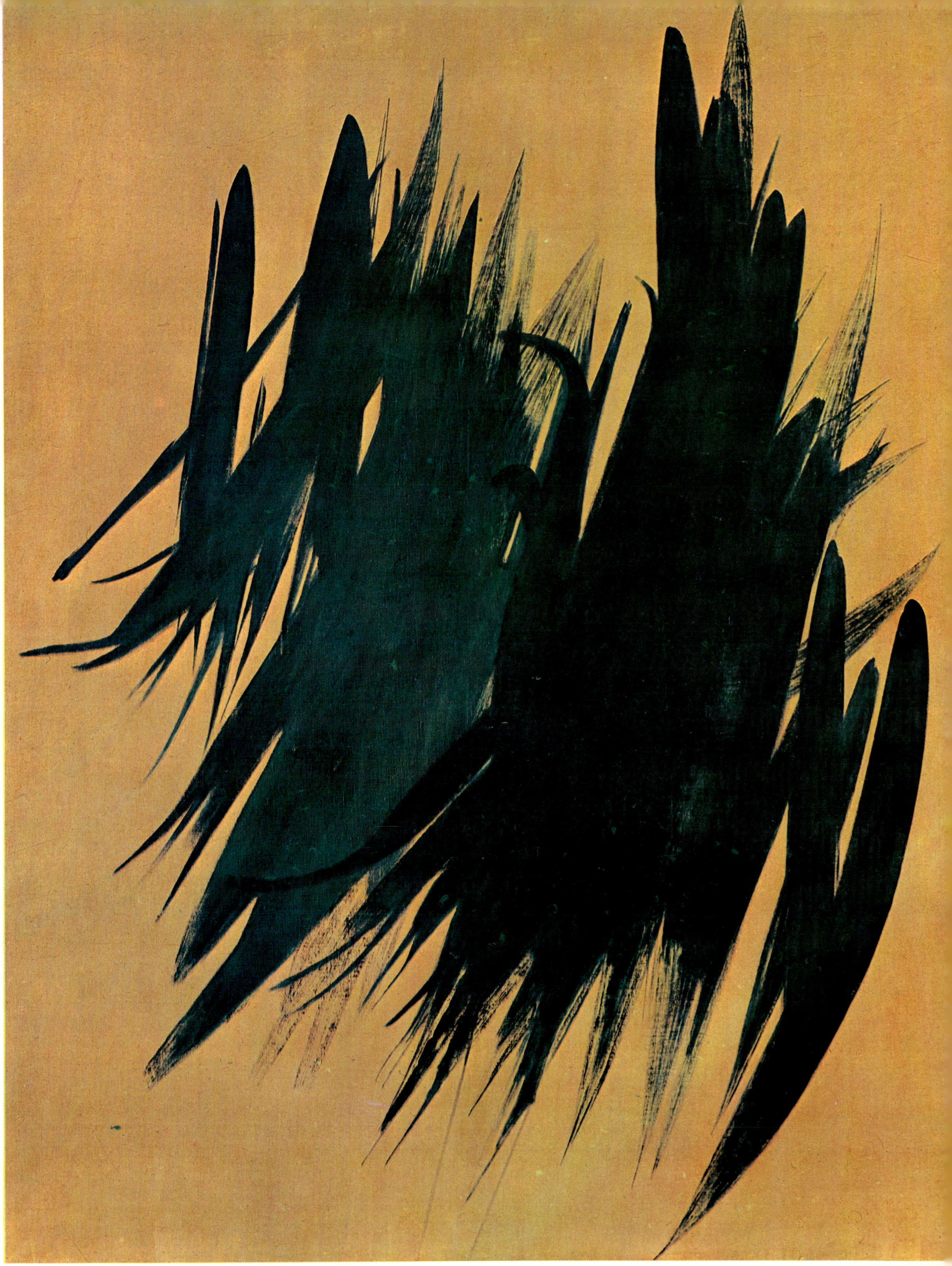

124 T. 1956-19

125 T. 1955-17

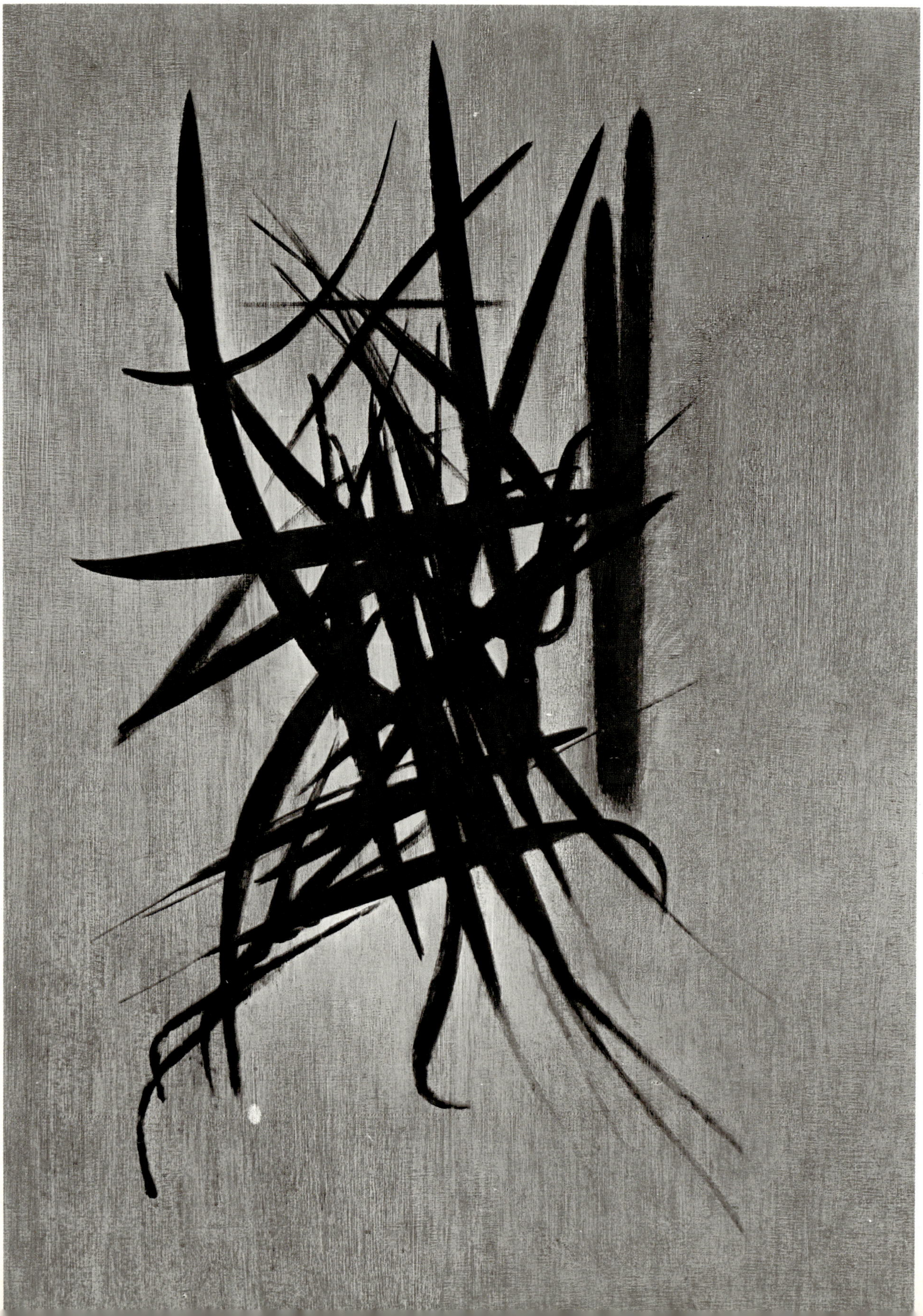

26 T. 1956-20

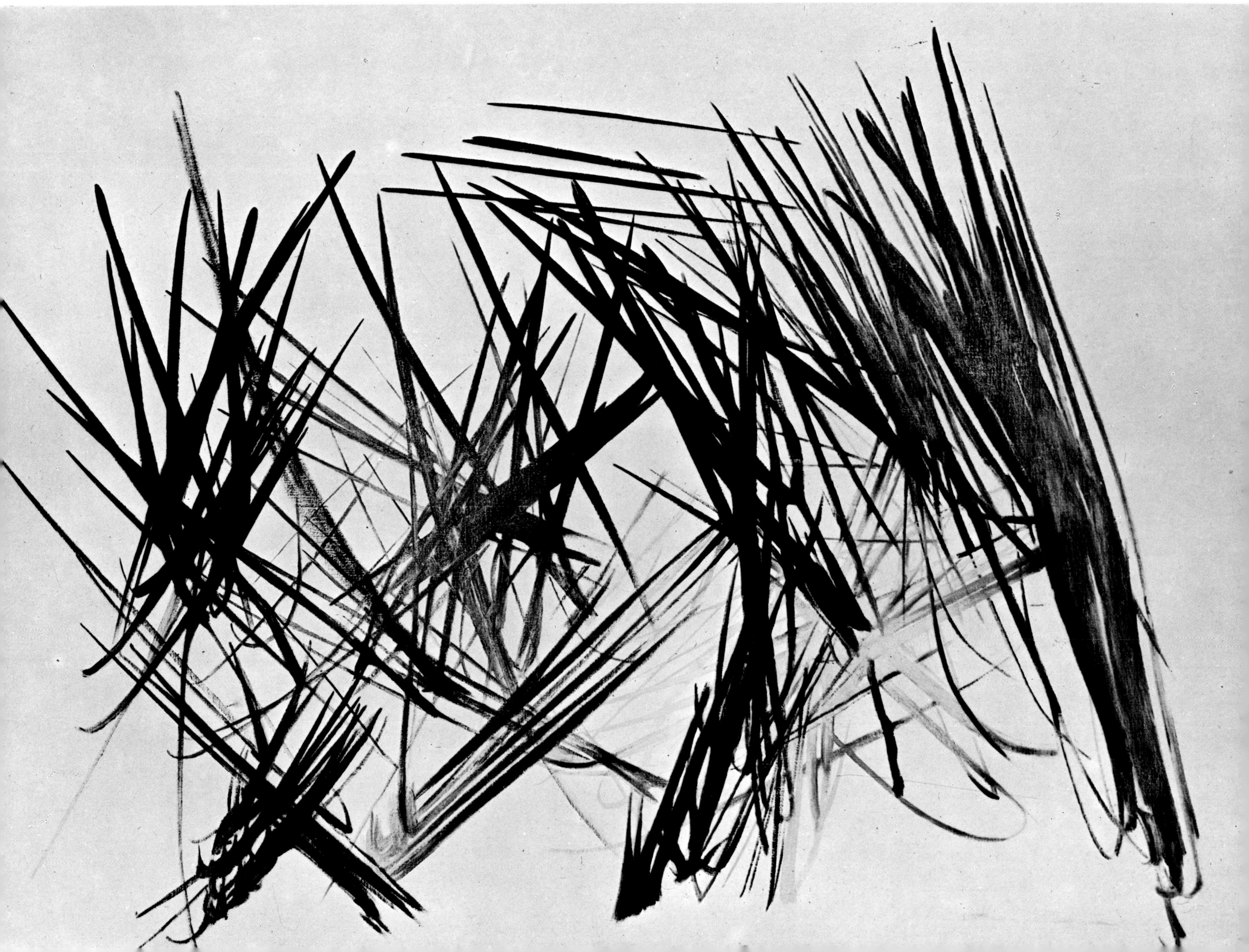

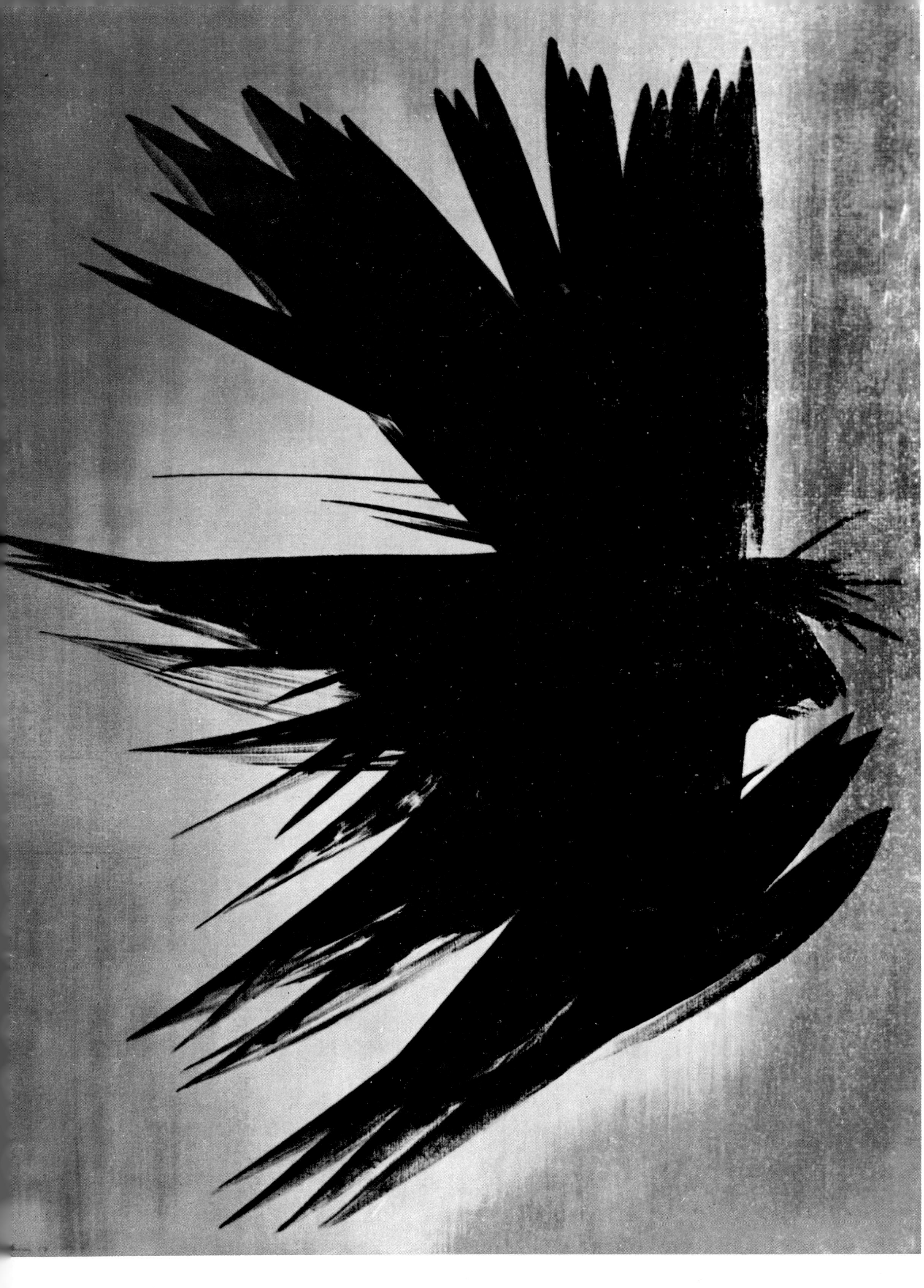

127 T. 1957-12

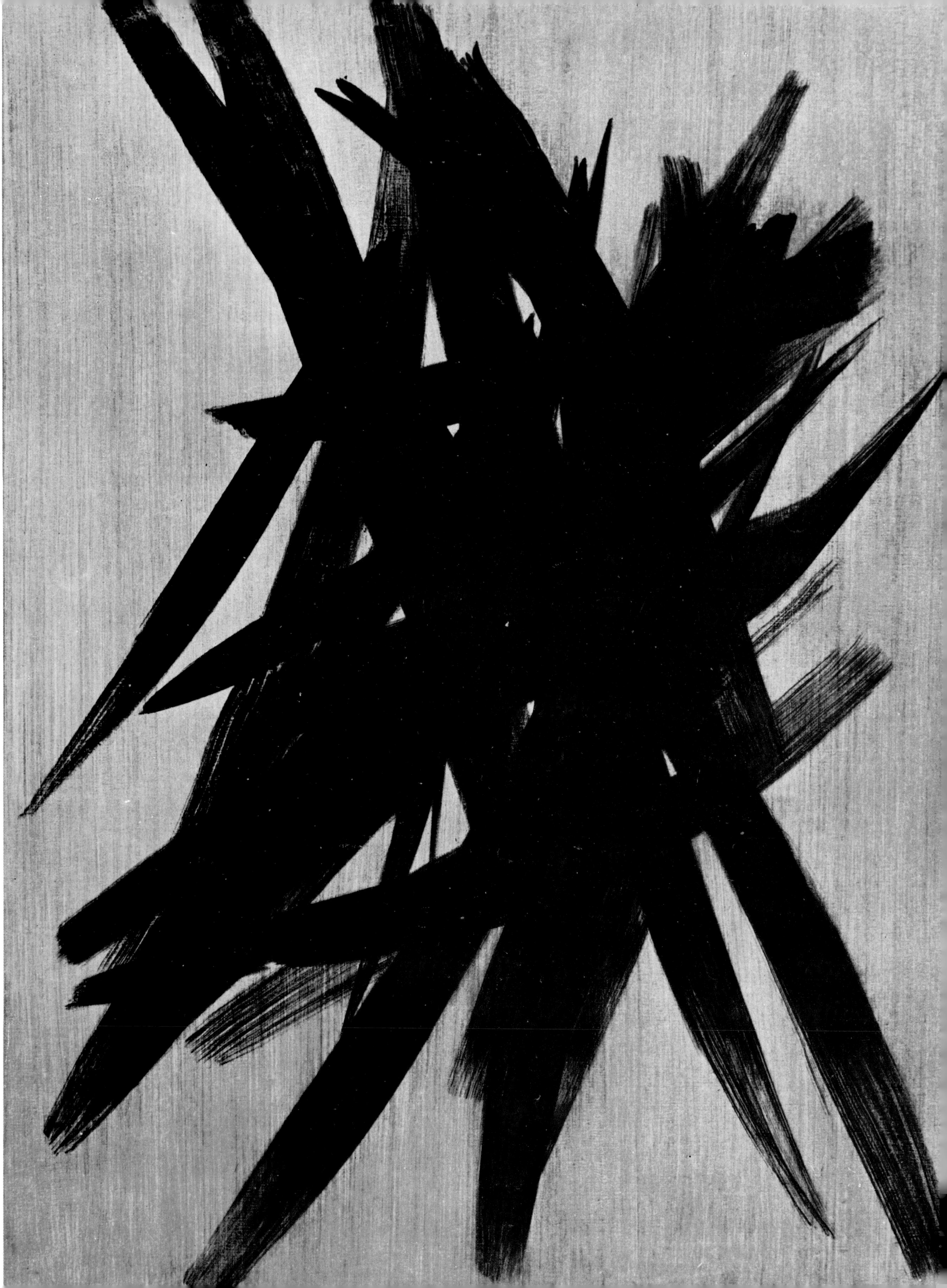

128
1955-23

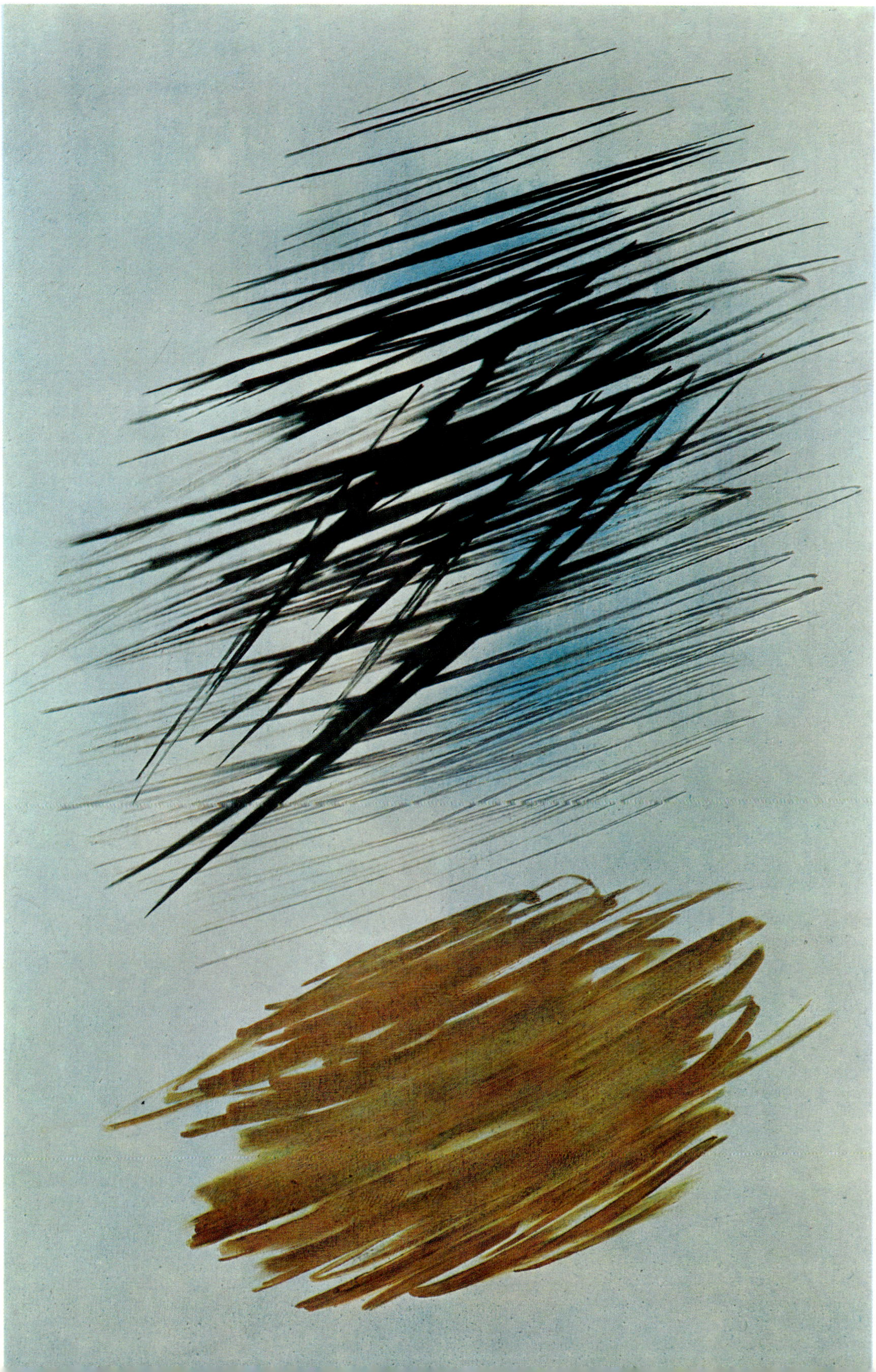

129 T. 1956-21

30 T. 1956-10

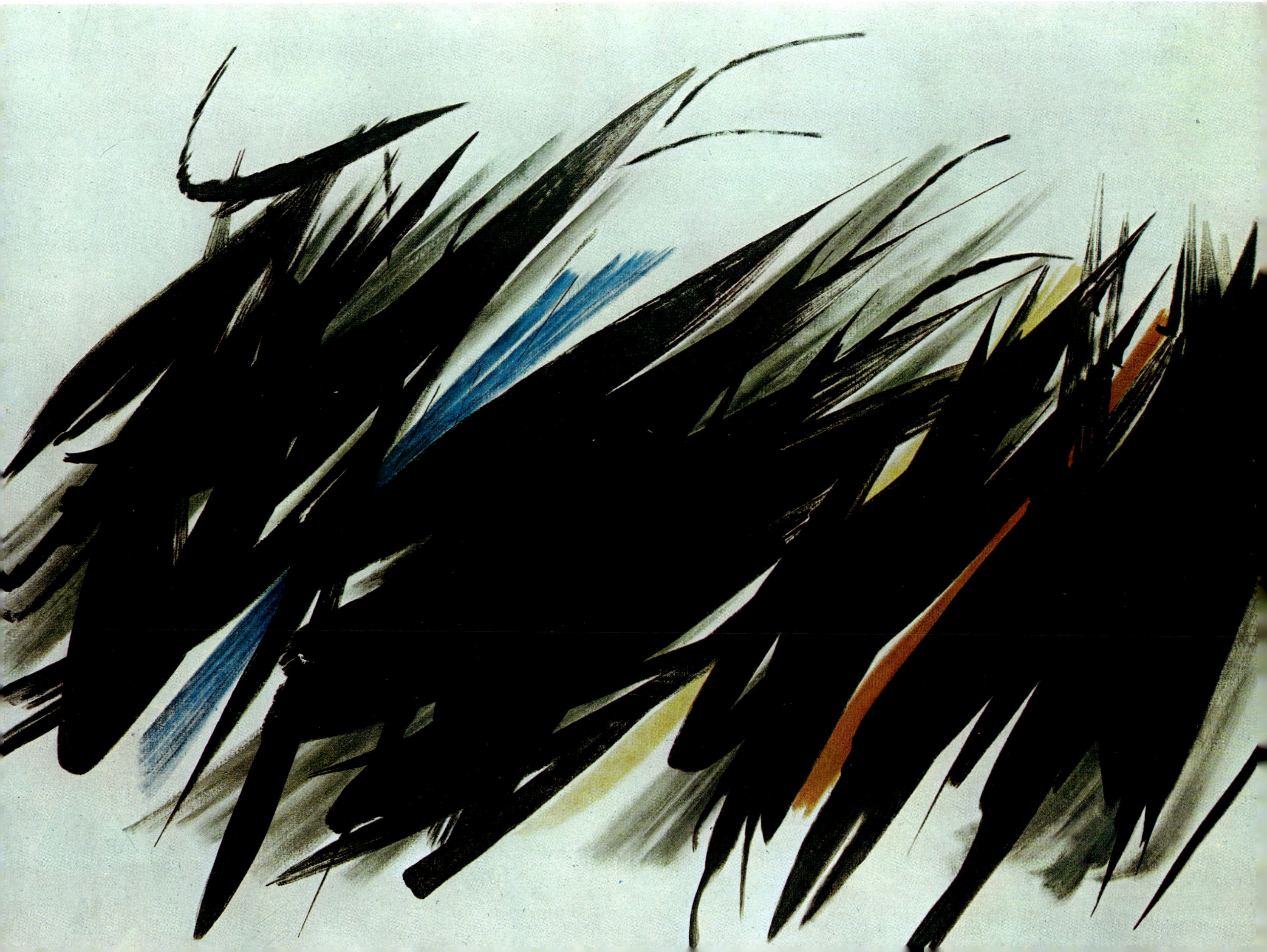

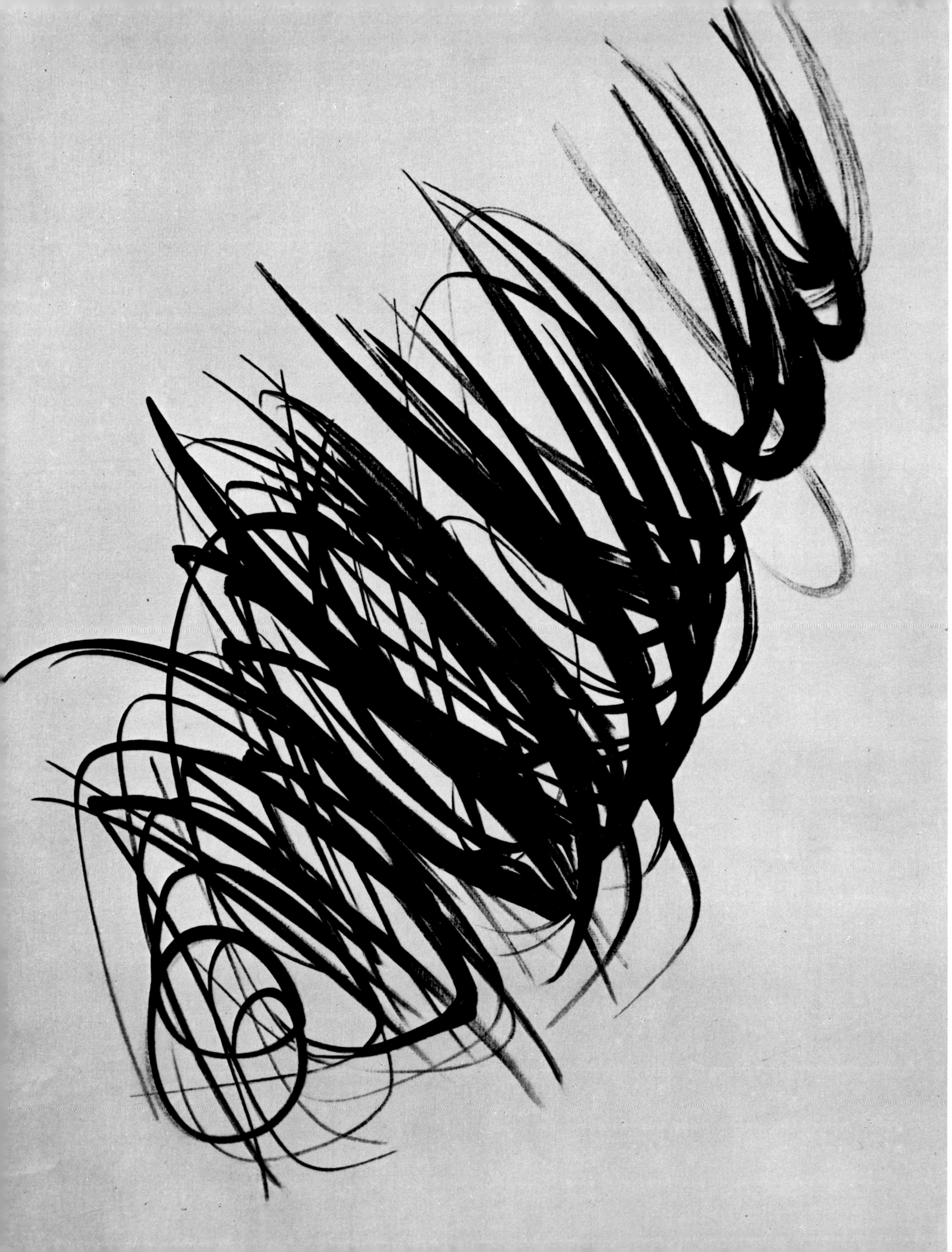

131
T.
195

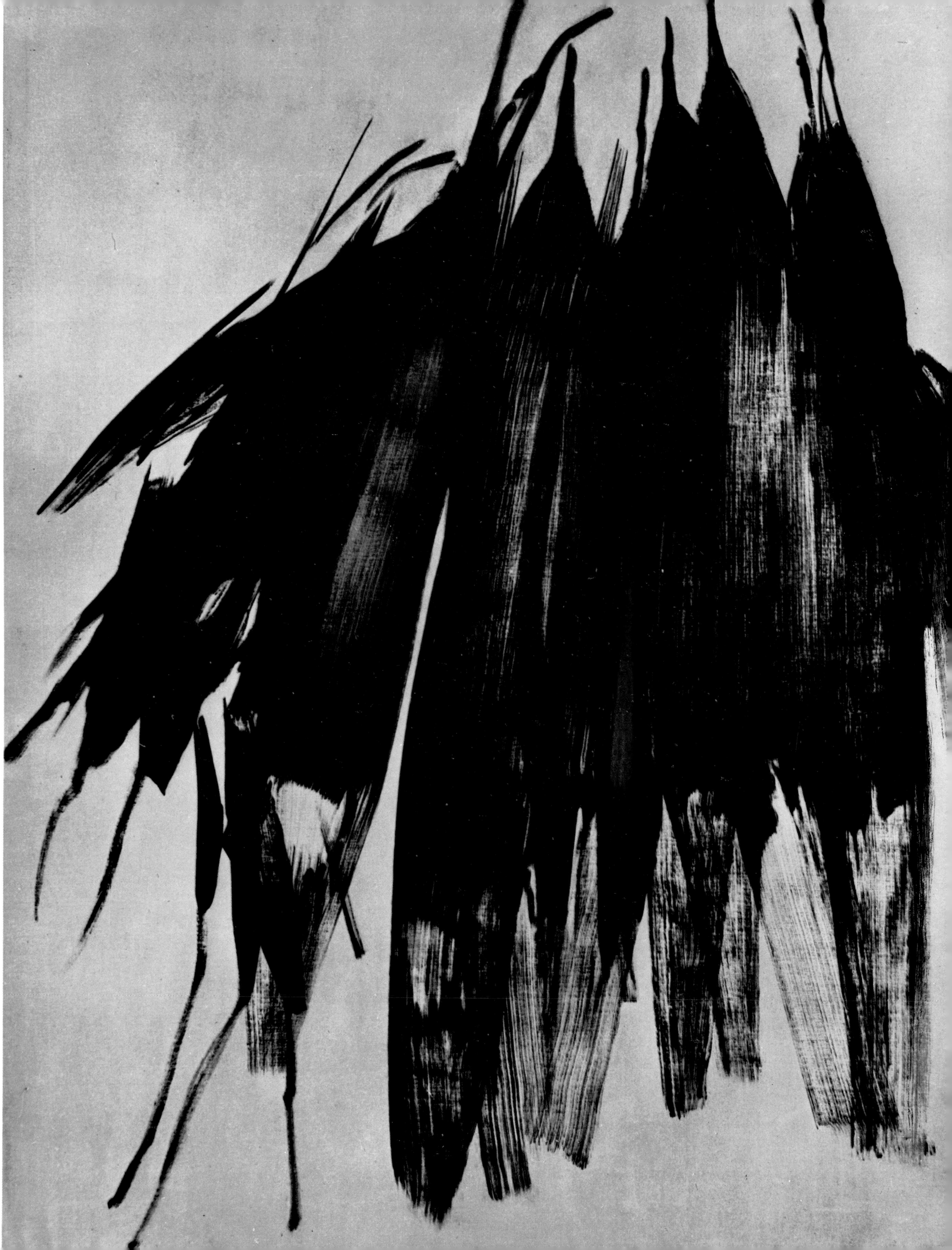

132
T.
-10

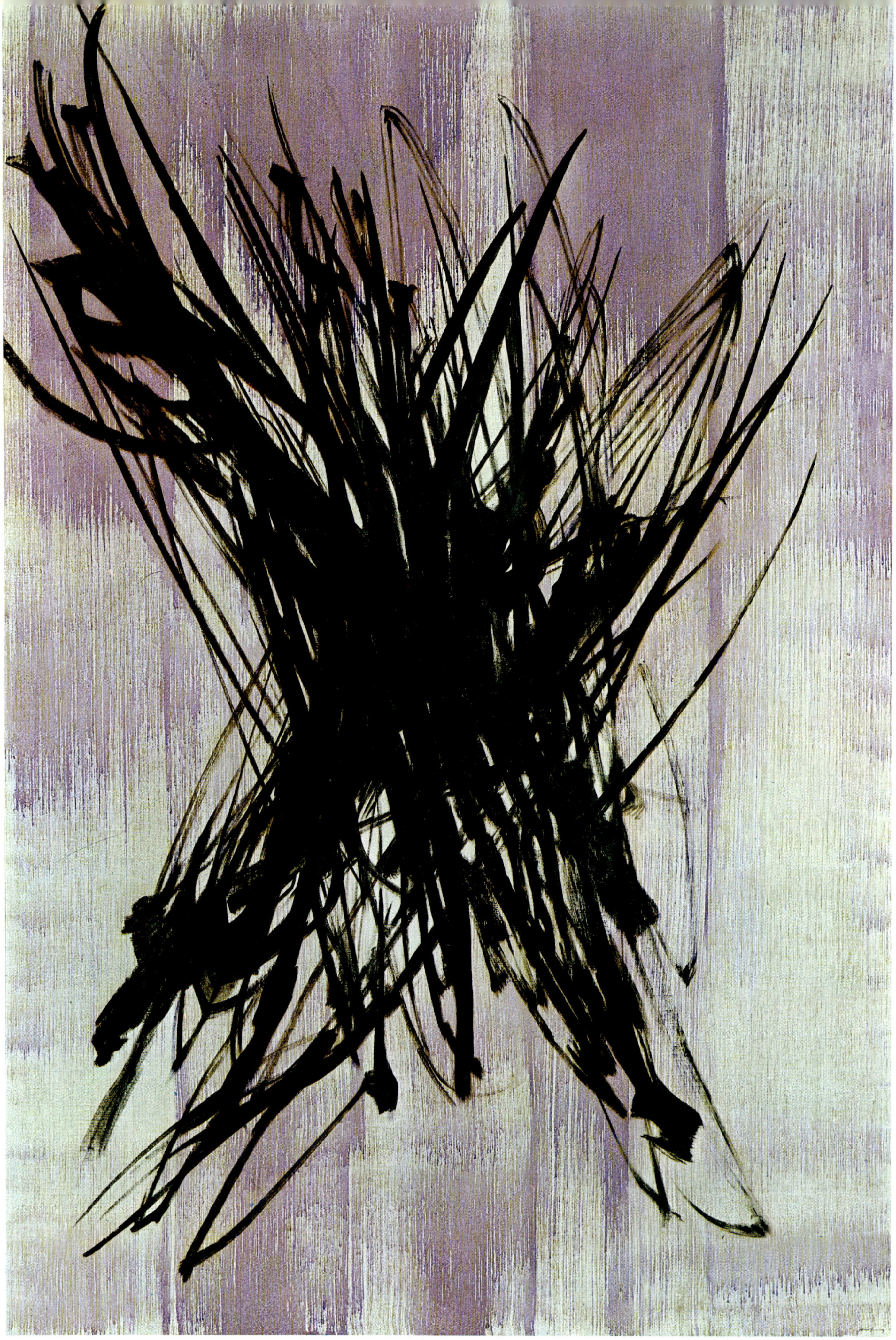

133 T. 1957-1

134 T. 1959-2

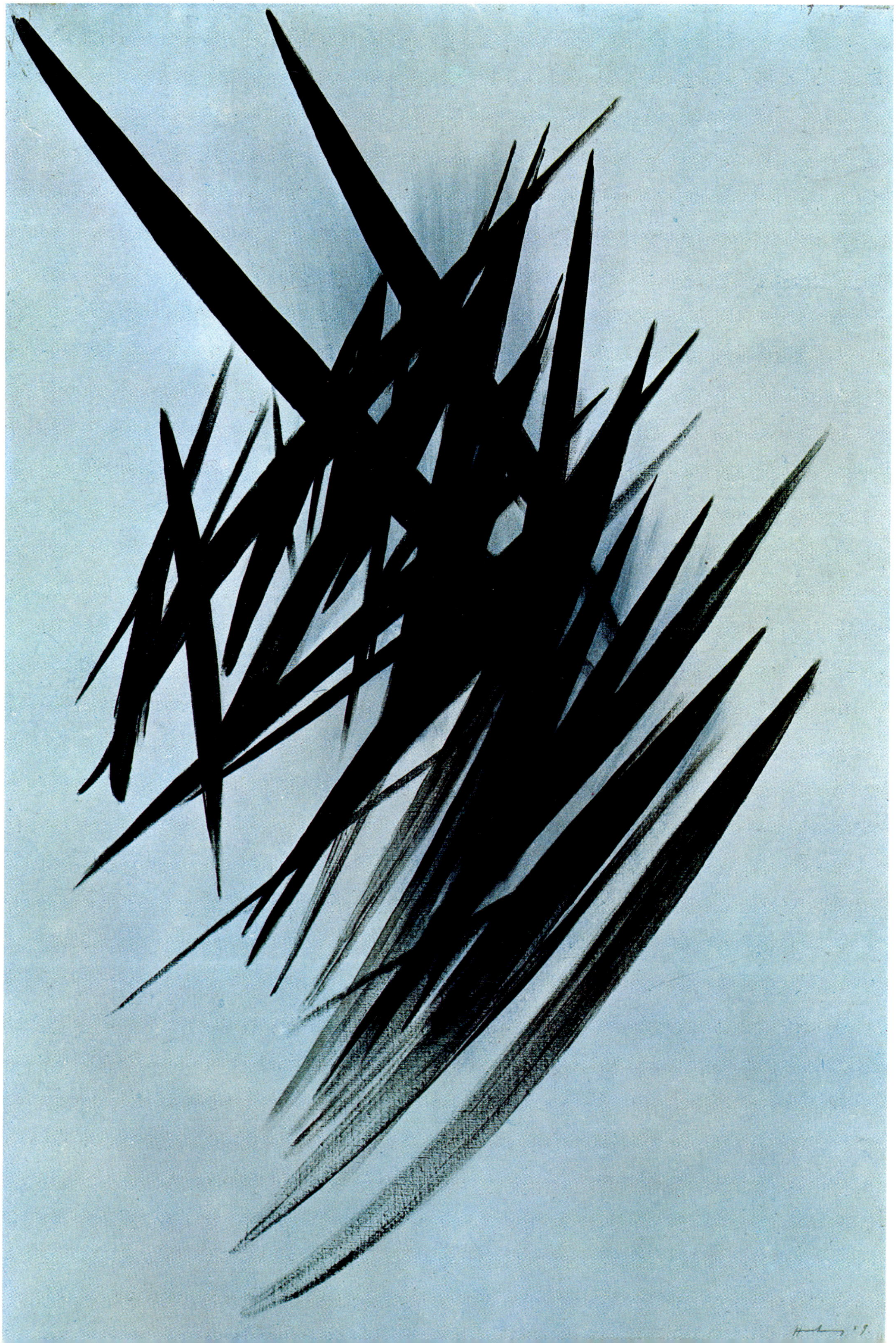

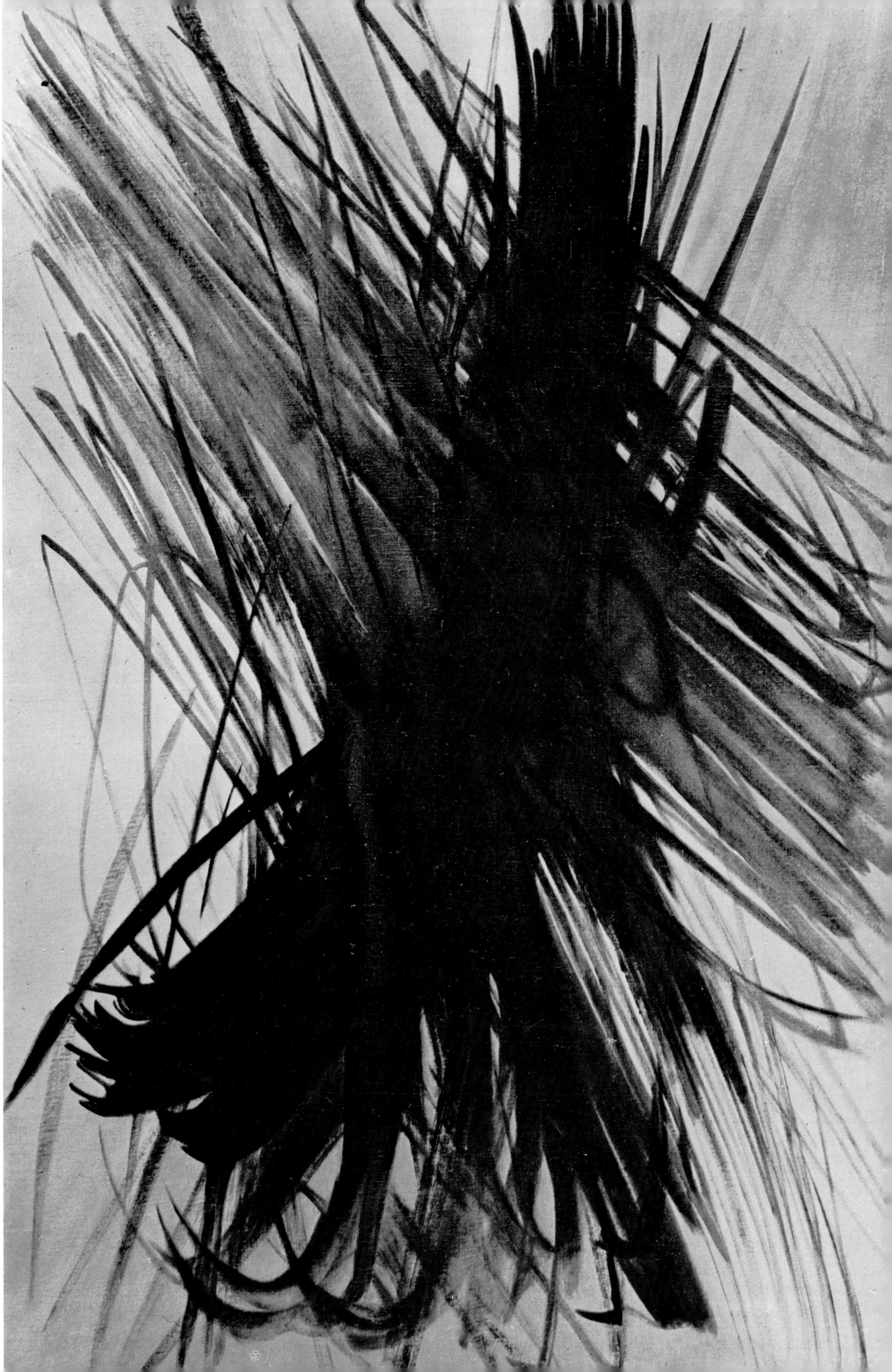

135 T. 1956-18

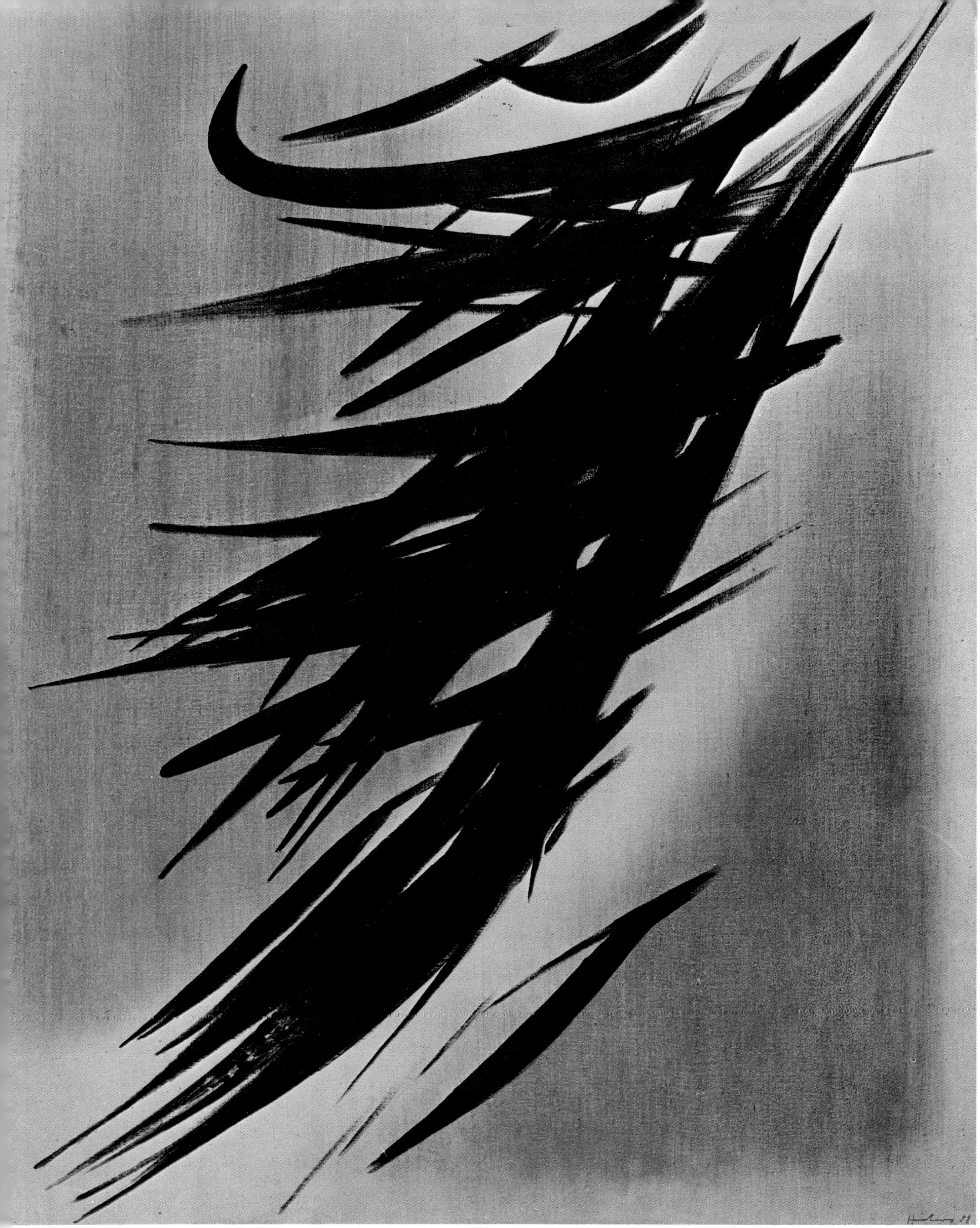

136 T. 1958-3

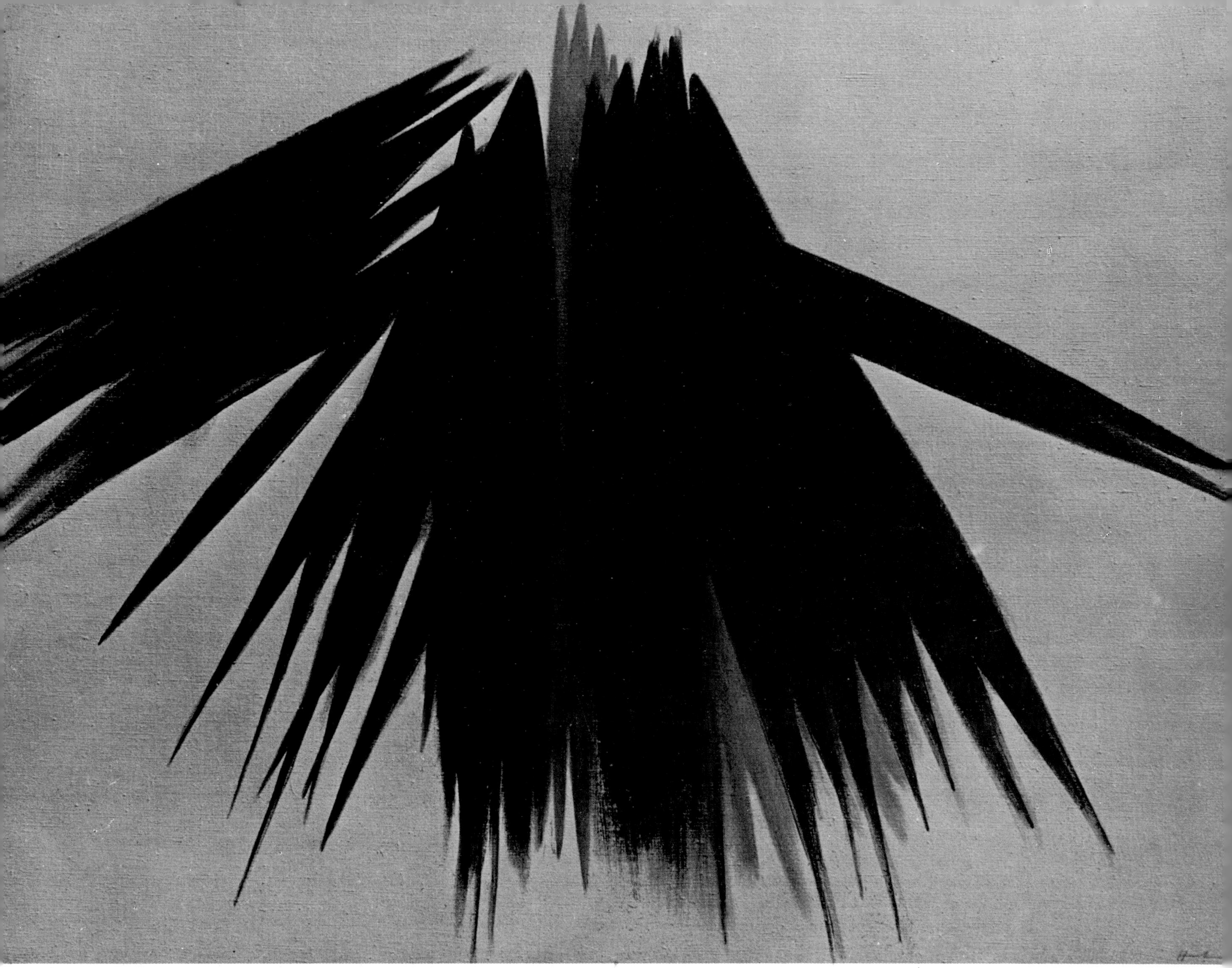

37 T. 1958-15

138 T. 1958-1

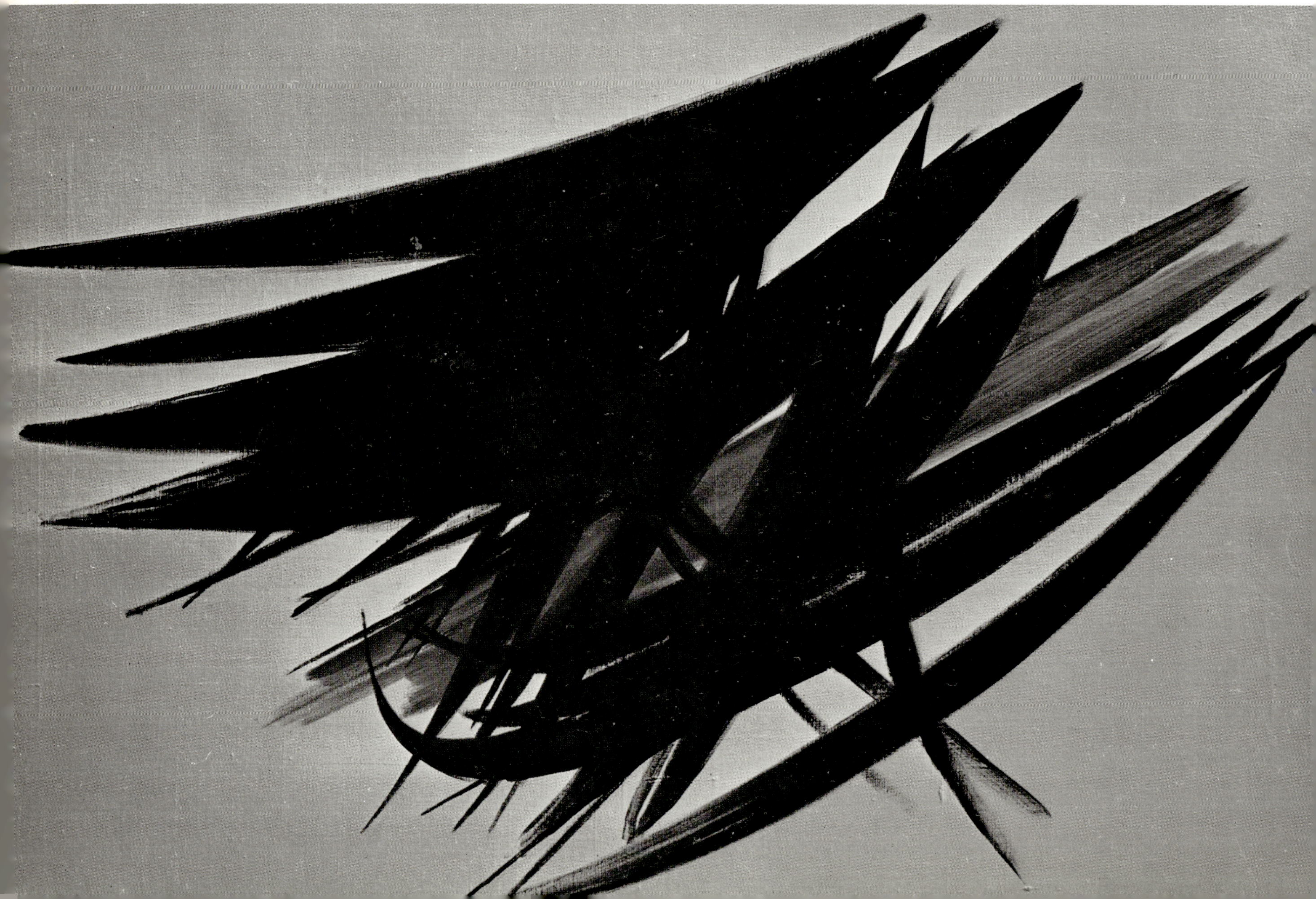

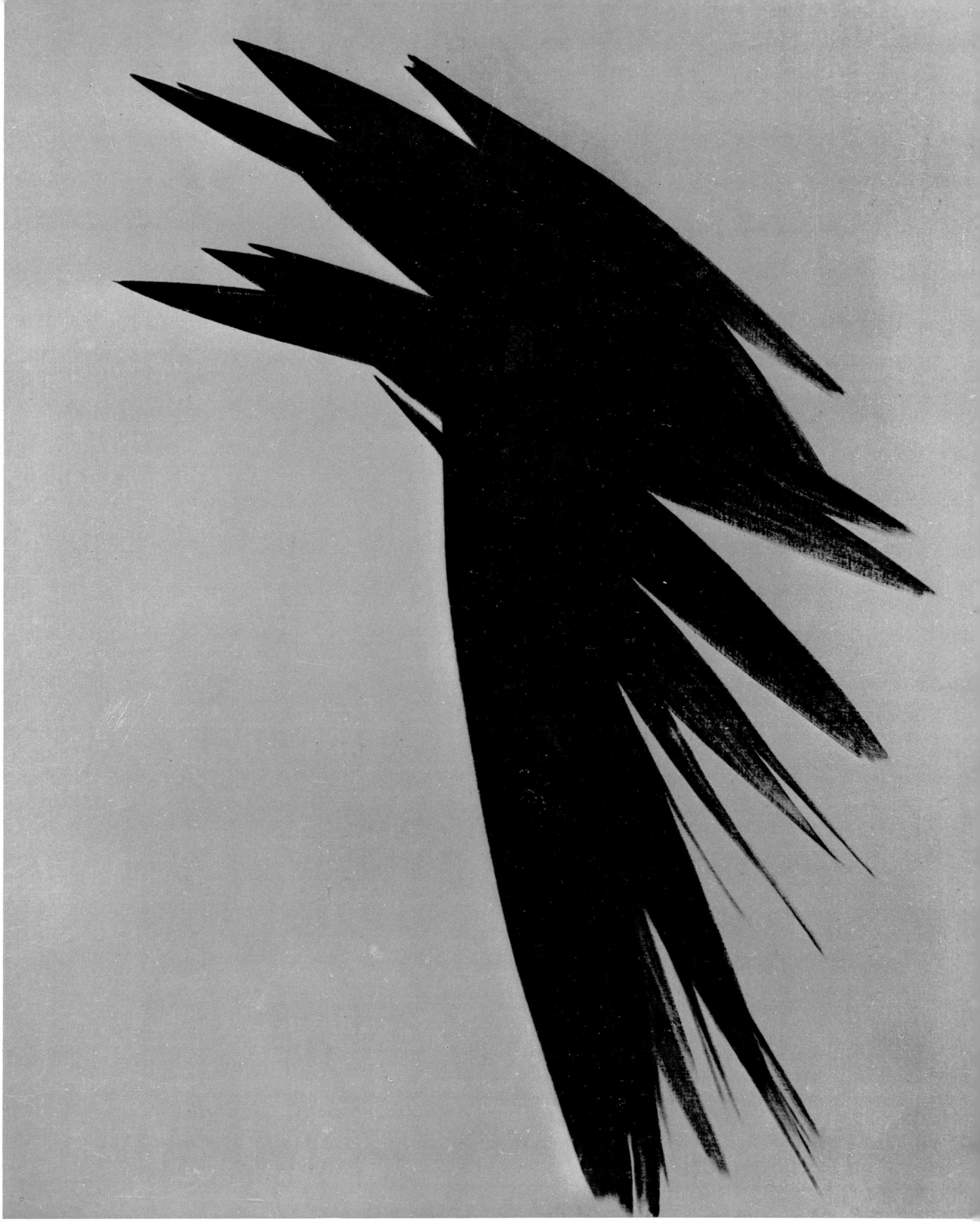

139 T. 1957-8

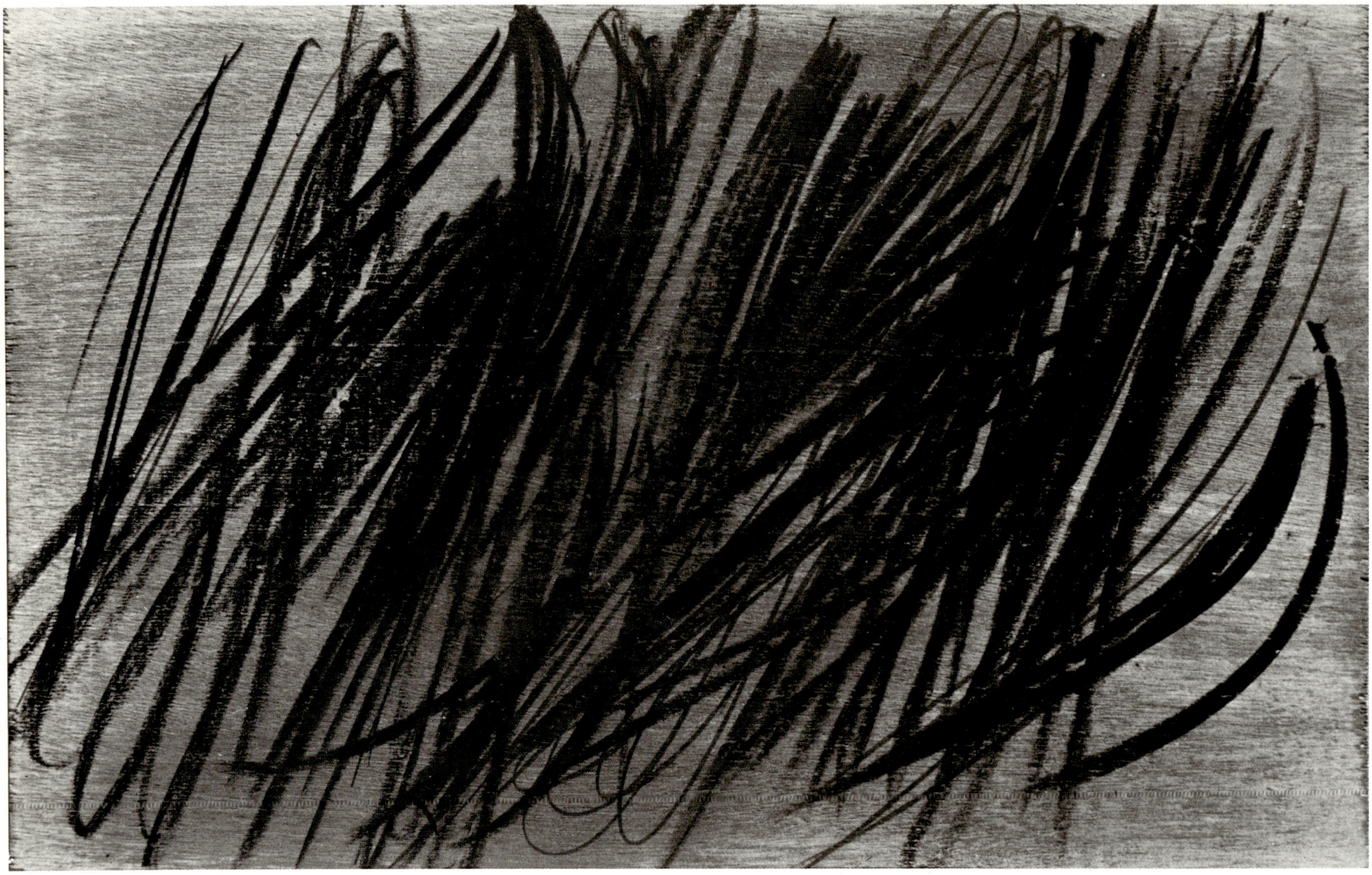

140 T. 1960-20

1960-1966

141 T. 1961-H4

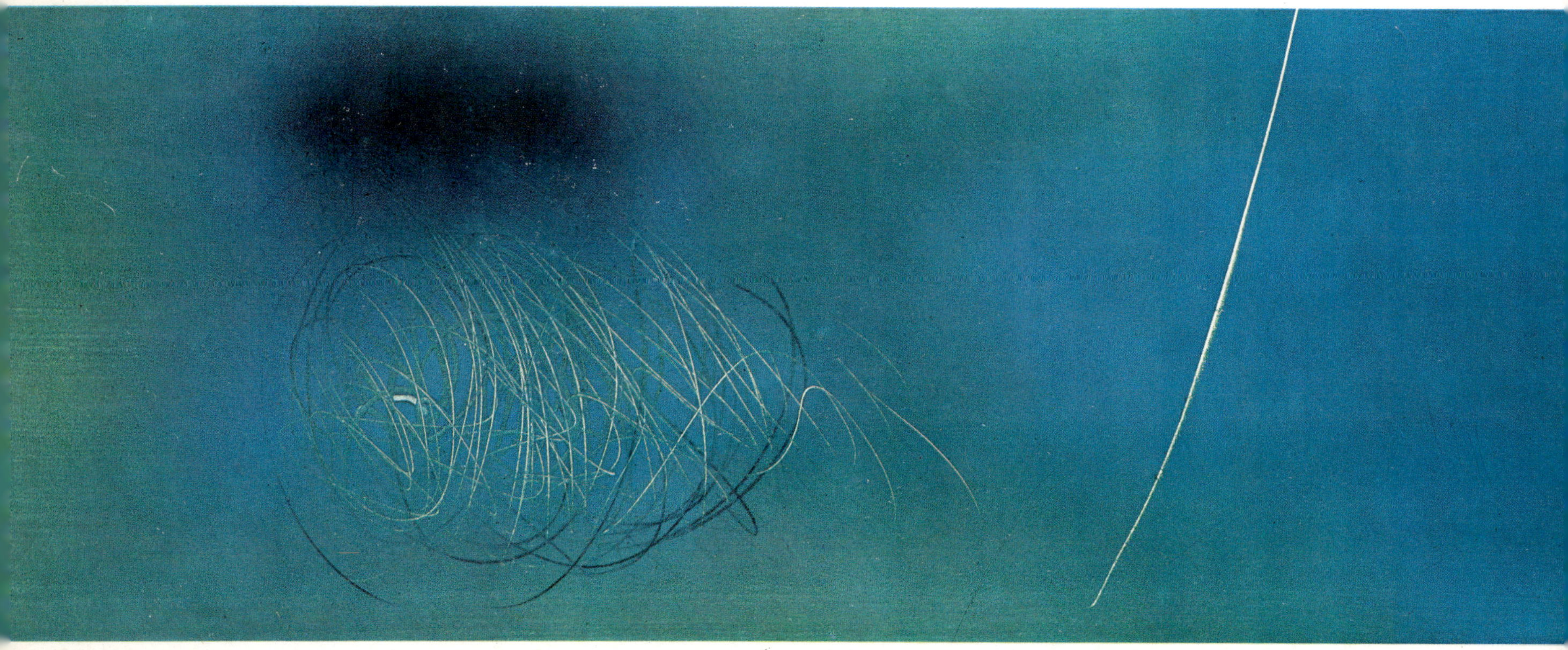

42 T. 1961-66

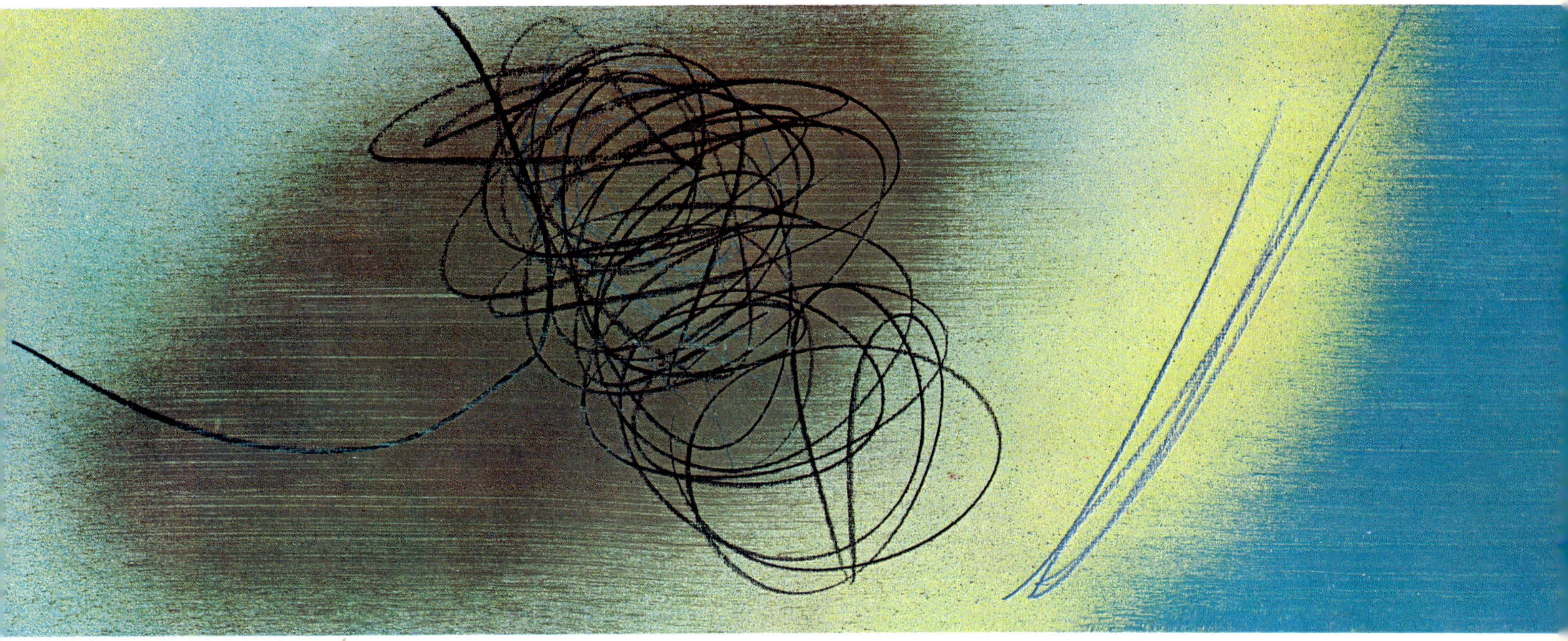

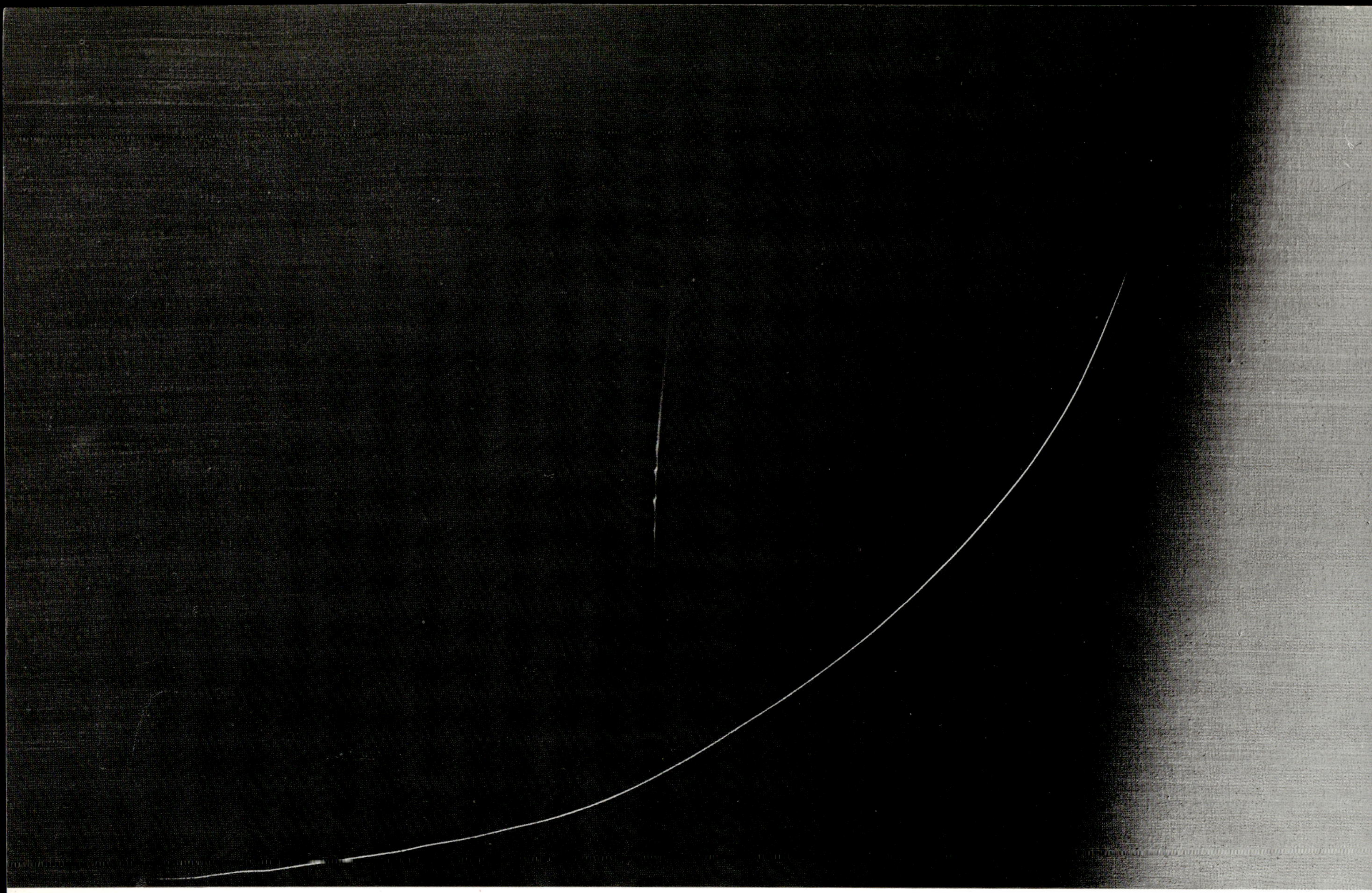

143 T. 1962-H9

44 T. 1961-H48

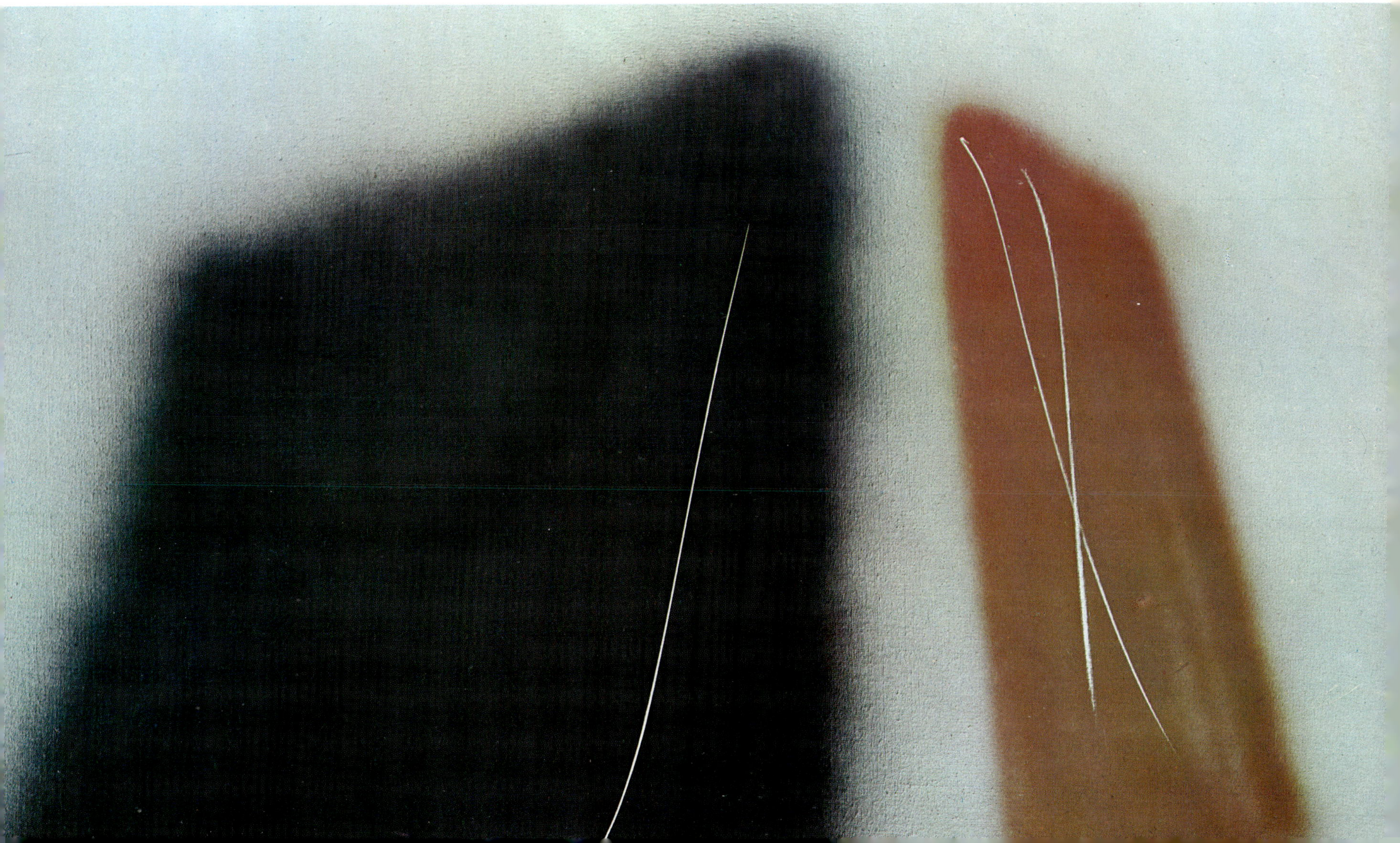

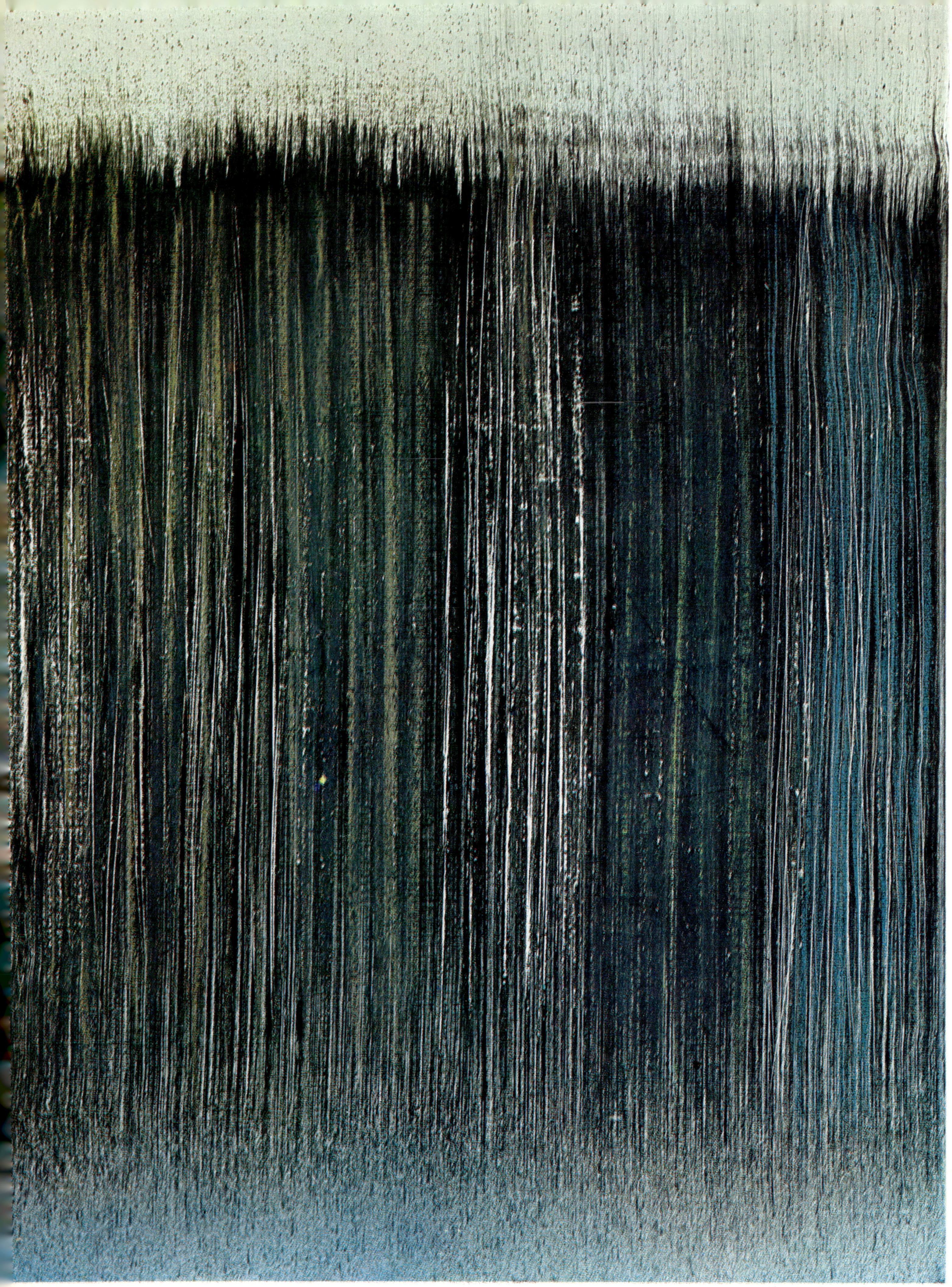

145 T. 1961-H23

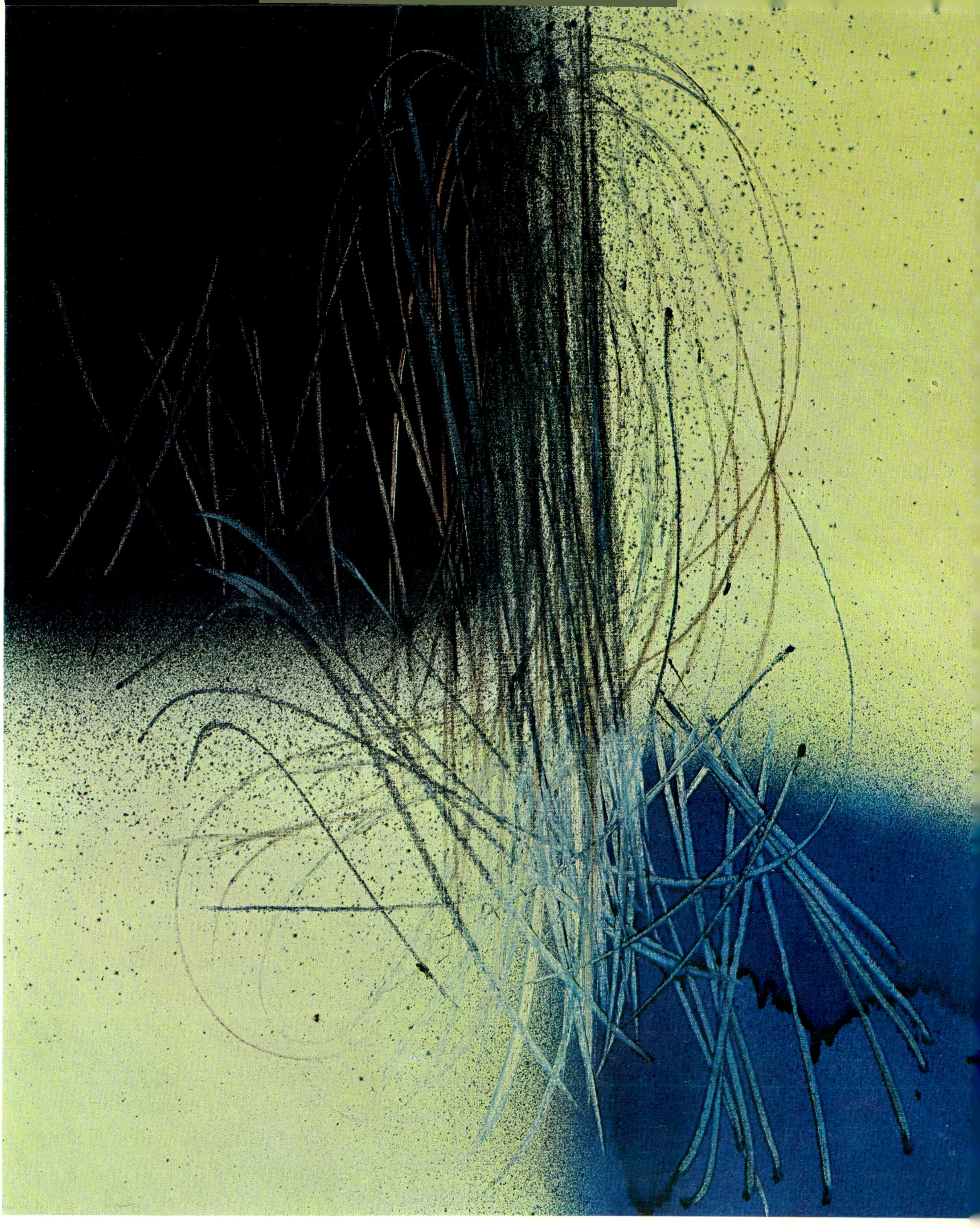

146 T. 1962-R33

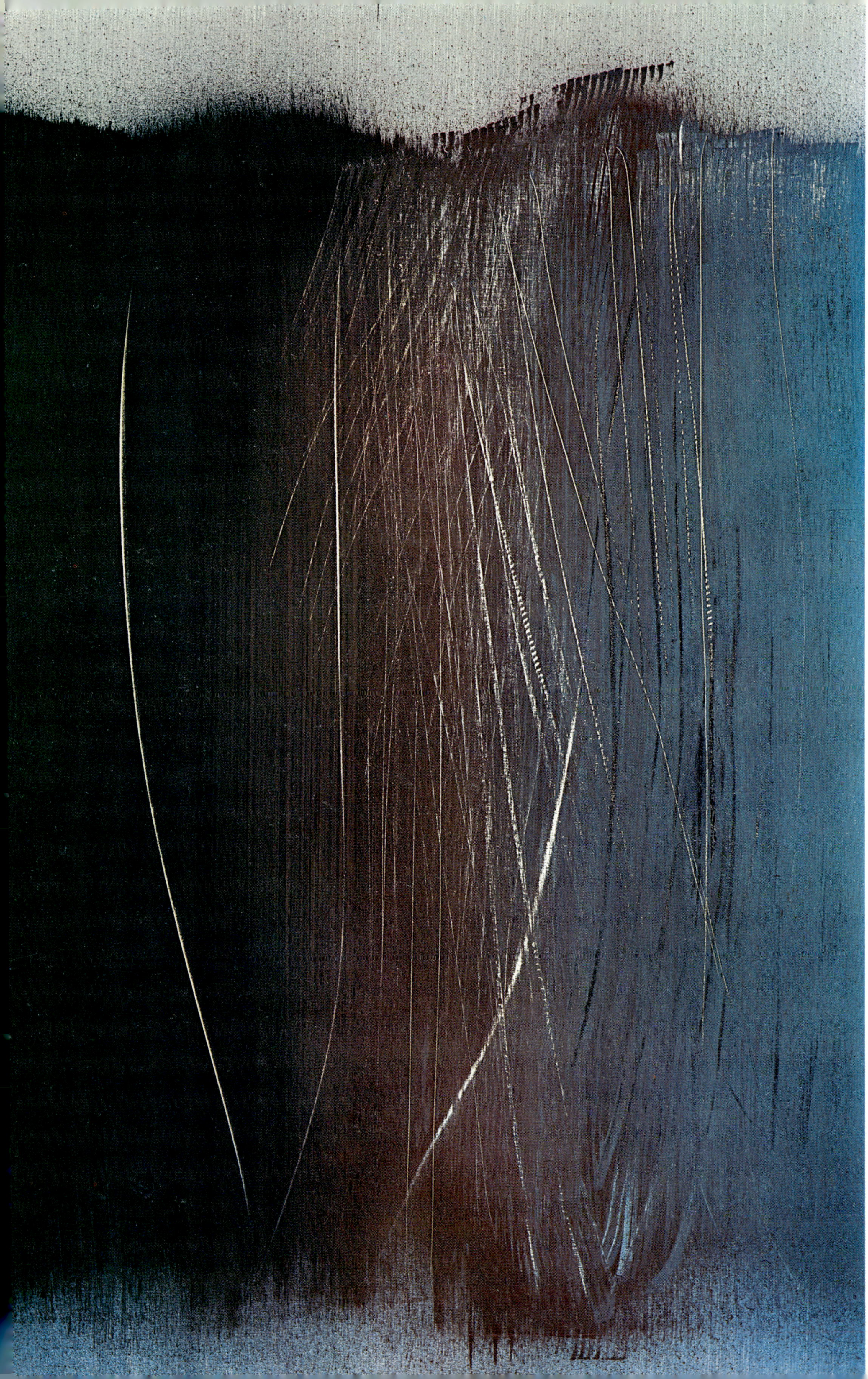

147 T. 1962-R12

148 T. 1962-F

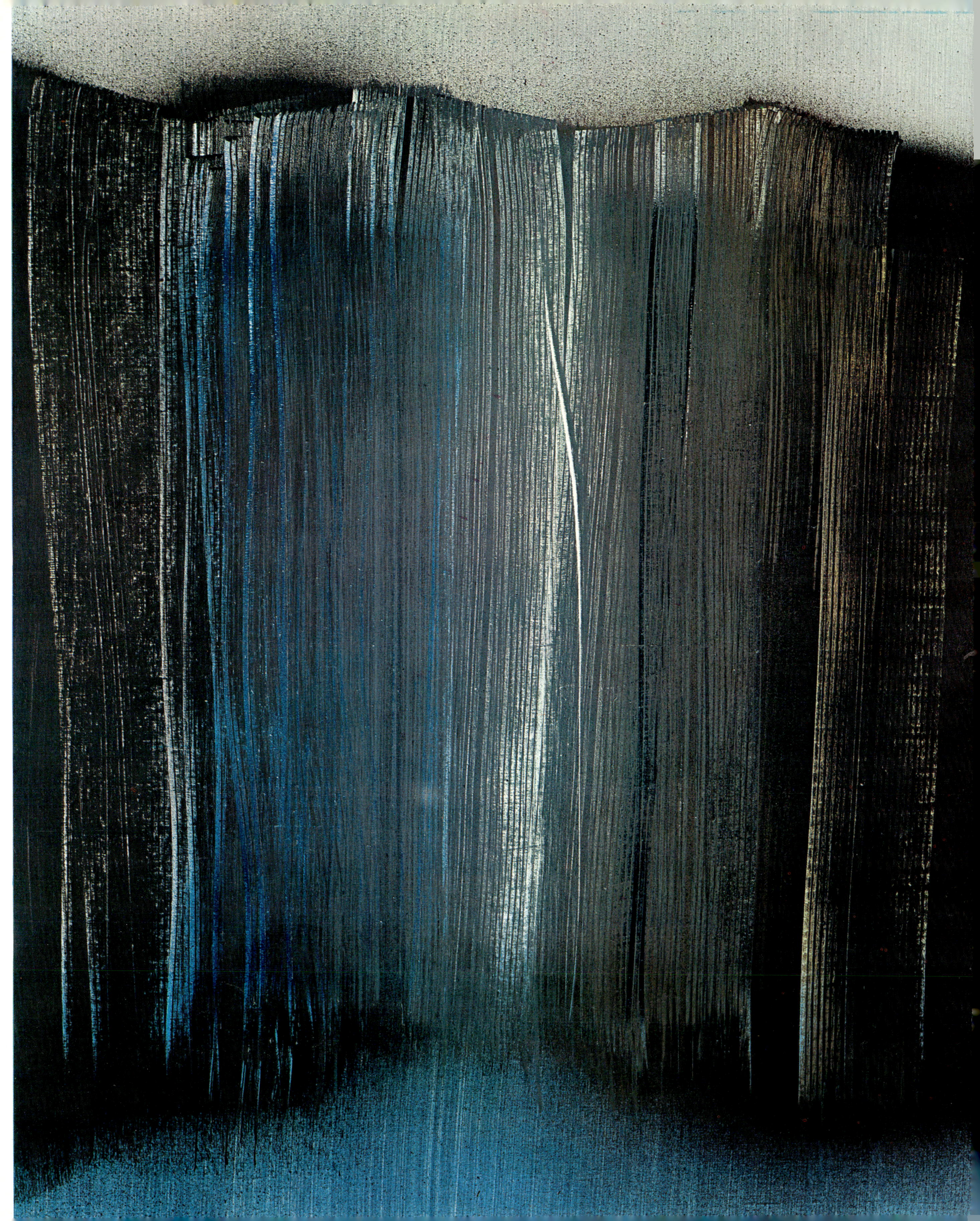

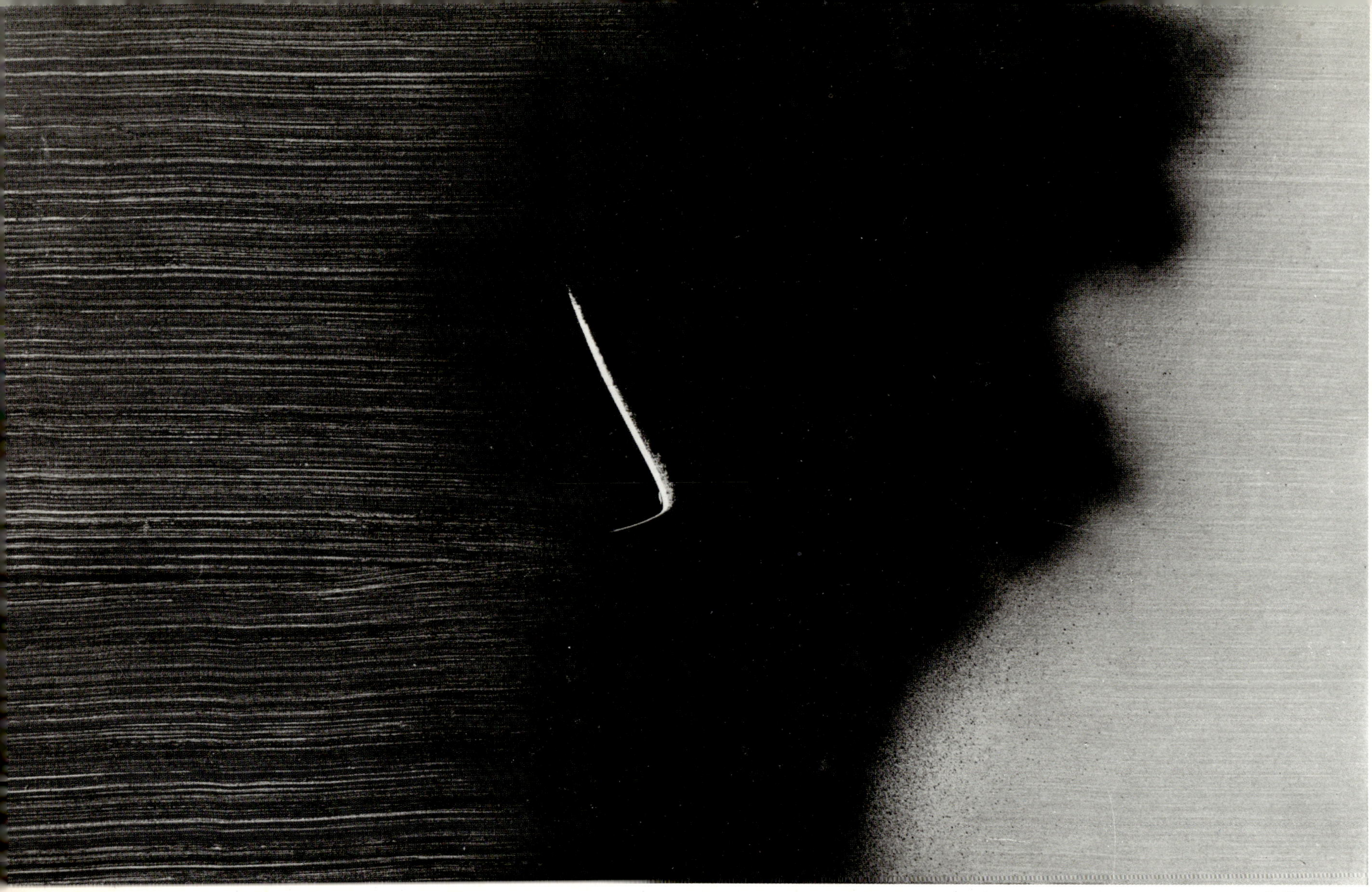

149 T. 1962-E1

150 T. 1962-E8

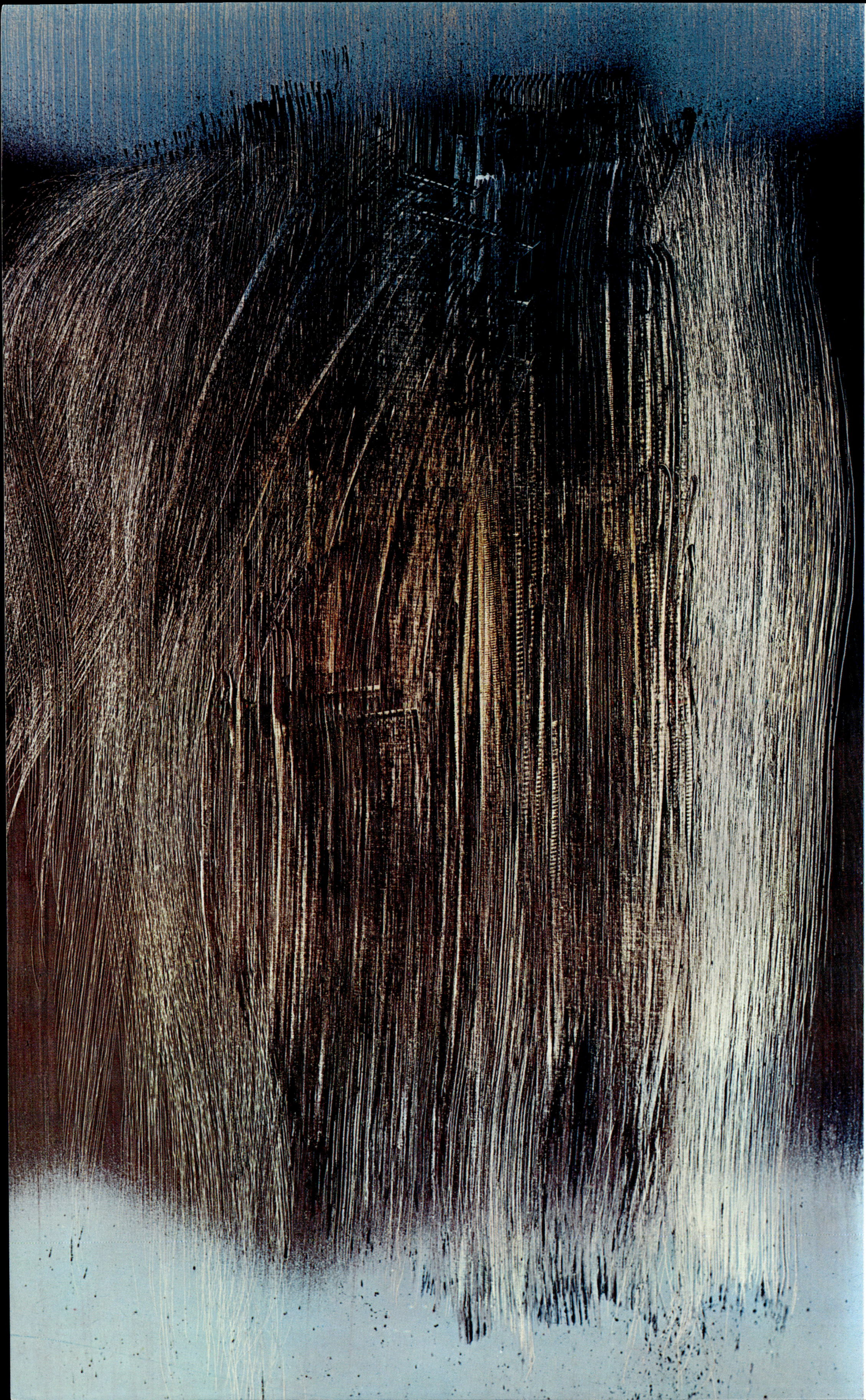

151 T. 1962-U4

152 T. 1963-H

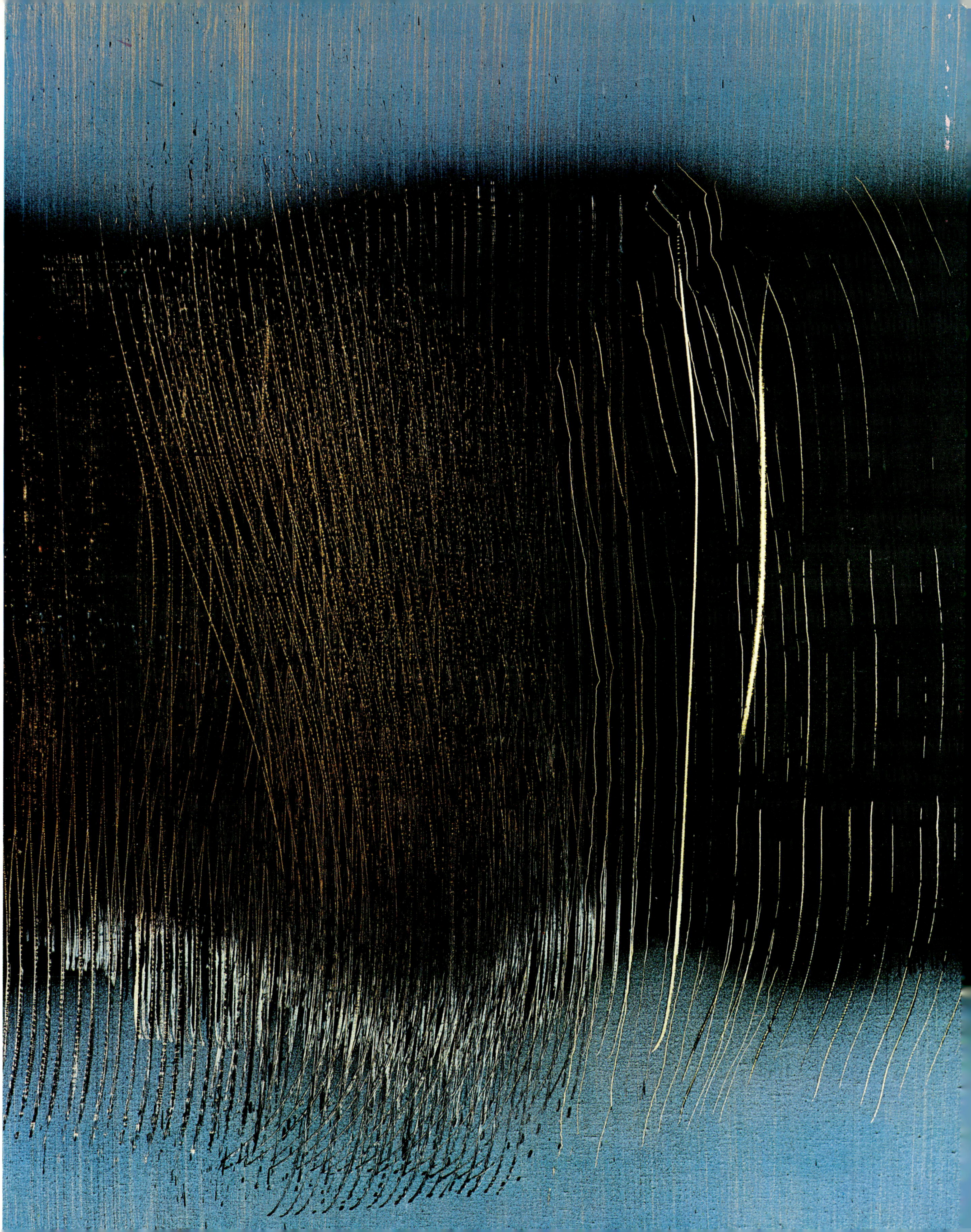

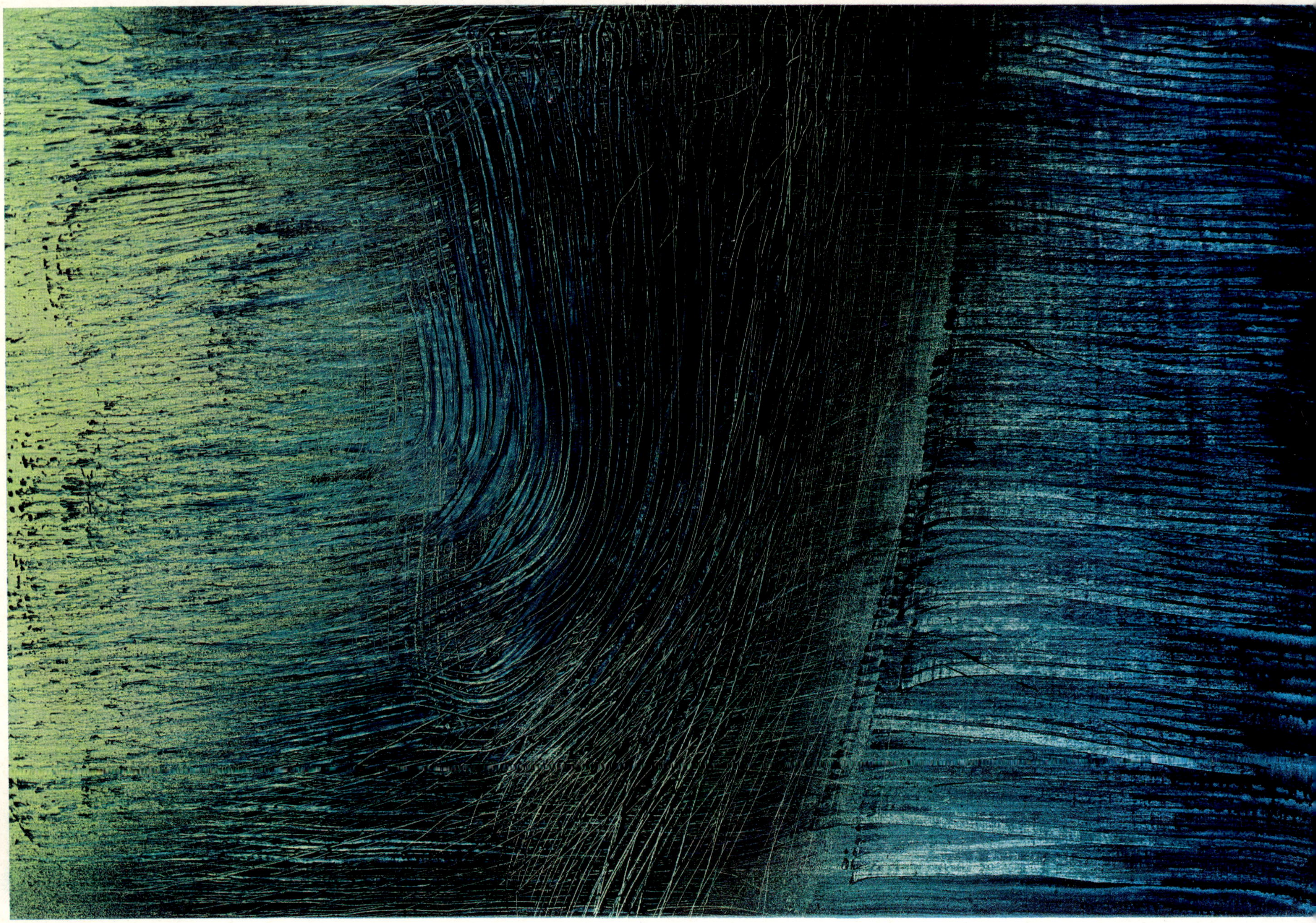

153 T. 1962-U5

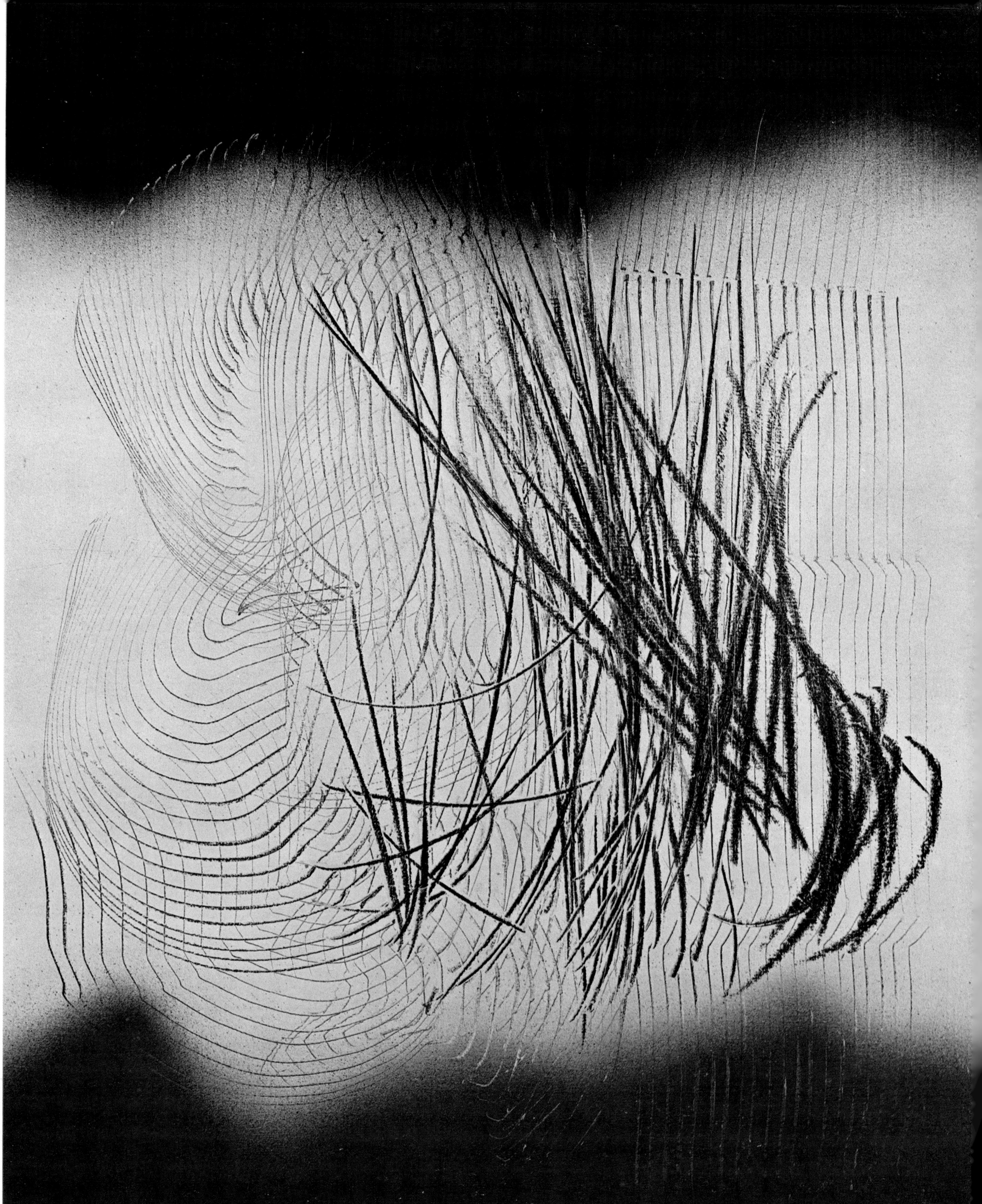

6
3
8

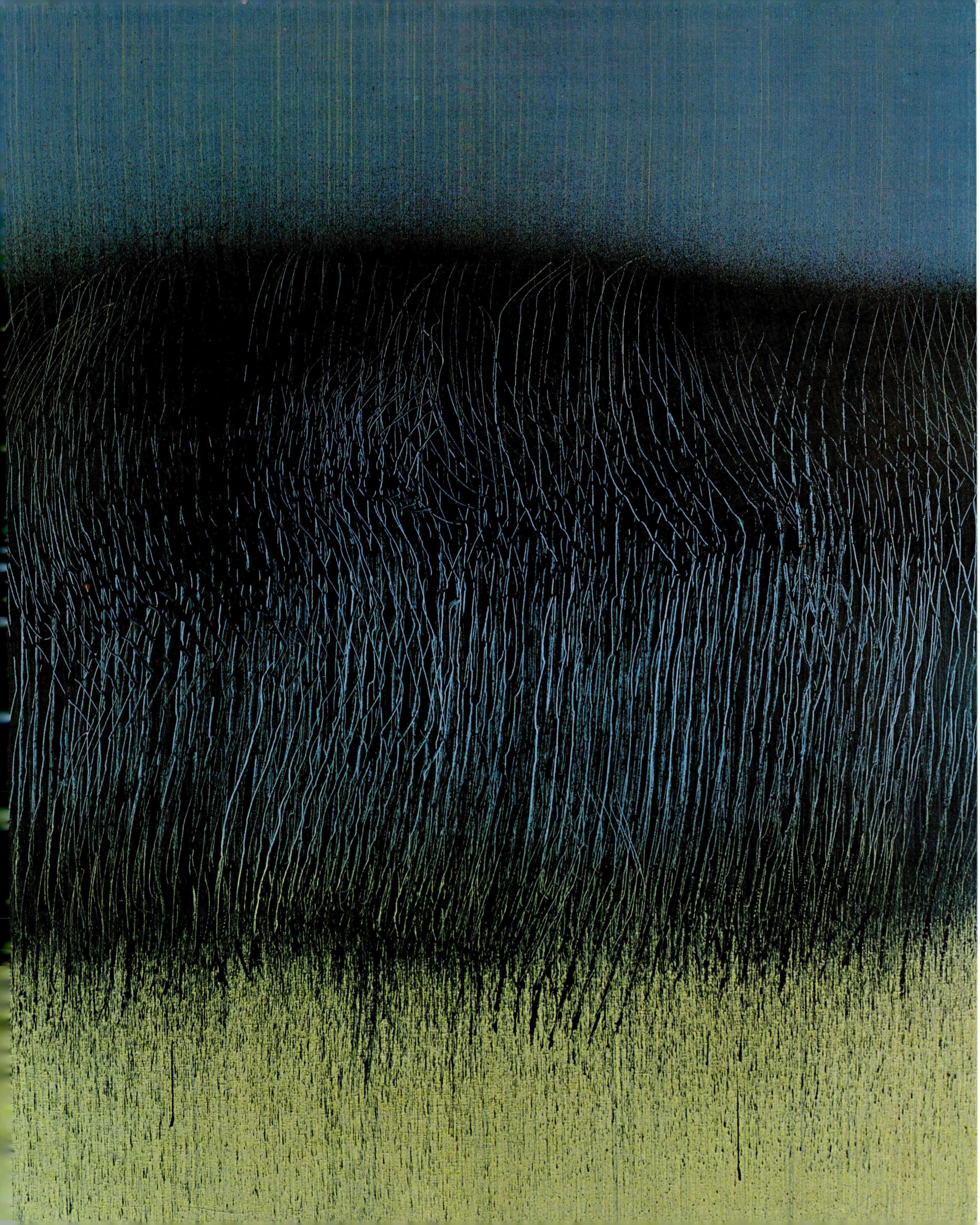

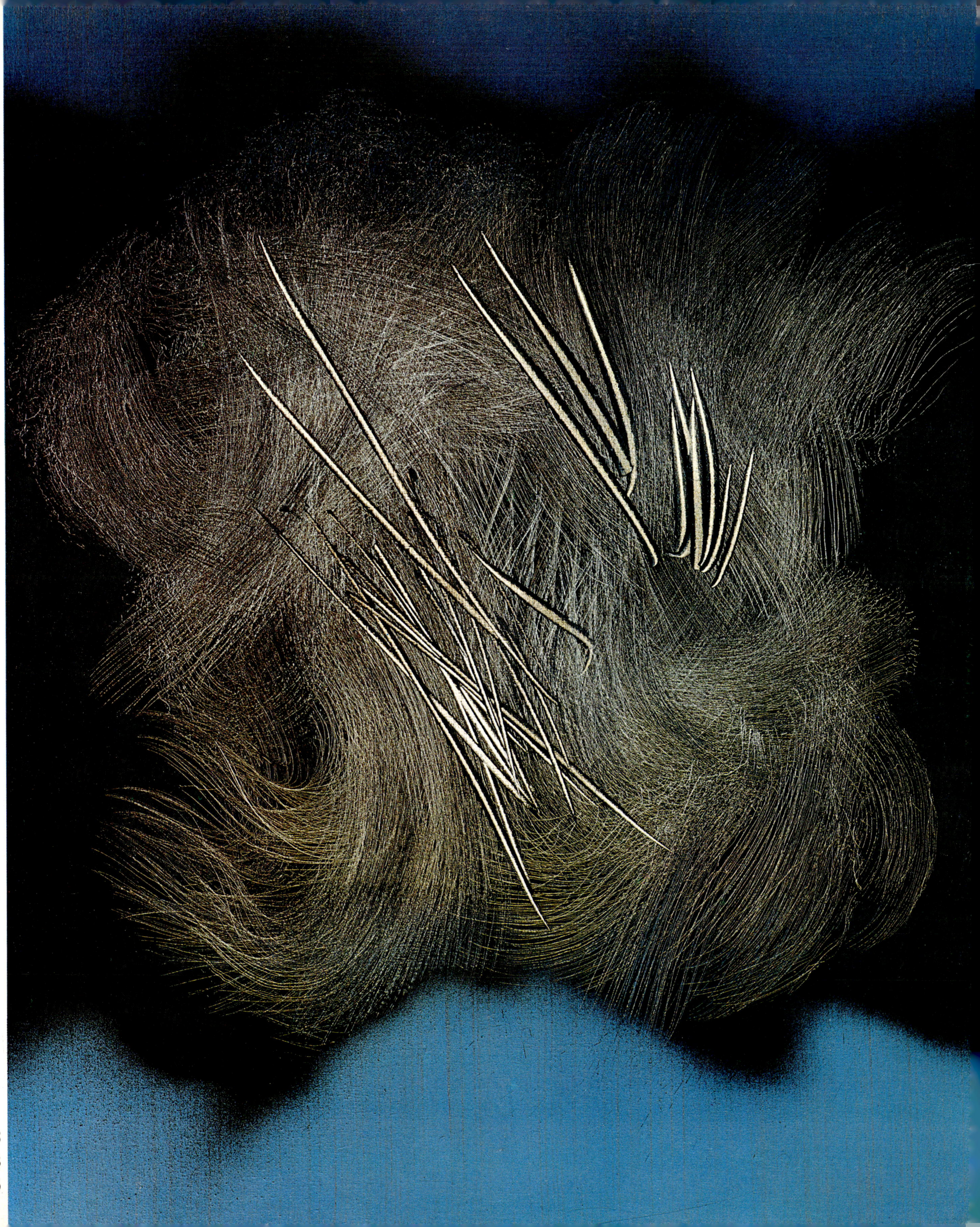

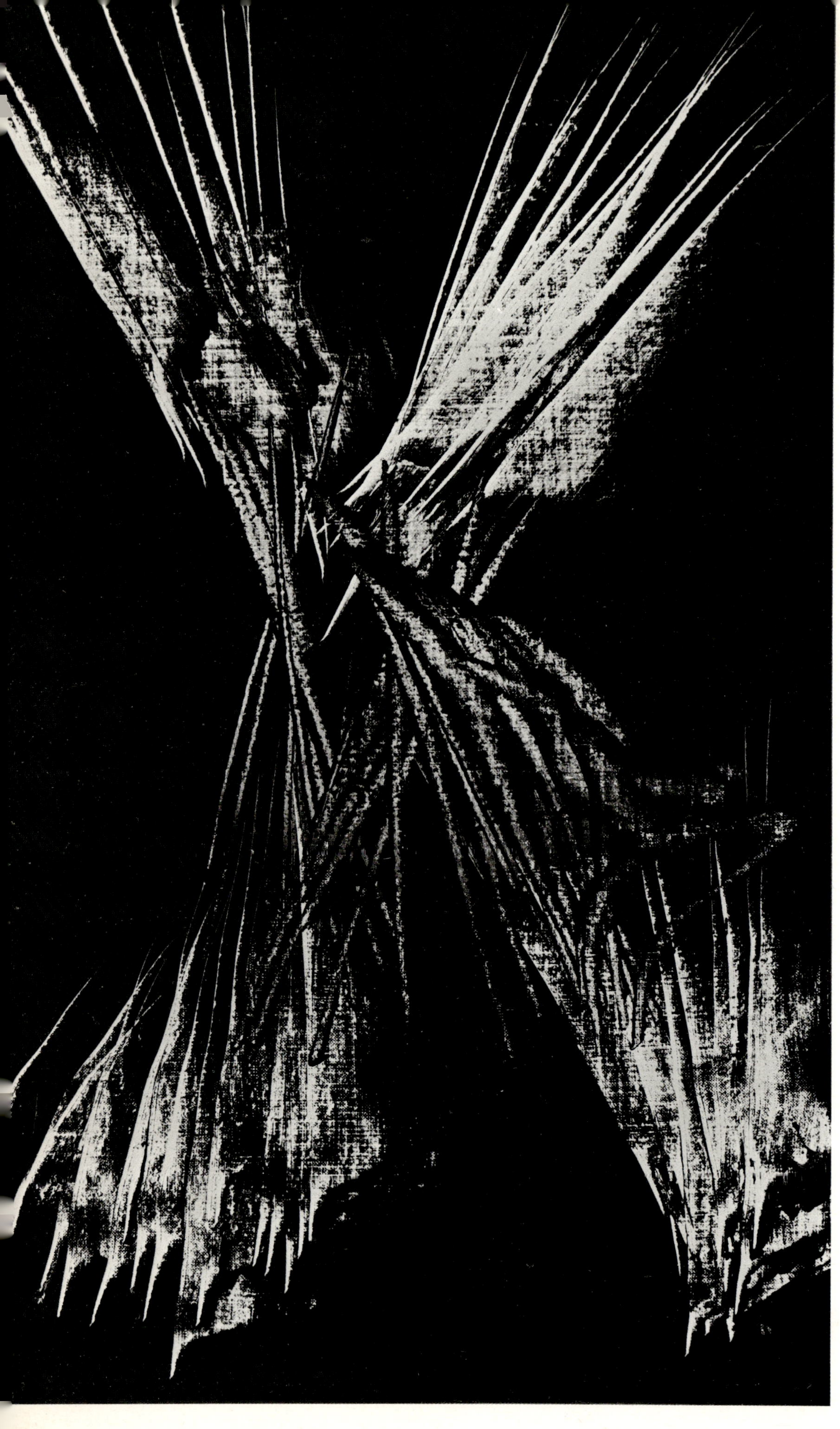

159 T. 1963-U28

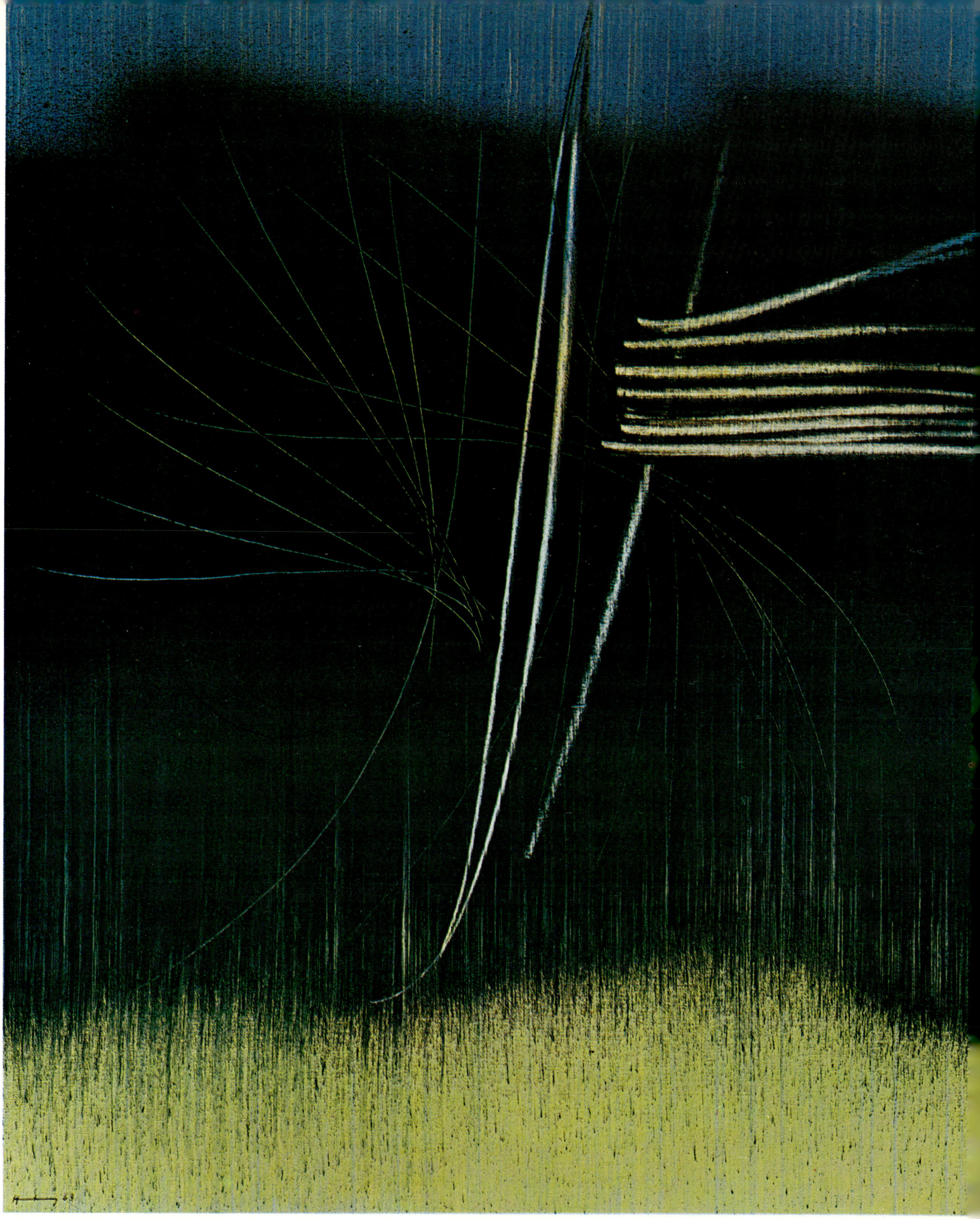

160 T. 1963-H48

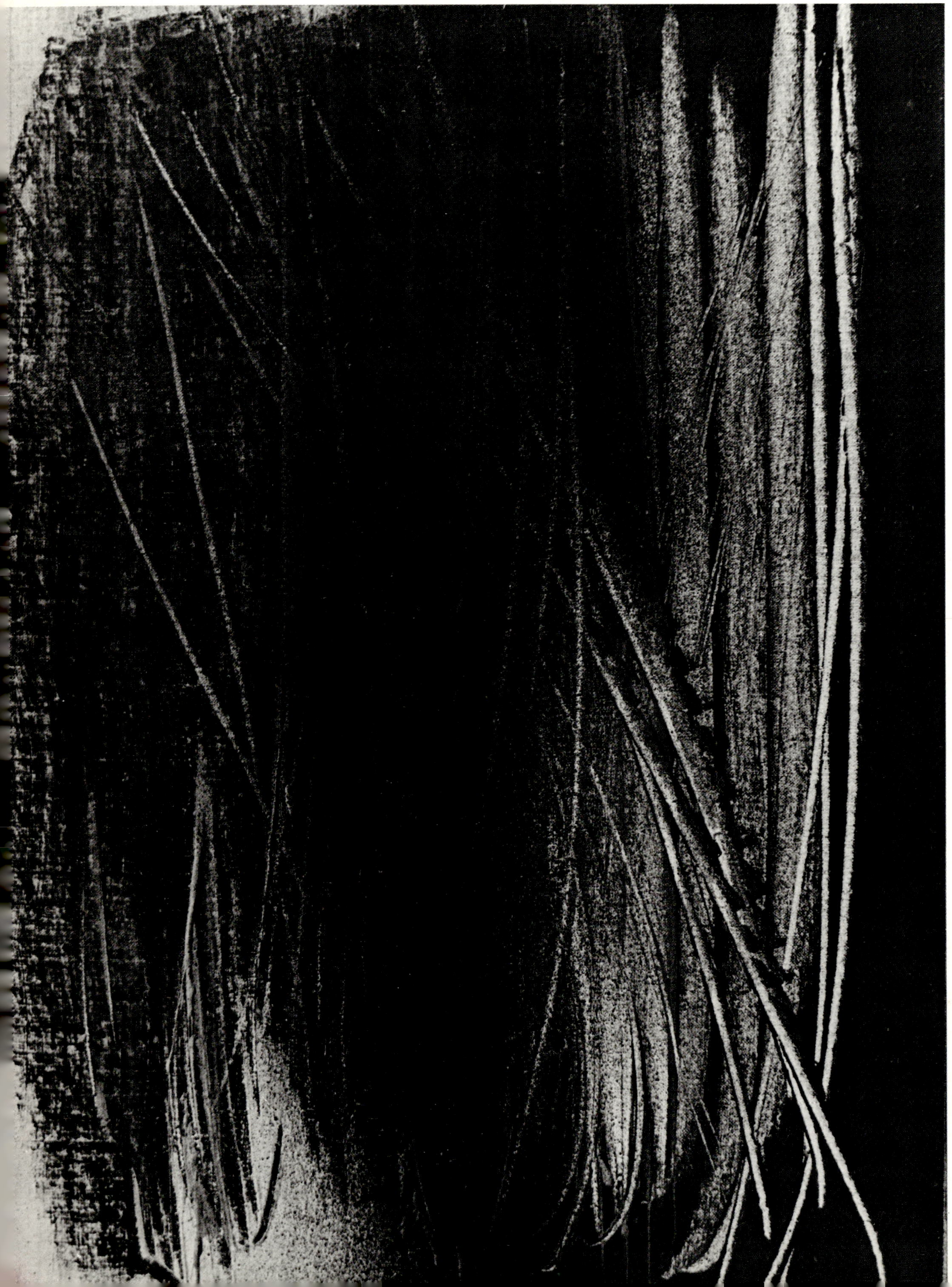

161 T. 1962-L46

162 T. 1963-U17

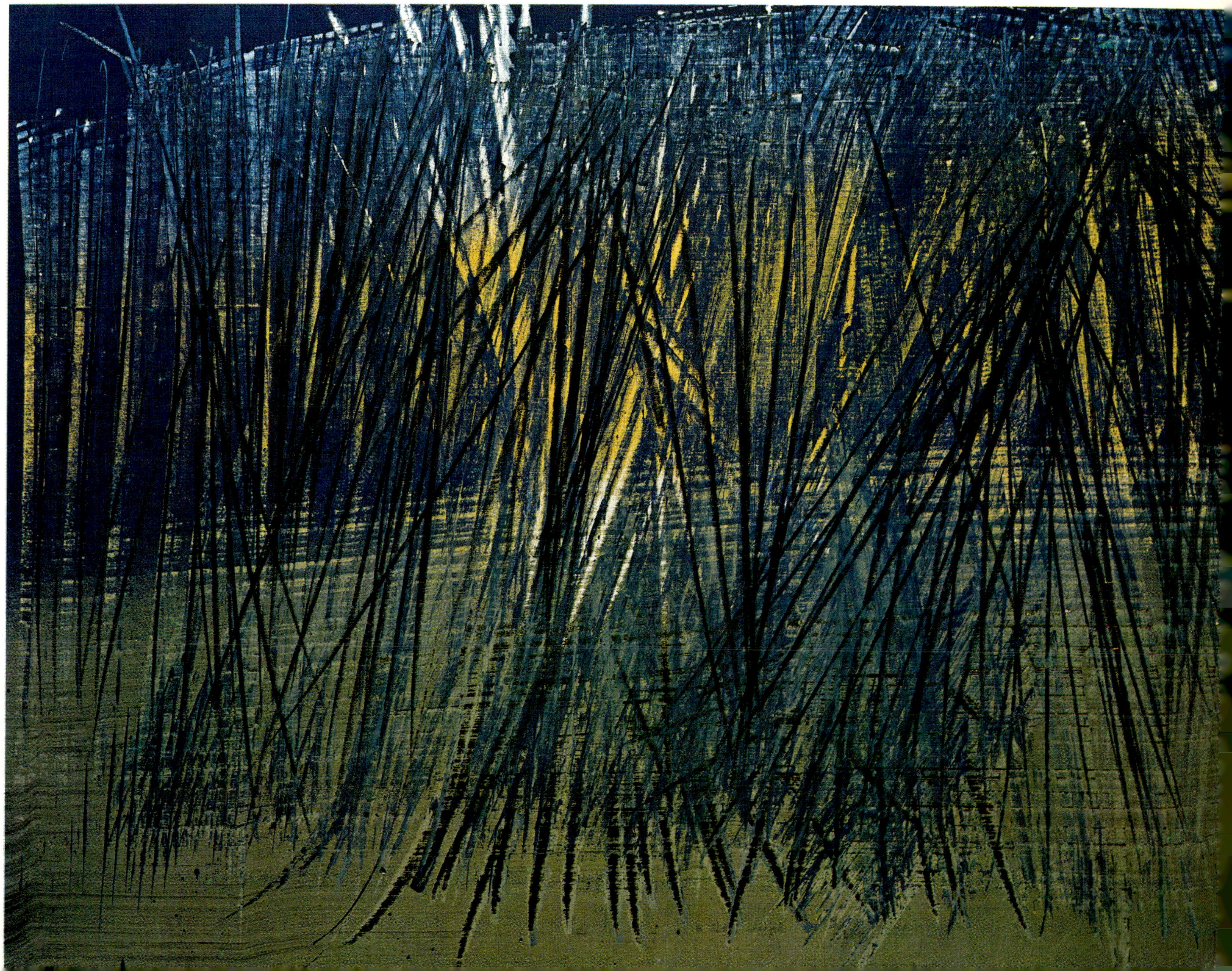

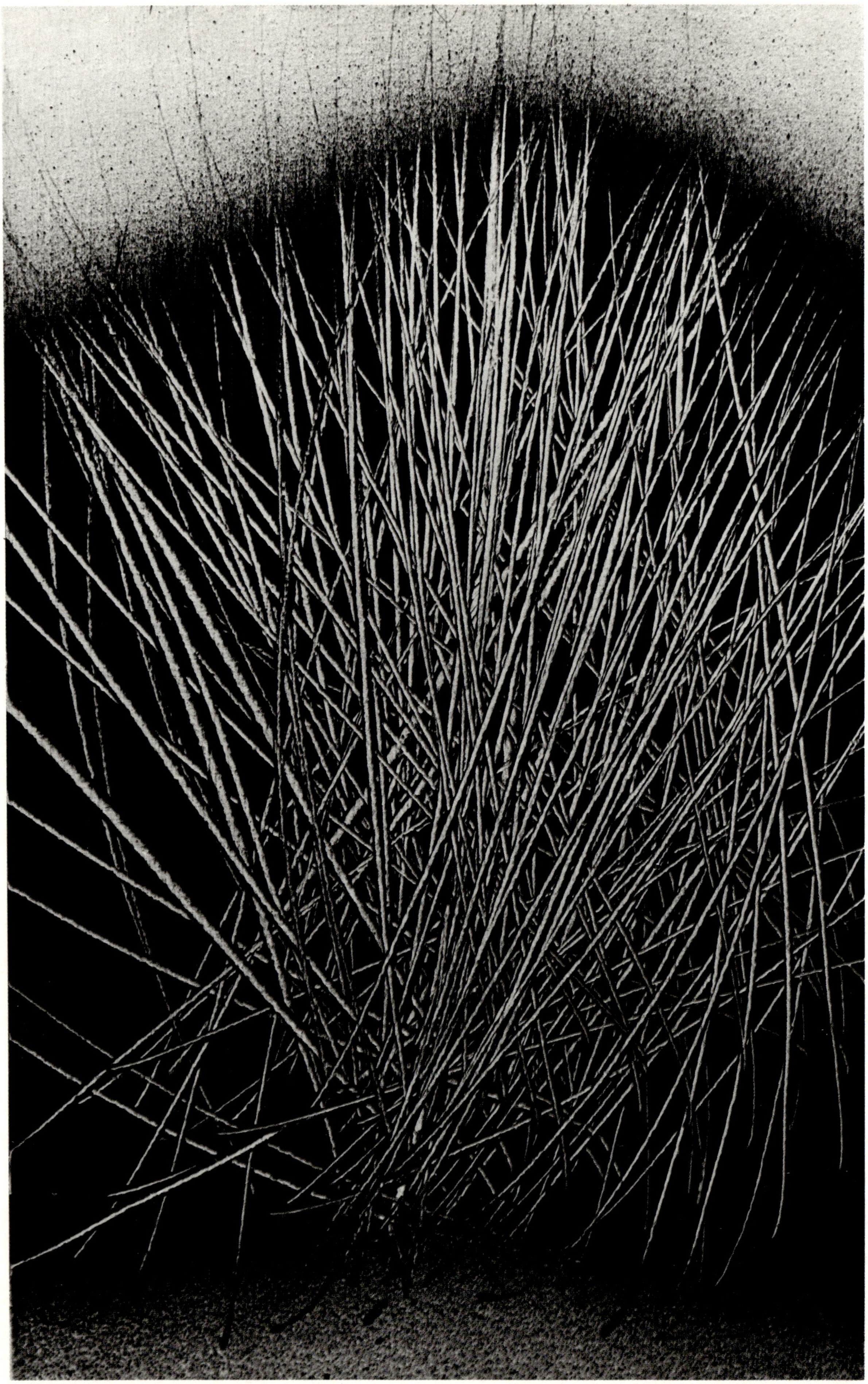

163 T. 1962-A1

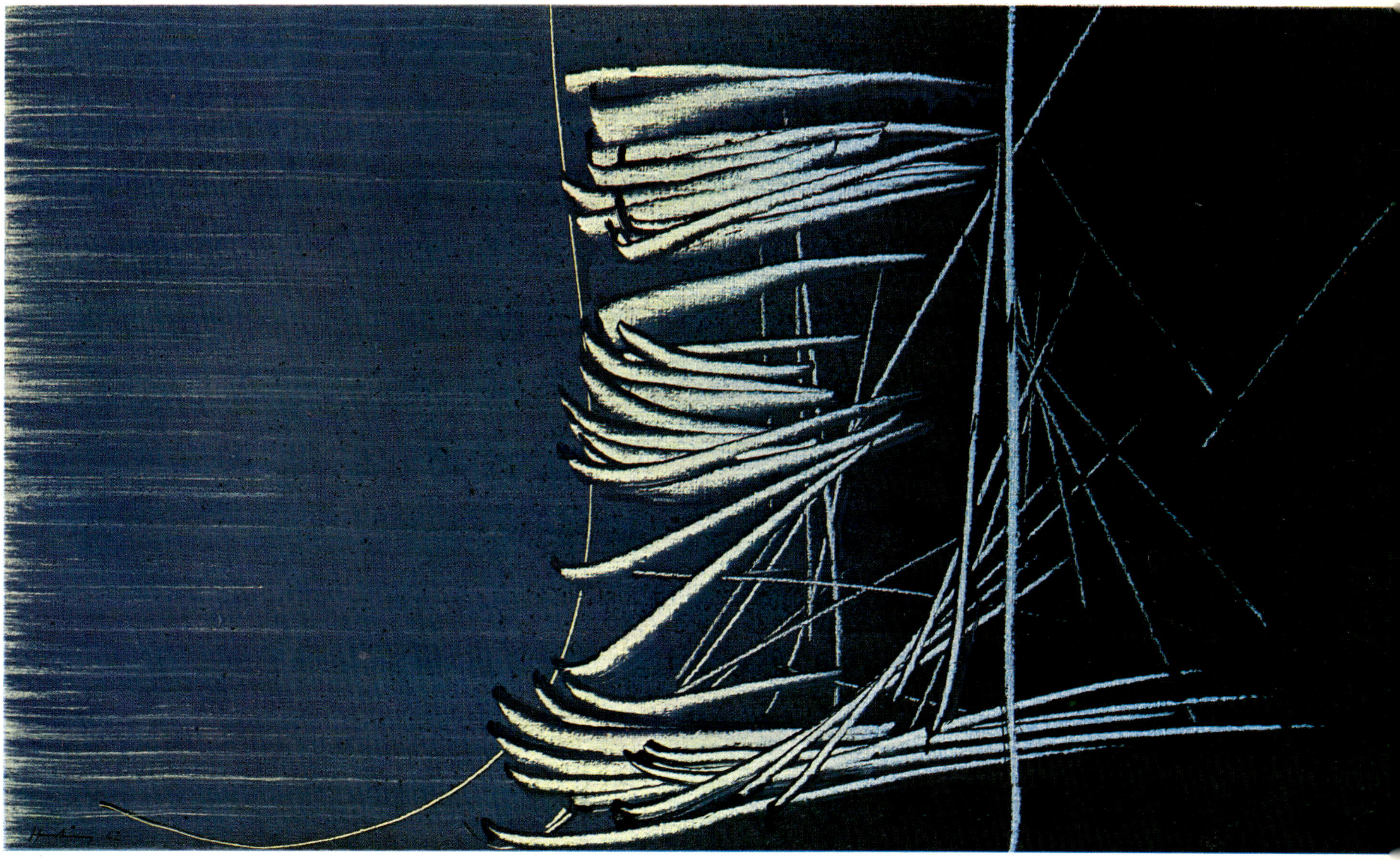

164 T. 1962-A20

165 T. 1963-U40

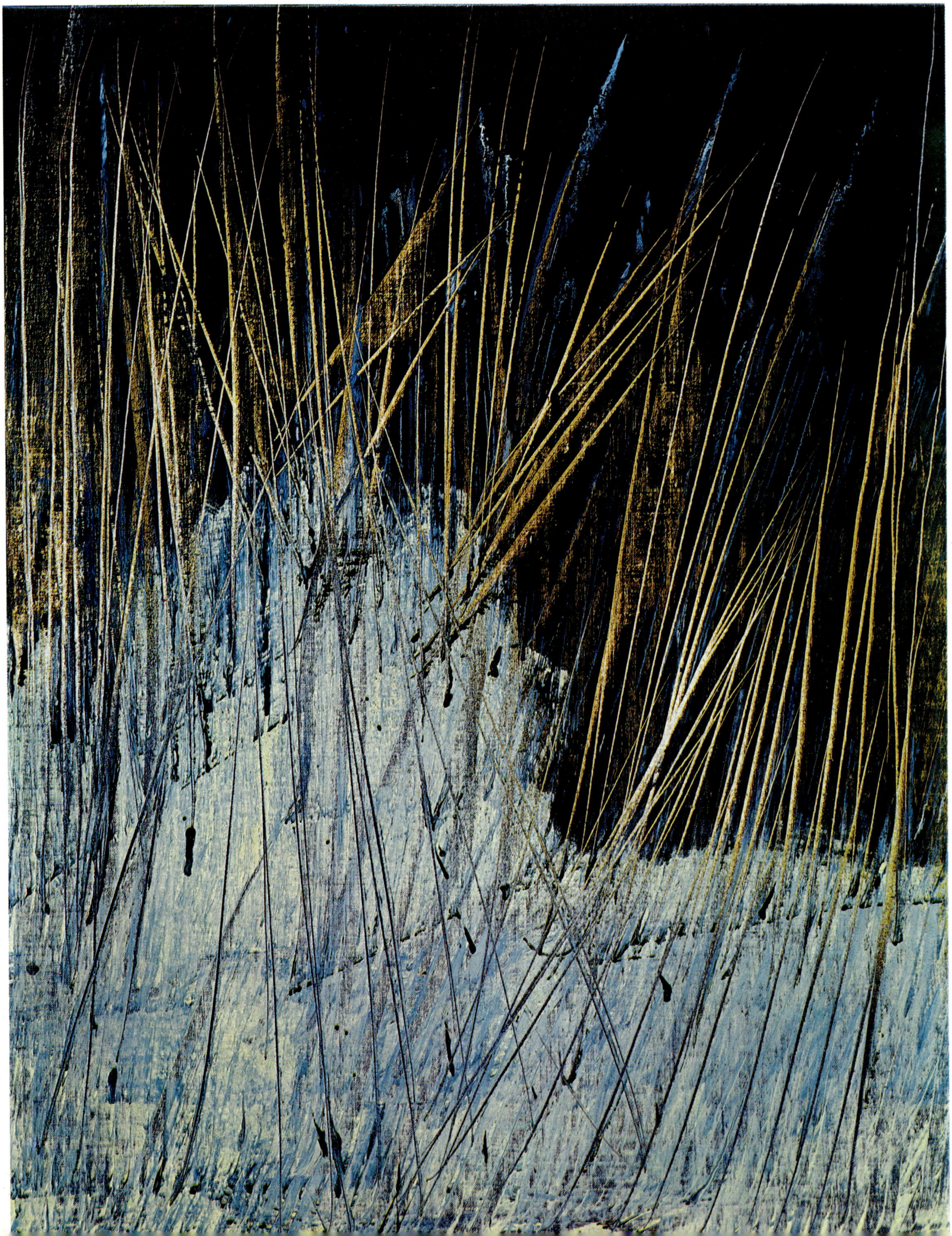

166 T. 1963-U18

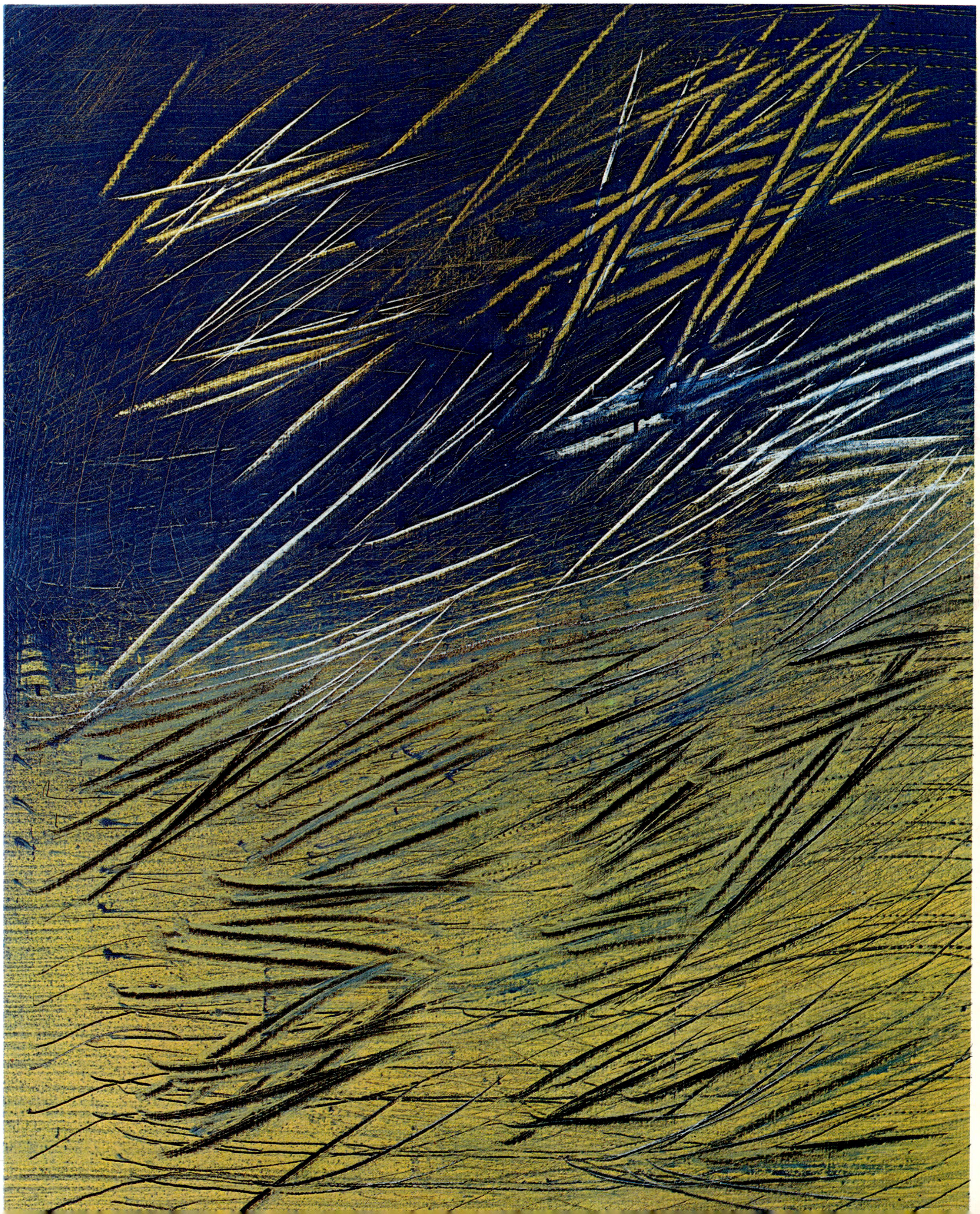

167 T. 1964-E1

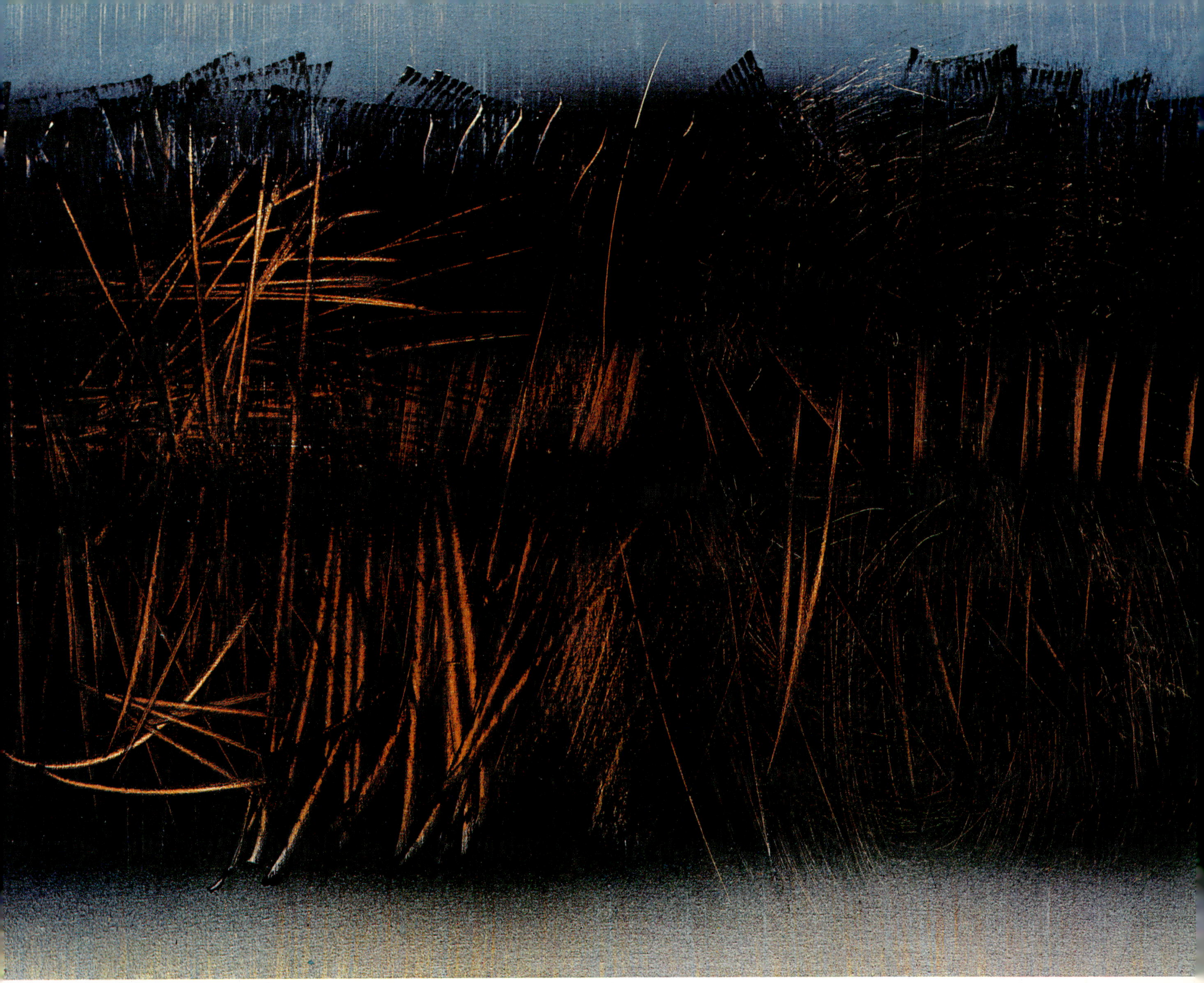

68 T. 1963-R23

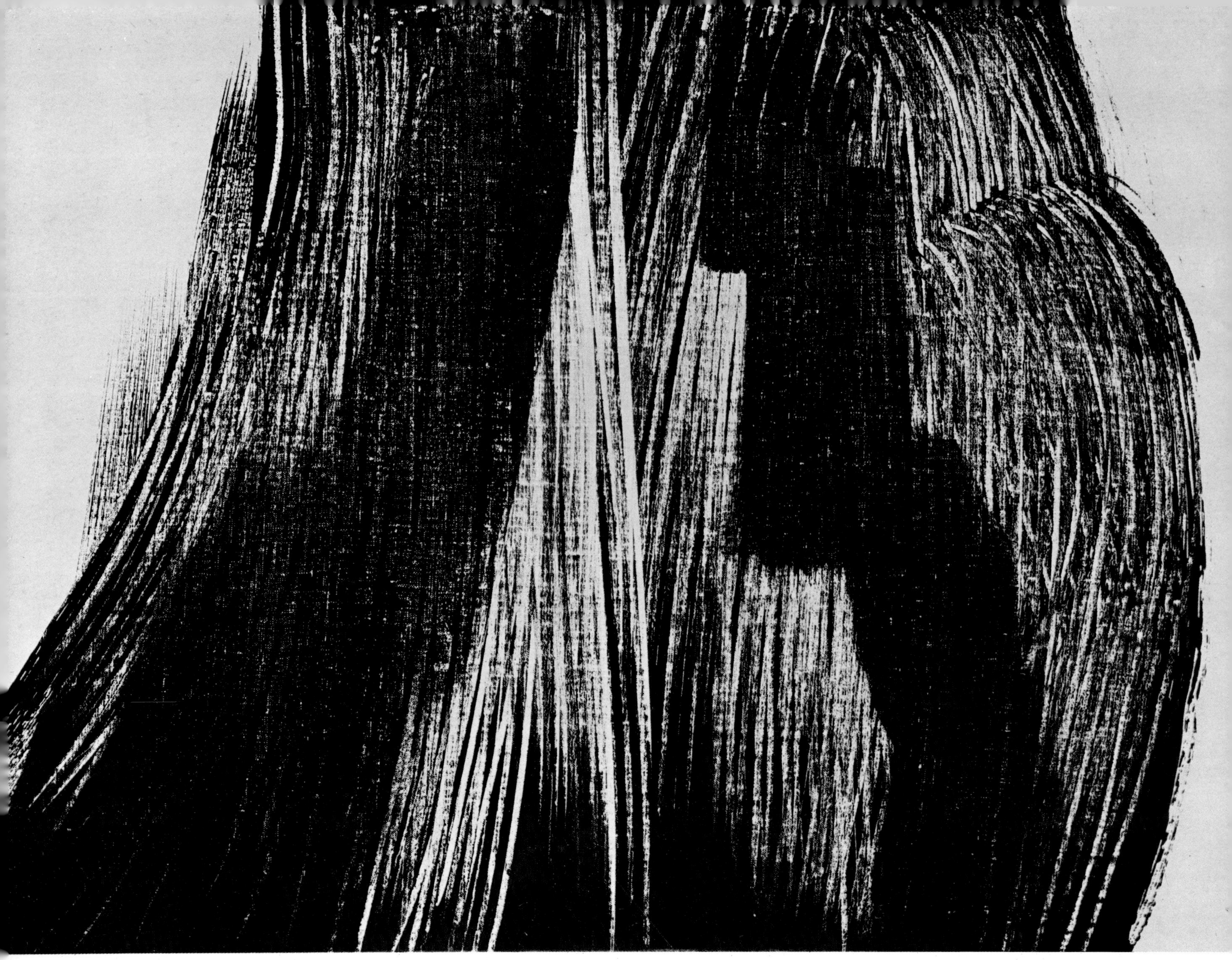

169 T. 1963-U4

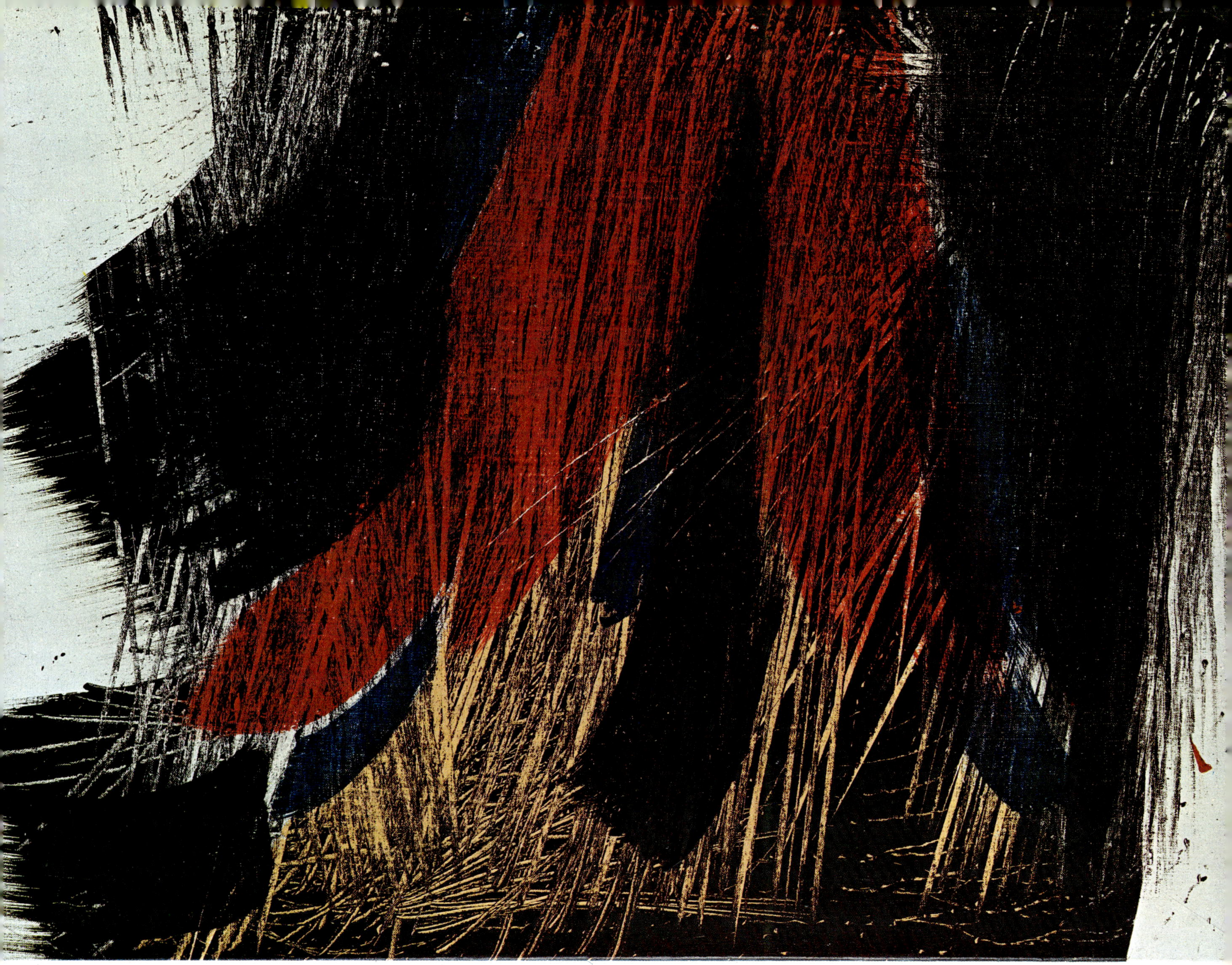

70 T. 1963-U45

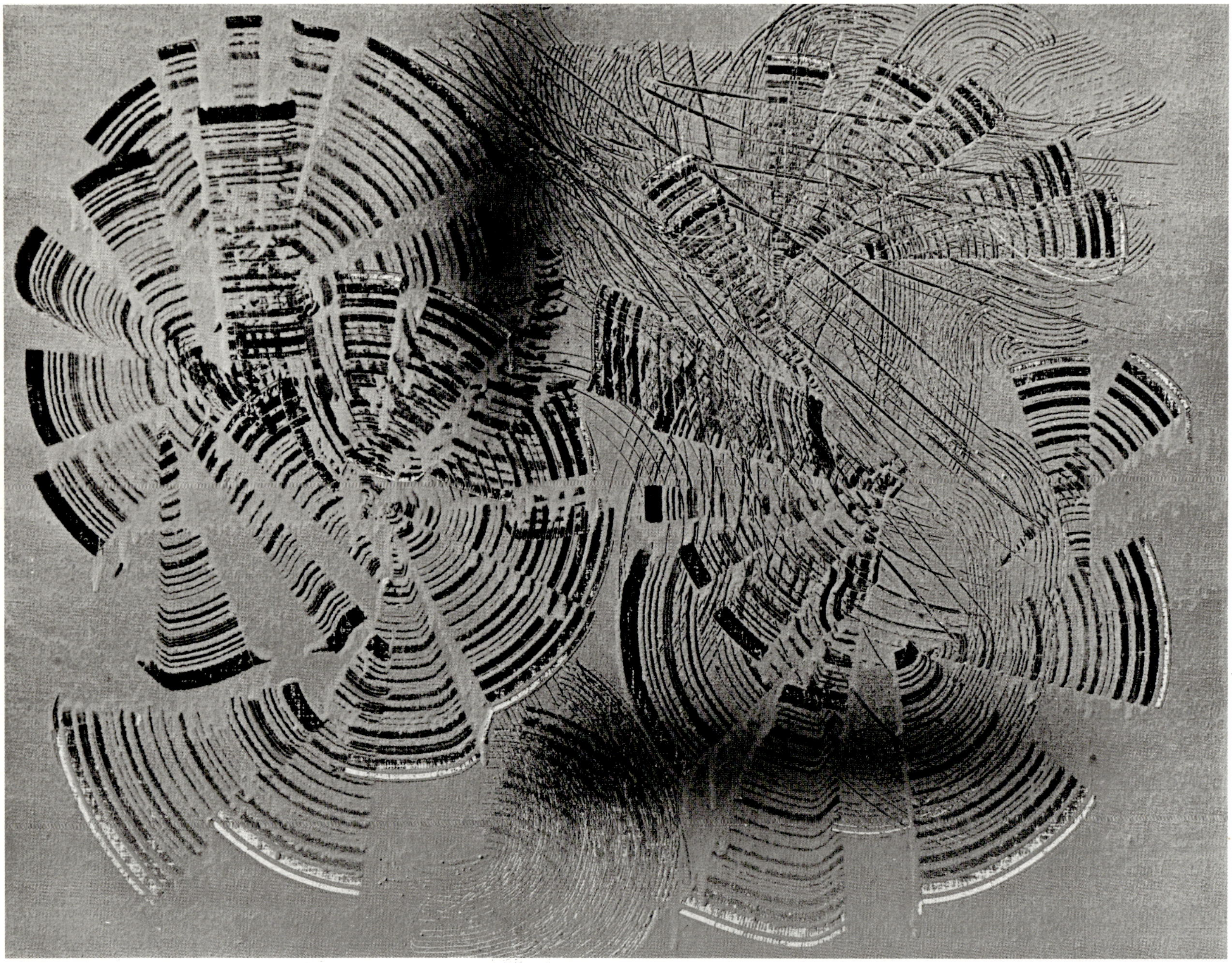

171 T. 1964-E31

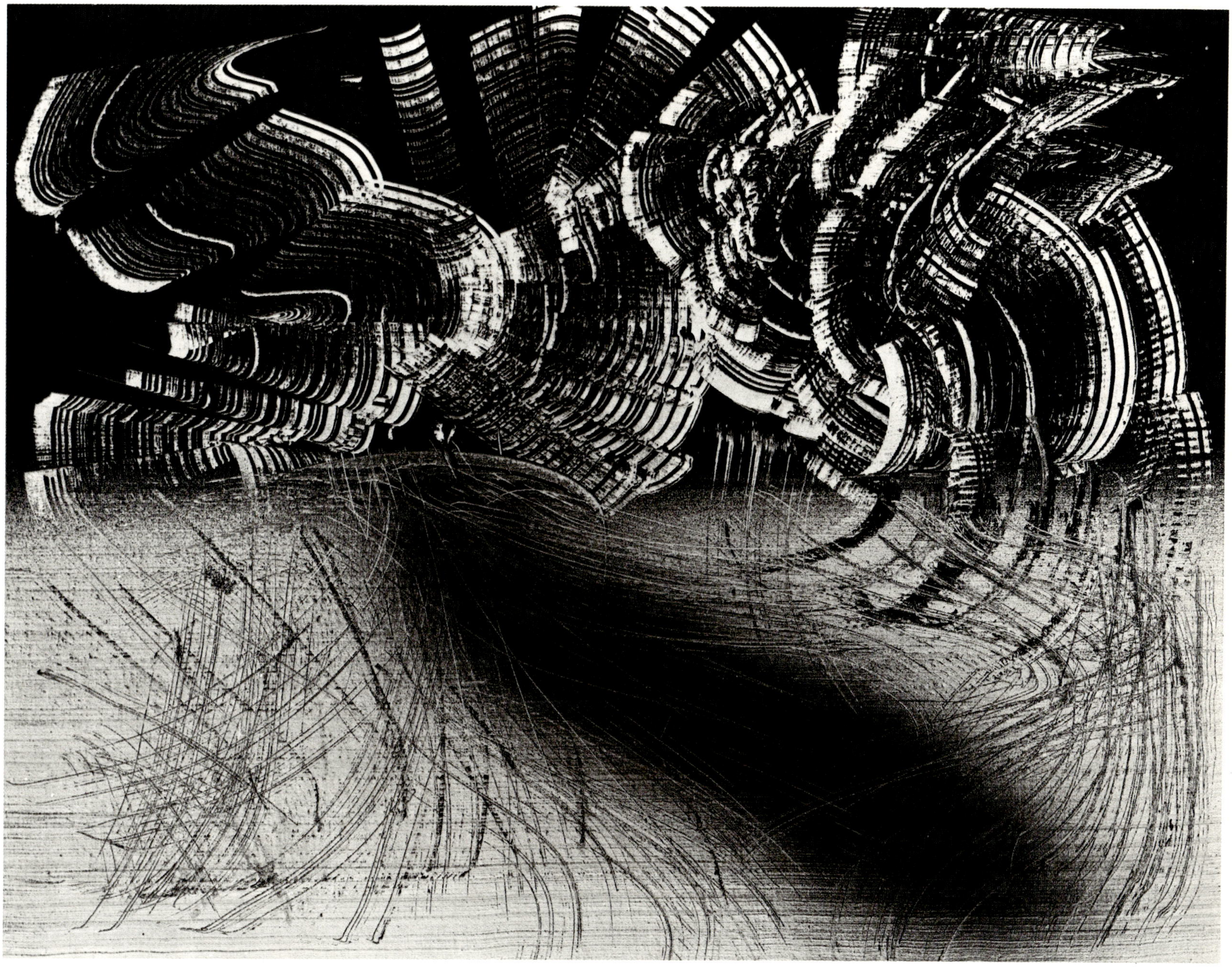

172 T. 1964-E27

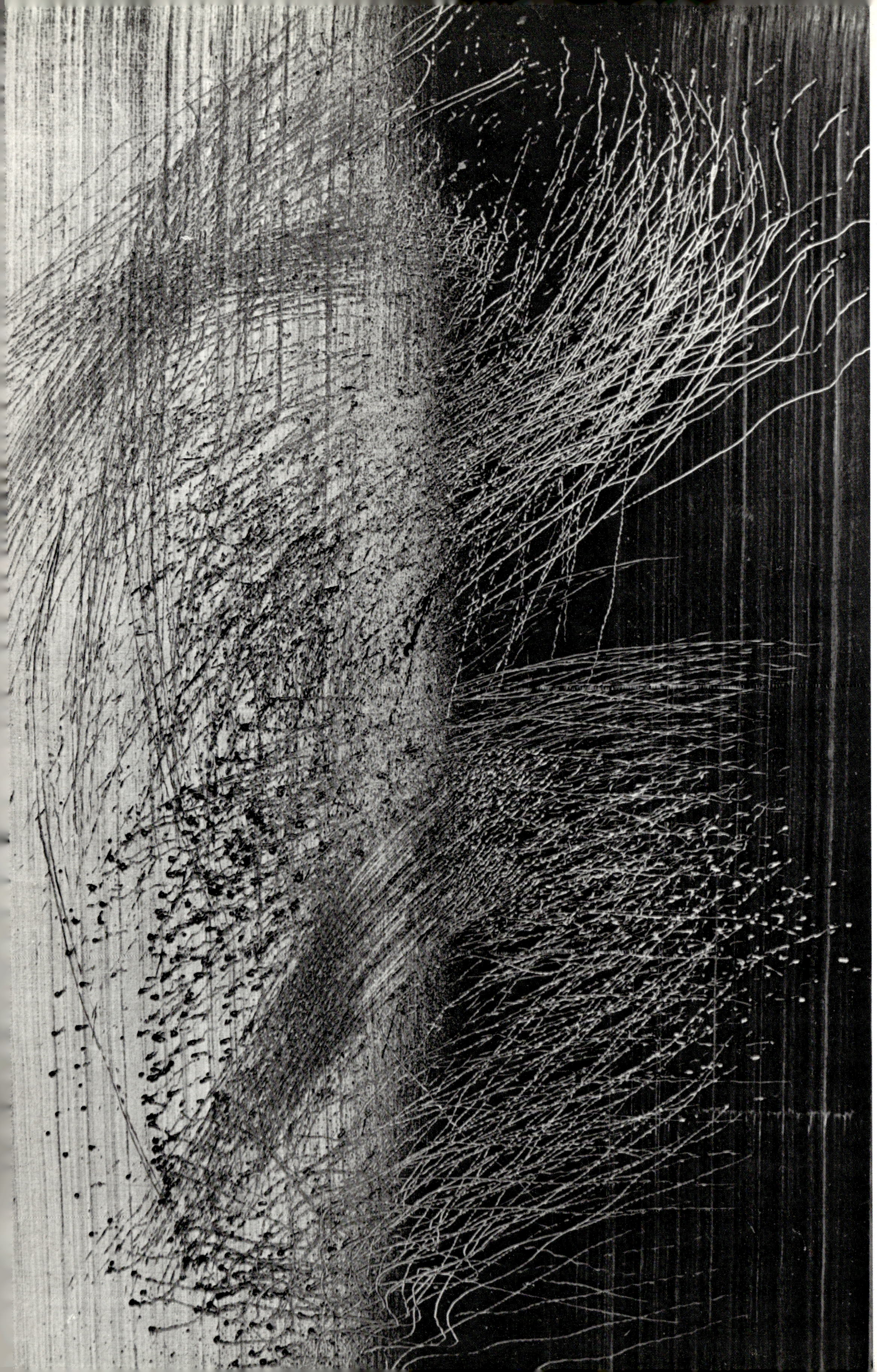

173 T. 1963-E7

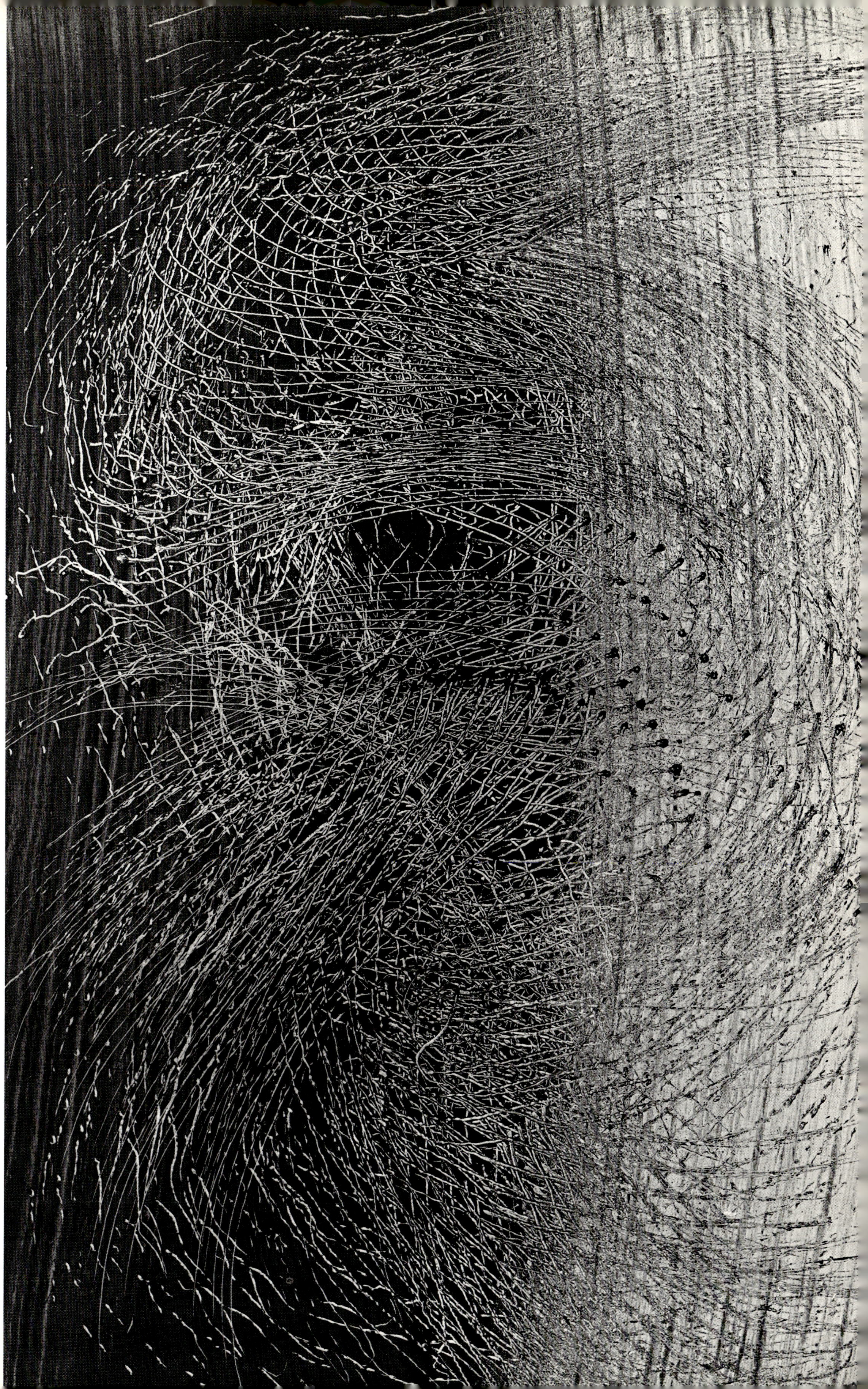

174 T. 1963-E6

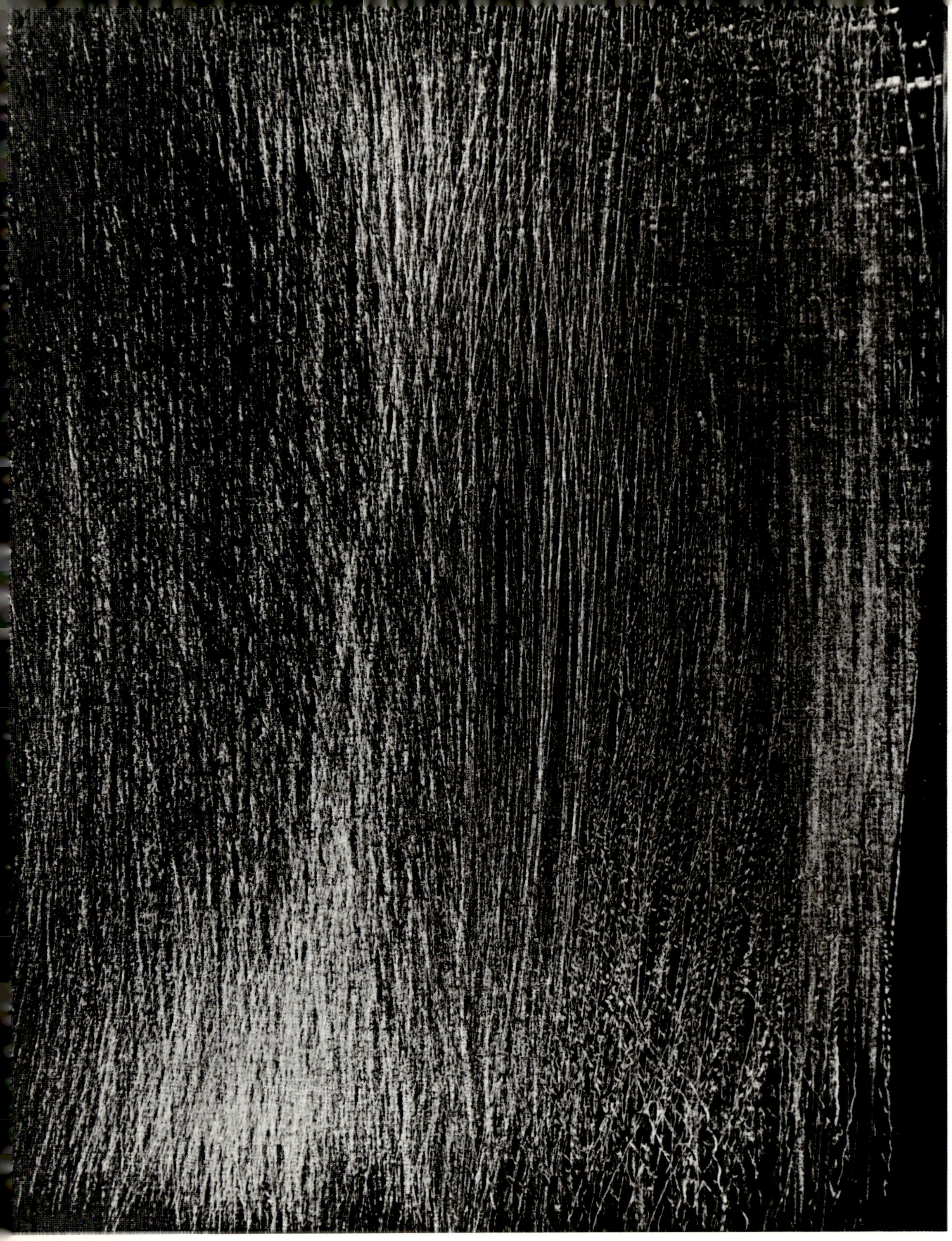

175 T. 1963-H21

176 T. 1963-E40

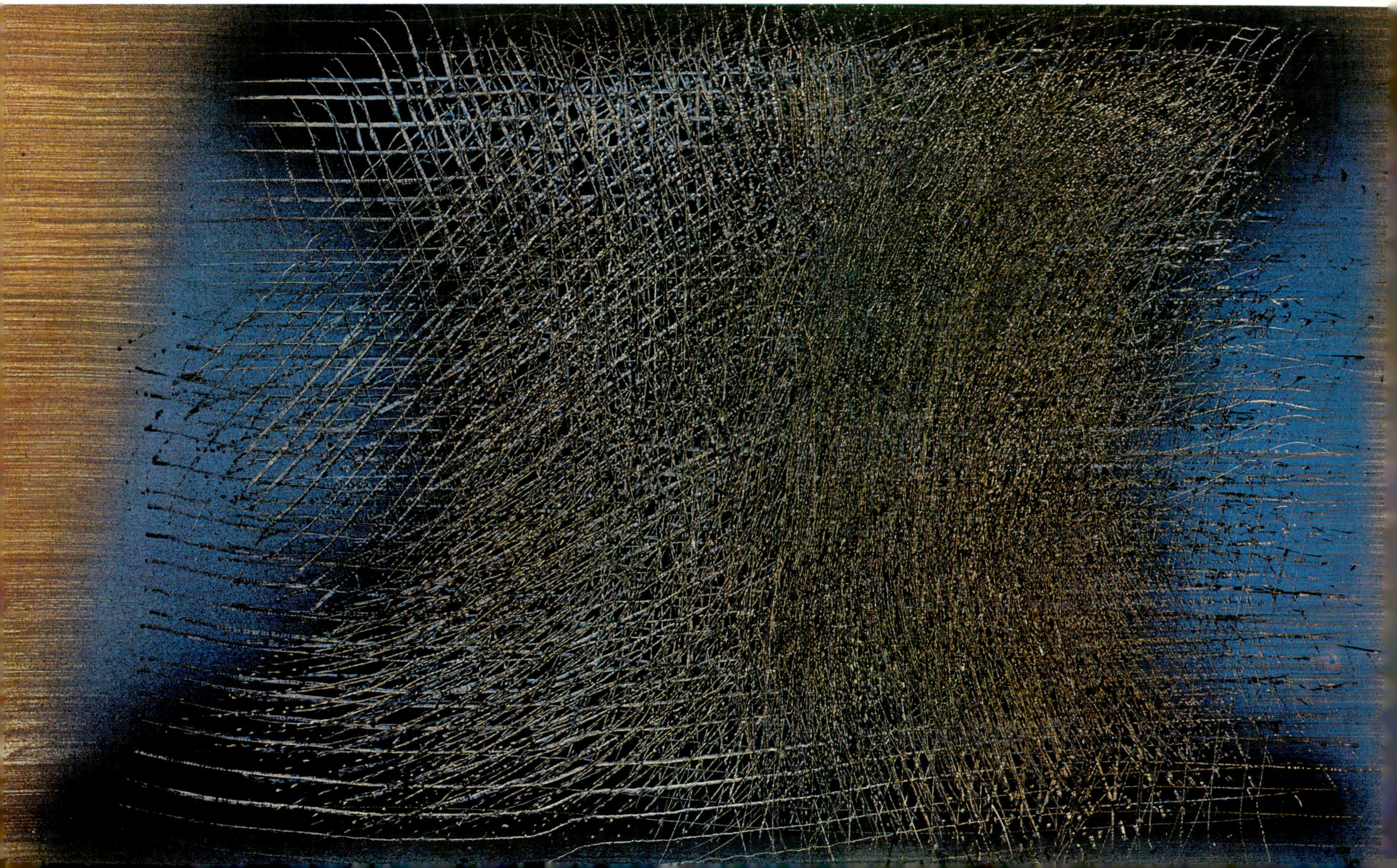

177 T. 1962-K1

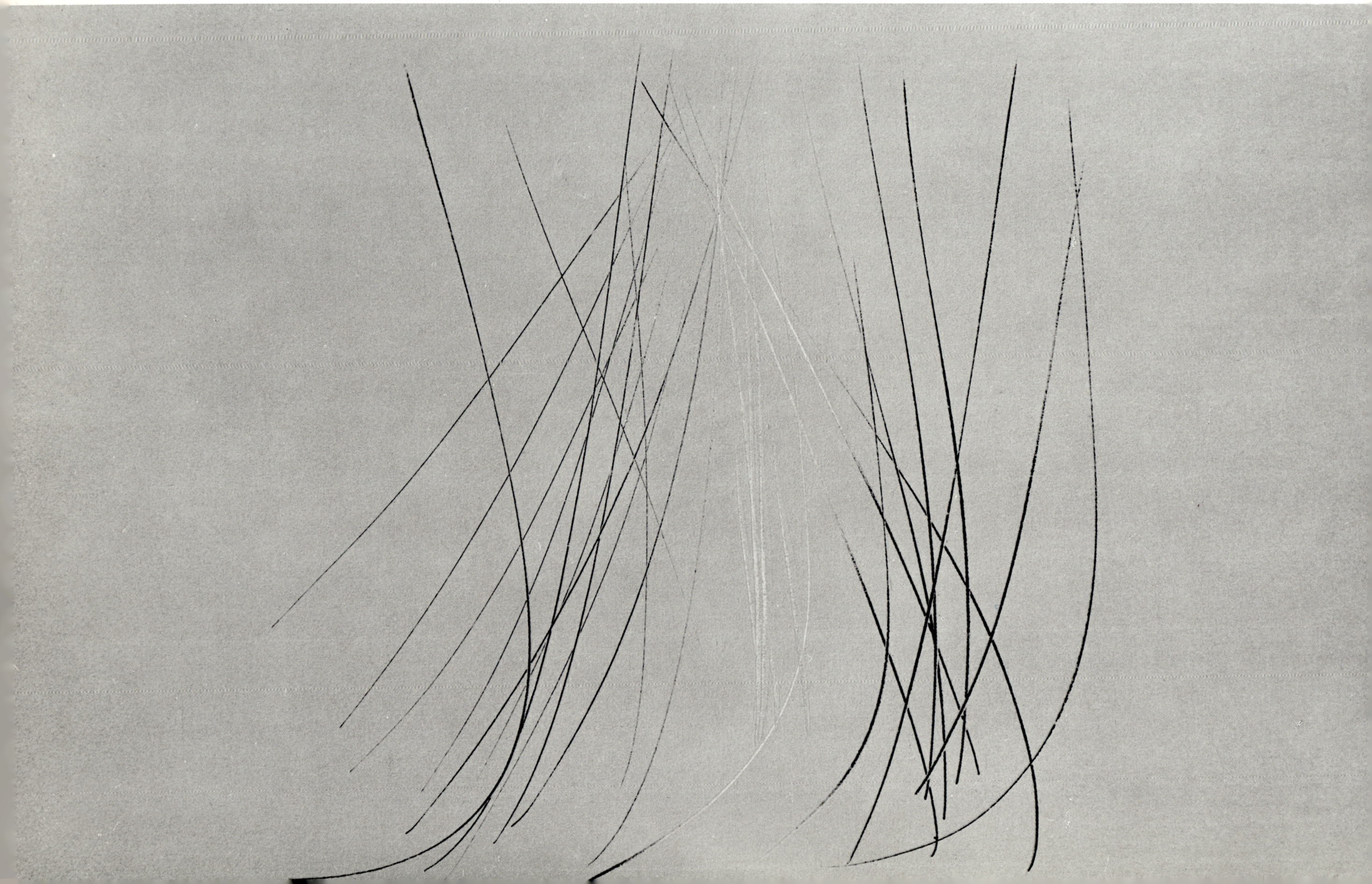

178 T. 1965-H9

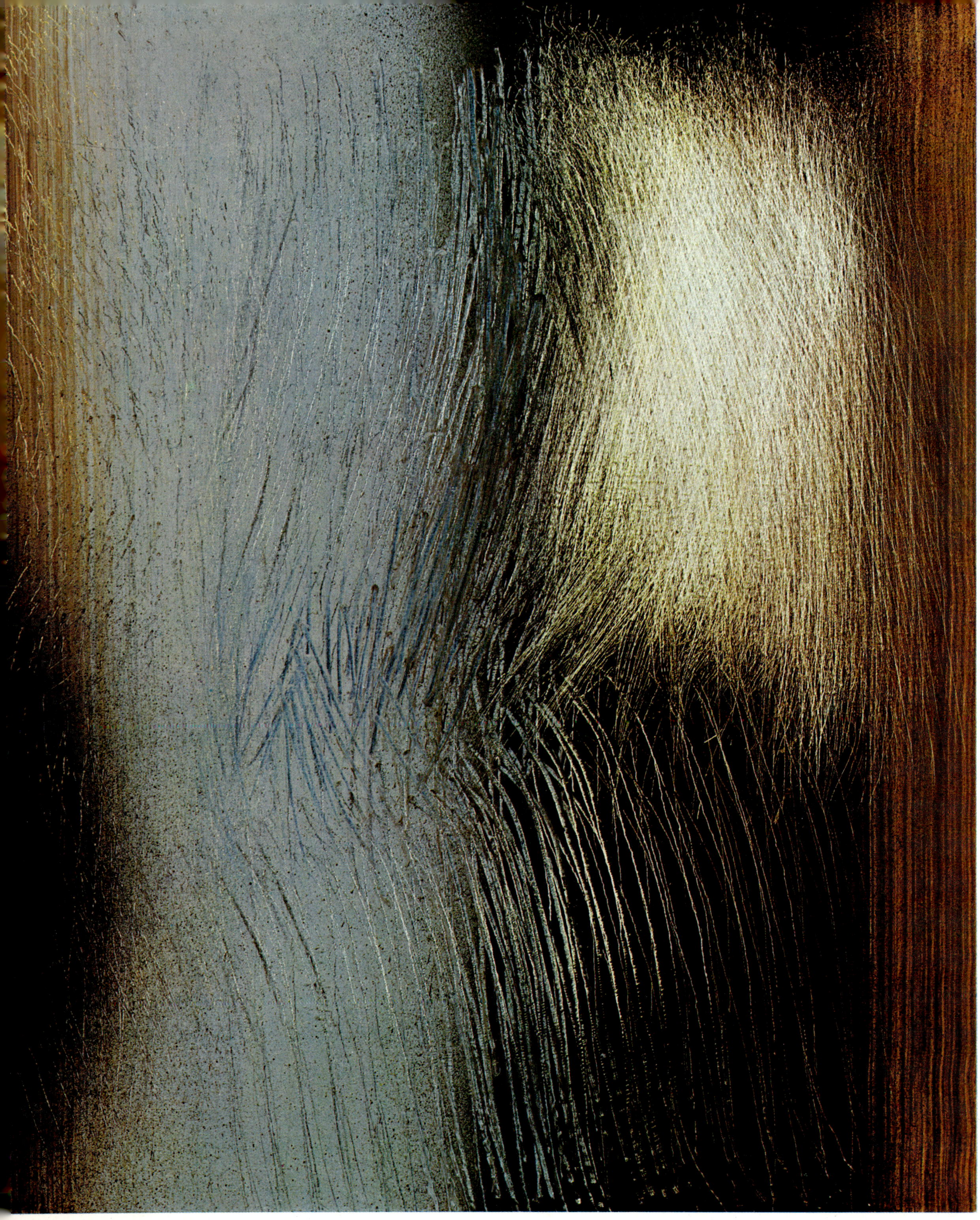

179 T. 1963-H26

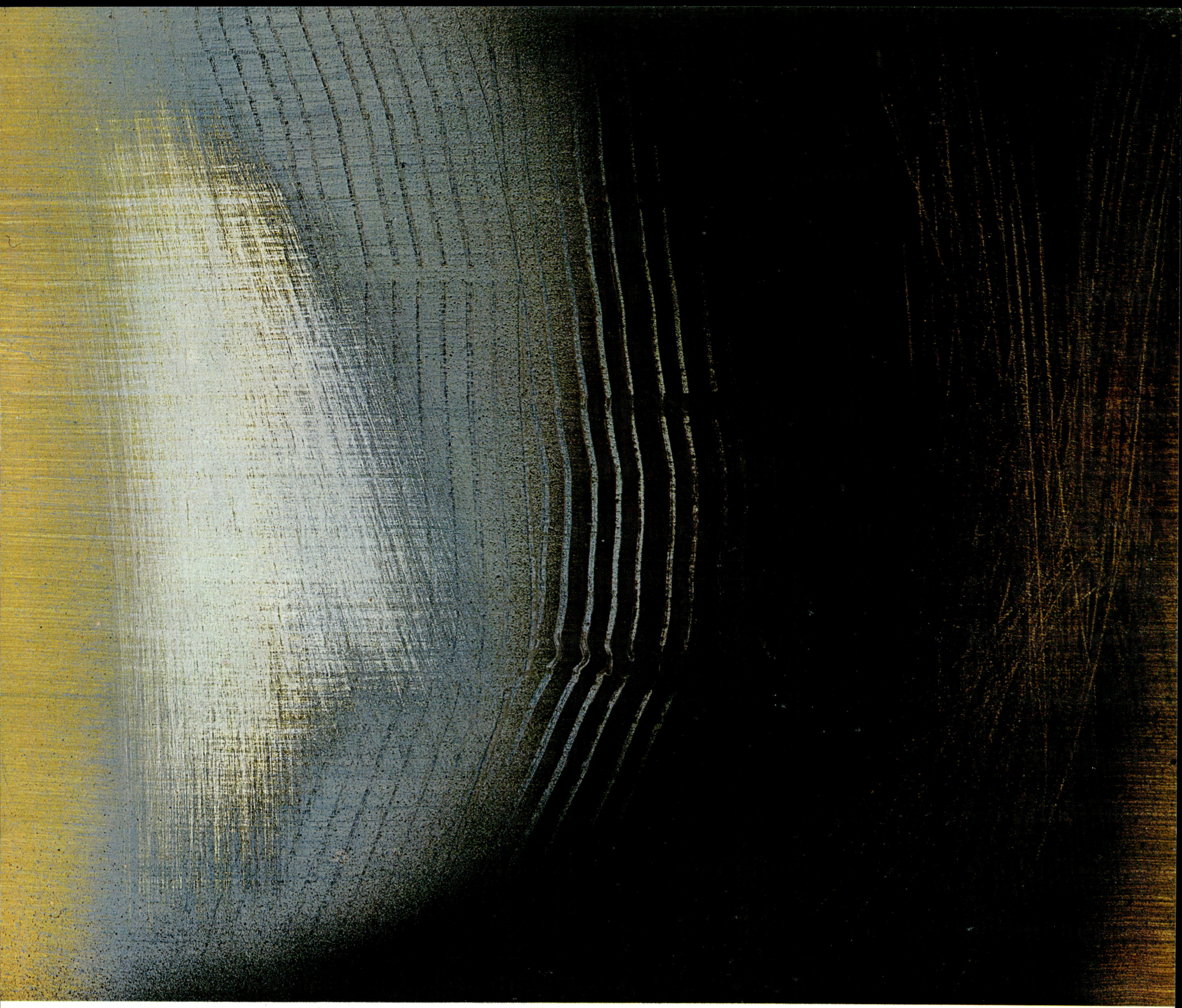

80 T. 1963-H24

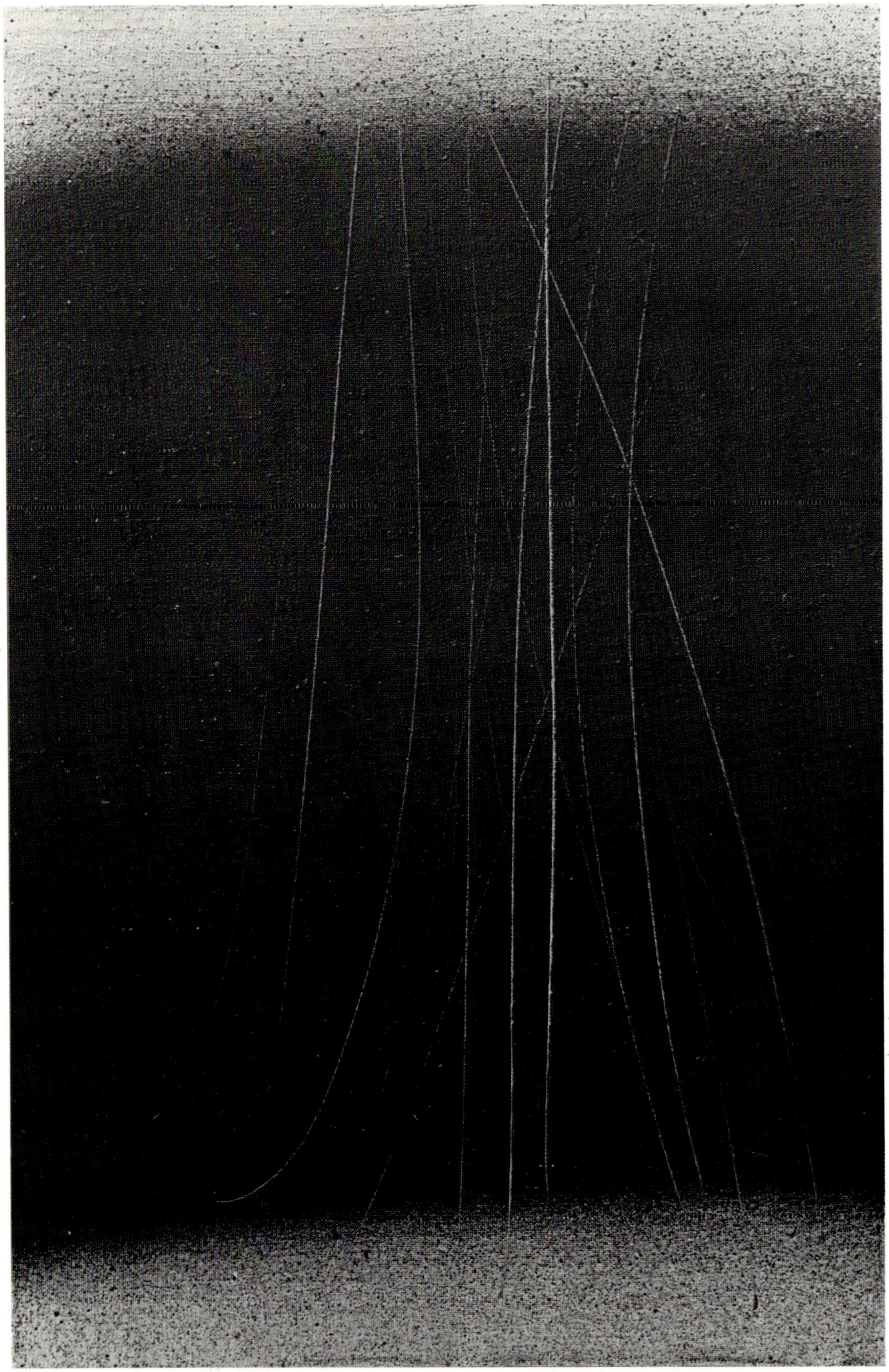

181 T. 1965-H19

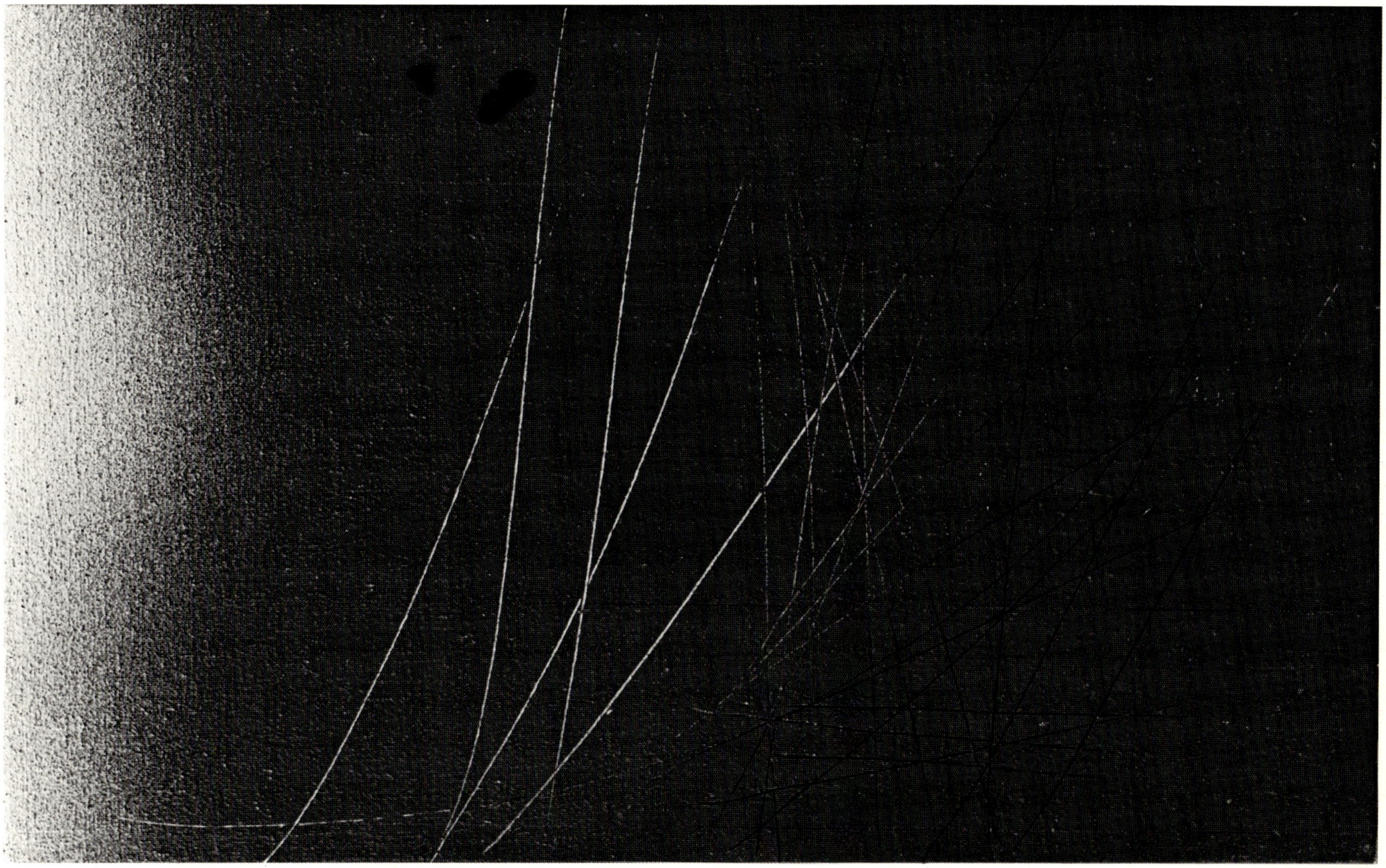

182 T. 1965-E9

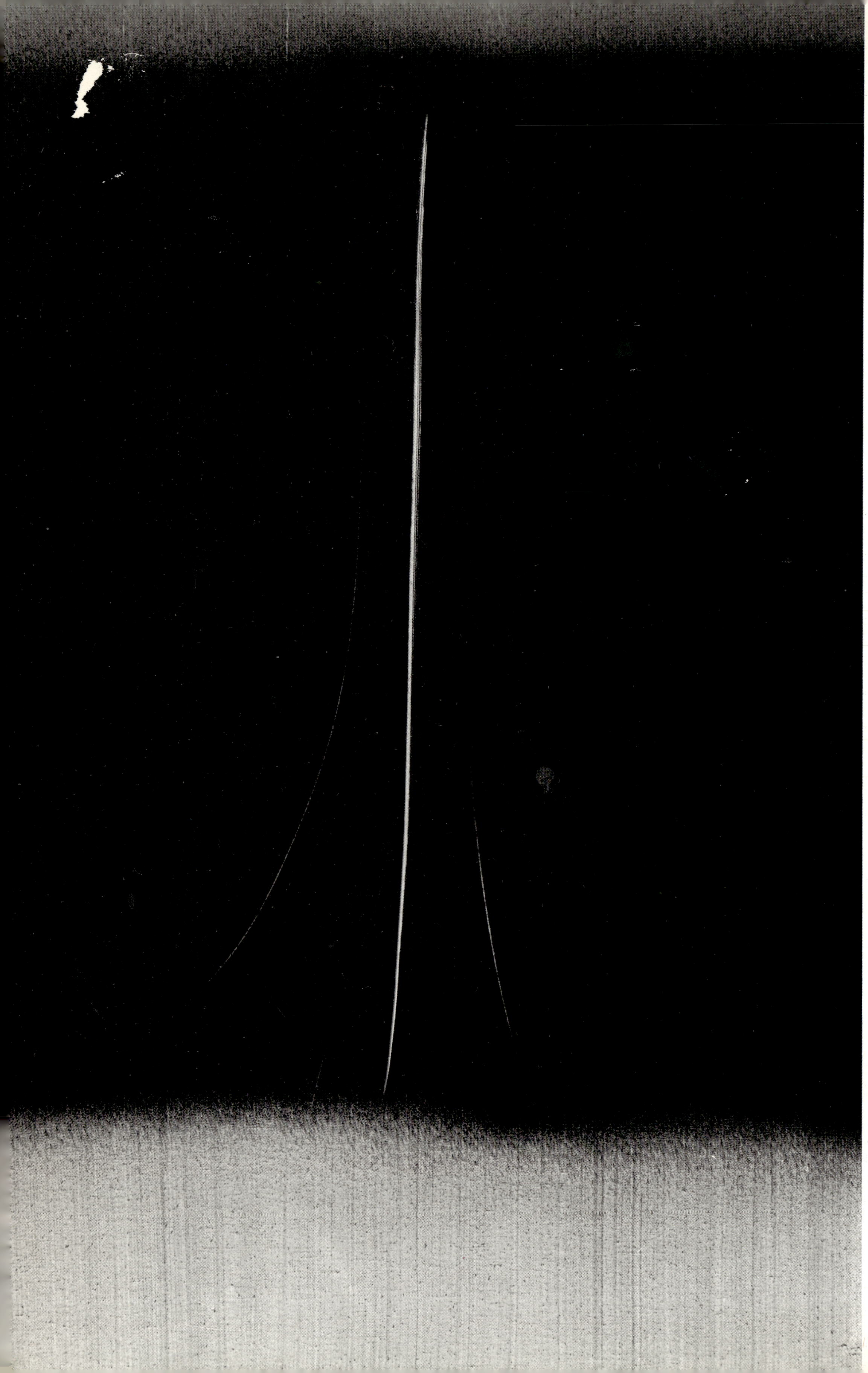

183 T. 1964-H45

184 T. 1964-H

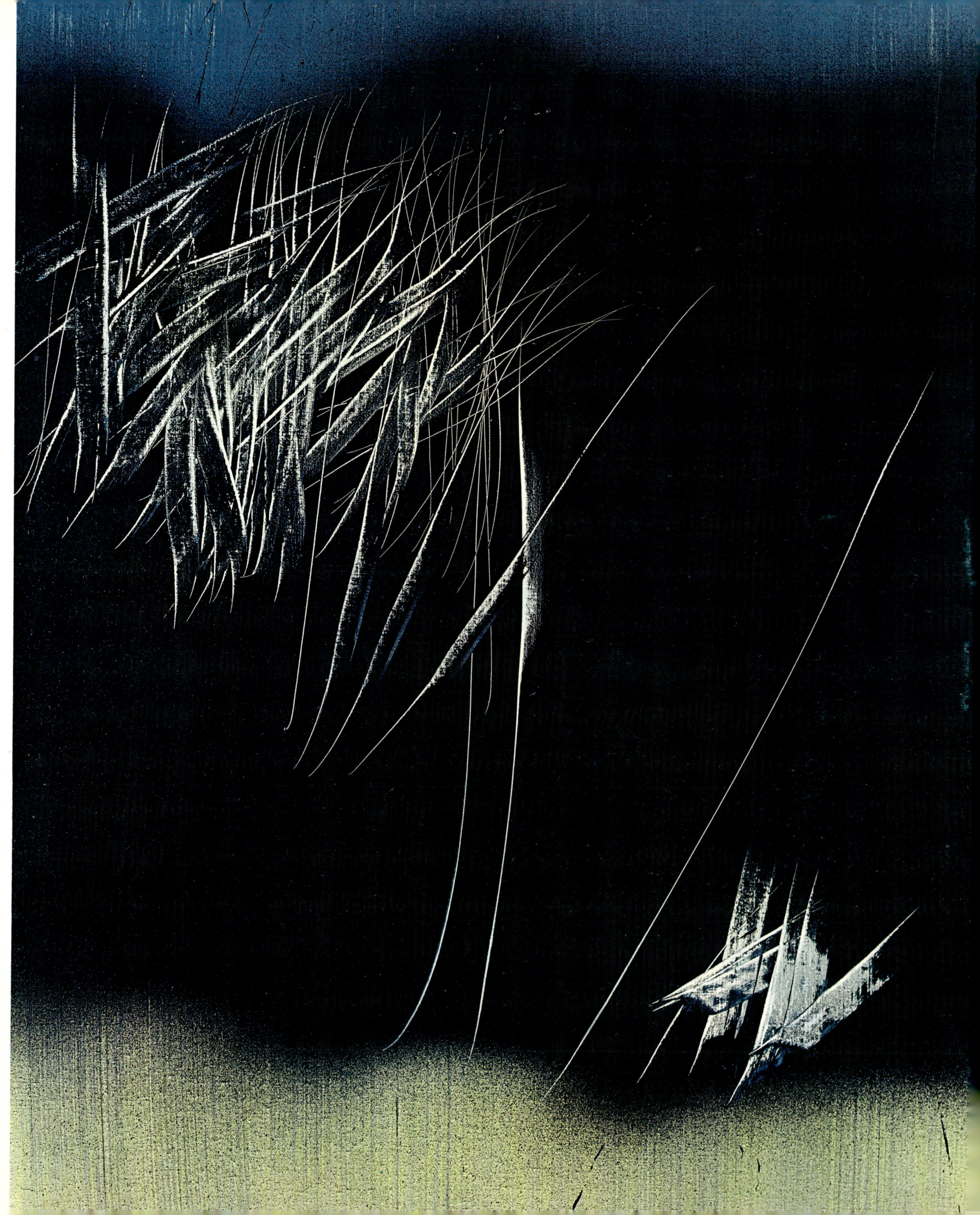

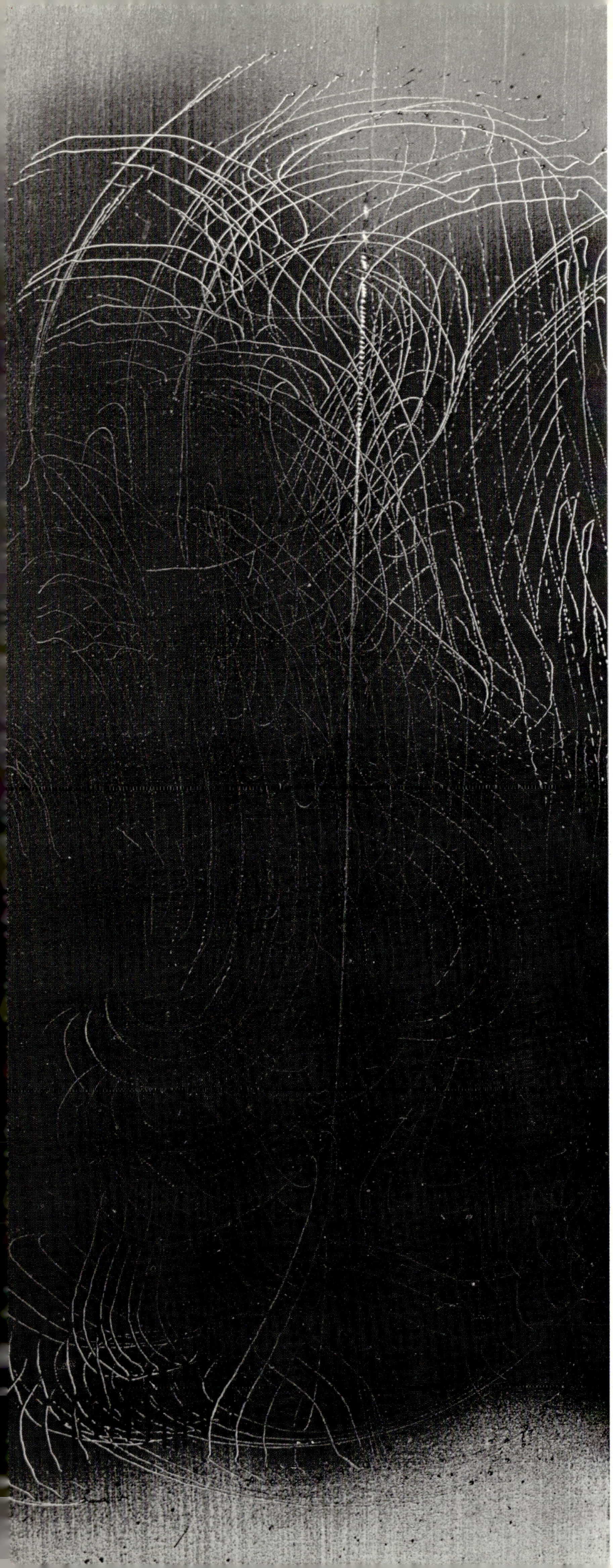

◄ T. 1963-R18

► T. 1963-R19

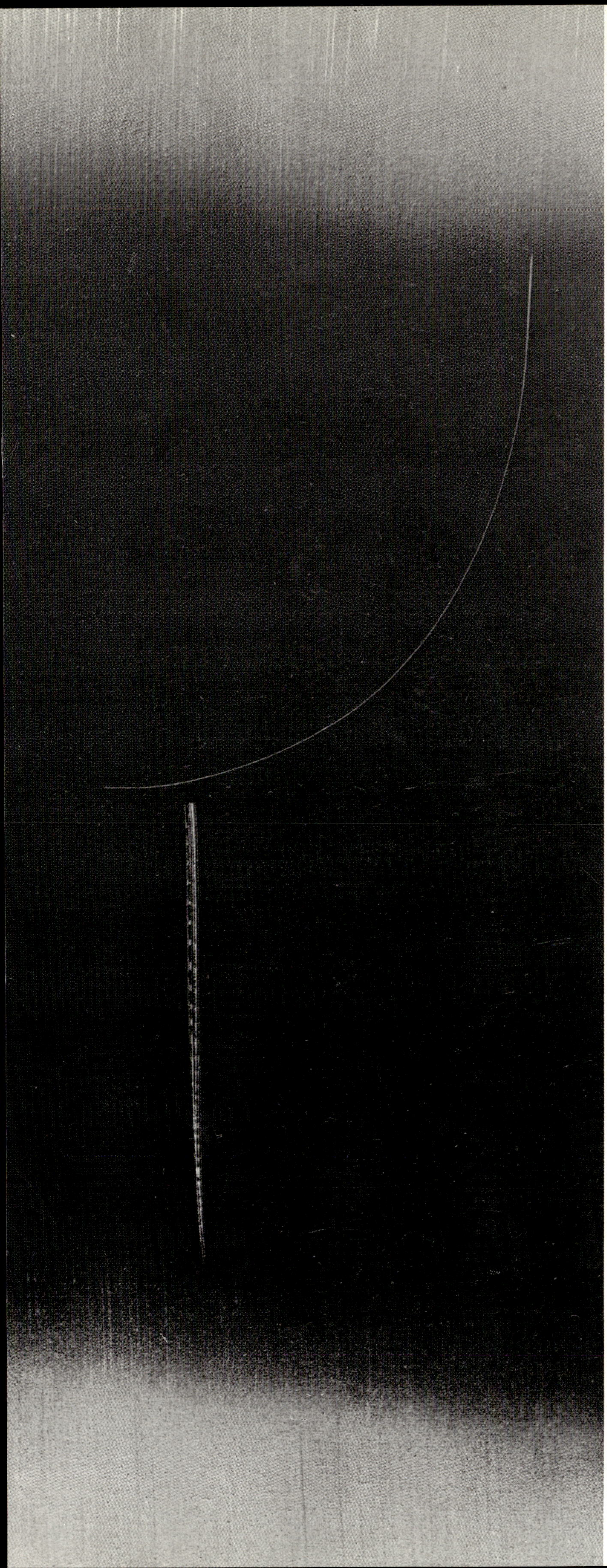

T. 1963-R20

T. 1963-R21

186 T. 1963-K45

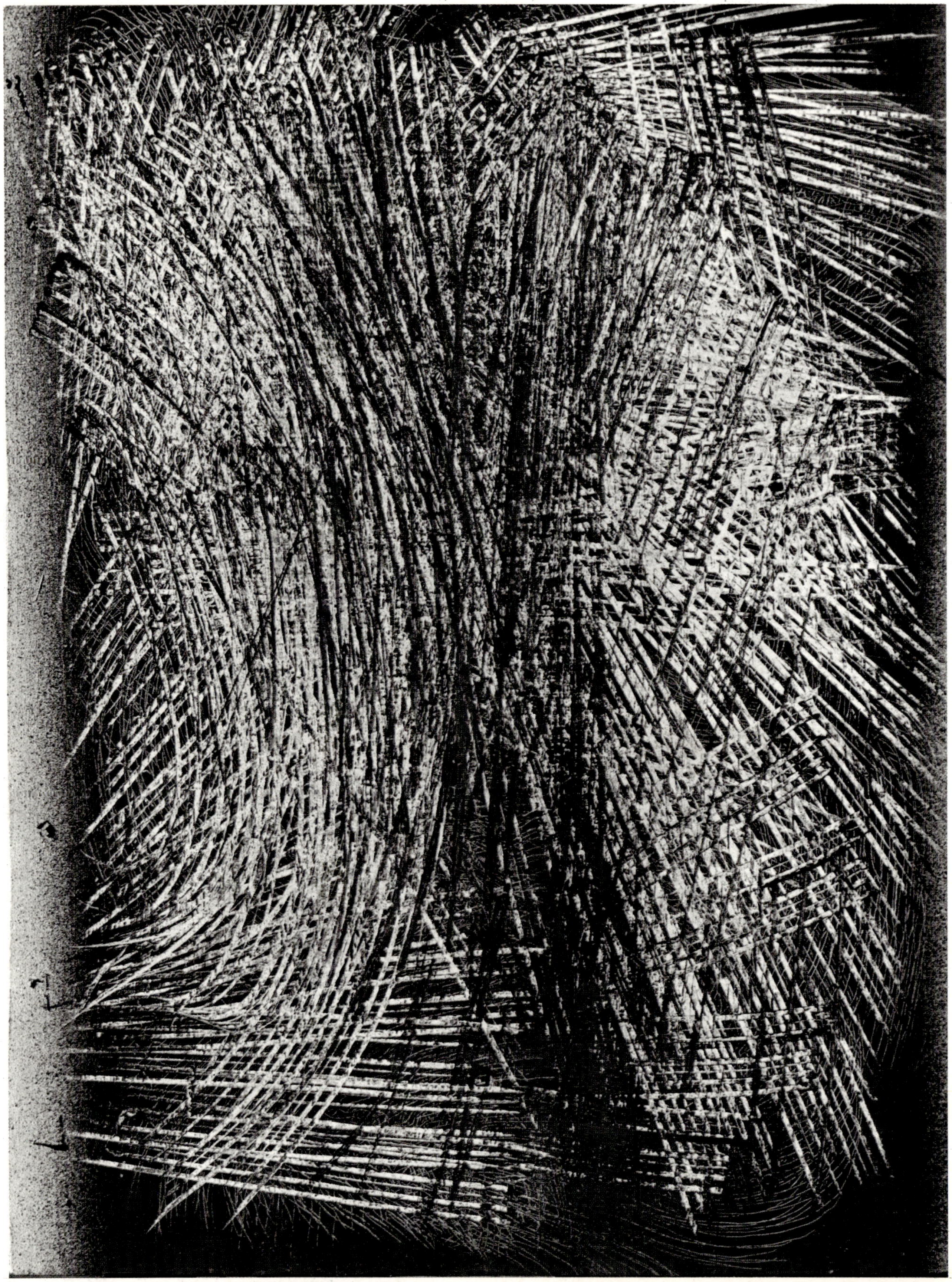

187 T. 1963-K33

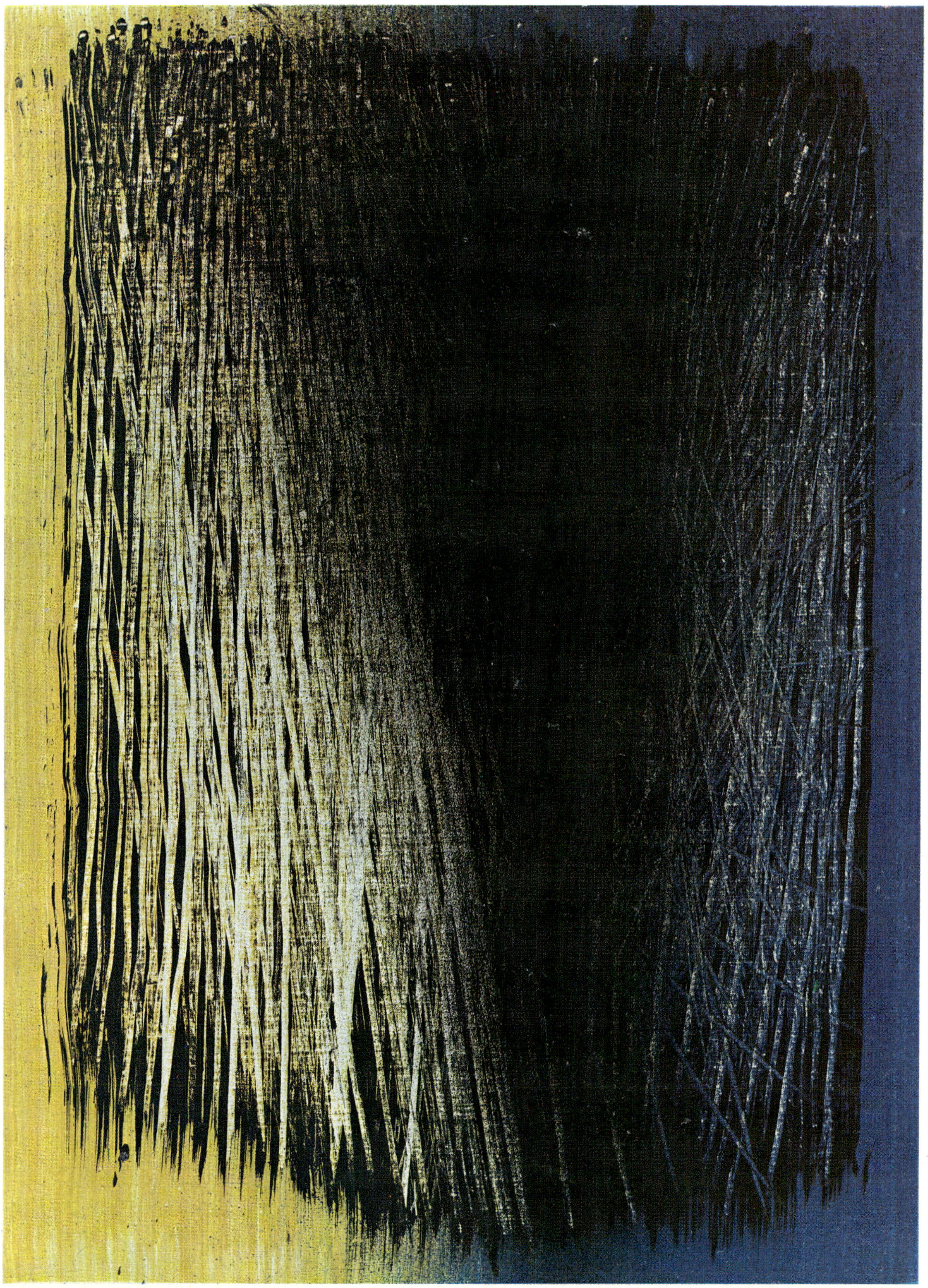

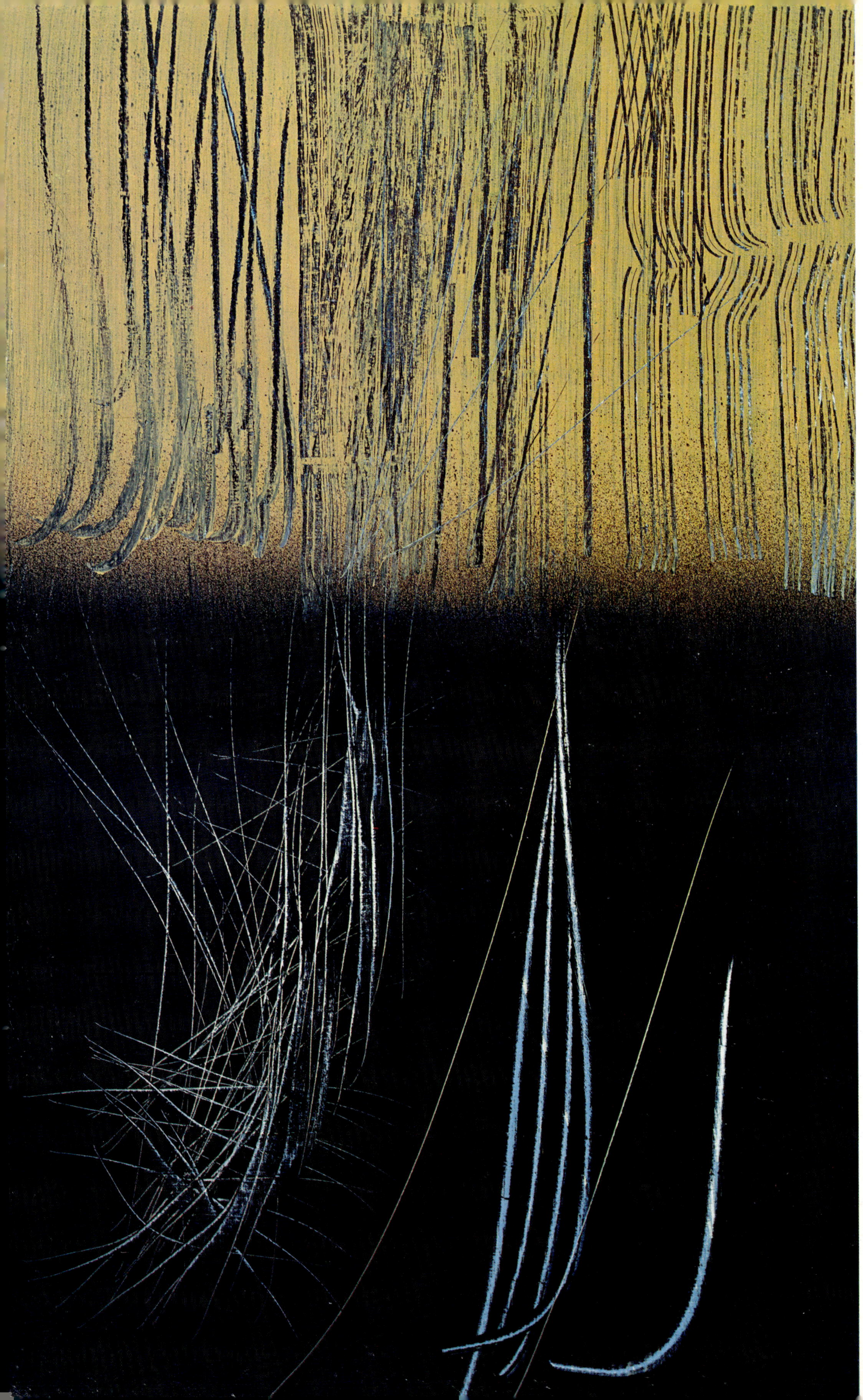

188 T. 1964-H35

189 T. 1964-H

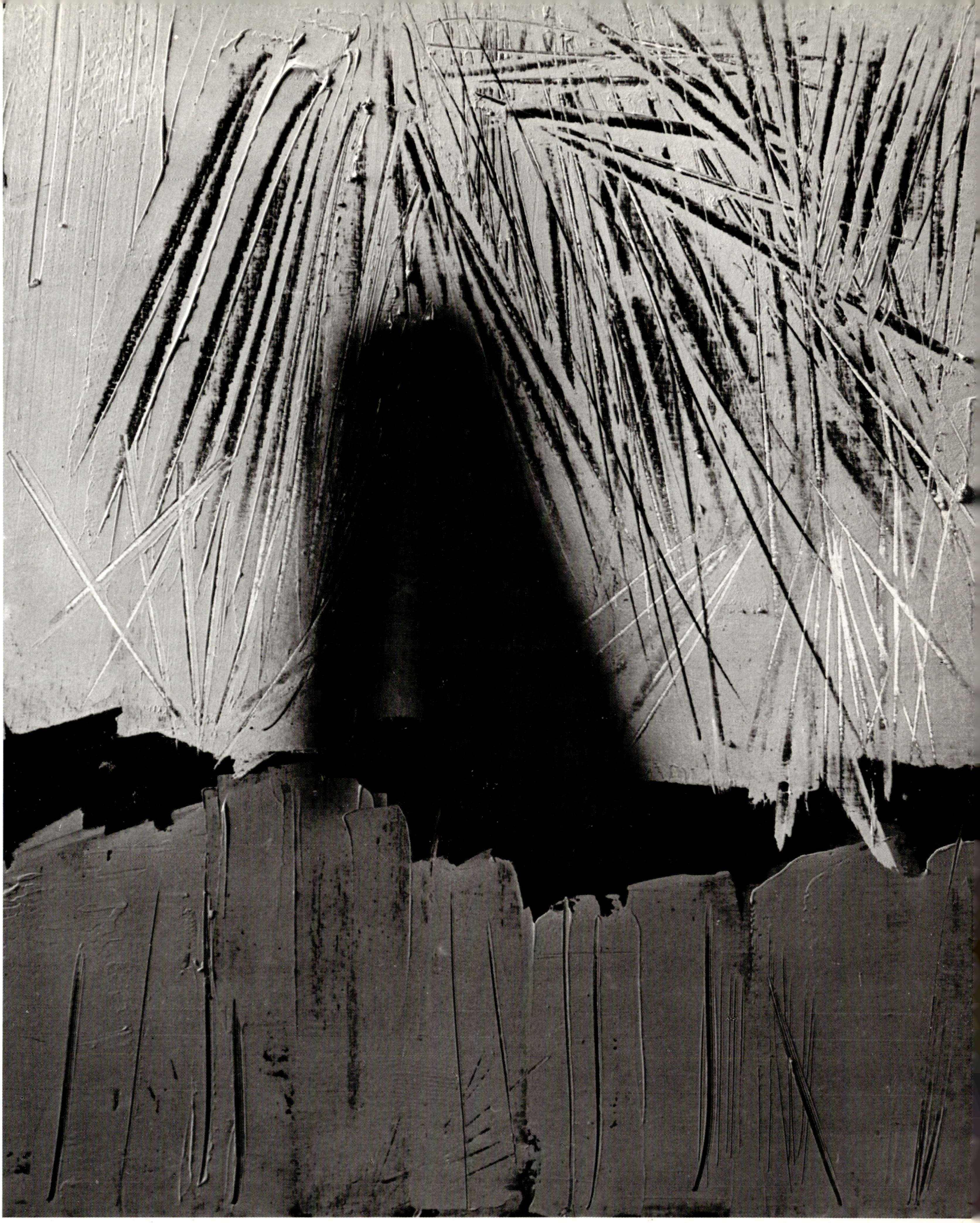

192 T. 1964-R15

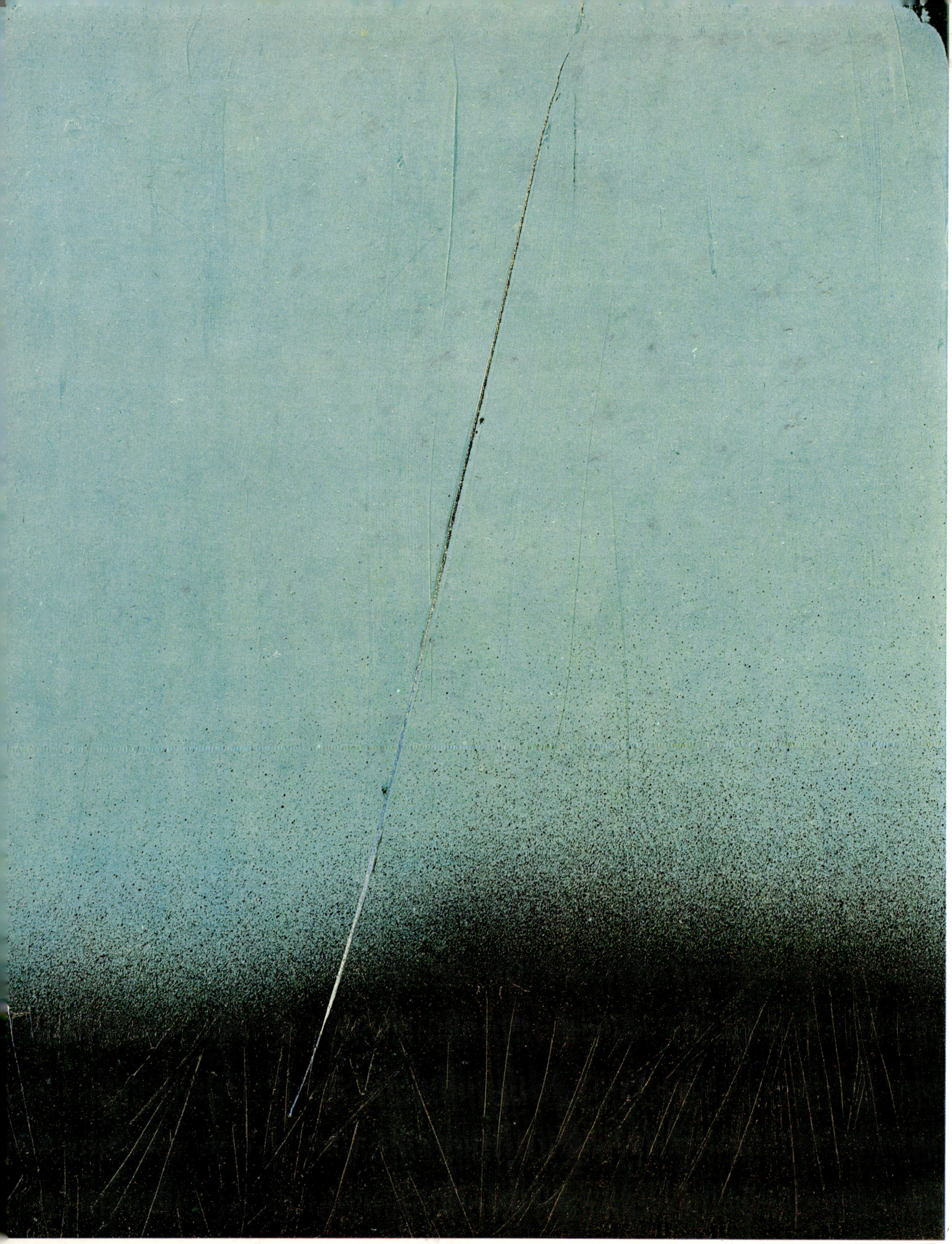

193 T. 1964-R1

200 T. 1964-R24

201
T. 1966
H33

202 T. 1966-H1